Volume Three

Sherida K. Eddlemon

HERITAGE BOOKS, INC.

Other Heritage Books and CDs by the author

Index to the Arkansas General Land Office, 1820-1907, Volumes 1-6
A Genealogical Collection of Kentucky Birth and Death Records, Volume 1
Kentucky Genealogical Records & Abstracts, Volume 1 & 2
Missouri Birth and Death Records, Volumes 1 & 2
Missouri Genealogical Gleanings and Beyond, Volumes 1-7
The "Show-Me" Guide to Missouri: Sources for Genealogical and Historical Research
Ten Thousand Missouri Taxpayers
Tennesee Genealogical Records and Abstracts, 1787-1839, Volume 1
Dickson County, Tennessee, Marriages
*HB Archives: Missouri Volume 1 *CD**
*Tennessee Genealogical Records *CD**

Published 2001 by

HERITAGE BOOKS, INC.
1540E Pointer Ridge Place, Bowie, Maryland 20716
1-800-398-7709
www.heritagebooks.com

ISBN 0-7884-1752-5

PREFACE

Missouri did not have complete compliance of the registration of births and deaths until 1911. Registration began as early as 1863 in some areas of the State. Records from 1910 maybe obtained from the Bureau of Vital Records, P.O. Box 570, Jefferson City, MO 65102. Please contact the Bureau of Vital Records for current fee rates.

County Clerks were required to register births and deaths from 1883 to 1893. These records are available from the Missouri State Archives, P. O. Box 778, Jefferson City, MO 65102. Although registration was required, it was not enforced. In some counties very few births or deaths were recorded.

Since mandatory registration was not in complete compliance until 1911, sources such as newspapers, census, church, military, cemetery, tax and probate records are the researcher's tools in establishing dates of birth and death.

The birth and death records in this third volume in this series are arranged in alphabetically order. The only surnames in the index are names which appeared in the comment section.

Abbreviations used in this volume are:

C	Cemetery
CO	County
B	Birth Date
MD	Marriage Date
B	Birth Date
D	Death Date
PRTS	Parents
CMTS	Comments
A	Age
MIL	Military
BUR	Burial Information
NWS	Newspaper
DP	Place of Death
BP	Place of Birth
RES	Residence
Y	Year
M	Month
D	Day

Good Luck in your search for you ancestors

Aaron, Joseph: (B) 1838, (CO) Pulaski, (A) 22, (BP) KY, (CMTS) 1860 Census
Aaron, Malaga: (B) 1840, (CO) Pulaski, (A) 20, (BP) KY, (CMTS) 1860 Census
Abbott, Miles: (D) Aug. 30, 1917, (CO) Livingston, (C) Edgewood Cemetery, (MIL) WWI
Abbott, Sampson: (B) 1838, (CO) Pulaski, (A) 22, (BP) MO, (CMTS) 1860 Census
Abernathy, Cora: (B) Aug. 19, 1807, (D) Nov.21, 1872, (CO) Barry, (C) Cassville Cemetery
Abernathy, Nancy: (B) Mar, 36, 1839, (D) Jul. 30, 1879, (CO) Barry, (C) Cassville Cemetery
Able, Agnes: (D) Jul. 22, 1879, (CO) St. Louis, (C) Calvary Cemetery, (A) 22
Aches, Eliza: (B) 1851, (CO) Pulaski, (A) 9, (BP) MO, (CMTS) 1860 Census
Aches, Esabel: (B) 1854, (CO) Pulaski, (A) 6, (BP) MO, (CMTS) 1860 Census
Aches, Mary A.: (B) 1856, (CO) Pulaski, (A) 4, (BP) MO, (CMTS) 1860 Census
Aches, Mellissa: (B) 1838, (CO) Pulaski, (A) 22, (BP) IL, (CMTS) 1860 Census
Aches, William: (B) 1830, (CO) Pulaski, (A) 30, (BP) KY, (CMTS) 1860 Census
Ackers, Isabel: (B) 1852, (CO) Cedar, (C) Brashear Cemetery
Ackers, Jacob: (B) 1846, (D) 1915, (CO) Cedar, (C) Brashear Cemetery
Acuff, Andy D.: (B) 1828, (CO) Pulaski, (A) 32, (BP) TN, (CMTS) 1860 Census
Acuff, Delphia: (B) Oct. 17, 1900, (D) May 2, 1997, (CO) Pemiscot, (DP) Caruthersville, MO.
Acuff, Dolores: (B) Jun. 21, 1921, (D) Jan. 3, 1998, (CO) Jackson, (DP) Blue Springs, MO.
Acuff, Edgar: (B) Apr. 18, 1924, (D) Jan. 19, 2000, (CO) St. Louis, (DP) St. Louis
Acuff, Elizabeth: (B) Apr. 30, 1895, (D) Dec., 1972, (CO) Audrain, (DP) Mexico, MO.
Acuff, Elsie: (B) May 26, 1913, (D) Sep., 1985, (CO) Greene, (DP) Springfield, MO.
Acuff, Ernest: (B) Feb. 2, 1919, (D) Aug. 18, 1996, (CO) Jackson, (DP) Blue Springs, MO.
Acuff, Ernest: (B) Mar. 11, 1923, (D) Apr. 24, 2000, (CO) Audrain, (DP) Mexico, MO.
Acuff, Gene: (B) Sep. 9, 1916, (D) Apr., 1987, (CO) St. Louis, (RES) St.

Louis, MO.
Acuff, Horace: (B) Apr. 29, 1910, (D) Jan. 14, 1994, (CO) Morgan, (DP) Versailles, MO.
Acuff, Howard: (B) Aug. 15, 1924, (D) Sep. 24, 1994, (CO) Cass, (DP) Harrisonville, MO.
Acuff, Ida: (B) Apr. 1, 1913, (D) Jul. 19, 1994, (CO) Cass, (DP) Harrisonville, MO.
Acuff, Nancy K.: (B) 1832, (CO) Pulaski, (A) 28, (BP) TN, (CMTS) 1860 Census
Acuff, Sarah: (B) 1856, (CO) Pulaski, (A) 4, (BP) MO, (CMTS) 1860 Census
Acuff, Sorena: (B) 1849, (CO) Pulaski, (A) 11, (BP) TN, (CMTS) 1860 Census
Ada, James Q: (B) 1844, (CO) Stone, (A) 6, (BP) MO, (CMTS) 1870 Census
Ada, John: (B) 1841, (CO) Stone, (A) 9, (BP) MO, (CMTS) 1870 Census
Ada, Polly Ann: (B) 1848, (CO) Stone, (A) 2, (BP) MO, (CMTS) 1870 Census
Ada, William H.: (B) 1821, (CO) Stone, (A) 29, (BP) AR, (CMTS) 1870 Census
Adair, Alfred F: (B) 1840, (CO) Stone, (A) 10, (BP) MO, (CMTS) 1870 Census
Adair, Allen: (B) Oct. 21, 1913, (D) Mar. 26, 1993, (CO) St. Charles, (RES) St. Peters, St. Charles, MO.
Adair, Allene: (B) Oct. 20, 1887, (D) 1967, (CO) St. Francois, (RES) Farmington, MO.
Adair, Alta: (B) Sep. 26, 1910, (D) Apr., 1992, (CO) St. Charles, (RES) St. Charles, MO.
Adair, Earlene: (B) Jul. 7, 1926, (D) Feb., 1973, (CO) Crawford, (RES) Cuba. MO.
Adair, Edwin: (B) Aug. 4, 1890, (D) Jan., 1980, (CO) Grundy, (DP) Trenton, MO,
Adair, Elzie: (B) Jul. 1, 1897, (D) Aug. 12, 1992, (CO) Henry, (RES) Windsor, MO.
Adair, Emmett: (B) Feb. 20, 1905, (D) Sep. 11, 1990, (CO) New Madrid, (RES) New Madrid, MO.
Adair, Fannie: (B) May 3, 1915, (D) Mar. 10, 1998, (CO) Johnson, (RES) Warrensburg, MO.
Adair, Floyd: (B) Jul. 10, 1885, (D) Oct. 6, 1998, (CO) Linn, (RES) Marceline, MO.
Adair, Georgerge: (B) Sep. 4, 1905, (D) Jul. 25, 1991, (CO) Johnson, (RES) Chilhowee, MO.
Adair, George H.: (B) 1846, (CO) Stone, (A) 4, (BP) MO, (CMTS) 1870

Census

Adair, Gladys: (B) Nov. 13, 1902, (D) Mar. 23, 1992, (CO) Jackson, (RES) Lees Summit, MO.

Adair, James: (B) 1827, (CO) Stone, (A) 23, (BP) MO, (CMTS) 1870 Census

Adair, John Perry: (B) 1837, (CO) Stone, (A) 13, (BP) MO, (CMTS) 1870 Census

Adair, Mary E.: (B) Nov. 30, 1873, (CO) Morgan,

Adair, Peggy Jane: (B) 1840, (CO) Stone, (A) 10, (BP) MO, (CMTS) 1870 Census

Adair, Rebecca J.: (B) 1817, (CO) Stone, (A) 33, (BP) IN, (CMTS) 1870 Census

Adair, Susan: (B) 1827, (CO) Stone, (A) 23, (BP) TN, (CMTS) 1870 Census

Adair, William: (B) 1838, (CO) Stone, (A) 12, (BP) MO, (CMTS) 1870 Census

Adams, Benjamin H.: (B) 1851, (CO) Pulaski, (A) 9, (BP) TN, (CMTS) 1860 Census

Adams, Catharine J.: (B) 1851, (CO) Pulaski, (A) 9, (BP) TN, (CMTS) 1860 Census

Adams, Charlotte: (B) 1832, (CO) Pulaski, (A) 28, (BP) TN, (CMTS) 1860 Census

Adams, Elizabeth: (B) 1829, (CO) Pulaski, (A) 31, (BP) NC, (CMTS) 1860 Census

Adams, Ella: (B) Nov. 24, 1889, (D) Nov., 1969, (CO) Stone, (DP) Crane, MO.

Adams, Evelyn: (B) Jun. 14, 1896, (D) Jul. 15, 1974, (CO) Texas, (DP) Houston, MO.

Adams, George F.: (B) 1855, (CO) Pulaski, (A) 5, (BP) TN, (CMTS) 1860 Census

Adams, Glen: (B) Jan. 23, 1917, (D) 1987, (CO) Texas

Adams, Icy: (B) 1911, (D) 1976, (CO) Texas

Adams, Jacob: (B) 1837, (CO) Pulaski, (A) 23, (BP) NC, (CMTS) 1860 Census

Adams, James: (B) 1830, (CO) Pulaski, (A) 30, (BP) SC, (CMTS) 1860 Census

Adams, James R.: (B) 1840, (CO) Pulaski, (A) 20, (BP) TN, (CMTS) 1860 Census

Adams, James R.: (B) 1843, (CO) Pulaski, (A) 17, (BP) TN, (CMTS) 1860 Census

Adams, Jesse: (B) 1847, (CO) Pulaski, (A) 13, (BP) TN, (CMTS) 1860 Census

Adams, Laura Land: (B) Aug. 26, 1863, (D) Jul. 6, 1947, (CO) Henry,

(C) Knights of Pythias Cemetery, Deepwater, MO
Adams, Louis: (B) Feb. 14, 1924, (D) May 16, 1996, (CO) Texas, (DP) Summersville, MO.
Adams, Margaret: (B) 1840, (CO) Pulaski, (A) 20, (BP) MO, (CMTS) 1860 Census
Adams, Margaret A.: (B) 1844, (CO) Pulaski, (A) 16, (BP) TN, (CMTS) 1860 Census
Adams, Marion: (B) 1821, (CO) Pulaski, (A) 39, (BP) TN, (CMTS) 1860 Census
Adams, Martha: (B) Dec. 31, 1812, (D) Dec. 9, 1872, (CO) Barry, (C) Old Corsicana Cemetery
Adams, Martha J.: (B) 1846, (CO) Pulaski, (A) 14, (BP) TN, (CMTS) 1860 Census
Adams, Mary: (B) 1894, (D) 1976, (CO) Texas
Adams, Mernerva: (B) 1843, (CO) Stone, (A) 27, (BP) TN, (CMTS) 1870 Census
Adams, Mildred: (B) Nov. 1, 1927, (D) Mar. 5, 1998, (CO) Texas, (DP) Houston, MO.
Adams, Monroe E.: (B) 1845, (CO) Stone, (A) 25, (BP) MO, (CMTS) 1870 Census
Adams, Morenva: (B) 1830, (CO) Pulaski, (A) 30, (BP) TN, (CMTS) 1860 Census
Adams, Napoleon: (B) 1849, (CO) Pulaski, (A) 11, (BP) TN, (CMTS) 1860 Census
Adams, Patsy C.: (B) 1854, (CO) Pulaski, (A) 6, (BP) TN, (CMTS) 1860 Census
Adams, Robert: (B) 1796, (CO) Pulaski, (A) 64, (BP) SC, (CMTS) 1860 Census
Adams, Sally A.: (B) 1843, (CO) Pulaski, (A) 17, (BP) TN, (CMTS) 1860 Census
Adams, Silas: (B) May 17, 1802, (D) May 22, 1873, (CO) Barry, (C) Old Corsicana Cemetery
Adams, Thomas N.: (B) 1840, (CO) Pulaski, (A) 20, (BP) TN, (CMTS) 1860 Census
Adams, Uriah: (B) 1849, (CO) Pulaski, (A) 11, (BP) TN, (CMTS) 1860 Census
Adams, William: (B) 1820, (CO) Pulaski, (A) 40, (BP) NC, (CMTS) 1860 Census
Adams, William H.: (B) 1845, (CO) Pulaski, (A) 15, (BP) TN, (CMTS) 1860 Census
Adams, William H.: (B) 1854, (CO) Pulaski, (A) 6, (BP) TN, (CMTS) 1860 Census
Adams, Wilma: (B) Sep. 23, 1923, (D) Sep., 1983, (CO) Texas, (DP)

Houston, MO.
Adamson, Elijah: (B) 1851, (CO) Pulaski, (A) 9, (BP) MO, (CMTS) 1860 Census
Aday, Dollie: (B) Sep. 19, 1910, (D) Sep. 19, 1993, (CO) Taney, (DP) Point Lookout, MO.
Aday, Edward: (B) 1818, (CO) Stone, (A) 52, (BP) TN, (CMTS) 1870 Census
Aday, John: (B) Jan. 15, 1861, (CO) Barry, (PRTS) William G. H. Aday
Aday, Lucinda J.: (B) 1855, (CO) Stone, (A) 15, (BP) AR, (CMTS) 1870 Census
Aday, Ralph: (B) Oct. 8, 1927, (D) Nov. 20, 1999, (CO) Newton, (DP) Granby, MO.
Aday, Rebecca: (B) 1828, (CO) Stone, (A) 42, (BP) TN, (CMTS) 1870 Census
Aday, Roger: (B) Feb. 2, 1959, (D) Feb. 22, 1990, (CO) Jackson, (DP) Kansas City, MO.
Aday, Wade: (B) 1850, (CO) Stone, (A) 20, (BP) AR, (CMTS) 1870 Census
Aday, William A.: (B) Sep. 5, 1886, (CO) Atchison, (PRTS) Nathaniel J. Aday and Anna C. Berrier
Ader, Mary Ellen: (B) May 12, 1879, (CO) Mercer
Adkins, George W.: (B) Jan. 20, 1857, (D) Aug. 15, 1951, (CO) Jackson
Adkins, John: (D) Nov. 1, 1852, (CO) Carroll
Adkins, John D.: (B) Nov. 3, 1857, (D) Mar. 20, 1900, (CO) Carroll
Adkins, Pelley: (B) Mar. 17, 1850, (D) May 1, 1928, (CO) Carroll
Admires, Catharine: (B) 1858, (CO) Pulaski, (A) 2, (BP) MO, (CMTS) 1860 Census
Admires, Matilda: (B) 1815, (CO) Pulaski, (A) 45, (BP) MO, (CMTS) 1860 Census
Admires, Ruth: (B) 1830, (CO) Pulaski, (A) 30, (BP) MO, (CMTS) 1860 Census
Admires, Squire: (B) 1838, (CO) Pulaski, (A) 22, (BP) MO, (CMTS) 1860 Census
Admires, Susan: (B) 1852, (CO) Pulaski, (A) 8, (BP) MO, (CMTS) 1860 Census
Admires, William: (B) 1856, (CO) Pulaski, (A) 4, (BP) MO, (CMTS) 1860 Census
Adrian, Herman : (B) 1836, (D) 1888, (CO) Audrain, (C) St. Joseph Catholic Cemetery
Agendee, John: (B) 1835, (CO) Pulaski, (A) 25, (BP) Ireland, (CMTS) 1860 Census
Ahlers, Egelbert: (B) 1850, (D) 1897, (CO) St. Louis, (C) Calvary

Cemetery

Ahrendt, Katherine: (B) Feb. 14, 1916, (D) 1974, (CO) Greene, (DP) Springfield, MO.

Ahrendt, Louis Julius: (B) Jul. 25, 1876, (D) Feb. 14, 1961, (CO) Henry, (C) Knights of Pythias Cemetery, Deepwater, MO

Ahrendt, Nannie: (B) Feb. 25, 1891, (D) May, 1979, (CO) Jackson, (DP) Kansas City, MO.

Ahrens, Elizabeth: (B) 1839, (D) 1888, (CO) Audrain, (C) St. Joseph Catholic Cemetery

Aka, Anna: (B) Aug. 26, 1892, (D) Oct., 19780, (CO) St. Louis, (DP) St. Louis, MO.

Akins, Martha J.: (B) 1821, (CO) Stone, (A) 29, (BP) MO, (CMTS) 1870 Census

Al-Shams, Akbar: (B) Jul. 1, 1920, (D) Jul. 19, 1999, (CO) Jackson, (DP) Kansas City, MO.

Alaman, Clarence: (B) Oct. 31, 1909, (D) Jan., 1982, (CO) Stone, (DP) Galena, MO.

Alberson, Benjamin: (B) 1850, (CO) Pulaski, (A) 10, (BP) MO, (CMTS) 1860 Census

Alberson, Elizabeth: (B) 1847, (CO) Pulaski, (A) 13, (BP) MO, (CMTS) 1860 Census

Alberson, Solomon: (B) 1843, (CO) Pulaski, (A) 17, (BP) MO, (CMTS) 1860 Census

Albert, Martin L.: (D) Dec. 10, 1928, (CO) Oregon, (C) Falling Springs Cemetery

Albert, Ralph: (B) Jan. 21, 1921, (D) Jan. 23, 1997, (CO) Texas, (DP) Houston, MO.

Albitz, Anna M.: , (D) Jan. 13, 1883, (CO) St. Louis, (C) Calvary Cemetery, (A) 70

Alcorn, Sadie Douglass: (B) Feb. 2, 1889, (D) Jan. 4, 1919, (CO) Oregon, (C) Falling Springs Cemetery

Alexander, Carlos R.: (D) Aug. 9, 1941, (CO) Grundy, (CMTS) A. F. & A. M. Trenton Lodge 111

Alexander, Catharine: (B) 1836, (CO) Pulaski, (A) 24, (BP) IL, (CMTS) 1860 Census

Alexander, Charles H.: (D) Oct. 17, 1916, (CO) Grundy, (CMTS) A. F. & A. M. Trenton Lodge 111

Alexander, Emily: (B) 1840, (CO) Pulaski, (A) 20, (BP) KY, (CMTS) 1860 Census

Alexander, James: (B) 1841, (CO) Pulaski, (A) 19, (BP) IL, (CMTS) 1860 Census

Alexander, John: (B) 1843, (CO) Pulaski, (A) 17, (BP) IL, (CMTS) 1860

Census
Alexander, Jonathan: (B) 1828, (CO) Pulaski, (A) 32, (BP) MO, (CMTS) 1860 Census
Alexander, William O.: (B) 1834, (CO) Pulaski, (A) 26, (BP) IL, (CMTS) 1860 Census
Alker, Finley: (B) 1838, (D) 1870, (CO) Adair, (A) 32, (CMTS) 1870 Mortality Schedule
Allee, Virginia: (B) Mar. 14, 1915, (CO) Moniteau, (PRTS) Lee and Clare Gray Allee
Allen, Ava: (B) 1834, (CO) Pulaski, (A) 26, (BP) KY, (CMTS) 1860 Census
Allen, Bailey: (B) 1840, (CO) Pulaski, (A) 20, (BP) KY, (CMTS) 1860 Census
Allen, Bailey: (B) 1847, (CO) Pulaski, (A) 13, (BP) KY, (CMTS) 1860 Census
Allen, Doretha: (B) 1826, (CO) Stone, (A) 24, (BP) MO, (CMTS) 1870 Census
Allen, Geneora: (B) 1845, (CO) Pulaski, (A) 15, (BP) KY, (CMTS) 1860 Census
Allen, James: (B) 1838, (CO) Pulaski, (A) 22, (BP) KY, (CMTS) 1860 Census
Allen, Jemimia: (B) 1849, (CO) Pulaski, (A) 11, (BP) MO, (CMTS) 1860 Census
Allen, John A.: (B) 1849, (CO) Stone, (A) 1, (BP) MO, (CMTS) 1870 Census
Allen, Laura: (B) 1842, (CO) Pulaski, (A) 18, (BP) KY, (CMTS) 1860 Census
Allen, Margaret: (B) 1856, (CO) Pulaski, (A) 4, (BP) MO, (CMTS) 1860 Census
Allen, Nancy: (B) 1841, (CO) Pulaski, (A) 19, (BP) KY, (CMTS) 1860 Census
Allen, Nathan: (B) 1821, (CO) Stone, (A) 29, (BP) AR, (CMTS) 1870 Census
Allen, Nicholas: (B) 1853, (CO) Pulaski, (A) 7, (BP) KY, (CMTS) 1860 Census
Allen, Polly: (B) 1844, (CO) Pulaski, (A) 16, (BP) KY, (CMTS) 1860 Census
Allen, Valentine: (B) 1854, (CO) Pulaski, (A) 6, (BP) KY, (CMTS) 1860 Census
Allen, William: (B) 1843, (CO) Pulaski, (A) 17, (BP) KY, (CMTS) 1860 Census
Allen, William T. J.: (B) 1848, (CO) Stone, (A) 2, (BP) MO, (CMTS) 1870 Census

Allman, James: (B) 1877, (D) 1879, (CO) Oregon, (C) Falling Springs Cemetery
Allman, Mary A.: (B) Nov. 11, 1835, (D) Feb. 15, 1866, (CO) Oregon, (C) Falling Springs Cemetery
Allmon, Chester Guy : (B) Apr. 17, 1906, (D) Oct. 7, 1961, (CO) Oregon, (C) Falling Springs Cemetery
Allmon, Douglas Doyle: (B) Jun. 2, 1958, (D) Jun. 2, 1958, (CO) Oregon, (C) Falling Springs Cemetery
Allmon, Joseph S.: (B) 1864, (D) 1954, (CO) Oregon, (C) Falling Springs Cemetery
Allmon, Kenneth Lee: (B) Aug. 18, 1925, (D) Apr. 4, 1942, (CO) Oregon, (C) Falling Springs Cemetery
Allmon, Maggie Marie: (B) 1911, (D) 1998, (CO) Oregon, (C) Falling Springs Cemetery
Allmon, Mahala E.: (B) 1863, (D) 1945, (CO) Oregon, (C) Falling Springs Cemetery
Allmon, Martha: (B) 1899, (D) 1901, (CO) Oregon, (C) Falling Springs Cemetery
Allmon, Richard Lee: (B) Jun. 21, 1943, (D) Sep. 15, 1943, (CO) Oregon, (C) Falling Springs Cemetery
Allmon, Ruby: (B) Apr. 21, 1889, (D) Jul. 28, 1916, (CO) Oregon, (C) Falling Springs Cemetery
Allmon, Terry Dale: (B) May 20, 1966, (D) May 20, 1966, (CO) Oregon, (C) Falling Springs Cemetery
Alvarez, Juan: (B) Aug. 10, 1951, (D) Aug. 19, 2000, (CO) Jackson, (NWS) *Kansas City, Missouri Star*, Aug. 22, 2000 (C) Mt. Olivet
Cemetery, (PRTS) Ben H. and Julia S. Alvarez, (SIBLINGS) Benny, Phillip, Don Carlos, Eugene, Rudolph, Fred, Anthony, Arthur, Victor, Virginia Renfro, Elizabeth Yalas, Helen Navarro, Dianna Ibarra, Evanline Kay, Amelia Navarro, Julia Ann Perez (CH) John, Phillip, Juan Carlos, Joshua, Daniel, Juan Valetin, Valencia, Bria, Jessica, Teresa, Desiree
Amann, Raymond: (B) Jan. 24, 1895, (D) 1977, (CO) Texas, (DP) Summersville, MO.
Amos, Gwen Mary: , (D) Apr. 18, 1999, (CO) St. Louis, (DP) St, Louis, MO, (NWS) *Allentown, Pennslyvania Morning Call*, Apr. 21, 1999.
Anawalt, Mary Jane: (B) Dec. 29, 1861, (D) Sep. 7, 1927, (CO) Camden, (DP) Climax Springs, MO
Anderson, Blanche Evens: , (D) Aug. 21, 2000, (CO) Jackson, (NWS) *Kansas City, Missouri Star*, Aug. 22, 2000 (C) Oak Hill Cemetery, Butler, MO
Anderson, Elizabeth: (B) 1827, (CO) Stone, (A) 43, (BP) TN, (CMTS)

1870 Census
Anderson, Fraces: (B) 1826, (CO) Pulaski, (A) 34, (BP) TN, (CMTS) 1860 Census
Anderson, Geneva A.: (B) Nov. 28, 1929, (D) Aug. 20, 2000, (CO) Jackson, (NWS) *Kansas City, Missouri Star*, Aug. 22, 2000 (C) Corinth Cemetery, (PRTS) Frederick Wallderstandt and Emelia Leander
Anderson, James: (B) 1843, (CO) Stone, (A) 7, (BP) IL, (CMTS) 1870 Census
Anderson, John H.: (B) 1826, (CO) Stone, (A) 44, (BP) SC, (CMTS) 1870 Census
Anderson, Louisa: (B) 1854, (CO) Pulaski, (A) 6, (BP) KY, (CMTS) 1860 Census
Anderson, Ludinda: (B) 1848, (CO) Pulaski, (A) 12, (BP) TN, (CMTS) 1860 Census
Anderson, Margarett: (B) 1841, (CO) Stone, (A) 9, (BP) IL, (CMTS) 1870 Census
Anderson, Martha E.: (B) 1856, (CO) Pulaski, (A) 4, (BP) KY, (CMTS) 1860 Census
Anderson, Mary M.: (B) 1852, (CO) Pulaski, (A) 8, (BP) TN, (CMTS) 1860 Census
Anderson, Nancy J.: (B) 1846, (CO) Pulaski, (A) 14, (BP) TN, (CMTS) 1860 Census
Anderson, Sarah C.: (B) 1850, (CO) Pulaski, (A) 10, (BP) TN, (CMTS) 1860 Census
Anderson, Sarah E.: (B) 1817, (CO) Stone, (A) 33, (BP) KY, (CMTS) 1870 Census
Anderson, Sena F.: (B) 1857, (CO) Pulaski, (A) 3, (BP) KY, (CMTS) 1860 Census
Anderson, William: (B) 1841, (CO) Pulaski, (A) 19, (BP) MO, (CMTS) 1860 Census
Anderson, Robert R.: , (D) Oct. 31, 1943, (CO) Grundy, (CMTS) A. F. & A. M. Trenton Lodge 111
Applegate, Aletha: (B) May 4, 1893, (D) 1980, (CO) Gentry, (DP) Albany, MO
Applegate, Arland: (B) Sep. 5, 1897, (D) Oct. 3, 1989, (CO) Marion, (DP) Philadelphia, MO.
Applegate, Bertha: (B) Feb. 1, 1907, (D) Jan. 2, 1994, (CO) Christian, (DP) Sparta, MO.
Applegate, Birdie (B) Nov. 20, 1883, (D) 1967, (CO) St. Louis, (DP) St. Louis, MO.
Applegate, Carl: (B) Sep. 16, 1924, (D) 1984, (CO) Greene, (DP) Springfield, MO.

Applegate, Catherine: (B) 1845, (CO) Stone, (A) 25, (BP) TN, (CMTS) 1870 Census
Applegate, Charles: (B) 1901, (D) 1979, (CO) Boone, (DP) Columbia, MO.
Applegate, Charles: (B) Mar. 23, 1885, (D) 1965, (CO) Nodaway, (DP) Maryville, MO.
Applegate, Ebenezer: (B) Jan. 30, 1840, (D) Mar. 3, 1915, (CO) Vernon, (DP) Schell City, MO.
Applegate, Edith: (B) Jul. 30, 1899, (D) Oct. 15, 1967, (CO) Vernon, (DP) Nevada, MO.
Applegate, Edith: (B) Nov. 19, 1906, (D) Dec. 20, 1997, (CO) Marion, (DP) Palmyra, MO.
Applegate, Gilbert: (B) 1846, (CO) Stone, (A) 24, (BP) MO, (CMTS) 1870 Census
Applegate, John: (B) Jun. 13, 1877, (D) Oct. 13, 1878, (CO) Ray, (DP) Orrick, MO, (C) Riffe Cemetery.
Applegate, John Henry: (B) Feb. 23, 1895, (D) Jul. 13, 1961, (CO) Buchanan, (DP) St. Joseph, MO.
Applegate, Mary Molly: (B) Aug. 15, 1850, (D) Jan. 2, 1936, (CO) Jackson, (DP) Kansas City, MO, (C) Calvary Cemetery.
Archer, Thomas B.: (B) 1834, (D) 1901, (CO) Oregon, (C) Cave Springs Cemetery
Arcldrain, Rebecca: (B) 1825, (D) 1870, (CO) Adair, (A) 45, (CMTS) 1870 Mortality Schedule
Arcldrain, Robert: (B) 1820, (D) 1870, (CO) Adair, (A) 50, (CMTS) 1870 Mortality Schedule
Armistead, Francis: (B) Apr. 27, 1790 , (CO) Audrain, (C) Old Village Cemetery
Armstrong, Robert: , (D) Dec. 10, 1902, (CO) St. Louis, (C) Calvary Cemetery (A) 63
Arnold, Leander: (B) 1839, (CO) Pulaski, (A) 21, (BP) MO, (CMTS) 1860 Census
Arnold, Mary Ann: (B) 1842, (CO) Pulaski, (A) 18, (BP) MO, (CMTS) 1860 Census
Arterbury, James: (B) 1818, (CO) Stone, (A) 32, (BP) AR, (CMTS) 1870 Census
Arterbury, Pamelia: (B) 1830, (CO) Stone, (A) 20, (BP) MO, (CMTS) 1870 Census
Arterbury, Samuel: (B) 1846, (CO) Stone, (A) 4, (BP) MO, (CMTS) 1870 Census
Arterbury, William S.: (B) 1849, (CO) Stone, (A) 1, (BP) MO, (CMTS) 1870 Census
Ash, Cynthia: (B) 1823, (CO) Stone, (A) 27, (BP) MO, (CMTS) 1870

Census

Ash, James: (B) 1847, (CO) Stone, (A) 3, (BP) MO, (CMTS) 1870 Census

Ash, John B.: (B) 1847, (CO) Stone, (A) 3, (BP) MO, (CMTS) 1870 Census

Asher, Milton C.: , (D) Apr. 16, 1891, (CO) Grundy, (CMTS) A. F. & A. M. Trenton Lodge 111

Ashly, Hopkins: (B) 1850, (CO) Stone, (A) 20, (BP) IN, (CMTS) 1870 Census

Ashly, Mary Jane: (B) 1852, (CO) Stone, (A) 18, (BP) KY, (CMTS) 1870 Census

Asman, Sr., Frederick: (D) Jul. 6, 1949, (CO) Grundy, (CMTS) A. F. & A. M. Trenton Lodge 111

Aspromonte, Sam Vincent: (B) 1875, (D) 1964, (CO) St. Louis, (C) Calvary Cemetery

Auer, Donna Sutton: (B) Aug. 21, 1941, (D) Aug. 19, 2000, (CO) Jackson, (NWS) *Kansas City, Missouri Star*, Aug. 22, 2000

Augna, Alvin: (B) 1792, (D) 1870, (CO) Adair, (A) 78, (CMTS) 1870 Mortality Schedule

Austin, James: (D) Mar. 8, 1885, (CO) Grundy, (CMTS) A. F. & A. M. Trenton Lodge 111

Ax, Clarence: (B) Aug. 17, 1907, (D) Dec., 1983, (CO) St. Louis, (DP) St. Louis, MO.

Ay, Mary: (B) Sep. 8, 1914, (D) Sep. 19, 1999, (CO) Lafayette, (DP) Lexington, MO.

Ayers, Alzira: (B) 1792, (CO) Stone, (A) 58, (BP) GA, (CMTS) 1870 Census

Ayers, Elizabeth: (B) 1829, (CO) Stone, (A) 21, (BP) MO, (CMTS) 1870 Census

Ayers, John L.: (B) 1835, (CO) Stone, (A) 15, (BP) MO, (CMTS) 1870 Census

Ayers, Moses: (B) 1828, (CO) Stone, (A) 22, (BP) TN, (CMTS) 1870 Census

Ayers, Sarah C.: (B) 1830, (CO) Stone, (A) 20, (BP) TN, (CMTS) 1870 Census

Ayers, William C.: (B) 1792, (CO) Stone, (A) 58, (BP) GA, (CMTS) 1870 Census

Aylward, Catherine: (D) Mar. 14, 1896, (CO) St. Louis, (C) Calvary Cemetery

Aylward, John: (D) Jan. 14, 1895, (CO) St. Louis, (C) Calvary Cemetery

Babb, William: (B) Nov. 7, 1835, (D) Nov. 9, 1911, (CO) Cape Girardeau, (DP) TX

Babler, Sarah Salome: (D) Jan. 20, 1918, (CO) St. Louis, (NWS) *St. Louis*

Post Dispatch, Jan. 22, 1918, (SPOUSE) Henry J. Babler, (CMTS) Jacob L. Babler, son; Henry J. Babler, Jr., son; Mrs. G. A. A. Deane, Jr., daughter; Mrs. Mary S. Gettings, daughter; Mrs. O.A. Wall, daughter

Bacigalupo, Angeline: (B) May 8, 1836, (D) Apr. 9, 1907, (CO) St. Louis, (C) Calvary Cemetery

Back, Caroline: (B) 1833, (CO) Pulaski, (A) 27, (BP) IL, (CMTS) 1860 Census

Back, Mahala: (B) 1854, (CO) Pulaski, (A) 6, (BP) MO, (CMTS) 1860 Census

Back, William: (B) 1829, (CO) Pulaski, (A) 31, (BP) KY, (CMTS) 1860 Census

Backer, Lucinda: (B) 1845, (CO) Pulaski, (A) 15, (BP) MO, (CMTS) 1860 Census

Bagley, Elias: (D) Mar. 14, 1921, (CO) Grundy, (CMTS) A. F. & A. M. Trenton Lodge 111

Bagley, Phyllis A.: (B) 1918, (D) 1988, (CO) St. Louis, (C) Calvary Cemetery

Bagley, William: (B) 1917,, (CO) St. Louis, (C) Calvary Cemetery

Bailey, Cornelia: (B) 1842, (CO) Pulaski, (A) 18, (BP) IN, (CMTS) 1860 Census

Bailey, Euna V.: (B) Feb. 21, 1880, (D) Feb. 24, 1883, (CO) Henry, (C) Knights of Pythias Cemetery, Deepwater, MO

Bailey, Henry: (B) 1844, (CO) Pulaski, (A) 16, (BP) KY, (CMTS) 1860 Census

Bailey, Henry S.: (B) Aug. 3, 1847, (D) Feb. 21, 1933, (CO) Henry, (C) Knights of Pythias Cemetery, Deepwater, MO

Bailey, Herbert: (B) Aug. 7, 1882, (D) Oct. 12, 1933, (CO) Henry, (C) Knights of Pythias Cemetery, Deepwater, MO

Bailey, James M.: (D) Nov. 1, 1901, (CO) Grundy, (CMTS) A. F. & A. M. Trenton Lodge 111

Bailey, Joseph William: (B) Oct. 1, 1886, (CO) Macon, (PRTS) Joseph M. Bailey

Bailey, Norris Jacob: (B) Aug. 5, 1888, (CO) Macon, (PRTS) Joseph M. Bailey

Bailey, Obadiah: (B) 1833, (CO) Pulaski, (A) 27, (BP) IN, (CMTS) 1860 Census

Bailey, Theophilus: (B) 1831, (CO) Pulaski, (A) 29, (BP) IN, (CMTS) 1860 Census

Bailey, Thomas Fulton: (B) Sep. 2, 1852, (CO) St. Charles

Bailey, William: (B) Oct. 1, 1854, (CO) Barry

Bailey, William A.: (B) Mar. 11, 1861, (CO) Barton

Bailey, William Elmer: (B) Jan. 25, 1872, (D) Dec. 30, 1930, (CO)

Atchison
Bailey, William H.: (B) Oct. 22, 1824, (D) Oct. 23, 1873, (CO) Linn, (DP) Bucklin, MO
Bailey, William Henry: (B) Sep. 24, 1882, (CO) Barry
Bailey, William Moses: (B) Jun. 10, 1836, (CO) Missouri
Bailey, William T.: (B) Feb. 4, 1869, (D) Jun. 19, 1952, (CO) Henry, (C) Knights of Pythias Cemetery, Deepwater, MO
Bain, Louis J.: (D) Mar. 28, 1937, (CO) Grundy, (CMTS) A. F. & A. M. Trenton Lodge 111
Baize, Anna C.: (B) 1835, (CO) Stone, (A) 35, (BP) TN, (CMTS) 1870 Census
Baize, Squire W.: (B) 1847, (CO) Stone, (A) 23, (BP) MO, (CMTS) 1870 Census
Baize, Worthy A.: (B) 1847, (CO) Stone, (A) 23, (BP) OH, (CMTS) 1870 Census
Baker, Alvis: (B) 1849, (CO) Stone, (A) 21, (BP) MO, (CMTS) 1870 Census
Baker, Archie: (B) 1851, (CO) Pulaski, (A) 9, (BP) MO, (CMTS) 1860 Census
Baker, Balim: (B) 1837, (CO) Stone, (A) 13, (BP) MO, (CMTS) 1870 Census
Baker, Charity E.: (B) 1846, (CO) Stone, (A) 4, (BP) MO, (CMTS) 1870 Census
Baker, Daniel: (B) 1835, (CO) Stone, (A) 15, (BP) MO, (CMTS) 1870 Census
Baker, Enos: (B) 1837, (CO) Stone, (A) 13, (BP) MO, (CMTS) 1870 Census
Baker, George W.: (B) 1851, (CO) Stone, (A) 19, (BP) MO, (CMTS) 1870 Census
Baker, Hannah: (D) Oct. 9, 1905, (CO) St. Louis, (C) Calvary Cemetery
Baker, Henry: (B) 1842, (CO) Stone, (A) 8, (BP) MO, (CMTS) 1870 Census
Baker, James: (B) 1821, (CO) Stone, (A) 49, (BP) TN, (CMTS) 1870 Census
Baker, Joel: (B) 1849, (CO) Stone, (A) 1, (BP) MO, (CMTS) 1870 Census
Baker, Louis J.: (B) 1862, (D) 1900, (CO) St. Louis, (C) Calvary Cemetery
Baker, Margaret E.: (B) 1854, (CO) Pulaski, (A) 6, (BP) MO, (CMTS) 1860 Census
Baker, Mary: (B) 1829, (CO) Pulaski, (A) 31, (BP) IN, (CMTS) 1860 Census
Baker, Mary: (B) 1841, (CO) Stone, (A) 9, (BP) MO, (CMTS) 1870

Census
Baker, Mary A.: (B) 1838, (CO) Stone, (A) 12, (BP) MO, (CMTS) 1870
Census
Baker, Mary C.: (B) 1854, (CO) Stone, (A) 16, (BP) MO, (CMTS) 1870
Census
Baker, Nancy A.: (B) 1821, (CO) Stone, (A) 49, (BP) TN, (CMTS) 1870
Census
Baker, Nancy Jane: (B) 1840, (CO) Stone, (A) 10, (BP) MO, (CMTS)
1870 Census
Baker, Octavia: (B) 1846, (CO) Stone, (A) 4, (BP) MO, (CMTS) 1870
Census
Baker, Samuel: (B) 1850, (CO) Pulaski, (A) 10, (BP) MO, (CMTS) 1860
Census
Baker, Sarah: (B) 1843, (CO) Stone, (A) 7, (BP) MO, (CMTS) 1870
Census
Baker, Sarah A.: (B) 1818, (CO) Stone, (A) 32, (BP) MO, (CMTS) 1870
Census
Baker, Sarah A.: (B) 1841, (CO) Pulaski, (A) 19, (BP) MO, (CMTS) 1860
Census
Baker, Sarah J.: (B) 1846, (CO) Stone, (A) 4, (BP) MO, (CMTS) 1870
Census
Baker, Thomas: (B) 1848, (CO) Stone, (A) 2, (BP) MO, (CMTS) 1870
Census
Baker, W.: (B) 1838, (CO) Pulaski, (A) 22, (BP) MO, (CMTS) 1860
Census
Baker, William: (B) 1838, (CO) Stone, (A) 12, (BP) MO, (CMTS) 1870
Census
Baker, William: (D) 1914, (CO) St. Louis, (C) Calvary Cemetery
Baker, William H.: (B) 1848, (CO) Pulaski, (A) 12, (BP) MO, (CMTS)
1860 Census
Baker, Willie M.: (B) 1841, (CO) Stone, (A) 9, (BP) MO, (CMTS) 1870
Census
Baland, Charles Augustus: (B) Jul. 18, 1871, (D) Jul. 27, 1957, (CO)
Greene, (DP) Springfield, MO, (C) Maple Park Cemetery
Balducci, Angela: (B) 1896, (CO) St. Louis, (C) Calvary Cemetery
Balducci, Patrick: (B) 1894, (D) 1966, (CO) St. Louis, (C) Calvary
Cemetery
Ball, Martha: (B) 1844, (D) 1919, (CO) Cedar, (C) Brashear Cemetery
Ballard, George W.: (B) 1852, (CO) Pulaski, (A) 8, (BP) TN, (CMTS)
1860 Census
Ballard, Jesse J.: (B) 1844, (CO) Pulaski, (A) 16, (BP) NC, (CMTS) 1860
Census
Ballard, John: (B) 1850, (CO) Pulaski, (A) 10, (BP) TN, (CMTS) 1860

Census
Ballard, Mary M.: (B) 1847, (CO) Pulaski, (A) 13, (BP) TN, (CMTS) 1860 Census
Ballard, Minerva: (B) 1843, (CO) Pulaski, (A) 17, (BP) MO, (CMTS) 1860 Census
Ballard, Tonssa J.: (B) 1837, (CO) Pulaski, (A) 23, (BP) NC, (CMTS) 1860 Census
Ballard, William L.: (B) 1839, (CO) Pulaski, (A) 21, (BP) NC, (CMTS) 1860 Census
Ballard, Jr., N.: (B) 1834, (CO) Pulaski, (A) 26, (BP) IL, (CMTS) 1860 Census
Ballon, John: (B) 1835, (CO) Pulaski, (A) 25, (BP) IL, (CMTS) 1860 Census
Ballow, Maria: (B) 1842, (CO) Pulaski, (A) 18, (BP) MO, (CMTS) 1860 Census
Ballow, Newton: (B) 1838, (CO) Pulaski, (A) 22, (BP) MO, (CMTS) 1860 Census
Balsiger, Elizabeth: (D) Sep. 26, 1896, (CO) Andrew, (C) Oak Ridge Cemetery (A) 67Y 4M 15D
Bambrick, Andrew: (B) 1847, (D) 1883, (CO) St. Louis, (C) Calvary Cemetery
Bambrick, Annie M.: (B) 1875, (D) 1938, (CO) St. Louis, (C) Calvary Cemetery
Bambrick, Catherine: (B) May 15, 1854, (D) Aug. 24, 1894, (CO) St. Louis, (C) Calavary Cemetery
Bambrick, Dr. Thomas J.: (B) 1903, (D) 1967, (CO) St. Louis, (C) Calvary Cemetery
Bambrick, John F.: (B) 1882, (D) 1959, (CO) St. Louis, (C) Calvary Cemetery
Bambrick, Mary: (B) 1878, (D) 1882, (CO) St. Louis, (C) Calvary Cemetery
Bambrick, Patrick W.: (B) 1877, (D) 1931, (CO) St. Louis, (C) Calvary Cemetery
Bannis, Euphrates: (B) 1842, (CO) Pulaski, (A) 18, (BP) MO, (CMTS)] 1860 Census
Bannister, Elsie F.: (B) 1900, (D) 1965, (CO) St. Louis, (C) Calvary Cemetery
Bannister, Florence: (B) Mar. 9, 1866, (D) Mar. 26, 1908, (CO) St. Louis, (C) Calvary Cemetery
Bannister, Joseph B.: (B) 1891, (D) 1965, (CO) St. Louis, (C) Calvary Cemetery
Barcus, Warner: (B) Aug. 23, 1814, (D) Oct. 18, 1898, (CO) Barry, (C) Cassville Cemetery

Barker, Birtha Edna: (B) Dec. 27, 1874, (D) Oct. 3, 1943, (CO) Henry, (C) Knights of Pythias Cemetery, Deepwater, MO
Barker, Frances D.: (B) Dec. 22, 1925, (D) Jul. 20, 1986, (CO) Henry, (C) Knights of Pythias Cemetery, Deepwater, MO
Barker, Rollo T.: (B) Feb. 17, 1901, (D) Jun. 10, 1988, (CO) Henry, (C) Knights of Pythias Cemetery, Deepwater, MO
Barlow, Stephen A.: (B) 1816, (D) 1895, (CO) St. Louis
Barnard, Elizabeth: (B) 1848, (CO) Pulaski, (A) 12, (BP) MO, (CMTS) 1860 Census
Barnard, Emily: (B) 1839, (CO) Pulaski, (A) 21, (BP) KY, (CMTS) 1860 Census
Barnard, Jesse: (B) 1846, (CO) Pulaski, (A) 14, (BP) MO, (CMTS) 1860 Census
Barnard, Nancy: (B) 1856, (CO) Pulaski, (A) 4, (BP) MO, (CMTS) 1860 Census
Barnard, Rose L.: (B) 1843, (CO) Pulaski, (A) 17, (BP) IN, (CMTS) 1860 Census
Barnard, William: (B) 1850, (CO) Pulaski, (A) 10, (BP) MO, (CMTS) 1860 Census
Barnes, Alfred: (B) Jun. 1, 1790, (D) May 6, 1888, (CO) Callaway, (NWS) *Fulton Telegraph*
Barnes, Bessie: (D) Jul. 16, 1905, (CO) Callaway, (NWS) *Fulton Telegraph*
Barnes, Charles (D) Nov. 22, 1894, (CO) Callaway, (NWS) *Callaway Weekly Gazette*
Barnes, Julia: (D) Feb. 9, 1899, (CO) Callaway, (NWS) *Fulton Telegraph*
Barnes, Martain Alexander: (B) Sep. 8, 1833, (D) Feb. 25, 1875, (CO) Oregon, (C) Falling Springs Cemetery
Barnes, Mrs. Charles: (D) Dec. 13, 1897, (CO) Callaway, (NWS) *Callaway Weekly Gazette*
Barnes, Mrs. Nancy: (D) Apr. 19, 1906, (CO) Callaway, (NWS) *Callaway Weekly Gazette*
Barnes, Mrs. Sarah: (D) Apr. 10, 1879, (CO) Callaway, (NWS) *Fulton Telegraph*
Barnes, Parker: (D) Mar. 15, 1904, (CO) Callaway, (NWS) *Callaway Weekly Gazette*
Barnes, Susan Jemma: (D) Oct. 28, 1860, (CO) Callaway, (NWS) *Callaway County, Missouri Telegrah*
Barnes,: (B) Feb. 15, 1896, (D) Oct. ??, 1968, (CO) Polk
Barnett, James A.: (B) 1848, (CO) Pulaski, (A) 12, (BP) MO, (CMTS) 1860 Census
Barnett, Joseph M.: (B) 1853, (CO) Pulaski, (A) 7, (BP) MO, (CMTS) 1860 Census

Barnett, Lincoln: (D) Dec. 22, 1944, (CO) Grundy, (CMTS) A. F. & A. M. Trenton Lodge 111
Barnett, Margaret: (B) 1823, (CO) Pulaski, (A) 37, (BP) TN, (CMTS) 1860 Census
Barnett, Martha A.: (B) 1844, (CO) Pulaski, (A) 16, (BP) MO, (CMTS) 1860 Census
Barnett, Martha J.: (B) 1851, (CO) Pulaski, (A) 9, (BP) MO, (CMTS) 1860 Census
Barnett, Mary J.: (B) 1842, (CO) Pulaski, (A) 18, (BP) MO, (CMTS) 1860 Census
Barnett, Melinda C.: (B) 1855, (CO) Pulaski, (A) 5, (BP) MO, (CMTS) 1860 Census
Barnett, Membra E.: (B) 1845, (CO) Pulaski, (A) 15, (BP) MO, (CMTS) 1860 Census
Barnett, Robert P.: (B) 1850, (CO) Pulaski, (A) 10, (BP) MO, (CMTS) 1860 Census
Barnidge, Edward: (D) Jan. 14, 1877, (CO) St. Louis, (C) Calvary Cemetery
Barns, Baalam: (B) 1858, (CO) Pulaski, (A) 2, (BP) MO, (CMTS) 1860 Census
Barns, Hezekiah: (B) 1851, (CO) Pulaski, (A) 9, (BP) MO, (CMTS) 1860 Census
Barns, Jane: (B) 1840, (CO) Pulaski, (A) 20, (BP) IN, (CMTS) 1860 Census
Barns, Lephaniah: (B) 1830, (CO) Pulaski, (A) 30, (BP) TN, (CMTS) 1860 Census
Barns, Margaret: (B) 1853, (CO) Pulaski, (A) 7, (BP) MO, (CMTS) 1860 Census
Barrett, Joel Lee: (B) 1866, (D) 1944, (CO) Oregon, (C) Falling Springs Cemetery
Barrett, May E.T.: (B) 1879, (D) 1948, (CO) St. Louis, (C) Calvary Cemetery
Barrett, Peter T.: (B) 1869, (D) 1960, (CO) St. Louis, (C) Calvary Cemetery
Barringer, Harriet: (B) 1828, (CO) Stone, (A) 42, (BP) AR, (CMTS) 1870 Census
Barringer, James: (B) 1848, (CO) Stone, (A) 22, (BP) AR, (CMTS) 1870 Census
Barringer, Martha A.: (B) 1853, (CO) Stone, (A) 17, (BP) AR, (CMTS) 1870 Census
Barry, Jeanette E.: (D) Sep., 1974, (CO) St. Louis, (C) Calvary Cemetery
Bartlett, Hiram: (B) 1845, (CO) Pulaski, (A) 15, (BP) MO, (CMTS) 1860 Census

Bartlett, James M.: (B) 1831, (CO) Pulaski, (A) 29, (BP) MO, (CMTS) 1860 Census
Bartlett, John G.: (B) 1841, (CO) Pulaski, (A) 19, (BP) MO, (CMTS) 1860 Census
Bartlett, Luthea: (B) 1854, (CO) Pulaski, (A) 6, (BP) MO, (CMTS) 1860 Census
Bartlett, Margaret: (B) 1856, (CO) Pulaski, (A) 4, (BP) MO, (CMTS) 1860 Census
Bartlett, Martha: (B) 1836, (CO) Pulaski, (A) 24, (BP) MO, (CMTS) 1860 Census
Bartlett, Mary: (B) 1818, (CO) Pulaski, (A) 42, (BP) MO, (CMTS) 1860 Census
Bartlett, Mary B.: (B) 1832, (CO) Pulaski, (A) 28, (BP) IN, (CMTS) 1860 Census
Bartlett, Rosannah: (B) 1850, (CO) Pulaski, (A) 10, (BP) MO, (CMTS) 1860 Census
Bartlett, Ruben: (B) 1848, (CO) Pulaski, (A) 12, (BP) MO, (CMTS) 1860 Census
Bartlett, Solomon: (B) 1831, (CO) Pulaski, (A) 29, (BP) MO, (CMTS) 1860 Census
Bartlett, Thomas: (B) 1837, (CO) Pulaski, (A) 23, (BP) MO, (CMTS) 1860 Census
Barton, Mary: (B) 1833, (CO) Stone, (A) 17, (BP) MO, (CMTS) 1870 Census
Barton, William: (B) 1829, (CO) Stone, (A) 21, (BP) AR, (CMTS) 1870 Census
Bass, Clara: (B) 1832, (CO) Stone, (A) 18, (BP) MO, (CMTS) 1870 Census
Bass, John: (B) 1827, (CO) Stone, (A) 23, (BP) MO, (CMTS) 1870 Census
Bates, Alice A.: (B) 1842, (CO) Pulaski, (A) 18, (BP) MO, (CMTS) 1860 Census
Bates, Almira M.: (B) 1855, (CO) Pulaski, (A) 5, (BP) MO, (CMTS) 1860 Census
Bates, H.: (B) 1828, (CO) Pulaski, (A) 32, (BP) MO, (CMTS) 1860 Census
Bates, James: (B) 1837, (CO) Pulaski, (A) 23, (BP) MO, (CMTS) 1860 Census
Bates, Larkin: (B) 1839, (CO) Pulaski, (A) 21, (BP) MO, (CMTS) 1860 Census
Bates, Lucy: (B) 1838, (CO) Pulaski, (A) 22, (BP) TN, (CMTS) 1860 Census
Bates, Mary: (B) 1830, (CO) Pulaski, (A) 30, (BP) VA, (CMTS) 1860

Census

Bates, William: (B) 1844, (CO) Pulaski, (A) 16, (BP) TN, (CMTS) 1860 Census

Bates, William S.: (B) 1853, (CO) Pulaski, (A) 7, (BP) MO, (CMTS) 1860 Census

Bath, Sarah A.: (B) 1846, (CO) Stone, (A) 24, (BP) MO, (CMTS) 1870 Census

Bath, Steven: (B) 1839, (CO) Stone, (A) 31, (BP) TN, (CMTS) 1870 Census

Baue, Hermann: (B) Nov. 30, 1817, (D) May 20, 1897, (CO) Jefferson, (C) Old St. John's Catholic Cemetery

Bauer, Alfred: (B) 1876, (D) 1918, (CO) St. Louis, (C) Calvary Cemetery

Bauer, Emma: (B) 1854, (D) 1930, (CO) St. Louis, (C) Calvary Cemetery

Bauer, Marthella: (B) 1886, (D) 1890, (CO) St. Louis, (C) Calvary Cemetery

Bauer, Mary E.: (B) 1891, (D) 1963, (CO) St. Louis, (C) Calvary Cemetery

Bauer, Sr., Raymond O.: (B) Nov. 16, 1901, (D) Jun. 27, 1993, (CO) St. Louis, (C) Calavary Cemetery

Baur, William M.: (B) 1887, (D) 1956, (CO) St. Louis, (C) Calvary Cemetery

Bayne, Forest H.: (D) Mar. 8, 1935, (CO) Grundy, (CMTS) A. F. & A. M. Trenton Lodge 111

Beacham, John C.: (D) Nov. 29, 1945, (CO) Grundy, (CMTS) A. F. & A. M. Trenton Lodge 111

Beagle, Sarah E.: (B) 1840, (CO) Pulaski, (A) 20, (BP) IL, (CMTS) 1860 Census

Beagle, William A.: (B) 1828, (CO) Pulaski, (A) 32, (BP) NY, (CMTS) 1860 Census

Beal, Ara M.: (B) 1849, (CO) Stone, (A) 1, (BP) MO, (CMTS) 1870 Census

Beal, Ellen: (B) 1840, (CO) Stone, (A) 10, (BP) AR, (CMTS) 1870 Census

Beal, James: (B) 1795, (CO) Stone, (A) 55, (BP) NC, (CMTS) 1870 Census

Beal, James: (B) 1838, (CO) Stone, (A) 12, (BP) MO, (CMTS) 1870 Census

Beal, Elizabeth: (B) 1845, (CO) Stone, (A) 5, (BP) MO, (CMTS) 1870 Census

Beal, Sarah J.: (B) 1815, (CO) Stone, (A) 35, (BP) MS, (CMTS) 1870 Census

Beal, Valeny: (B) 1834, (CO) Stone, (A) 16, (BP) AR, (CMTS) 1870 Census

Bearbow,: (B) 1832, (CO) Pulaski, (A) 28, (BP) NY, (CMTS) 1860 Census
Beard, Sarah Jane: (B) 1881, (D) 1925, (CO) St. Louis, (C) Calvary Cemetery
Beard, William J.: (B) 1881, (D) 1951, (CO) St. Louis, (C) Calvary Cemetery
Beaucham, Lawence: (B) Oct. 17, 1831, (D) Nov., 1870, (CO) Audrain, (C) Old Village Cemetery
Beck, John: (B) 1831, (CO) Pulaski, (A) 29, (BP) IN, (CMTS) 1860 Census
Beckley, Eileen: (B) 1890, (D) 1981, (CO) St. Louis, (C) Calvary Cemetery
Beckley, George W.: (B) 1883, (D) 1964, (CO) St. Louis, (C) Calvary Cemetery
Belche, Calvin: (D) Jun. 24, 1889, (CO) Grundy, (CMTS) A. F. & A. M. Trenton Lodge 111
Belk, Clarence C.: (D) Dec., 1909, (CO) St. Louis, (C) Calvary Cemetery
Belk, Norman: (D) Apr., 1911, (CO) St. Louis, (C) Calvary Cemetery
Belk, Pauline: (D) Oct., 1916, (CO) St. Louis, (C) Calvary Cemetery
Bell, Ann A.: (B) 1898, (D) 1983, (CO) St. Louis, (C) Calvary Cemetery
Bell, Betty: (B) 1904, (D) 1928, (CO) St. Louis, (C) Calvary Cemetery
Bell, Edward: (B) 1895, (D) 1917, (CO) Oregon, (C) Falling Springs Cemetery
Bell, Elmer J.: (B) 1893, (D) 1941, (CO) St. Louis, (C) Calvary Cemetery
Bell, James E.: (B) 1868, (D) 1943, (CO) Oregon, (C) Falling Springs Cemetery
Bell, Sarah Ann: (B) 1872, (D) 1939, (CO) Oregon, (C) Falling Springs Cemetery
Bell,George: (B) 1894, (D) 1925, (CO) Oregon, (C) Falling Springs Cemetery
Bench, Andy: (B) 1852, (CO) Pulaski, (A) 8, (BP) MO, (CMTS) 1860 Census
Bench, Daniel: (B) 1854, (CO) Pulaski, (A) 6, (BP) MO, (CMTS) 1860 Census
Bench, Henry: (B) 1833, (CO) Pulaski, (A) 27, (BP) IN, (CMTS) 1860 Census
Bench, Lucinda: (B) 1850, (CO) Pulaski, (A) 10, (BP) MO, (CMTS) 1860 Census
Bench, Lucy A.: (B) 1848, (CO) Pulaski, (A) 12, (BP) MO, (CMTS) 1860 Census
Bench, Mary: (B) 1834, (CO) Pulaski, (A) 26, (BP) MO, (CMTS) 1860 Census
Bench, Pulaski: (B) 1853, (CO) Pulaski, (A) 7, (BP) MO, (CMTS) 1860

Census
Bender, Eugene: (B) May 2, 1880, (D) Jul. 27, 1945, (CO) St. Louis, (C) Calavary Cemetery
Bengaman, Eliza: (B) 1830, (CO) Stone, (A) 20, (BP) OH, (CMTS) 1870 Census
Bengaman, Reubin: (B) 1820, (CO) Stone, (A) 30, (BP) IL, (CMTS) 1870 Census
Bengiman, James M.: (B) 1840, (CO) Stone, (A) 10, (BP) MO, (CMTS) 1870 Census
Bengiman, John: (B) 1795, (CO) Stone, (A) 55, (BP) IN, (CMTS) 1870 Census
Bengiman, Mary: (B) 1836, (CO) Stone, (A) 14, (BP) MO, (CMTS) 1870 Census
Bengiman, Thomas: (B) 1838, (CO) Stone, (A) 12, (BP) MO, (CMTS) 1870 Census
Benham, Alfred: (B) 1836, (CO) Stone, (A) 14, (BP) MO, (CMTS) 1870 Census
Benham, Caroline R.: (B) 1842, (CO) Stone, (A) 8, (BP) MO, (CMTS) 1870 Census
Benham, Fisla Ann: (B) 1837, (CO) Stone, (A) 13, (BP) IN, (CMTS) 1870 Census
Benham, James: (B) 1829, (CO) Stone, (A) 21, (BP) MO, (CMTS) 1870 Census
Benham, Malinda: (B) 1835, (CO) Stone, (A) 15, (BP) IN, (CMTS) 1870 Census
Benham, Mary Jane: (B) 1841, (CO) Stone, (A) 9, (BP) MO, (CMTS) 1870 Census
Benham, Robert: (B) 1826, (CO) Stone, (A) 24, (BP) MO, (CMTS) 1870 Census
Benham, Robert: (B) 1848, (CO) Stone, (A) 2, (BP) MO, (CMTS) 1870 Census
Benham, William: (B) 1845, (CO) Stone, (A) 5, (BP) MO, (CMTS) 1870 Census
Benham, Willliam: (B) 1831, (CO) Stone, (A) 19, (BP) MO, (CMTS) 1870 Census
Benhan, Donald Patrick: (B) Nov. 3, 1925, (D) Mar. 24, 1961, (CO) St. Louis, (C) Calavary Cemetery
Benne, Eugene: (D) 1976, (CO) St. Louis, (C) Calvary Cemetery
Benne, Henry: (D) 1916, (CO) St. Louis, (C) Calvary Cemetery
Benne, Henry L.: (D) 1964, (CO) St. Louis, (C) Calvary Cemetery
Benne, John: (D) 1966, (CO) St. Louis, (C) Calvary Cemetery
Benne, May F.: (D) 1970, (CO) St. Louis, (C) Calvary Cemetery
Benne, Rose: (D) 1976, (CO) St. Louis, (C) Calvary Cemetery

Benne, Rose: (D) 1937, (CO) St. Louis, (C) Calvary Cemetery
Bennett, Carl: (B) Feb. 11, 1892, (D) Sep. 9, 1950, (CO) Henry, (C) Knights of Pythias Cemetery, Deepwater, MO
Bentzen, Adolph J.: (B) 1868, (D) 1948, (CO) St. Louis, (C) Calvary Cemetery
Bentzen, Mary: (B) 1869, (D) 1948, (CO) St. Louis, (C) Calvary Cemetery
Bentzen, Mary L.: (B) 1893, (D) 1986, (CO) St. Louis, (C) Calvary Cemetery
Bergs, Ida M.: (B) 1874, (D) 1942, (CO) St. Louis, (C) Calvary Cemetery
Bergs, Jacob P.: (B) 1869, (D) 1939, (CO) St. Louis, (C) Calvary Cemetery
Bergs, Phillipine: (B) 1886, (D) 1908, (CO) St. Louis, (C) Calvary Cemetery
Berman, Edward T.: (B) 1883, (D) 1935, (CO) St. Louis, (C) Calvary Cemetery
Berman, Eleanor M.: (B) 1884, (D) 1958, (CO) St. Louis, (C) Calvary Cemetery
Bernheimer, Joan E.: (B) 1926, (D) 1981, (CO) St. Louis, (C) Calvary Cemetery
Berre, Lucy: (B) Aug. 8, 1808, (D) Sep. 6, 1872, (CO) Barry, (C) Cassville Cemetery
Berresheim, George J.: (B) 1864, (D) 1929, (CO) St. Louis, (C) Calvary Cemetery
Berry, Barbara A.: (B) 1832, (CO) Pulaski, (A) 28, (BP) Holland, (CMTS) 1860 Census
Berry, Carrie L.: (B) 1835, (CO) Stone, (A) 35, (BP) MO, (CMTS) 1870 Census
Berry, Charity E.: (B) 1856, (CO) Stone, (A) 14, (BP) MO, (CMTS) 1870 Census
Berry, Charles: (B) 1856, (CO) Stone, (A) 14, (BP) MO, (CMTS) 1870 Census
Berry, Charles: (B) 1835, (CO) Stone, (A) 35, (BP) MO, (CMTS) 1870 Census
Berry, Charles A.: (B) 1855, (CO) Stone, (A) 15, (BP) MO, (CMTS) 1870 Census
Berry, Charles Byron: (B) 1831, (CO) Stone, (A) 39, (BP) VA, (CMTS) 1870 Census
Berry, Charles D.: (B) 1841, (CO) Stone, (A) 29, (BP) GA, (CMTS) 1870 Census
Berry, Charles Edwin: (B) 1855, (CO) Stone, (A) 15, (BP) MO, (CMTS) 1870 Census
Berry, Charles H.: (B) 1858, (CO) Stone, (A) 12, (BP) MO, (CMTS) 1870 Census

Berry, Charles Lee: (B) 1820, (CO) Stone, (A) 50, (BP) KY, (CMTS) 1870 Census
Berry, Christian: (B) 1854, (CO) Pulaski, (A) 6, (BP) IN, (CMTS) 1860 Census
Berry, Eliza: (B) 1845, (CO) Stone, (A) 25, (BP) MO, (CMTS) 1870 Census
Berry, Isaac: (B) 1838, (CO) Stone, (A) 32, (BP) MO, (CMTS) 1870 Census
Berry, Mary: (B) 1818, (CO) Pulaski, (A) 42, (BP) KY, (CMTS) 1860 Census
Berry, Sebastian: (B) 1856, (CO) Pulaski, (A) 4, (BP) MO, (CMTS) 1860 Census
Berry, Silas J.: (B) 1821, (CO) Pulaski, (A) 39, (BP) KY, (CMTS) 1860 Census
Berry, Dr. W. R.: (D) Nov. 29,1893, (CO) Grundy, (CMTS) A. F. & A. M. Trenton Lodge 111
Berry, Guy N.: (D) Jan. 4, 1934, (CO) Grundy, (CMTS) A. F. & A. M. Trenton Lodge 111
Bert, Elbert: (B) Jan 18, 1836, (D) Jan. 25, 1898, (CO) Barry, (C) Cassville Cemetery
Berthold, Augustus: (D) Jan. 21, 1918, (CO) St. Louis, (NWS) *St. Louis Post Dispatch*, Jan. 22, 1918, (A) 75Y
Beydler, Charles T.: (B) 1833, (D) 1910, (CO) Cedar, (C) Brashear Cemetery
Bibles, Elizabeth: (B) 1846, (CO) Pulaski, (A) 14, (BP) TN, (CMTS) 1860 Census
Bibles, Jacob: (B) 1823, (CO) Pulaski, (A) 37, (BP) TN, (CMTS) 1860 Census
Bibles, James: (B) 1856, (CO) Pulaski, (A) 4, (BP) IL, (CMTS) 1860 Census
Bibles, John: (B) 1848, (CO) Pulaski, (A) 12, (BP) TN, (CMTS) 1860 Census
Bibles, Lusane: (B) 1847, (CO) Pulaski, (A) 13, (BP) TN, (CMTS) 1860 Census
Bibles, Mary E.: (B) 1854, (CO) Pulaski, (A) 6, (BP) TN, (CMTS) 1860 Census
Bibles, Ruth: (B) 1852, (CO) Pulaski, (A) 8, (BP) TN, (CMTS) 1860 Census
Bickel, Samuel C.: (D) Jul. 27, 1920, (CO) Grundy, (CMTS) A. F. & A. M. Trenton Lodge 111
Biery, Magdelena: (B) Aug. 16, 1834, (D) Nov. 3, 1869, (CO) Andrew, (C) Oak Ridge Cemetery
Biery, Ulrich: (B) 1825, (D) 1898, (CO) Andrew, (C) Oak Ridge Cemetery

Billberry, C.: (B) 1830, (CO) Pulaski, (A) 30, (BP) TN, (CMTS) 1860 Census
Billberry, Campbell: (B) 1852, (CO) Pulaski, (A) 8, (BP) TN, (CMTS) 1860 Census
Billberry, Edmund H.: (B) 1858, (CO) Pulaski, (A) 2, (BP) MO, (CMTS) 1860 Census
Billberry, Esau: (B) 1852, (CO) Pulaski, (A) 8, (BP) IL, (CMTS) 1860 Census
Billberry, Henry H.: (B) 1854, (CO) Pulaski, (A) 6, (BP) TN, (CMTS) 1860 Census
Billberry, Jane: (B) 1849, (CO) Pulaski, (A) 11, (BP) TN, (CMTS) 1860 Census
Billberry, John T.: (B) 1846, (CO) Pulaski, (A) 14, (BP) TN, (CMTS) 1860 Census
Billberry, Luthur M.: (B) 1856, (CO) Pulaski, (A) 4, (BP) TN, (CMTS) 1860 Census
Billberry, Margaret: (B) 1827, (CO) Pulaski, (A) 33, (BP) TN, (CMTS) 1860 Census
Billberry, Martha E.: (B) 1850, (CO) Pulaski, (A) 10, (BP) TN, (CMTS) 1860 Census
Billberry, Polly M.: (B) 1855, (CO) Pulaski, (A) 5, (BP) TN, (CMTS) 1860 Census
Billberry, Squire: (B) 1854, (CO) Pulaski, (A) 6, (BP) TN, (CMTS) 1860 Census
Billing, Mary T.: (B) 1854, (D) 1879, (CO) St. Louis, (C) Calvary Cemetery
Billings, John L.: (B) 1844, (D) 1904, (CO) St. Louis, (C) Calvary Cemetery
Bingaman, Emiline S.: (B) 1826, (CO) Stone, (A) 24, (BP) MO, (CMTS) 1870 Census
Bingaman, Louisa J.: (B) 1843, (CO) Stone, (A) 7, (BP) MO, (CMTS) 1870 Census
Bingaman, William T: (B) 1847, (CO) Stone, (A) 3, (BP) KS, (CMTS) 1870 Census
Birch, Chyntha J.: (B) 1850, (D) 1924, (CO) Henry, (C) Knights of Pythias Cemetery, Deepwater, MO
Bischoff, Sr., Charles E.: (D) Nov., 1963, (CO) St. Louis, (C) Calvary Cemetery
Bishop, Allie Osceloa: (D) May 3, 1862, (CO) Audrain, (C) Old Village Cemetery, Mexico, MO, (A) 1Y 8M 16D
Bishop, Ann Eliza: (D) Apr. 14, 1853, (CO) Audrain, (C) Old Village Cemetery, (A) 25Y

Bishop, Ann Eliza: (D) Apr. 14, 1853, (CO) Audrain, (C) Old Village Cemetery, (A) 25Y

Bishop, Clara: (B) 1842, (D) 1939, (CO) Cedar, (C) Brashear Cemetery

Bishop, James Wallace: (B) Apr. 14, 1840, (D) Aug. 10, 1851, (CO) Audrain, (C) Old Village Cemetery

Bishop, John: (B) 1837, (CO) Pulaski, (A) 23, (BP) TN, (CMTS) 1860 Census

Bishop, John L.: (B) 1855, (CO) Pulaski, (A) 5, (BP) MO, (CMTS) 1860 Census

Bishop, Louisa: (B) 1840, (CO) Pulaski, (A) 20, (BP) TN, (CMTS) 1860 Census

Bishop, Martha: (B) Nov. 1, 1846, (D) Feb. 18, 1890, (CO) Warren, (C) Hickory Grove Christian Church Cemetery

Bishop, Mary Isabel: (B) Jul. 13, 1846, (D) Oct. 6, 1847, (CO) Audrain, (C) Old Village Cemetery

Bishop, Napleon: (D) Mar. 2, 1878, (CO) Warren, (C) Hickory Grove Christian Church Cemetery

Bittner, John D.: (D) Jan. 21, 1918, (CO) St. Louis, (NWS) *St. Louis Post Dispatch*, Jan. 22, 1918, (A) 60, (SPOUSE) Lala L. Wilson; (CMTS) Audmore L. Bittner,son; Mrs. W. Wagoner, daughter; William Bittner, brother; Ella Bittner, sister; (C) Bellefontaine Cemetery

Blackby, Bailey: (B) Apr. 8, 1925, (D) Feb. 20, 1996, (CO) Stone, (DP) Reeds Spring, MO.

Blackwell, Lloyd Fisher: (B) Aug. 5, 1916, (D) Aug. 21, 2000, (CO) Jackson, (NWS) *Kansas City, Missouri Star*, Aug. 22, 2000

Blackwell, Roy: (B) Dec. 22, 1895, (D) Aug. 31, 1988, (CO) Stone, (DP) Crane, MO.

Blackwood, Martha A.: (B) 1826, (CO) Stone, (A) 24, (BP) MO, (CMTS) 1870 Census

Blackwood, Mary E.: (B) 1849, (CO) Stone, (A) 1, (BP) MO, (CMTS) 1870 Census

Blackwood, Sarah M.: (B) 1846, (CO) Stone, (A) 4, (BP) MO, (CMTS) 1870 Census

Blair, Eliza: (B) 1823, (CO) Pulaski, (A) 37, (BP) MO, (CMTS) 1860 Census

Blair, Francis A.: (B) 1818, (CO) Pulaski, (A) 42, (BP) MO, (CMTS) 1860 Census

Blair, Susan: (B) 1853, (CO) Pulaski, (A) 7, (BP) MO, (CMTS) 1860 Census

Blair, Wm.: (B) 1851, (CO) Pulaski, (A) 9, (BP) MO, (CMTS) 1860 Census

Blakey, Claude: (B) 1866, (D) 1946, (CO) Henry, (C) Knights of Pythias Cemetery, Deepwater, MO

Blankenship, Gilbert: (B) 1838, (D) 1912, (CO) Oregon, (C) Norman Cemetery

Blankenship, Martha: (B) May 1, 1830, (D) Nov. 16, 1897, (CO) Barry, (C) Old Corsicana Cemetery

Blannchard, Edson F.: (D) Jul. 15, 1941, (CO) Grundy, (CMTS) A. F. & A. M. Trenton Lodge 111

Blythe, Conrad: (B) 1839, (CO) Stone, (A) 31, (BP) IL, (CMTS) 1870 Census

Boatman, Nancy E.: (B) 1846, (CO) Pulaski, (A) 14, (BP) MO, (CMTS) 1860 Census

Boatman, William: (B) 1843, (CO) Pulaski, (A) 17, (BP) MO, (CMTS) 1860 Census

Boaz, David P.: (D) 1854, (CO) Audrain, (C) Old Village Cemetery (A) 42Y

Bockmon, John: (B) Nov. 25, 1882, (CO) Oregon, (C) Falling Springs Cemetery

Bockmon, Mary: (B) Mar. 2, 1843, (D) Mar. 12, 1908, (CO) Oregon, (C) Falling Springs Cemetery

Bode, Robert N.: (D) Sep. 7, 1934, (CO) St. Charles, (DP) New York City, NY, (OC) Vice-President George W. Luft Manufacturing Co.

Boggiana, John: (B) 1876, (D) 1933, (CO) St. Louis, (C) Calvary Cemetery

Boggiana, Orlena M.: (B) 1882, (D) 1969, (CO) St. Louis, (C) Calvary Cemetery

Boggiano, Catherine V.: (B) 1876, (D) 1957, (CO) St. Louis, (C) Calvary Cemetery

Boggiano, James L.: (B) 1884, (D) 1969, (CO) St. Louis, (C) Calvary Cemetery

Boggiano, Joseph J.: (B) 1861, (D) 1917, (CO) St. Louis, (C) Calvary Cemetery

Boggiano, Louis: (B) Nov. 1, 1834, (D) Sep. 1, 1906, (CO) St. Louis, (C) Calavary Cemetery

Boggiano, Louis J.: (B) Nov. 21, 1895, (D) Mar. 7, 1968, (CO) St. Louis, (C) Calavary Cemetery

Boggiano, Sr., Louis J.: (B) 1875, (D) 1960, (CO) St. Louis, (C) Calvary Cemetery

Boggiano, Marie: (B) 1841, (D) 1917, (CO) St. Louis, (C) Calvary Cemetery

Boggiano, Marie K.: (B) Sep. 27, 1905, (D) Sep. 26, 1991, (CO) St. Louis, (C) Calavary Cemetery

Boggiano, Mary: (B) 1867, (D) 1955, (CO) St. Louis, (C) Calvary Cemetery
Boggs, William: (B) 1844, (CO) Pulaski, (A) 16, (BP) MO, (CMTS) 1860 Census
Bogy, Joseph: (B) 1838, (D) 1907, (CO) St. Louis, (C) Calvary Cemetery
Boisseau, Oscar Gilliland: (B) Apr. 7, 1870, (D) Aug. 16, 1934, (CO) Johnson, (DP) Holden, MO
Boitano, Angelo A.: (B) 1864, (D) 1946, (CO) St. Louis, (C) Calvary Cemetery
Boland, Archibald J.: (B) 1840, (CO) Pulaski, (A) 20, (BP) MO, (CMTS) 1860 Census
Boland, Barrill: (B) 1819, (CO) Pulaski, (A) 41, (BP) mo, (CMTS) 1860 Census
Boland, Burrill P,: (B) 1845, (CO) Pulaski, (A) 15, (BP) MO, (CMTS) 1860 Census
Boland, Gilbert: (B) 1851, (CO) Pulaski, (A) 9, (BP) MO, (CMTS) 1860 Census
Boland, John: (B) 1838, (CO) Pulaski, (A) 22, (BP) MO, (CMTS) 1860 Census
Boland, Joseph F.: (B) 1853, (CO) Pulaski, (A) 7, (BP) MO, (CMTS) 1860 Census
Boland, Martha E.: (B) 1847, (CO) Pulaski, (A) 13, (BP) MO, (CMTS) 1860 Census
Boland, Mrs. John: (D) 1926, (CO) St. Louis, (C) Calvary Cemetery
Boland, Sarah A.: (B) 1839, (CO) Pulaski, (A) 21, (BP) MO, (CMTS) 1860 Census
Boland, Susan: (B) 1849, (CO) Pulaski, (A) 11, (BP) MO, (CMTS) 1860 Census
Boland, Susan C.: (B) 1819, (CO) Pulaski, (A) 41, (BP) KY, (CMTS) 1860 Census
Boldt, Cordelia B.: (D) Jun. 26, 2000, (CO) Jackson, (NWS) *Kansas City, Missouri Star*, July 12, 2000
Bolen, Cordelia B.: (B) 1848, (CO) Stone, (A) 22, (BP) TN, (CMTS) 1870 Census
Boley, Cory Domn: (B) 1845, (CO) Stone, (A) 25, (BP) MO, (CMTS) 1870 Census
Boley, Crystal O.: (B) 1828, (CO) Stone, (A) 42, (BP) TN, (CMTS) 1870 Census
Boley, Tennessee: (B) 1856, (CO) Stone, (A) 14, (BP) MO, (CMTS) 1870 Census
Bollinger, Samuel C.: (D) Aug. 29, 1942, (CO) Grundy, (CMTS) A. F. & A. M. Trenton Lodge 111
Bondurant, James: (B) 1836, (CO) Pulaski, (A) 24, (BP) VA, (CMTS)

1860 Census
Bonnett, Artemiesa: (B) 1848, (CO) Stone, (A) 22, (BP) TN, (CMTS) 1870 Census
Bonnett, Mongomery: (B) 1842, (CO) Stone, (A) 28, (BP) MO, (CMTS) 1870 Census
Booker, Edward: (B) 1836, (CO) Pulaski, (A) 24, (BP) TN, (CMTS) 1860 Census
Booker, Elizabeth: (B) 1856, (CO) Pulaski, (A) 4, (BP) TN, (CMTS) 1860 Census
Booker, Sarah: (B) 1842, (CO) Pulaski, (A) 18, (BP) TN, (CMTS) 1860 Census
Boone, Grace H.: (B) Jun. 5, 1922, (D) Apr. 2, 1953, (CO) Pettis, (C) Black Baptist Cemetery, Prairie Township
Borden, Aven S.: (B) 1855, (CO) Pulaski, (A) 5, (BP) IL, (CMTS) 1860 Census
Borden, Catharine: (B) 1847, (CO) Pulaski, (A) 13, (BP) TN, (CMTS) 1860 Census
Borden, Clarinda: (B) 1850, (CO) Pulaski, (A) 10, (BP) TN, (CMTS) 1860 Census
Borden, Elizabeth: (B) 1858, (CO) Pulaski, (A) 2, (BP) MO, (CMTS) 1860 Census
Borden, George W.: (B) 1848, (CO) Pulaski, (A) 12, (BP) TN, (CMTS) 1860 Census
Borden, Jesse: (B) 1819, (CO) Pulaski, (A) 41, (BP) TN, (CMTS) 1860 Census
Borden, Joanna: (B) 1830, (CO) Pulaski, (A) 30, (BP) TN, (CMTS) 1860 Census
Borden, John: (B) 1845, (CO) Pulaski, (A) 15, (BP) TN, (CMTS) 1860 Census
Bosch, Anna: (B) 1890, (D) 1966, (CO) St. Louis, (C) Calvary Cemetery
Bosch, John: (B) 1885, (D) 1945, (CO) St. Louis, (C) Calvary Cemetery
Bosley, Frank L.: (D) Jun. 5, 1937, (CO) Grundy, (CMTS) A. F. & A. M. Trenton Lodge 111
Boston, Mary: (B) 1840, (CO) Pulaski, (A) 20, (BP) KY, (CMTS) 1860 Census
Boston, Sarah C.: (B) 1856, (CO) Pulaski, (A) 4, (BP) KY, (CMTS) 1860 Census
Boston, William: (B) 1832, (CO) Pulaski, (A) 28, (BP) KY, (CMTS) 1860 Census
Bourne, James: (B) 1834, (CO) Pulaski, (A) 26, (BP) NC, (CMTS) 1860 Census
Bourne, Martha C.: (B) 1844, (CO) Pulaski, (A) 16, (BP) NC, (CMTS) 1860 Census

Bowen, Edward N.: (D) Nov. 24, 1880, (CO) St. Louis, (C) Calvary Cemetery
Bowen, James A.: (B) 1841, (CO) Pulaski, (A) 19, (BP) KY, (CMTS) 1860 Census
Bowen, John: (B) 1840, (CO) Pulaski, (A) 20, (BP) MO, (CMTS) 1860 Census
Bowman, Andrew: (B) 1849, (CO) Stone, (A) 1, (BP) MO, (CMTS) 1870 Census
Bowman, Andrew J.: (B) 1830, (CO) Stone, (A) 20, (BP) MO, (CMTS) 1870 Census
Bowman, China: (B) 1795, (CO) Stone, (A) 55, (BP) MO, (CMTS) 1870 Census
Bowman, Elizabeth: (B) 1794, (CO) Stone, (A) 56, (BP) IN, (CMTS) 1870 Census
Bowman, Elizabeth: (B) 1831, (CO) Stone, (A) 19, (BP) AR, (CMTS) 1870 Census
Bowman, Elizabeth C.: (B) 1841, (CO) Stone, (A) 9, (BP) MO, (CMTS) 1870 Census
Bowman, Elizy: (B) 1847, (CO) Stone, (A) 3, (BP) MO, (CMTS) 1870 Census
Bowman, H. D: (B) 1850, (CO) Stone, (A) 20, (BP) MO, (CMTS) 1870 Census
Bowman, Isaac: (B) 1838, (CO) Stone, (A) 12, (BP) MO, (CMTS) 1870 Census
Bowman, Jacob: (B) 1836, (CO) Stone, (A) 14, (BP) MO, (CMTS) 1870 Census
Bowman, Jane A.: (B) 1822, (CO) Stone, (A) 28, (BP) MO, (CMTS) 1870 Census
Bowman, Jeptha: (B) 1822, (CO) Stone, (A) 28, (BP) MO, (CMTS) 1870 Census
Bowman, Jeptha: (B) 1827, (CO) Stone, (A) 23, (BP) MO, (CMTS) 1870 Census
Bowman, John: (B) 1834, (CO) Stone, (A) 16, (BP) MO, (CMTS) 1870 Census
Bowman, John: (D) Mar. 16, 1856, (CO) Grundy, (CMTS) A. F. & A. M. Trenton Lodge 111
Bowman, John A.: (B) 1829, (CO) Stone, (A) 21, (BP) MO, (CMTS) 1870 Census
Bowman, John C.: (B) 1796, (CO) Stone, (A) 54, (BP) KY, (CMTS) 1870 Census
Bowman, Malinda J.: (B) 1827, (CO) Stone, (A) 23, (BP) MO, (CMTS) 1870 Census
Bowman, Margarette E.: (B) 1852, (CO) Stone, (A) 18, (BP) MO,

(CMTS) 1870 Census
Bowman, Martha J.: (B) 1845, (CO) Stone, (A) 5, (BP) MO, (CMTS) 1870 Census
Bowman, Noah: (B) 1840, (CO) Stone, (A) 10, (BP) MO, (CMTS) 1870 Census
Bowman, P. Elizabeth: (B) 1847, (CO) Stone, (A) 3, (BP) MO, (CMTS) 1870 Census
Bowman, Sarah C.: (B) 1840, (CO) Stone, (A) 10, (BP) MO, (CMTS) 1870 Census
Bowman, Sarah E.: (B) 1845, (CO) Stone, (A) 5, (BP) MO, (CMTS) 1870 Census
Bowman, Virginia C.: (B) 1845, (CO) Stone, (A) 5, (BP) MO, (CMTS) 1870 Census
Boyles, William W.: (D) May 13, 1919, (CO) Grundy, (CMTS) A. F. & A. M. Trenton Lodge 111
Boylan, Harry H.: (D) May 1, 1939, (CO) Grundy, (CMTS) A. F. & A. M. Trenton Lodge 111
Braden, Orris: (B) Nov. 5, 1901, (D) Jul. 15, 1974, (CO) Stone, (DP) Reeds Spring, MO.
Bradford, Elmira: (B) 1856, (CO) Pulaski, (A) 4, (BP) MO, (CMTS) 1860 Census
Bradford, Parmelia: (B) 1838, (CO) Pulaski, (A) 22, (BP) TN, (CMTS) 1860 Census
Bradford, W.: (B) 1819, (CO) Pulaski, (A) 41, (BP) KY, (CMTS) 1860 Census
Bradshaw, Renee: (B) 1887, (D) 1979, (CO) St. Louis, (C) Calvary Cemetery
Brady, Terrence: (D) Jan. 23, 1873, (CO) St. Louis, (C) Calvary Cemetery (A) 75
Brag, Artimessa: (B) 1858, (CO) Pulaski, (A) 2, (BP) MO, (CMTS) 1860 Census
Brag, Daniel: (B) 1794, (CO) Pulaski, (A) 66, (BP) NC, (CMTS) 1860 Census
Brag, Elizabeth: (B) 1842, (CO) Pulaski, (A) 18, (BP) TN, (CMTS) 1860 Census
Brag, Minerva: (B) 1847, (CO) Pulaski, (A) 13, (BP) MO, (CMTS) 1860 Census
Brag, Polly: (B) 1845, (CO) Pulaski, (A) 15, (BP) MO, (CMTS) 1860 Census
Brag, Rebecca: (B) 1849, (CO) Pulaski, (A) 11, (BP) MO, (CMTS) 1860 Census
Brag, Susannah: (B) 1817, (CO) Pulaski, (A) 43, (BP) TN, (CMTS) 1860 Census

Brainerd, Isaih: (D) Nov. 11, 1907, (CO) Grundy, (CMTS) A. F. & A. M. Trenton Lodge 111
Brake, Nancy: (B) 1830, (CO) Pulaski, (A) 30, (BP) NC, (CMTS) 1860 Census
Brake, Robert: (B) 1835, (CO) Pulaski, (A) 25, (BP) NC, (CMTS) 1860 Census
Branan, Hugh: (B) 1819, (D) Jun. 2, 1901, (CO) St. Louis, (C) Calvary Cemetery
Branan, Jr., Hugh: (B) 1857, (D) 1860, (CO) St. Louis, (C) Calvary Cemetery
Brandon, Cecile: (D) Sep. 18, 1892, (CO) St. Louis, (C) Calvary Cemetery (A) 84
Brannum, John P: (B) 1838, (CO) Stone, (A) 12, (BP) MO, (CMTS) 1870 Census
Brannum, Luke W.: (B) 1833, (CO) Stone, (A) 17, (BP) MO, (CMTS) 1870 Census
Brannum, Nancy: (B) 1830, (CO) Stone, (A) 20, (BP) MO, (CMTS) 1870 Census
Brannum, Nathan: (B) 1835, (CO) Stone, (A) 15, (BP) MO, (CMTS) 1870 Census
Brannum, Wilson: (B) 1796, (CO) Stone, (A) 54, (BP) KY, (CMTS) 1870 Census
Bransetter, S.: (D) Sep. 13, 1870, (CO) Audrain, (C) Old Village Cemetery (A) 59 Y. 11D
Branstuter, Allen T: (B) 1837, (CO) Stone, (A) 13, (BP) MO, (CMTS) 1870 Census
Branstuter, James M.: (B) 1833, (CO) Stone, (A) 17, (BP) MO, (CMTS) 1870 Census
Branstuter, John C.: (B) 1831, (CO) Stone, (A) 19, (BP) MO, (CMTS) 1870 Census
Branstuter, Mary Jane: (B) 1835, (CO) Stone, (A) 15, (BP) MO, (CMTS) 1870 Census
Branstuter, Morrow S.: (B) 1839, (CO) Stone, (A) 11, (BP) MO, (CMTS) 1870 Census
Branstuter, Nancy E.: (B) 1841, (CO) Stone, (A) 9, (BP) MO, (CMTS) 1870 Census
Branstuter, Thomas V: (B) 1843, (CO) Stone, (A) 7, (BP) MO, (CMTS) 1870 Census
Branstuter, William H.: (B) 1847, (CO) Stone, (A) 3, (BP) MO, (CMTS) 1870 Census
Brasher, Aquilla: (B) 1842, (D) 1912, (CO) Cedar, (C) Brashear Cemetery
Brasher, Earnest C.: (B) 1849, (D) 1908, (CO) Cedar, (C) Brashear Cemetery

Brasher, Green: (B) 1848, (D) 1860, (CO) Cedar, (C) Brashear Cemetery
Brasher, Julia: (B) 1845, (CO) Cedar, (C) Brashear Cemetery
Brasher, Larkin T: (B) 1841, (D) 1882, (CO) Cedar, (C) Brashear Cemetery
Brasher, M. I: (B) 1854, (CO) Cedar, (C) Brashear Cemetery
Brasher, Margaret: (B) 1852, (D) 1858, (CO) Cedar, (C) Brashear Cemetery
Brawley, Charley D.: (B) Nov. 25, 1866, (D) Jul. 18, 1929, (CO) Oregon, (C) Falling Springs Cemetery
Brawley, Faustine A.: (B) 11 May 1859, (D) Dec. 30, 1941, (CO) Oregon, (C) Falling Springs Cemetery
Brawley, Hettie: (B) Mar. 25, 1871, (D) Jul. 24, 1905, (CO) Oregon, (C) Falling Springs Cemetery
Brawley, John M.: (B) 29 April 1870, (D) 28 May 1937, (CO) Oregon, (C) Falling Springs Cemetery
Brawley, Martha: (B) 26 October 1871, (D) 25 Sepember 1932, (CO) Oregon, (C) Falling Springs Cemetery
Brawley, Polly: (B) 1880, (CO) Oregon, (C) Falling Springs Cemetery
Brawley, Sarah B.: (B) 1874, (D) 1938, (CO) Oregon, (C) Falling Springs Cemetery
Braziel, William: (B) 1848, (CO) Stone, (A) 22, (BP) MO, (CMTS) 1870 Census
Breen, John: (D) 1885, (CO) St. Louis, (C) Calvary Cemetery
Breen, Mary: (B) 1860, (D) 1887, (CO) St. Louis, (C) Calvary Cemetery
Breen, Stella: (D) 1893, (CO) St. Louis, (C) Calvary Cemetery
Bremels, Henry: (D) Jun. 30, 1909, (CO) St. Louis, (C) Calvary Cemetery, (A) 47
Bremmerman, Georgerge H.: (D) Jul. 4, 1950, (CO) Grundy, (CMTS) A. F. & A. M. Trenton Lodge 111
Brennan, Allen P.: (B) 1885, (D) 1955, (CO) St. Louis, (C) Calvary Cemetery
Brennan, Cecelia: (B) 1865, (D) 1945, (CO) St. Louis, (C) Calvary Cemetery
Brennan, George A.: (B) 1890, (D) 1971, (CO) St. Louis, (C) Calvary Cemetery
Brennan, Isabelle: (B) 1868, (D) 1927, (CO) St. Louis, (C) Calvary Cemetery
Brennan, John: (B) Mar. 7, 1846, (D) 1896, (CO) St. Louis, (C) Calavary Cemetery
Brennan, Mamie M.: (B) 1887, (D) 1969, (CO) St. Louis, (C) Calvary Cemetery
Brennan, Patrick W.: (B) 1868, (D) 1943, (CO) St. Louis, (C) Calvary Cemetery

Brennan, Thomas: (B) 1861, (D) 1923, (CO) St. Louis, (C) Calvary Cemetery
Brennan, William: (B) 1882, (D) 1911, (CO) St. Louis, (C) Calvary Cemetery
Breunig, Wenzel: (B) May 21, 1821, (D) Feb. 18, 1863, (CO) St. Louis, (C) Calvary Cemetery
Brevator, Anna Louise: (D) Aug. 25, 1864, (CO) St. Louis, (C) Calvary Cemetery
Brevator, Willie: (D) Dec. 14, 1863, (CO) St. Louis, (C) Calvary Cemetery (A) 3
Brewer, Delilah: (B) 1833, (CO) Pulaski, (A) 27, (BP) MO, (CMTS) 1860 Census
Brewer, Felix: (B) 1830, (CO) Pulaski, (A) 30, (BP) IL, (CMTS) 1860 Census
Brewer, Jackson: (B) 1830, (CO) Pulaski, (A) 30, (BP) MO, (CMTS) 1860 Census
Brewer, Mary H.: (B) 1855, (CO) Pulaski, (A) 5, (BP) MO, (CMTS) 1860 Census
Brickey, Mary: (B) 1838, (CO) Pulaski, (A) 22, (BP) MO, (CMTS) 1860 Census
Brickey, Mary: (B) 1838, (CO) Pulaski, (A) 22, (BP) MO, (CMTS) 1860 Census
Briggs, David: (B) 1849, (CO) Pulaski, (A) 11, (BP) IL, (CMTS) 1860 Census
Briggs, Margaret: (B) 1823, (CO) Pulaski, (A) 37, (BP) NC, (CMTS) 1860 Census
Briggs, William: (B) 1846, (CO) Pulaski, (A) 14, (BP) IL, (CMTS) 1860 Census
Briles, Larkin: (B) Oct. 19, 1874, (CO) Missouri, (CMTS) Draft Registration WWI in Modoc Co., CA.
Briscoe, Francis M.: (B) 1849, (CO) Pulaski, (A) 11, (BP) MO, (CMTS) 1860 Census
Briscoe, John H.: (B) 1851, (CO) Pulaski, (A) 9, (BP) MO, (CMTS) 1860 Census
Briscoe, Julia A.: (B) 1829, (CO) Pulaski, (A) 31, (BP) MO, (CMTS) 1860 Census
Brisolara, Augustine: (D) 1937, (CO) St. Louis, (C) Calvary Cemetery
Brisolara, Jennie: (D) 1955, (CO) St. Louis, (C) Calvary Cemetery
Brisolara, Mary L.: (D) 1920, (CO) St. Louis, (C) Calvary Cemetery
Brisolara, Nettie J.: (D) 1972, (CO) St. Louis, (C) Calvary Cemetery
Brisolara, Theresa L.: (D) 1946, (CO) St. Louis, (C) Calvary Cemetery
Brissolara, Dominick J.: (B) 1876, (D) 1940, (CO) St. Louis, (C) Calvary Cemetery

Brissolara, Mary V.: (B) 1880, (D) 1952, (CO) St. Louis, (C) Calvary Cemetery
Brittain, John H.: (B) 1837, (CO) Pulaski, (A) 23, (BP) TN, (CMTS) 1860 Census
Brittain, Missouri A.: (B) 1842, (CO) Pulaski, (A) 18, (BP) TN, (CMTS) 1860 Census
Brittam, James E.: (B) 1848, (CO) Pulaski, (A) 12, (BP) MO, (CMTS) 1860 Census
Brittam, Margaret J.: (B) 1850, (CO) Pulaski, (A) 10, (BP) MO, (CMTS) 1860 Census
Brittam, Mary E.: (B) 1853, (CO) Pulaski, (A) 7, (BP) MO, (CMTS) 1860 Census
Brittam, Nancy: (B) 1838, (CO) Pulaski, (A) 22, (BP) TN, (CMTS) 1860 Census
Brittam, Nancy A.: (B) 1855, (CO) Pulaski, (A) 5, (BP) ., (CMTS) 1860 Census
Brittam, Sarah A.: (B) 1857, (CO) Pulaski, (A) 3, (BP) MO, (CMTS) 1860 Census
Brittam, W.: (B) 1826, (CO) Pulaski, (A) 34, (BP) TN, (CMTS) 1860 Census
Brittam, William H.: (B) 1853, (CO) Pulaski, (A) 7, (BP) MO, (CMTS) 1860 Census
Brittan, Cynthia A.: (B) 1855, (CO) Pulaski, (A) 5, (BP) MO, (CMTS) 1860 Census
Brittan, Eliza J.: (B) 1837, (CO) Pulaski, (A) 23, (BP) KY, (CMTS) 1860 Census
Brittan, James P.: (B) 1831, (CO) Pulaski, (A) 29, (BP) TN, (CMTS) 1860 Census
Brittan, Mary M.: (B) 1853, (CO) Pulaski, (A) 7, (BP) MO, (CMTS) 1860 Census
Britton, Clementine: (B) 1904, (D) 1970, (CO) St. Louis, (C) Calvary Cemetery
Britton, Clementine J.: (B) 1866, (D) 1950, (CO) St. Louis, (C) Calvary Cemetery
Britton, Edward J.: (B) 1865, (D) 1945, (CO) St. Louis, (C) Calvary Cemetery
Britton, Edward J.: (B) 1895, (D) 1977, (CO) St. Louis, (C) Calvary Cemetery
Britton, Janet: (B) 1899, (D) 1983, (CO) St. Louis, (C) Calvary Cemetery
Britton, Melissa: (B) 1850, (CO) Pulaski, (A) 10, (BP) MO, (CMTS) 1860 Census
Britton, Newton: (B) 1847, (CO) Pulaski, (A) 13, (BP) MO, (CMTS) 1860 Census

Broaddus, Jerry: (B) ????, (D) Oct. 15, 1918, (CO) Livingston, (C) Edgewood Cemetery, (MIL) WWI, (PRTS) Joseph and Jessie Broaddus

Brocklen, Elizabeth: (B) 1832, (CO) Pulaski, (A) 28, (BP) TN, (CMTS) 1860 Census

Brook, Johnnie W.: (B) Jun. 28, 1922, (D) Apr. 13, 1999, (CO) Barry, (PRTS) Albert Washington Brock and Lulu Jimerson

Brooks, James: (B) 1850, (CO) Pulaski, (A) 10, (BP) MO, (CMTS) 1860 Census

Brooks, Milly: (B) 1818, (CO) Pulaski, (A) 42, (BP) IL, (CMTS) 1860 Census

Brooks, NeWilliaman: (B) 1853, (CO) Pulaski, (A) 7, (BP) IL, (CMTS) 1860 Census

Brooks, Ruth J.: (B) 1842, (CO) Pulaski, (A) 18, (BP) IL, (CMTS) 1860 Census

Brooks, Sarah E.: (B) 1847, (CO) Pulaski, (A) 13, (BP) IL, (CMTS) 1860 Census

Brooks, T.: (B) 1815, (CO) Pulaski, (A) 45, (BP) KY, (CMTS) 1860 Census

Brooks, William D.: (B) 1850, (CO) Pulaski, (A) 10, (BP) MO, (CMTS) 1860 Census

Brown, David S.: (B) 1837, (CO) Stone, (A) 33, (BP) NC, (CMTS) 1870 Census

Brown, DeWitt C.: (B) 1826, (D) 1884, (CO) St. Louis, (C) Calvary Cemetery

Brown, Eliza: (B) 1851, (CO) Stone, (A) 19, (BP) MO, (CMTS) 1870 Census

Brown, Eliza J.: (B) 1846, (CO) Stone, (A) 24, (BP) TN, (CMTS) 1870 Census

Brown, Ellis L.: (B) Nov. 17, 1915, (D) Feb. 15, 1992, (CO) St. Louis, (C) Calavary Cemetery

Brown, George L.: (B) Apr. 6, 1923, (D) Aug. 19, 2000, (CO) Jackson, (NWS) *Kansas City, Missouri Star*, Aug. 22, 2000

Brown, Harold L.: (B) Oct. 17, 1918, (D) 24 April 1934, (CO) Oregon, (C) Falling Springs Cemetery

Brown, Jane P.: (B) 1814, (D) Jan. 18, 1868, (CO) Oregon, (C) Falling Springs Cemetery

Brown, John H.: (B) 1840, (CO) Stone, (A) 30, (BP) TN, (CMTS) 1870 Census

Brown, Louis M.: (D) Feb. 7, 1917, (CO) Grundy, (CMTS) A. F. & A. M. Trenton Lodge 111

Brown, Lucy: (B) 1853, (CO) Stone, (A) 17, (BP) MO, (CMTS) 1870 Census

Brown, Mary E.: (B) 1845, (CO) Stone, (A) 25, (BP) TN, (CMTS) 1870 Census
Brown, Mrs. H. H.: (D) Jan. 22, 1863, (CO) Audrain, (C) Old Village Cemetery (A) 62Y 11M
Brown, Nancy: (B) 1818, (CO) Pulaski, (A) 42, (BP) TN, (CMTS) 1860 Census
Brown, Nancy: (B) 1839, (CO) Pulaski, (A) 21, (BP) MO, (CMTS) 1860 Census
Brown, Nancy: (B) 1850, (CO) Stone, (A) 20, (BP) AL, (CMTS) 1870 Census
Brown, Rebecca: (B) 1846, (CO) Pulaski, (A) 14, (BP) TN, (CMTS) 1860 Census
Brown, Rebecca: (B) 1831, (D) 1904, (CO) St. Louis, (C) Calvary Cemetery
Brown, Richard: (B) 1817, (CO) Pulaski, (A) 43, (BP) TN, (CMTS) 1860 Census
Brown, Richard: (B) 1856, (CO) Pulaski, (A) 4, (BP) TN, (CMTS) 1860 Census
Brown, Robert: (B) 1831, (CO) Stone, (A) 19, (BP) TN, (CMTS) 1870 Census
Brown, Robert L.: (B) Sep. 1, 1911, (D) Jan. 24, 1956, (CO) St. Louis, (C) Calvary Cemetery
Brown, Rufus B.: (B) 1819, (CO) Stone, (A) 51, (BP) NC, (CMTS) 1870 Census
Brown, Ruth: (B) 1815, (CO) Stone, (A) 55, (BP) NC, (CMTS) 1870 Census
Brown, Sarah A.: (B) Apr. 2, 1831, (D) Apr. 7, 1863, (CO) Audrain, (C) Old Village Cemetery
Brown, Sarah J.: (B) 1833, (CO) Stone, (A) 17, (BP) TN, (CMTS) 1870 Census
Brown, Shirley Mae: (D) Aug. 21, 2000, (CO) Jackson, (NWS) *Kansas City, Missouri Star*, Aug. 22, 2000
Brown, Thomas: (B) 1814, (D) 1896, (CO) Douglas
Brown, Thomas E.: (B) Mar. 16, 1911, (CO) Wayne
Brown, William: (B) 1845, (CO) Stone, (A) 25, (BP) NC, (CMTS) 1870 Census
Brown, William: (D) Aug. 9, 1884, (CO) Grundy, (CMTS) A. F. & A. M. Trenton Lodge 111
Brownfield, Elizabeth: (B) 1821, (CO) Pulaski, (A) 39, (BP) KY, (CMTS) 1860 Census
Brownfield, Frances M.: (B) 1854, (CO) Pulaski, (A) 6, (BP) MO, (CMTS) 1860 Census
Brownfield, James P.: (B) 1851, (CO) Pulaski, (A) 9, (BP) MO, (CMTS)

1860 Census
Brownfield, Joseph: (B) 1848, (CO) Pulaski, (A) 12, (BP) MO, (CMTS) 1860 Census
Brownfield, Thomas: (B) 1840, (CO) Pulaski, (A) 20, (BP) MO, (CMTS) 1860 Census
Brownlee, Margarette: (B) 1852, (D) 1913, (CO) Cedar, (C) Brashear Cemetery
Brubeck, Faye: (B) Jul. 20, 1907, (D) Jun. 9, 1991, (CO) Henry, (C) Knights of Pythias Cemetery, Deepwater, MO
Brubeck, John Robert: (B) Sep. 26, 1920, (CO) St. Clair, (PRTS) William A. Brubeck and Alma Breeze
Brubeck, William L.: (B) Mar. 21, 1916, (D) Jul. 17, 1932, (CO) Cedar,
Bruening, Frank: (B) 1871, (D) 1923, (CO) St. Louis, (C) Calvary Cemetery
Bruening, Joseph: (B) 1840, (D) 1906, (CO) St. Louis, (C) Calvary Cemetery
Bruening, Joseph: (B) 1879, (D) 1927, (CO) St. Louis, (C) Calvary Cemetery
Bruening, Katherine: (B) 1842, (D) 1902, (CO) St. Louis, (C) Calvary Cemetery
Bruessler, William H.: (D) 1895, (CO) St. Louis, (C) Calvary Cemetery
Brungard, Andrew: (D) Feb. 27, 1877, (CO) St. Louis, (C) Calvary Cemetery (A) 47
Bryan, Alexander: (B) 1831, (CO) Pulaski, (A) 29, (BP) TN, (CMTS) 1860 Census
Bryan, Arter: (B) 1852, (CO) Pulaski, (A) 8, (BP) MO, (CMTS) 1860 Census
Bryan, Bethel: (B) 1846, (CO) Pulaski, (A) 14, (BP) MO, (CMTS) 1860 Census
Bryan, Celia: (B) 1821, (CO) Pulaski, (A) 39, (BP) TN, (CMTS) 1860 Census
Bryan, Clàrinda: (B) 1849, (CO) Pulaski, (A) 11, (BP) MO, (CMTS) 1860 Census
Bryan, Daniel: (B) 1852, (CO) Pulaski, (A) 8, (BP) TN, (CMTS) 1860 Census
Bryan, Eliza: (B) 1849, (CO) Pulaski, (A) 11, (BP) MO, (CMTS) 1860 Census
Bryan, Elizabeth: (B) 1820, (CO) Pulaski, (A) 40, (BP) NC, (CMTS) 1860 Census
Bryan, Elizabeth: (B) 1852, (CO) Pulaski, (A) 8, (BP) MO, (CMTS) 1860 Census
Bryan, Everett: (D) Sep. 25, 1918, (CO) Livingston, (PRTS) William

Columbus and Scottie Bell Bryan (MIL) WWI, (C) Bethel Church Cemetery, Ludlow, MO
Bryan, Frances: (B) 1849, (CO) Pulaski, (A) 11, (BP) MO, (CMTS) 1860 Census
Bryan, George: (B) 1853, (CO) Pulaski, (A) 7, (BP) MO, (CMTS) 1860 Census
Bryan, Isaac: (B) 1821, (CO) Pulaski, (A) 39, (BP) TN, (CMTS) 1860 Census
Bryan, Jabez: (B) 1845, (CO) Pulaski, (A) 15, (BP) MO, (CMTS) 1860 Census
Bryan, James R.: (B) 1852, (CO) Pulaski, (A) 8, (BP) MO, (CMTS) 1860 Census
Bryan, John W.: (B) 1823, (CO) Pulaski, (A) 37, (BP) TN, (CMTS) 1860 Census
Bryan, Mary A.: (B) 1839, (CO) Pulaski, (A) 21, (BP) MO, (CMTS) 1860 Census
Bryan, Plotema: (B) 1854, (CO) Pulaski, (A) 6, (BP) TN, (CMTS) 1860 Census
Bryan, Priscilla: (B) 1845, (CO) Pulaski, (A) 15, (BP) MO, (CMTS) 1860 Census
Bryan, Rachael: (B) 1830, (CO) Pulaski, (A) 30, (BP) MO, (CMTS) 1860 Census
Bryan, Rachel: (B) 1818, (CO) Pulaski, (A) 42, (BP) TN, (CMTS) 1860 Census
Bryan, Rachel: (B) 1848, (CO) Pulaski, (A) 12, (BP) TN, (CMTS) 1860 Census
Bryan, William Allen: (B) 1856, (CO) Pulaski, (A) 4, (BP) MO, (CMTS) 1860 Census
Bryant, Emily: (B) 1846, (CO) Pulaski, (A) 14, (BP) MO, (CMTS) 1860 Census
Bryant, Gibson: (B) 1853, (CO) Pulaski, (A) 7, (BP) MO, (CMTS) 1860 Census
Bryant, Howell: (B) 1835, (CO) Pulaski, (A) 25, (BP) IN, (CMTS) 1860 Census
Bryant, Jasper: (B) 1838, (CO) Pulaski, (A) 22, (BP) MO, (CMTS) 1860 Census
Bryant, John: (B) 1845, (CO) Pulaski, (A) 15, (BP) MO, (CMTS) 1860 Census
Bryant, John J.: (B) 1835, (CO) Stone, (A) 15, (BP) MO, (CMTS) 1870 Census
Bryant, Josaphine: (B) 1853, (CO) Pulaski, (A) 7, (BP) MO, (CMTS) 1860 Census
Bryant, Joseph: (B) 1848, (CO) Pulaski, (A) 12, (BP) MO, (CMTS) 1860

Census
Bryant, Mahala: (B) 1848, (CO) Pulaski, (A) 12, (BP) MO, (CMTS) 1860 Census
Bryant, Margaret: (B) 1850, (CO) Pulaski, (A) 10, (BP) MO, (CMTS) 1860 Census
Bryant, Mary E.: (B) 1917, (D) 1983, (CO) St. Louis, (C) Calvary Cemetery
Bryant, Mary J.: (B) 1848, (CO) Pulaski, (A) 12, (BP) MO, (CMTS) 1860 Census
Bryant, Matilda: (B) 1842, (CO) Pulaski, (A) 18, (BP) MO, (CMTS) 1860 Census
Bryant, Missouri: (B) 1854, (CO) Pulaski, (A) 6, (BP) MO, (CMTS) 1860 Census
Bryant, Nancy A.: (B) 1850, (CO) Pulaski, (A) 10, (BP) MO, (CMTS) 1860 Census
Bryant, Nancy J.: (B) 1845, (CO) Stone, (A) 5, (BP) A, (CMTS) 1870 Census
Bryant, Permelia: (B) 1853, (CO) Pulaski, (A) 7, (BP) MO, (CMTS) 1860 Census
Bryant, Phillip: (B) 1852, (CO) Pulaski, (A) 8, (BP) MO, (CMTS) 1860 Census
Bryant, Polk: (B) 1847, (CO) Pulaski, (A) 13, (BP) MO, (CMTS) 1860 Census
Bryant, Priscilla: (B) 1844, (CO) Pulaski, (A) 16, (BP) MO, (CMTS) 1860 Census
Bryant, Rebecca: (B) 1826, (CO) Pulaski, (A) 34, (BP) IL, (CMTS) 1860 Census
Bryant, Richard: (B) 1855, (CO) Pulaski, (A) 5, (BP) MO, (CMTS) 1860 Census
Bryant, Rubin: (B) 1856, (CO) Pulaski, (A) 4, (BP) MO, (CMTS) 1860 Census
Bryant, Susan: (B) 1826, (CO) Pulaski, (A) 34, (BP) TN, (CMTS) 1860 Census
Bryant, Susan: (B) 1856, (CO) Pulaski, (A) 4, (BP) MO, (CMTS) 1860 Census
Bryant, Susannah: (B) 1841, (CO) Pulaski, (A) 19, (BP) MO, (CMTS) 1860 Census
Bryant, Thomas E.: (B) 1851, (CO) Pulaski, (A) 9, (BP) MO, (CMTS) 1860 Census
Bryant, Troy E . Sr.: (B) 1918, (CO) St. Louis, (C) Calvary Cemetery
Bryant, William: (B) 1845, (CO) Pulaski, (A) 15, (BP) MO, (CMTS) 1860 Census
Brynan, Mitchell: (B) 1836, (CO) Pulaski, (A) 24, (BP) Ireland, (CMTS)

1860 Census

Buerman, Fred S.: (B) 1924, (D) 1942, (CO) St. Louis, (C) Calvary Cemetery

Buford, Nancy: (B) 1830, (CO) Pulaski, (A) 30, (BP) TN, (CMTS) 1860 Census

Buford, Stanton: (B) 1838, (CO) Pulaski, (A) 22, (BP) TN, (CMTS) 1860 Census

Bull, Claire M.: (B) 1918, (D) 1978, (CO) St. Louis, (C) Calvary Cemetery

Bull, Walter C.: (B) 1911, (CO) St. Louis, (C) Calvary Cemetery

Bumpas, Elija J.: (B) 1839, (CO) Pulaski, (A) 21, (BP) TN, (CMTS) 1860 Census

Bunch, Annie M.: (B) 1878, (CO) Missouri, (RES) Graves Co., TX, (CMTS) 1920 Census, p. 103

Bunch, Leo C.: (B) Dec. 24, 1910, (D) May 23, 1980, (CO) Henry, (C) Knights of Pythias Cemetery, Deepwater, MO

Bunnell, Lewis W.: (D) Aug. 19, 1939, (CO) Grundy, (CMTS) A. F. & A. M. Trenton Lodge 111

Burchard, John R.: (B) 1848, (CO) Pulaski, (A) 12, (BP) MO, (CMTS) 1860 Census

Burchard, Margaret: (B) 1825, (CO) Pulaski, (A) 35, (BP) KY, (CMTS) 1860 Census

Burchard, Margaret J.: (B) 1854, (CO) Pulaski, (A) 6, (BP) MO, (CMTS) 1860 Census

Burchard, Mary E.: (B) 1851, (CO) Pulaski, (A) 9, (BP) MO, (CMTS) 1860 Census

Burchard, Samuel J.: (B) 1847, (CO) Pulaski, (A) 13, (BP) MO, (CMTS) 1860 Census

Burchit, Alexander: (B) 1848, (CO) Stone, (A) 22, (BP) MO, (CMTS) 1870 Census

Burchit, Doctor L. C.: (B) 1854, (CO) Stone, (A) 16, (BP) MO, (CMTS) 1870 Census

Burchit, Hiram E.: (B) 1845, (CO) Stone, (A) 25, (BP) KY, (CMTS) 1870 Census

Burchit, Isaac N: (B) 1849, (CO) Stone, (A) 21, (BP) MO, (CMTS) 1870 Census

Burchit, James P: (B) 1852, (CO) Stone, (A) 18, (BP) MO, (CMTS) 1870 Census

Burchit, Nancy A.: (B) 1853, (CO) Stone, (A) 17, (BP) MO, (CMTS) 1870 Census

Burchit, Rebecca J.: (B) 1857, (CO) Stone, (A) 13, (BP) MO, (CMTS) 1870 Census

Burgard, Lester C.: (B) ????, (D) Sep. 26, 1918, (CO) Livingston, (MIL)

WWI, Killed at the Battle of Argonne Forest, (BUR) France, (PRTS) Samuel H. and Charity R. Burgard

Burgess, Elizabeth: (B) 1850, (CO) Pulaski, (A) 10, (BP) MO, (CMTS) 1860 Census

Burgess, Ferriday: (B) 1846, (CO) Pulaski, (A) 14, (BP) MO, (CMTS) 1860 Census

Burgess, James: (B) 1840, (CO) Pulaski, (A) 20, (BP) MO, (CMTS) 1860 Census

Burgess, Louisa: (B) 1848, (CO) Pulaski, (A) 12, (BP) MO, (CMTS) 1860 Census

Burgess, P. D.: (B) 1846, (CO) Pulaski, (A) 14, (BP) MO, (CMTS) 1860 Census

Burgess, Ruth: (B) 1844, (CO) Pulaski, (A) 16, (BP) MO, (CMTS) 1860 Census

Burgess, Sanford: (B) 1853, (CO) Pulaski, (A) 7, (BP) MO, (CMTS) 1860 Census

Burgess, William S.: (B) 1842, (CO) Pulaski, (A) 18, (BP) MO, (CMTS) 1860 Census

Burkart, George: (B) 1904, (D) 1990, (CO) St. Louis, (C) Calvary Cemetery

Burkart, Helen: (B) 1914, (D) 1990, (CO) St. Louis, (C) Calvary Cemetery

Burke, Frank: (D) Nov.11, 1880, (CO) St. Louis, (C) Calvary Cemetery (A) 55

Burkeholder, Walcott H.: (D) Feb. 19, 1917, (CO) Grundy, (CMTS) A. F. & A. M. Trenton Lodge 111

Burkett, Roy: (D) Sep. 23, 1918, (CO) Livingston, (MIL) WWI, Killed at Charpentry, France, (BUR) France, (PRTS) Allen L. and Maggie Burkett

Burkhead, Clifton Dallas: (B) Dec. 24, 1907, (D) Oct. 12, 1980, (CO) Jackson, (DP) Kansas City, MO

Burnam, Squire: (D) Nov. 24, 1869, (CO) Missouri, (DP) Ashland, MO

Burnett, Daniel W.: (B) 1842, (CO) Pulaski, (A) 18, (BP) TN, (CMTS) 1860 Census

Burnett, John G.: (B) 1846, (CO) Pulaski, (A) 14, (BP) TN, (CMTS) 1860 Census

Burnett, Margaret: (B) 1848, (CO) Pulaski, (A) 12, (BP) TN, (CMTS) 1860 Census

Burnett, Minerva: (B) 1844, (CO) Pulaski, (A) 16, (BP) TN, (CMTS) 1860 Census

Burnett, Rebecca M.: (B) 1822, (CO) Pulaski, (A) 38, (BP) NC, (CMTS) 1860 Census

Burnett, Sarah Ann: (B) 1852, (CO) Pulaski, (A) 8, (BP) TN, (CMTS) 1860 Census

Burnett, William P.: (B) 1850, (CO) Pulaski, (A) 10, (BP) TN, (CMTS) 1860 Census
Burns, Francis: (D) May 15, 1892, (CO) St. Louis, (C) Calvary Cemetery (A) 30
Burns, James: (D) Apr. 12, 1890, (CO) St. Louis, (C) Calvary Cemetery (A) 27
Burns, Matthew: (D) Aug. 26, 1892, (CO) St. Louis, (C) Calvary Cemetery (A) 58
Burns, William J.: (D) 1928, (CO) St. Louis, (C) Calvary Cemetery
Burrill, Forest C.: (D) Jun. 8, 1938, (CO) Grundy, (CMTS) A. F. & A. M. Trenton Lodge 111
Burris, Mat.: (B) 1836, (CO) Pulaski, (A) 24, (BP) Ireland, (CMTS) 1860 Census
Burrowes, Michael: (B) 1829, (D) 1865, (CO) St. Louis, (C) Calvary Cemetery
Burt, Emma C.: (B) Jul. 12, 1829, (D) Feb. 14, 1908, (CO) Henry, (C) Knights of Pythias Cemetery, Deepwater, MO
Bush, Martin: (B) 1832, (CO) Pulaski, (A) 28, (BP) Ruttenburg, (CMTS) 1860 Census
Butcher, Cyntha: (B) Feb. 12, 1865, (D) Dec. 2, 1881, (CO) Polk, (C) Turkey Creek Cemetery
Butcher, Jonas: (B) 1859, (D) Jun. 14, 1914, (CO) Polk, (C) Turkey Creek Cemetery
Butcher, Nathaniel: (B) 1847, (D) 1917, (CO) Polk, (C) Turkey Creek Cemetery
Butcher, Thomas J.: (B) 1902, (D) Apr. 29, 1922, (CO) Polk, (C) Turkey Creek Cemetery
Butcher, William S.: (B) May 4, 1818, (D) Novmber 24, 1888, (CO) Polk, (C) Turkey Creek Cemetery
Butler, Elbert N: (B) 1845, (CO) Stone, (A) 25, (BP) AR, (CMTS) 1870 Census
Butler, Elizabeth: (B) 1852, (CO) Stone, (A) 18, (BP) TN, (CMTS) 1870 Census
Butler, Emma: (B) 1795, (CO) Stone, (A) 75, (BP) NC, (CMTS) 1870 Census
Butler, James L.: (B) 1848, (CO) Stone, (A) 22, (BP) AR, (CMTS) 1870 Census
Butler, John W.: (B) Oct. 14, 1873, (D) Nob. 18, 18883, (CO) Stone,
Butler, Margarette T: (B) 1848, (CO) Stone, (A) 22, (BP) MO, (CMTS) 1870 Census
Butler, Margarette: (B) 1825, (CO) Stone, (A) 45, (BP) GA, (CMTS) 1870 Census
Butler, Mary J. C.: (B) 1846, (CO) Stone, (A) 24, (BP) TN, (CMTS) 1870

Census
Butler, Nellie: (B) 1852, (CO) Stone, (A) 18, (BP) AR, (CMTS) 1870 Census
Butler, Seneca: (B) 1853, (CO) Stone, (A) 17, (BP) AR, (CMTS) 1870 Census
Butler, Thos.: (B) 1837, (CO) Stone, (A) 33, (BP) TN, (CMTS) 1870 Census
Butler, Wilson: (B) 1856, (CO) Stone, (A) 14, (BP) AR, (CMTS) 1870 Census
Butler, Wilson S.: (B) 1820, (CO) Stone, (A) 50, (BP) NC, (CMTS) 1870 Census
Butner, Edna: (B) Sep. 12, 1899, (D) Aug. 30, 1944, (CO) Jackson, (C) Elwood Cemetery, Kansas City, MO
Byer, James W.: (B) Jun. 7, 1811, (CO) Audrain, (C) Old Village Cemetery
Byrne, Ann: (D) Jun. 5, 1916, (CO) St. Louis, (C) Calvary Cemetery
Byrne, Catherine: (D) Jul. 27, 1896, (CO) St. Louis, (C) Calvary Cemetery
Byrne, Hugh Edward: (D) Mar. 31, 1949, (CO) St. Louis, (C) Calvary Cemetery
Byrne, Nancy Nangle: (B) 1931, (D) 1987, (CO) St. Louis, (C) Calvary Cemetery
Bysor, Mary Evelyn: (B) Dec. 22, 1945, (D) Jun. 29, 1998, (CO) Henry, (C) Knights of Pythias Cemetery, Deepwater, MO
Cabanne, Jean Pierre: (B) 1773, (D) Nov. 27, 1811, (CO) St. Louis, (C) Calvary Cemetery
Cabanne, Virginia Eliot: (B) 1816, (D) 1899, (CO) St. Louis, (C) Calvary Cemetery
Cabrilliac, Paul: (D) Jun. 30, 1909, (CO) St. Louis, (C) Calvary Cemetery
Caine, Bridget: (D) May, 1897, (CO) St. Louis, (C) Calvary Cemetery, (A) 55
Caine, Ellen: (D) May, 1879, (CO) St. Louis, (C) Calvary Cemetery, (A) 12
Caine, John: (D) Aug., 1924, (CO) St. Louis, (C) Calvary Cemetery
Caine, Patrick: (D) Mar.,1905, (CO) St. Louis, (C) Calvary Cemetery
Caine, Reginald: (D) Jun., 1975, (CO) St. Louis, (C) Calvary Cemetery, (A) 31
Caira, Sr., Therese: (D) Jun., 1995, (CO) St. Louis, (C) Calvary Cemetery, (A) 80
Cairns, Blanche A.: (D) Oct., 1960, (CO) St. Louis, (C) Calvary Cemetery, (A) 70
Cairns, Frank J.: (D) Feb., 1942, (CO) St. Louis, (C) Calvary Cemetery
Cairns, James: (D) Nov., 1925, (CO) St. Louis, (C) Calvary Cemetery,

(A) 57
Cairns, James F.: (D) Jun., 1936, (CO) St. Louis, (C) Calvary Cemetery, (A) 47
Cairns, James F.: (D) Oct., 1926, (CO) St. Louis, (C) Calvary Cemetery, (A) 74
Caise, Elizabeth: (B) 1822, (CO) Pulaski, (A) 38, (BP) SC, (CMTS) 1860 Census
Caise, Frances: (B) 1854, (CO) Pulaski, (A) 6, (BP) MO, (CMTS) 1860 Census
Caise, George: (B) 1823, (CO) Pulaski, (A) 37, (BP) MO, (CMTS) 1860 Census
Caise, George W.: (B) 1852, (CO) Pulaski, (A) 8, (BP) MO, (CMTS) 1860 Census
Caise, Jesse: (B) 1855, (CO) Pulaski, (A) 5, (BP) MO, (CMTS) 1860 Census
Caise, John: (B) 1850, (CO) Pulaski, (A) 10, (BP) MO, (CMTS) 1860 Census
Caise, Jonathan: (B) 1848, (CO) Pulaski, (A) 12, (BP) MO, (CMTS) 1860 Census
Caise, Mary: (B) 1846, (CO) Pulaski, (A) 14, (BP) MO, (CMTS) 1860 Census
Caldwell, Berry: (B) 1858, (CO) Pulaski, (A) 2, (BP) MO, (CMTS) 1860 Census
Caldwell, Frank S.: (D) Jul. 14, 1925, (CO) Grundy, (CMTS) A. F. & A. M. Trenton Lodge 111
Caldwell, George: (B) 1846, (CO) Pulaski, (A) 14, (BP) MO, (CMTS) 1860 Census
Caldwell, James: (B) 1845, (CO) Pulaski, (A) 15, (BP) MO, (CMTS) 1860 Census
Caldwell, John H.: (B) 1851, (CO) Pulaski, (A) 9, (BP) MO, (CMTS) 1860 Census
Caldwell, Joseph L.: (B) 1835, (CO) Pulaski, (A) 25, (BP) MO, (CMTS) 1860 Census
Caldwell, Malinda: (B) 1837, (CO) Pulaski, (A) 23, (BP) MO, (CMTS) 1860 Census
Caldwell, Malinda J.: (B) 1853, (CO) Pulaski, (A) 7, (BP) MO, (CMTS) 1860 Census
Caldwell, Martha: (B) 1856, (CO) Pulaski, (A) 4, (BP) MO, (CMTS) 1860 Census
Caldwell, Mary C.: (B) 1849, (CO) Pulaski, (A) 11, (BP) MO, (CMTS) 1860 Census
Caldwell, Rachel: (B) 1825, (CO) Pulaski, (A) 35, (BP) MO, (CMTS) 1860 Census

Caldwell, Ruben: (B) 1830, (CO) Pulaski, (A) 30, (BP) MO, (CMTS) 1860 Census
Caldwell, Zechariah: (B) 1825, (CO) Pulaski, (A) 35, (BP) MO, (CMTS) 1860 Census
Calistone, John: (B) 1834, (CO) Stone, (A) 36, (BP) IL, (CMTS) 1870 Census
Calistone, Martha C.: (B) 1855, (CO) Stone, (A) 15, (BP) MO, (CMTS) 1870 Census
Calistone, Mary A.: (B) 1854, (CO) Stone, (A) 16, (BP) MO, (CMTS) 1870 Census
Calistone, Nancy J.: (B) 1837, (CO) Stone, (A) 33, (BP) IL, (CMTS) 1870 Census
Callahan, Johanna: (D) Apr. 3, 1898, (CO) St. Louis, (C) Calvary Cemetery, (A) 48
Callahan, John: (B) 1839, (CO) Pulaski, (A) 21, (BP) Ireland, (CMTS) 1860 Census
Calmes, Betty Salome: (D) Jul. 11, 2000, (CO) Jackson, (NWS) *Kansas City, Missouri Star*, July 12, 2000
Cammarata, Anthony: (B) 1871, (D) 1935, (CO) St. Louis, (C) Calvary Cemetery
Cammarata, Charles: (B) 1899, (D) 1974, (CO) St. Louis, (C) Calvary Cemetery
Cammarata, Maria: (B) 1880, (D) 1964, (CO) St. Louis, (C) Calvary Cemetery
Campbell, Amanda A.: (B) 1841, (CO) Pulaski, (A) 19, (BP) MO, (CMTS) 1860 Census
Campbell, Andrew J.: (B) 1856, (CO) Pulaski, (A) 4, (BP) TN, (CMTS) 1860 Census
Campbell, Cornelius: (B) 1854, (CO) Pulaski, (A) 6, (BP) MO, (CMTS) 1860 Census
Campbell, Diana: (B) 1822, (CO) Pulaski, (A) 38, (BP) TN, (CMTS) 1860 Census
Campbell, Elizabeth: (B) 1834, (CO) Pulaski, (A) 26, (BP) TN, (CMTS) 1860 Census
Campbell, Elizabeth: (B) 1854, (CO) Pulaski, (A) 6, (BP) TN, (CMTS) 1860 Census
Campbell, Emily: (B) 1854, (CO) Pulaski, (A) 6, (BP) MO, (CMTS) 1860 Census
Campbell, George: (B) 1833, (CO) Pulaski, (A) 27, (BP) TN, (CMTS) 1860 Census
Campbell, Ham H.: (B) 1843, (CO) Pulaski, (A) 17, (BP) MO, (CMTS) 1860 Census
Campbell, Isaac: (B) 1840, (CO) Pulaski, (A) 20, (BP) TN, (CMTS) 1860

Census
Campbell, James: (B) 1836, (CO) Pulaski, (A) 24, (BP) TN, (CMTS) 1860 Census
Campbell, James H.: (B) 1849, (CO) Pulaski, (A) 11, (BP) MO, (CMTS) 1860 Census
Campbell, John M.: (B) 1820, (CO) Stone, (A) 30, (BP) IN, (CMTS) 1870 Census
Campbell, Joshua: (B) 1822, (CO) Pulaski, (A) 38, (BP) TN, (CMTS) 1860 Census
Campbell, Joshua: (B) 1843, (CO) Pulaski, (A) 17, (BP) TN, (CMTS) 1860 Census
Campbell, Lucinda: (B) 1829, (CO) Pulaski, (A) 31, (BP) TN, (CMTS) 1860 Census
Campbell, Luna: (B) 1856, (CO) Pulaski, (A) 4, (BP) MO, (CMTS) 1860 Census
Campbell, Martha: (B) 1841, (CO) Pulaski, (A) 19, (BP) TN, (CMTS) 1860 Census
Campbell, Martha J.: (B) 1826, (CO) Stone, (A) 24, (BP) AR, (CMTS) 1870 Census
Campbell, Mary E.: (B) 1854, (CO) Pulaski, (A) 6, (BP) MO, (CMTS) 1860 Census
Campbell, Nancy H.: (B) 1851, (CO) Pulaski, (A) 9, (BP) MO, (CMTS) 1860 Census
Campbell, Nancy J.: (B) 1856, (CO) Pulaski, (A) 4, (BP) MO, (CMTS) 1860 Census
Campbell, Rebecca: (B) 1857, (CO) Pulaski, (A) 3, (BP) MO, (CMTS) 1860 Census
Campbell, Robert N.: (B) 1851, (CO) Pulaski, (A) 9, (BP) MO, (CMTS) 1860 Census
Campbell, Samuel: (B) 1823, (CO) Pulaski, (A) 37, (BP) TN, (CMTS) 1860 Census
Campbell, Sarah E.: (B) 1835, (CO) Pulaski, (A) 25, (BP) TN, (CMTS) 1860 Census
Campbell, Sarah J.: (B) 1857, (CO) Pulaski, (A) 3, (BP) MO, (CMTS) 1860 Census
Campbell, William F.: (B) 1857, (CO) Pulaski, (A) 3, (BP) MO, (CMTS) 1860 Census
Campbell,: (B) 1832, (CO) Pulaski, (A) 28, (BP) NY, (CMTS) 1860 Census
Campton, Nancy J.: (B) 1840, (CO) Stone, (A) 10, (BP) MO, (CMTS) 1870 Census
Campton, Sylfronia: (B) 1849, (CO) Stone, (A) 1, (BP) MO, (CMTS) 1870 Census

Campton, Thomas: (B) 1831, (CO) Stone, (A) 19, (BP) MO, (CMTS) 1870 Census

Canada, Eliza J.: (B) Aug. 24, 1827, (D) Jul. 12, 1876, (CO) Audrain, (C) Pisgah Cemetery

Canada, John Thomas: (B) Mar. 4, 1861, (CO) Henry, (PRTS) William Canada

Canaday, John M.: (B) Jul. 1, 1848, (CO) Gentry

Canavan, Helen English: (B) 1900, (D) 1922, (CO) St. Louis, (C) Calvary Cemetery

Canavan, Thomas: (D) Nov. 9, 1901, (CO) St. Louis, (C) Calvary Cemetery

Canefax, Rebecca C.: (B) 1855, (CO) Stone, (A) 15, (BP) MO, (CMTS) 1870 Census

Canimore, Caroline: (B) 1840, (CO) Pulaski, (A) 20, (BP) MO, (CMTS) 1860 Census

Canimore, Levi: (B) 1836, (CO) Pulaski, (A) 24, (BP) MO, (CMTS) 1860 Census

Cannady, Arthur R.: (D) Nov. 6, 1921, (CO) Grundy, (CMTS) A. F. & A. M. Trenton Lodge 111

Cannon, Ellen: (B) 1844, (D) 1887, (CO) St. Louis, (C) Calvary Cemetery

Cantrel, Francis: (B) 1816, (CO) Pulaski, (A) 44, (BP) KY, (CMTS) 1860 Census

Cantrel, Jason: (B) 1842, (CO) Pulaski, (A) 18, (BP) TN, (CMTS) 1860 Census

Cantrel, Keziah: (B) 1848, (CO) Pulaski, (A) 12, (BP) TN, (CMTS) 1860 Census

Cantrel, Martha: (B) 1852, (CO) Pulaski, (A) 8, (BP) TN, (CMTS) 1860 Census

Capone, Filippa: (B) 1873, (D) 1934, (CO) St. Louis, (C) Calvary Cemetery

Capone, Peter: (B) 1864, (D) 1933, (CO) St. Louis, (C) Calvary Cemetery

Capps, Jacob: (B) 1855, (CO) Pulaski, (A) 5, (BP) IL, (CMTS) 1860 Census

Capps, Mathew: (B) 1835, (CO) Pulaski, (A) 25, (BP) KY, (CMTS) 1860 Census

Capps, Nancy: (B) 1831, (CO) Pulaski, (A) 29, (BP) IL, (CMTS) 1860 Census

Capps, Ranson: (B) 1853, (CO) Pulaski, (A) 7, (BP) IL, (CMTS) 1860 Census

Capps, Sarah J.: (B) 1849, (CO) Pulaski, (A) 11, (BP) IL, (CMTS) 1860 Census

Cards, Isabella: (B) 1846, (CO) Pulaski, (A) 14, (BP) MO, (CMTS) 1860 Census

Cards, Leonard: (B) 1844, (CO) Pulaski, (A) 16, (BP) MO, (CMTS) 1860 Census
Cards, Robt A.: (B) 1843, (CO) Pulaski, (A) 17, (BP) MO, (CMTS) 1860 Census
Carey, Emily: (B) 1832, (CO) Pulaski, (A) 28, (BP) VA, (CMTS) 1860 Census
Carey, Hamilton: (B) 1850, (CO) Pulaski, (A) 10, (BP) VA, (CMTS) 1860 Census
Carey, James: (B) 1827, (CO) Pulaski, (A) 33, (BP) NC, (CMTS) 1860 Census
Carey, Jane: (B) 1853, (CO) Pulaski, (A) 7, (BP) VA, (CMTS) 1860 Census
Carey, John W.: (B) 1835, (CO) Stone, (A) 35, (BP) AR, (CMTS) 1870 Census
Carey, Martha A.: (B) 1856, (CO) Stone, (A) 14, (BP) MO, (CMTS) 1870 Census
Carey, Mary: (B) 1856, (CO) Pulaski, (A) 4, (BP) KY, (CMTS) 1860 Census
Carey, Octavia J.: (B) 1854, (CO) Stone, (A) 16, (BP) MO, (CMTS) 1870 Census
Carey, Sarah: (B) 1854, (CO) Pulaski, (A) 6, (BP) KY, (CMTS) 1860 Census
Carey, Susanna: (B) 1844, (CO) Stone, (A) 26, (BP) KY, (CMTS) 1870 Census
Carley, Wesley: (B) 1841, (CO) Pulaski, (A) 19, (BP) MO, (CMTS) 1860 Census
Carmack, Elizabeth: (B) 1843, (CO) Pulaski, (A) 17, (BP) TN, (CMTS) 1860 Census
Carmack, Henry: (B) 1846, (CO) Pulaski, (A) 14, (BP) TN, (CMTS) 1860 Census
Carmack, Jesse: (B) 1841, (CO) Pulaski, (A) 19, (BP) TN, (CMTS) 1860 Census
Carmack, Louisa: (B) 1819, (CO) Pulaski, (A) 41, (BP) KY, (CMTS) 1860 Census
Carmack, William: (B) 1848, (CO) Pulaski, (A) 12, (BP) TN, (CMTS) 1860 Census
Carney, Ann: (B) Nov. 2, 1894, (D) Aug. 5, 1968, (CO) St. Louis, (C) Calvary Cemetery
Carney, Bridget: (D) Sep. 6, 1926, (CO) St. Louis, (C) Calvary Cemetery
Carney, Burton: (B) 1838, (CO) Stone, (A) 32, (BP) IL, (CMTS) 1870 Census
Carney, David: (B) 1828, (CO) Stone, (A) 22, (BP) MO, (CMTS) 1870 Census

Carney, Forrest C.: (B) 1842, (CO) Stone, (A) 28, (BP) MO, (CMTS) 1870 Census
Carney, William: (B) 1846, (CO) Stone, (A) 4, (BP) MO, (CMTS) 1870 Census
Carpenter, Archie: (B) 1830, (CO) Pulaski, (A) 30, (BP) IL, (CMTS) 1860 Census
Carpenter, Nancy J.: (B) 1854, (CO) Pulaski, (A) 6, (BP) MO, (CMTS) 1860 Census
Carpenter, Silas: (B) 1853, (CO) Pulaski, (A) 7, (BP) MO, (CMTS) 1860 Census
Carpenter, William: (B) 1849, (CO) Pulaski, (A) 11, (BP) MO, (CMTS) 1860 Census
Carr, Angeline: (B) 1849, (CO) Pulaski, (A) 11, (BP) IL, (CMTS) 1860 Census
Carr, Bethena: (B) 1849, (CO) Stone, (A) 21, (BP) AL, (CMTS) 1870 Census
Carr, Byron: (B) 1845, (CO) Stone, (A) 25, (BP) TN, (CMTS) 1870 Census
Carr, Clementine: (B) 1855, (CO) Stone, (A) 15, (BP) MO, (CMTS) 1870 Census
Carr, Elihu: (B) 1847, (CO) Stone, (A) 23, (BP) AL, (CMTS) 1870 Census
Carr, Ellender: (B) 1836, (CO) Pulaski, (A) 24, (BP) IL, (CMTS) 1860 Census
Carr, Jackson: (B) 1851, (CO) Pulaski, (A) 9, (BP) IL, (CMTS) 1860 Census
Carr, James: (B) 1828, (CO) Pulaski, (A) 32, (BP) IL, (CMTS) 1860 Census
Carr, Levi: (B) 1852, (CO) Pulaski, (A) 8, (BP) IL, (CMTS) 1860 Census
Carr, Louisa: (B) 1851, (CO) Pulaski, (A) 9, (BP) IL, (CMTS) 1860 Census
Carr, Nancy: (B) 1820, (CO) Stone, (A) 50, (BP) MO, (CMTS) 1870 Census
Carr, Rosa R.: (B) 1845, (CO) Stone, (A) 25, (BP) MO, (CMTS) 1870 Census
Carr, William: (B) 1830, (CO) Pulaski, (A) 30, (BP) IL, (CMTS) 1860 Census
Carr, William: (B) 1855, (CO) Pulaski, (A) 5, (BP) MO, (CMTS) 1860 Census
Carreras, Catherine: (D) May 30, 1910, (CO) St. Louis, (C) Calvary Cemetery
Carreras, Ida C.: (B) 1871, (D) 1946, (CO) St. Louis, (C) Calvary

Cemetery
Carreras, Louis T.: (B) 1861, (D) 1947, (CO) St. Louis, (C) Calvary Cemetery
Carrico, Bernice P.: (D) Aug. 19, 2000, (CO) Jackson, (NWS) *Kansas City, Missouri Star*, Aug. 22, 2000 (RES) Blue Springs
Carroll Bridget: (B) 1835, (CO) Pulaski, (A) 25, (BP) Ireland, (CMTS) 1860 Census
Carroll Catherine G.: (B) 1898, (D) 1937, (CO) St. Louis, (C) Calvary Cemetery
Carroll Chester F.: (B) 1901, (D) 1963, (CO) St. Louis, (C) Calvary Cemetery
Carroll John: (B) 1833, (CO) Pulaski, (A) 27, (BP) Ireland, (CMTS) 1860 Census
Carroll John: (D) Jan. 7, 1881, (CO) St. Louis, (C) Calvary Cemetery, (A) 65
Carroll Magdalena: (B) 1856, (D) 1888, (CO) St. Louis, (C) Calvary Cemetery
Carroll Marie F.: (B) 1902, (D) 1989, (CO) St. Louis, (C) Calvary Cemetery
Carroll Michael: (B) 1830, (CO) Pulaski, (A) 30, (BP) Ireland, (CMTS) 1860 Census
Carroll Michael: (B) 1833, (CO) Pulaski, (A) 27, (BP) Ireland, (CMTS) 1860 Census
Carroll Nellie J.: (B) 1869, (D) 1945, (CO) St. Louis, (C) Calvary Cemetery
Carroll Sarah: (D) 11, 19, 1889, (CO) St. Louis, (C) Calvary Cemetery
Carroll Thomas J.: (B) 1865, (D) 1943, (CO) St. Louis, (C) Calvary Cemetery
Carson, Nancy M.: (B) 1835, (CO) Pulaski, (A) 25, (BP) AL, (CMTS) 1860 Census
Carson, Polly: (B) 1828, (CO) Pulaski, (A) 32, (BP) TN, (CMTS) 1860 Census
Carson, Sally: (B) 1844, (CO) Pulaski, (A) 16, (BP) AL, (CMTS) 1860 Census
Carson, Samuel: (B) 1827, (CO) Pulaski, (A) 33, (BP) TN, (CMTS) 1860 Census
Carter, Alfred: (B) 1847, (CO) Pulaski, (A) 13, (BP) TN, (CMTS) 1860 Census
Carter, Eliza M.: (B) 1838, (CO) Pulaski, (A) 22, (BP) TN, (CMTS) 1860 Census
Carter, Elizabeth: (B) 1797, (CO) Pulaski, (A) 63, (BP) TN, (CMTS) 1860 Census
Carter, Elizabeth: (B) 1833, (CO) Pulaski, (A) 27, (BP) TN, (CMTS) 1860

Census
Carter, John: (B) 1823, (CO) Pulaski, (A) 37, (BP) TN, (CMTS) 1860 Census
Carter, Mollie B.: (B) 1866, (D) 1959, (CO) Henry, (C) Knights of Pythias Cemetery, Deepwater, MO
Carver, Mary E.: (B) Aug. 5, 1829, (D) Mar. 23, 1892, (CO) Barry, (C) Cassville Cemetery
Case, Celia A.: (B) 1823, (CO) Stone, (A) 27, (BP) NC, (CMTS) 1870 Census
Case, Elizabeth: (B) 1838, (CO) Pulaski, (A) 22, (BP) GA, (CMTS) 1860 Census
Case, George M.: (B) 1848, (CO) Pulaski, (A) 12, (BP) MO, (CMTS) 1860 Census
Case, Hannah: (B) 1816, (CO) Pulaski, (A) 44, (BP) KY, (CMTS) 1860 Census
Case, J. Milos: (B) 1846, (CO) Stone, (A) 4, (BP) MO, (CMTS) 1870 Census
Case, James: (B) 1840, (CO) Pulaski, (A) 20, (BP) GA, (CMTS) 1860 Census
Case, James L.: (B) 1848, (CO) Stone, (A) 2, (BP) MO, (CMTS) 1870 Census
Case, Jesse: (B) 1850, (CO) Pulaski, (A) 10, (BP) MO, (CMTS) 1860 Census
Case, Jesse M.: (B) 1850, (CO) Pulaski, (A) 10, (BP) MO, (CMTS) 1860 Census
Case, John: (B) 1846, (CO) Pulaski, (A) 14, (BP) MO, (CMTS) 1860 Census
Case, John: (B) 1847, (CO) Pulaski, (A) 13, (BP) MO, (CMTS) 1860 Census
Case, John J.: (B) 1843, (CO) Pulaski, (A) 17, (BP) MO, (CMTS) 1860 Census
Case, Josiah: (B) 1846, (CO) Pulaski, (A) 14, (BP) MO, (CMTS) 1860 Census
Case, Lewellen: (B) 1839, (CO) Stone, (A) 11, (BP) NC, (CMTS) 1870 Census
Case, Margaretta: (B) 1845, (CO) Stone, (A) 5, (BP) NC, (CMTS) 1870 Census
Case, Martha A.: (B) 1843, (CO) Stone, (A) 7, (BP) NC, (CMTS) 1870 Census
Case, Nancy: (B) 1848, (CO) Pulaski, (A) 12, (BP) MO, (CMTS) 1860 Census
Case, Robert M.: (B) 1848, (CO) Pulaski, (A) 12, (BP) MO, (CMTS) 1860 Census

Case, Robert: (B) 1857, (CO) Pulaski, (A) 3, (BP) MO, (CMTS) 1860 Census
Case, Sarah J.: (B) 1853, (CO) Pulaski, (A) 7, (BP) MO, (CMTS) 1860 Census
Case, Susan C.: (B) 1854, (CO) Pulaski, (A) 6, (BP) MO, (CMTS) 1860 Census
Case, William: (B) 1820, (CO) Pulaski, (A) 40, (BP) TN, (CMTS) 1860 Census
Case, William: (B) 1845, (CO) Pulaski, (A) 15, (BP) MO, (CMTS) 1860 Census
Case, William L.: (B) 1841, (CO) Stone, (A) 9, (BP) NC, (CMTS) 1870 Census
Casey, Ellen: (B) 1843, (D) 1914, (CO) St. Louis, (C) Calvary Cemetery
Casey, James P.: (D) Jan. 24, 1941, (CO) St. Louis, (C) Calvary Cemetery
Casey, John: (B) 1828, (D) 1903, (CO) St. Louis, (C) Calvary Cemetery
Casey, Kate: (B) 1868, (D) 1958, (CO) St. Louis, (C) Calvary Cemetery
Casey, Margaret: (B) 1884, (D) 1938, (CO) St. Louis, (C) Calvary Cemetery
Casey, Mary: (B) 1818, (D) 1902, (CO) St. Louis, (C) Calvary Cemetery
Casey, Mary L.: (D) Mar. 29, 1926, (CO) St. Louis, (C) Calvary Cemetery
Casey, Mollie: (D) Mar. 11, 1967, (CO) St. Louis, (C) Calvary Cemetery
Casey, Walter E.: (B) 1868, (D) 1958, (CO) St. Louis, (C) Calvary Cemetery
Cashin, Nicholas J.: (B) 1862, (D) 1933, (CO) St. Louis, (C) Calvary Cemetery
Cass, Frank Lyle: (B) Jun. 2, 1914, (CO) Jackson, (PRTS) Irs Milton Cass and Emma Bell, (SPOUSE) Mary S. Cass
Cassidy, Mary A.: (B) 1834, (CO) Pulaski, (A) 26, (BP) MO, (CMTS) 1860 Census
Cassidy, Thomas: (B) 1834, (CO) Pulaski, (A) 26, (BP) Ireland, (CMTS) 1860 Census
Cassidy, William T.: (B) 1856, (CO) Pulaski, (A) 4, (BP) MO, (CMTS) 1860 Census
Caulfield, John J.: (B) 1874, (D) 1919, (CO) St. Louis, (C) Calvary Cemetery
Cavagnaro, Anthony: (D) Sep. 10, 1937, (CO) St. Louis, (C) Calvary Cemetery
Cavagnaro, Rose: (D) Feb. 15, 1946, (CO) St. Louis, (C) Calvary Cemetery
Cavender, Martha L.: (B) 1840, (CO) Stone, (A) 30, (BP) TN, (CMTS) 1870 Census
Cavender, Timothy: (B) 1842, (CO) Stone, (A) 28, (BP) TN, (CMTS)

1870 Census
Cavener, Frances: (B) 1851, (CO) Stone, (A) 19, (BP) TN, (CMTS) 1870 Census
Cavener, William: (B) 1847, (CO) Stone, (A) 23, (BP) TN, (CMTS) 1870 Census
Cento, Dorothy: (D) Aug., 19, 1933, (CO) St. Louis, (C) Calvary Cemetery
Chabot, Clarissa Randall: (B) Aug. 5, 1804, (D) Jan. 15, 1881, (CO) Audrain, (C) Pisgah Cemetery
Chapel, Ann: (B) 1849, (CO) Pulaski, (A) 11, (BP) MO, (CMTS) 1860 Census
Chapel, Elizabeth: (B) 1852, (CO) Pulaski, (A) 8, (BP) MO, (CMTS) 1860 Census
Chapel, Lydia: (B) 1847, (CO) Pulaski, (A) 13, (BP) MO, (CMTS) 1860 Census
Chapel, Martha J.: (B) 1844, (CO) Pulaski, (A) 16, (BP) MO, (CMTS) 1860 Census
Chapel, Mary: (B) 1825, (CO) Pulaski, (A) 35, (BP) MO, (CMTS) 1860 Census
Chapel, Nancy: (B) 1855, (CO) Pulaski, (A) 5, (BP) MO, (CMTS) 1860 Census
Chapel, Thomas: (B) 1855, (CO) Pulaski, (A) 5, (BP) MO, (CMTS) 1860 Census
Chapman, Arthur J.: (B) 1841, (CO) Pulaski, (A) 19, (BP) NY, (CMTS) 1860 Census
Chapman, Harriet: (B) 1848, (CO) Pulaski, (A) 12, (BP) NY, (CMTS) 1860 Census
Chapman, Herman: (B) 1839, (CO) Pulaski, (A) 21, (BP) NY, (CMTS) 1860 Census
Charles, James Litz: (B) 1835, (CO) Pulaski, (A) 25, (BP) Ireland, (CMTS) 1860 Census
Chauvin, Joseph Jerome: (B) May 17, 1848, (D) Dec. 23, 1912, (CO) St. Louis, (C) Calavary Cemetery
Chesser, Al H.: (B) Feb. 26, 1914, (CO) Pettis, (SPOUSE) Rose Chesser
Childers, Betty: (B) 1848, (CO) Stone, (A) 2, (BP) MO, (CMTS) 1870 Census
Childers, Henry Franklin: (B) Sep. 5, 1859, (D) Aug. 16, 1934, (CO) Wahsington, (DP) Columbia, MO
Childers, John T: (B) 1841, (CO) Stone, (A) 9, (BP) AR, (CMTS) 1870 Census
Childers, Major: (B) 1839, (CO) Stone, (A) 11, (BP) AR, (CMTS) 1870 Census
Childers, Margaret: (B) 1815, (CO) Stone, (A) 35, (BP) AL, (CMTS)

1870 Census
Christesson, Bowers: (B) 1837, (CO) Pulaski, (A) 23, (BP) MO, (CMTS) 1860 Census
Christesson, Cynthia: (B) 1835, (CO) Pulaski, (A) 25, (BP) MO, (CMTS) 1860 Census
Christesson, Jemima: (B) 1844, (CO) Pulaski, (A) 16, (BP) MO, (CMTS) 1860 Census
Christesson, Robert: (B) 1825, (CO) Pulaski, (A) 35, (BP) KY, (CMTS) 1860 Census
Christesson, Walker: (B) 1839, (CO) Pulaski, (A) 21, (BP) MO, (CMTS) 1860 Census
Christison, Elisha E.: (B) 1852, (CO) Pulaski, (A) 8, (BP) KY, (CMTS) 1860 Census
Christison, Elizabeth: (B) 1854, (CO) Pulaski, (A) 6, (BP) KY, (CMTS) 1860 Census
Christison, George: (B) 1856, (CO) Pulaski, (A) 4, (BP) KY, (CMTS) 1860 Census
Christison, J.: (B) 1819, (CO) Pulaski, (A) 41, (BP) KY, (CMTS) 1860 Census
Christison, James N. B.: (B) 1848, (CO) Pulaski, (A) 12, (BP) KY, (CMTS) 1860 Census
Christison, John L.: (B) 1844, (CO) Pulaski, (A) 16, (BP) KY, (CMTS) 1860 Census
Christison, Martha E.: (B) 1846, (CO) Pulaski, (A) 14, (BP) KY, (CMTS) 1860 Census
Christison, Mary A.: (B) 1827, (CO) Pulaski, (A) 33, (BP) KY, (CMTS) 1860 Census
Christison, Sally C.: (B) 1826, (CO) Pulaski, (A) 34, (BP) KY, (CMTS) 1860 Census
Christison, Thomas J.: (B) 1850, (CO) Pulaski, (A) 10, (BP) KY, (CMTS) 1860 Census
Christman, Erwine: (B) 1918, (D) 1990, (CO) St. Louis, (C) Calvary Cemetery
Christman, Phyllis A.: (B) 1919, (CO) St. Louis, (C) Calvary Cemetery
Chuley, James N.: (B) 1856, (CO) Pulaski, (A) 4, (BP) MO, (CMTS) 1860 Census
Chuley, Sarah: (B) 1825, (CO) Pulaski, (A) 35, (BP) MO, (CMTS) 1860 Census
Chuley, Sarah A.: (B) 1853, (CO) Pulaski, (A) 7, (BP) MO, (CMTS) 1860 Census
Chuley, Waller S.: (B) 1851, (CO) Pulaski, (A) 9, (BP) MO, (CMTS) 1860 Census
Chuley, William J.: (B) 1856, (CO) Pulaski, (A) 4, (BP) MO, (CMTS)

1860 Census
Chuley, William W.: (B) 1848, (CO) Pulaski, (A) 12, (BP) MO, (CMTS) 1860 Census
Churchill, Douglas: (D) Jul. 14, 1957, (CO) St. Louis, (C) Calvary Cemetery
Clark, Artemesa: (B) 1848, (CO) Pulaski, (A) 12, (BP) MO, (CMTS) 1860 Census
Clark, Barbara: (B) 1832, (CO) Pulaski, (A) 28, (BP) TN, (CMTS) 1860 Census
Clark, Eliza: (B) 1849, (CO) Pulaski, (A) 11, (BP) MO, (CMTS) 1860 Census
Clark, Emeline: (B) 1816, (CO) Pulaski, (A) 44, (BP) SC, (CMTS) 1860 Census
Clark, Fannie: (B) 1853, (CO) Stone, (A) 17, (BP) MO, (CMTS) 1870 Census
Clark, George H.: (B) 1858, (CO) Pulaski, (A) 2, (BP) MO, (CMTS) 1860 Census
Clark, J. G.: (B) 1829, (CO) Pulaski, (A) 31, (BP) IA, (CMTS) 1860 Census
Clark, James T.: (B) 1830, (CO) Pulaski, (A) 30, (BP) MS, (CMTS) 1860 Census
Clark, John: (B) 1823, (CO) Stone, (A) 47, (BP) MO, (CMTS) 1870 Census
Clark, John J.: (B) 1843, (CO) Pulaski, (A) 17, (BP) MO, (CMTS) 1860 Census
Clark, Johnny: (B) 1897, (D) 1904, (CO) St. Louis, (C) Calvary Cemetery
Clark, Littleton: (B) 1856, (CO) Pulaski, (A) 4, (BP) MO, (CMTS) 1860 Census
Clark, Martha E.: (B) 1841, (CO) Pulaski, (A) 19, (BP) MO, (CMTS) 1860 Census
Clark, Mary: (B) 1820, (CO) Pulaski, (A) 40, (BP) TN, (CMTS) 1860 Census
Clark, Mary: (B) 1835, (CO) Pulaski, (A) 25, (BP) MO, (CMTS) 1860 Census
Clark, Nancy: (B) 1830, (CO) Stone, (A) 40, (BP) TN, (CMTS) 1870 Census
Clark, Narcissa: (B) 1835, (CO) Pulaski, (A) 25, (BP) MO, (CMTS) 1860 Census
Clark, Patrick: (B) 1835, (D) 1897, (CO) St. Louis, (C) Calvary Cemetery
Clark, Rebecca A.: (B) 1850, (CO) Pulaski, (A) 10, (BP) MO, (CMTS) 1860 Census
Clark, Richard: (B) 1845, (CO) Pulaski, (A) 15, (BP) MO, (CMTS) 1860 Census

Clark, Richard: (B) 1854, (CO) Pulaski, (A) 6, (BP) MO, (CMTS) 1860 Census
Clark, Sarah: (B) 1851, (CO) Pulaski, (A) 9, (BP) MO, (CMTS) 1860 Census
Clark, Susan F.: (B) 1856, (CO) Pulaski, (A) 4, (BP) MO, (CMTS) 1860 Census
Clark, Thomas: (B) 1845, (CO) Pulaski, (A) 15, (BP) MO, (CMTS) 1860 Census
Clark, William: (B) 1847, (CO) Pulaski, (A) 13, (BP) MO, (CMTS) 1860 Census
Clark, William J.: (B) 1850, (CO) Pulaski, (A) 10, (BP) MO, (CMTS) 1860 Census
Clark, Yarney: (B) 1856, (CO) Stone, (A) 14, (BP) MO, (CMTS) 1870 Census
Clay, Glenwood Wilson: (B) Jan. 17, 1919, (CO), (PRTS) Finis Curran and Verda Louis Clay, (SPOUSE) Elizabeth Mary Clay, (MIL) Sgt. U.S. Army, 1941-1945.
Clifton, Cyrena E.: (B) 1838, (CO) Stone, (A) 12, (BP) MO, (CMTS) 1870 Census
Clifton, Fannie: (B) 1823, (CO) Stone, (A) 27, (BP) MO, (CMTS) 1870 Census
Clifton, Frances: (B) 1826, (CO) Stone, (A) 24, (BP) TN, (CMTS) 1870 Census
Clifton, James R.: (B) 1836, (CO) Stone, (A) 14, (BP) MO, (CMTS) 1870 Census
Clifton, John: (B) 1847, (CO) Stone, (A) 3, (BP) MO, (CMTS) 1870 Census
Clifton, John: (B) 1848, (CO) Stone, (A) 2, (BP) MO, (CMTS) 1870 Census
Clifton, Martha A.: (B) 1818, (CO) Stone, (A) 32, (BP) TN, (CMTS) 1870 Census
Clifton, Melinda: (B) 1852, (CO) Stone, (A) 18, (BP) MO, (CMTS) 1870 Census
Clifton, Rhoda: (B) 1835, (CO) Stone, (A) 15, (BP) MO, (CMTS) 1870 Census
Clifton, Rhoda: (B) 1836, (CO) Stone, (A) 14, (BP) AR, (CMTS) 1870 Census
Clifton, Sarah E.: (B) 1838, (CO) Stone, (A) 12, (BP) MO, (CMTS) 1870 Census
Clifton, Silas D: (B) 1831, (CO) Stone, (A) 19, (BP) MO, (CMTS) 1870 Census
Clifton, Thomas: (B) 1825, (CO) Stone, (A) 25, (BP) AR, (CMTS) 1870 Census

Clifton, William: (B) 1794, (CO) Stone, (A) 56, (BP) TN, (CMTS) 1870 Census
Clifton, William: (B) 1841, (CO) Stone, (A) 9, (BP) MO, (CMTS) 1870 Census
Cline, Rheva L.: (B) 1918, (D) 1949, (CO) Oregon, (C) Falling Springs Cemetery
Clinkingbeard, Elizabeth: (B) 1834, (CO) Stone, (A) 16, (BP) MO, (CMTS) 1870 Census
Clinkingbeard, Jacob: (B) 1836, (CO) Stone, (A) 14, (BP) MO, (CMTS) 1870 Census
Clinkingbeard, John: (B) 1821, (CO) Stone, (A) 29, (BP) MO, (CMTS) 1870 Census
Clinkingbeard, John: (B) 1833, (CO) Stone, (A) 17, (BP) MO, (CMTS) 1870 Census
Clinkingbeard, Samuel M.: (B) 1846, (CO) Stone, (A) 4, (BP) MO, (CMTS) 1870 Census
Cloud, George C.: (B) 1858, (CO) Stone, (A) 12, (BP) MO, (CMTS) 1870 Census
Cloud, Green: (B) 1845, (CO) Stone, (A) 25, (BP) MO, (CMTS) 1870 Census
Cloud, John B.: (B) 1843, (CO) Stone, (A) 27, (BP) MO, (CMTS) 1870 Census
Cloud, Joseph B.: (B) 1835, (CO) Stone, (A) 35, (BP) TN, (CMTS) 1870 Census
Cloud, Mary J.: (B) 1840, (CO) Stone, (A) 30, (BP) TN, (CMTS) 1870 Census
Cloud, Nancy: (B) 1844, (CO) Stone, (A) 26, (BP) TN, (CMTS) 1870 Census
Cloud, Pryor F: (B) 1856, (CO) Stone, (A) 14, (BP) MO, (CMTS) 1870 Census
Cloud, Sarah E.: (B) 1843, (CO) Stone, (A) 27, (BP) TN, (CMTS) 1870 Census
Cloud, SarahC: (B) 1837, (CO) Stone, (A) 33, (BP) TN, (CMTS) 1870 Census
Cloud, Wiley: (B) 1840, (CO) Stone, (A) 30, (BP) TN, (CMTS) 1870 Census
Cloyd, William: (B) Oct. 24, 1894, (D) Jan. ??, 1954, (CO) Jackson, (DP) Kansas City, MO;, (BP) Birmingham, TX
Coakey, Agnes: (D) Jul. 24, 1883, (CO) St. Louis, (C) Calvary Cemetery
Coates, Thomas A . M*: (B) 1908, (D) 1922, (CO) St. Louis, (C) Calvary Cemetery
Coates, Virginia O.: (B) 1916, (D) 1995, (CO) St. Louis, (C) Calvary Cemetery

Cockhoyl, Charles R.: (B) 1856, (CO) Stone, (A) 14, (BP) AR, (CMTS) 1870 Census
Cockland, Ellen: (B) 1834, (CO) Pulaski, (A) 26, (BP) Ireland, (CMTS) 1860 Census
Cockland, Jerry: (B) 1844, (CO) Pulaski, (A) 16, (BP) Ireland, (CMTS) 1860 Census
Cockland, John: (B) 1838, (CO) Pulaski, (A) 22, (BP) Ireland, (CMTS) 1860 Census
Cockland, Patrick: (B) 1833, (CO) Pulaski, (A) 27, (BP) Ireland, (CMTS) 1860 Census
Cockland, Susan: (B) 1792, (CO) Pulaski, (A) 68, (BP) Ireland, (CMTS) 1860 Census
Cockland, William: (B) 1825, (CO) Pulaski, (A) 35, (BP) Ireland, (CMTS) 1860 Census
Cockland, William: (B) 1836, (CO) Pulaski, (A) 24, (BP) Ireland, (CMTS) 1860 Census
Cockrell, Ehbert Railey: (B) Apr. 2, 1873, (D) Sep. 13, 1934, (CO) Platte, (DP) Fayetteville, AR
Cody, Edward F.: (D) Oct. 1, 1865, (CO) St. Louis, (C) Calvary Cemetery, (A) 37
Cofer, Davis A.: (B) 1858, (CO) Stone, (A) 12, (BP) MO, (CMTS) 1870 Census
Cofer, Harold C.: (B) 1846, (CO) Stone, (A) 24, (BP) TN, (CMTS) 1870 Census
Cofer, Sarah: (B) 1856, (CO) Stone, (A) 14, (BP) MO, (CMTS) 1870 Census
Coffey, Bridget: (B) 1839, (D) 1917, (CO) St. Louis, (C) Calvary Cemetery
Coffey, Michael J.: (B) 1869, (D) 1887, (CO) St. Louis, (C) Calvary Cemetery
Cohen, Gerald Leroy: (B) Apr. 11, 1928, (CO) St. Louis, (PRTS) Max and Sophie Cohen, (CMTS) Member of the Missouri Bar Association and St. Louis Bar Association.
Cohn, Mrs. Caroline: ((D) Jan. 21, 1918, (CO) St. Louis, (NWS) *St. Louis Post Dispatch*, Jan. 22, 1918,
Cohorse, John: (B) 1834, (CO) Pulaski, (A) 26, (BP) IL, (CMTS) 1860 Census
Cohorse, Susan: (B) 1839, (CO) Pulaski, (A) 21, (BP) IN, (CMTS) 1860 Census
Cole, Bridget: (B) 1862, (D) 1890, (CO) St. Louis, (C) Calvary Cemetery
Cole, Eliza J.: (B) 1841, (CO) Pulaski, (A) 19, (BP) IL, (CMTS) 1860 Census
Cole, Giles M.: (B) 1828, (CO) Pulaski, (A) 32, (BP) AL, (CMTS) 1860

Census
Cole, Jane: (B) 1829, (CO) Pulaski, (A) 31, (BP) TN, (CMTS) 1860 Census
Cole, John: (B) 1856, (CO) Pulaski, (A) 4, (BP) MO, (CMTS) 1860 Census
Cole, Malinda: (B) 1850, (CO) Pulaski, (A) 10, (BP) IL, (CMTS) 1860 Census
Cole, Robern J.: (B) 1930, (D) 1987, (CO) St. Louis, (C) Calvary Cemetery
Cole, Warner: (B) 1853, (CO) Pulaski, (A) 7, (BP) MO, (CMTS) 1860 Census
Colley, Colburn: (B) 1844, (CO) Pulaski, (A) 16, (BP) MO, (CMTS) 1860 Census
Colley, Daniel: (B) 1835, (CO) Pulaski, (A) 25, (BP) MO, (CMTS) 1860 Census
Colley, Elarisa: (B) 1840, (CO) Pulaski, (A) 20, (BP) MO, (CMTS) 1860 Census
Colley, Francis: (B) 1836, (CO) Pulaski, (A) 24, (BP) MO, (CMTS) 1860 Census
Colley, George: (B) 1829, (CO) Pulaski, (A) 31, (BP) KY, (CMTS) 1860 Census
Colley, John H.: (B) 1839, (CO) Pulaski, (A) 21, (BP) MO, (CMTS) 1860 Census
Colley, Mary: (B) 1846, (CO) Pulaski, (A) 14, (BP) MO, (CMTS) 1860 Census
Collier, Harry L.: (B) Nov. 26, 1881, (D) Jul. 11, 1893, (CO) St. Louis, (C) Calavary Cemetery
Collier, Mary: (B) 1838, (CO) Pulaski, (A) 22, (BP) MO, (CMTS) 1860 Census
Collier, Robert: (B) 1838, (CO) Pulaski, (A) 22, (BP) KY, (CMTS) 1860 Census
Collins, Estelle: (B) 1900, (CO) St. Louis, (C) Calvary Cemetery
Collins, Grace M.: (B) 1893, (D) 1978, (CO) St. Louis, (C) Calvary Cemetery
Collins, H. Thomas: (B) 1887, (D) 1950, (CO) St. Louis, (C) Calvary Cemetery
Collins, Joe: (B) Jun. 30, 1946, (D) Apr. 14, 1999, (CO) Barry, (RES) Purdy, MO, (PRTS) Benjamin Collins and Della Mae Bell, (C) Ruhamah Cemetery, Rantaul, KS
Collins, John: (B) 1820, (CO) Pulaski, (A) 40, (BP) Ireland, (CMTS) 1860 Census
Collins, Monette M.: (B) 1910, (D) 1968, (CO) St. Louis, (C) Calvary Cemetery

Collins, Jr., Raymond: (B) Oct. 31, 1920, (D) Apr. 22, 1928, (CO) St. Louis, (C) Calvary Cemetery
Collins, Rebecca: (B) 1849, (CO) Stone, (A) 21, (BP) MO, (CMTS) 1870 Census
Collins, Thomas B.: (B) 1845, (CO) Stone, (A) 25, (BP) MO, (CMTS) 1870 Census
Collins, Tommy: (B) 1925, (D) 1943, (CO) St. Louis, (C) Calvary Cemetery
Colyer, Edward A.: (B) 1927, (D) 1979, (CO) St. Louis, (C) Calvary Cemetery
Colyer, Marie F.: (B) 1928, (CO) St. Louis, (C) Calvary Cemetery
Combs, Alma: (B) 1880, (D) 1906, (CO) St. Louis, (C) Calvary Cemetery
Combs, Pauline H.: (B) 1876, (D) 1940, (CO) St. Louis, (C) Calvary Cemetery
Combs, Robert H.: (B) 1875, (D) 1941, (CO) St. Louis, (C) Calvary Cemetery
Comorsises, Patrick: (B) 1827, (CO) Pulaski, (A) 33, (BP) Ireland, (CMTS) 1860 Census
Conidi, Margaret J.: (B) 1893, (D) 1957, (CO) St. Louis, (C) Calvary Cemetery
Conidi, Sylvester J.: (B) 1925, (D) 1974, (CO) St. Louis, (C) Calvary Cemetery
Conidi, Thomas: (B) 1878, (D) 1954, (CO) St. Louis, (C) Calvary Cemetery
Conkling, Elizabeth: (B) 1856, (CO) Pulaski, (A) 4, (BP) MO, (CMTS) 1860 Census
Conkling, Mary J.: (B) 1826, (CO) Pulaski, (A) 34, (BP) KY, (CMTS) 1860 Census
Conkling, William: (B) 1830, (CO) Pulaski, (A) 30, (BP) NY, (CMTS) 1860 Census
Conley, Antoinette F.: (B) 1923, (CO) St. Louis, (C) Calvary Cemetery
Conley, Sr., William L.: (B) 1923, (CO) St. Louis, (C) Calvary Cemetery
Conlon, Stella M.: (D) May 13, 1954, (CO) St. Louis, (C) Calvary Cemetery
Connell, Phillip: (B) 1828, (CO) Pulaski, (A) 32, (BP) Ireland, (CMTS) 1860 Census
Conner, Benjamin T.: (B) Apr. 3, 1892, (D) Jan. 4, 1990, (CO) Andrew, (DP) Savannah, MO, (C) Savannah City Cemetery.
Conner, Clarence: (D) Aug. 19, 2000, (CO) Cole, (NWS) *Jefferson City, Missouri News-Tribune*, Aug. 22, 2000, (RES) St. Elisabeth
Conner, Mary Alice: (B) Sep. 17, 1893, (D) Apr. 1, 1986, (CO) Andrew, (DP) Savannah, MO, (C) Savannah City Cemetery.
Connestone, Anton: (B) 1832, (CO) Pulaski, (A) 28, (BP) Hessia, (CMTS)

1860 Census
Connor, Averilla: (B) 1854, (CO) Pulaski, (A) 6, (BP) MO, (CMTS) 1860 Census
Connor, Bridgett: (B) 1844, (CO) Pulaski, (A) 16, (BP) Ireland, (CMTS) 1860 Census
Connor, Cynthia: (B) 1842, (CO) Pulaski, (A) 18, (BP) MO, (CMTS) 1860 Census
Connor, Deborah: (B) 1851, (CO) Pulaski, (A) 9, (BP) Ireland, (CMTS) 1860 Census
Connor, Elijah: (B) 1838, (CO) Pulaski, (A) 22, (BP) MO, (CMTS) 1860 Census
Connor, Elizabeth: (B) 1843, (CO) Pulaski, (A) 17, (BP) MO, (CMTS) 1860 Census
Connor, Elizabeth: (B) 1854, (CO) Pulaski, (A) 6, (BP) Ireland, (CMTS) 1860 Census
Connor, Johanna: (B) 1819, (CO) Pulaski, (A) 41, (BP) Ireland, (CMTS) 1860 Census
Connor, Mary: (B) 1839, (CO) Pulaski, (A) 21, (BP) Ireland, (CMTS) 1860 Census
Connor, Mitchell: (B) 1815, (CO) Pulaski, (A) 45, (BP) Ireland, (CMTS) 1860 Census
Connors, Hazel E.: (B) Nov. 27, 1915, (D) Nov. 25, 1977, (CO) St. Louis, (C) Calvary Cemetery
Cook, Charlotte: (B) 1842, (CO) Pulaski, (A) 18, (BP) MO, (CMTS) 1860 Census
Cook, Green: (B) 1839, (CO) Pulaski, (A) 21, (BP) MO, (CMTS) 1860 Census
Cook, Henry: (B) 1850, (CO) Pulaski, (A) 10, (BP) MO, (CMTS) 1860 Census
Cook, Henry C.: (B) 1845, (CO) Pulaski, (A) 15, (BP) MO, (CMTS) 1860 Census
Cook, Lorenzo: (B) 1856, (CO) Pulaski, (A) 4, (BP) MO, (CMTS) 1860 Census
Cook, Lydia A.: (B) 1844, (CO) Pulaski, (A) 16, (BP) MO, (CMTS) 1860 Census
Cook, Margaret: (B) 1834, (CO) Pulaski, (A) 26, (BP) IL, (CMTS) 1860 Census
Cook, Martha J.: (B) 1846, (CO) Pulaski, (A) 14, (BP) MO, (CMTS) 1860 Census
Cook, Mary J.: (B) 1853, (CO) Pulaski, (A) 7, (BP) MO, (CMTS) 1860 Census
Cook, Mary T.: (B) 1843, (CO) Pulaski, (A) 17, (BP) MO, (CMTS) 1860 Census

Cook, Sally A.: (B) 1851, (CO) Pulaski, (A) 9, (BP) MO, (CMTS) 1860 Census
Cook, Sarah E.: (B) Nov. 29, 1830, (D) Aug. 3, 1883, (CO) Barry, (C) Old Corsicana Cemetery
Cook, Thomas: (B) 1827, (CO) Pulaski, (A) 33, (BP) MO, (CMTS) 1860 Census
Cook, Welton: (B) 1840, (CO) Pulaski, (A) 20, (BP) MO, (CMTS) 1860 Census
Cook, William: (B) 1833, (CO) Stone, (A) 17, (BP) TX, (CMTS) 1870 Census
Cook, Williams: (B) 1842, (CO) Pulaski, (A) 18, (BP) MO, (CMTS) 1860 Census
Cooley, James F.: (B) Apr. 20, 1901, (D) Aug. 20, 1902, (CO) Oregon, (C) Falling Springs Cemetery
Cooley, Runey: (B) 1909, (CO) Oregon, (C) Falling Springs Cemetery
Cooley, Viola May: (B) Jun. 14, 1899, (D) Aug. 4, 1902, (CO) Oregon, (C) Falling Springs Cemetery
Coons, Sarah W.: (B) Jun. 4, 1827, (D) Jan. 4, 1855, (CO) Audrain, (C) Old Village Cemetery
Coons, Sarah W.: (B) Jun. 4, 1827, (D) Jan. 4, 1855, (CO) Audrain, (C) Old Village Cemetery
Cooper, George: (B) 1850, (CO) Pulaski, (A) 10, (BP) MO, (CMTS) 1860 Census
Cooper, Jane: (B) 1846, (CO) Pulaski, (A) 14, (BP) MO, (CMTS) 1860 Census
Corbett, Nell: (D) Dec. 5-, (CO) St. Louis, (C) Calvary Cemetery
Corcoran, James: (D) Sep. 7, 1902, (CO) St. Louis, (C) Calvary Cemetery (A) 50
Cordell, David: (B) 1842, (CO) Pulaski, (A) 18, (BP) MO, (CMTS) 1860 Census
Cordell, Nancy: (B) 1849, (CO) Pulaski, (A) 11, (BP) MO, (CMTS) 1860 Census
Cordell, William: (B) 1843, (CO) Pulaski, (A) 17, (BP) MO, (CMTS) 1860 Census
Corder, Frank: (B) 1847, (CO) Pulaski, (A) 13, (BP) MO, (CMTS) 1860 Census
Cork, Patrick: (B) 1820, (CO) Pulaski, (A) 40, (BP) Ireland, (CMTS) 1860 Census
Cornelius, Lydia E.: (D) Aug. 20, 2000, (CO) Jackson, (NWS) *Kansas City, Missouri Star*, Aug. 22, 2000
Cornett, Thomas: (B) 1831, (CO) Pulaski, (A) 29, (BP) Ireland, (CMTS) 1860 Census
Cornforth, Charles P.: (B) Apr. 20, 1837, (D) Nov. 23, 1892, (CO)

Audrain, (C) Old Village Cemetery
Cornforth, Mary A.: (D) Jul. 31, 1863, (CO) Audrain, (C) Old Village Cemetery, (A) 37Y. 8M. 12D
Corrigan, Mathilda P.: (D) Jun. 30, 1909, (CO) St. Louis, (C) Calvary Cemetery
Costello, Con C.: (B) 1879, (D) 1924, (CO) St. Louis, (C) Calvary Cemetery
Costello, Johanna: (B) 1840, (D) 1924, (CO) St. Louis, (C) Calvary Cemetery
Costello, Michael: (B) 1830, (D) 1903, (CO) St. Louis, (C) Calvary Cemetery
Costello, Michael J.: (B) 1868, (D) 1934, (CO) St. Louis, (C) Calvary Cemetery
Costlow, Edward 2: (B) 1841, (CO) Stone, (A) 9, (BP) MO, (CMTS) 1870 Census
Costlow, John: (B) 1849, (CO) Stone, (A) 1, (BP) MO, (CMTS) 1870 Census
Costlow, Mary: (B) 1826, (CO) Stone, (A) 24, (BP) MO, (CMTS) 1870 Census
Costlow, Susan: (B) 1847, (CO) Stone, (A) 3, (BP) MO, (CMTS) 1870 Census
Cotes, James: (B) 1843, (CO) Stone, (A) 27, (BP) IL, (CMTS) 1870 Census
Cotes, Sarah: (B) 1849, (CO) Stone, (A) 21, (BP) MO, (CMTS) 1870 Census
Couch, George W.: (B) Mar. 6, 1847, (D) Jul. 5, 1912, (CO) Oregon, (C) New Salem Cemetery
Coutheard, Consley: (B) 1828, (CO) Stone, (A) 22, (BP) VA, (CMTS) 1870 Census
Coutheard, Henry: (B) 1827, (CO) Stone, (A) 23, (BP) AL, (CMTS) 1870 Census
Cowan, Margaret: (B) 1837, (CO) Pulaski, (A) 23, (BP) KY, (CMTS) 1860 Census
Cowen, Grace: (B) 1833, (CO) Pulaski, (A) 27, (BP) MO, (CMTS) 1860 Census
Cowherd, William Strother: (B) Sept. 1, 1860, (CO) Jackson,
Cox, Allen: (B) 1849, (D) 1922, (CO) Cedar, (C) Brashear Cemetery
Cox, Archie J.: (D) Sep. 21, 1918, (CO) Livingston, (PRTS) Joseph B. and Lee A. Cox, (DP) Great Lakes Training Station, Chicago, IL
Cox, Caroline: (B) 1855, (CO) Pulaski, (A) 5, (BP) MO, (CMTS) 1860 Census
Cox, Columbia: (B) 1843, (CO) Pulaski, (A) 17, (BP) MO, (CMTS) 1860 Census

Cox, Elizabeth: (B) 1823, (CO) Stone, (A) 27, (BP) MO, (CMTS) 1870 Census
Cox, Elizabeth G: (B) 1849, (CO) Stone, (A) 1, (BP) MO, (CMTS) 1870 Census
Cox, Francis: (B) 1855, (CO) Cedar, (C) Brashear Cemetery
Cox, Gallant: (B) 1830, (CO) Pulaski, (A) 30, (BP) KY, (CMTS) 1860 Census
Cox, Ginerva: (B) 1842, (CO) Pulaski, (A) 18, (BP) TN, (CMTS) 1860 Census
Cox, Henry B.: (B) 1846, (CO) Stone, (A) 4, (BP) MO, (CMTS) 1870 Census
Cox, Isaac S.: (B) 1856, (CO) Pulaski, (A) 4, (BP) MO, (CMTS) 1860 Census
Cox, James F.: (B) 1850, (CO) Pulaski, (A) 10, (BP) NC, (CMTS) 1860 Census
Cox, James H.: (B) 1823, (CO) Stone, (A) 27, (BP) MO, (CMTS) 1870 Census
Cox, John E.: (B) 1845, (CO) Pulaski, (A) 15, (BP) NC, (CMTS) 1860 Census
Cox, John L.: (B) 1841, (CO) Stone, (A) 9, (BP) MO, (CMTS) 1870 Census
Cox, John T.: (B) 1847, (CO) Stone, (A) 3, (BP) MO, (CMTS) 1870 Census
Cox, Joseph: (B) 1838, (CO) Pulaski, (A) 22, (BP) KY, (CMTS) 1860 Census
Cox, Laura J.: (B) 1852, (CO) Pulaski, (A) 8, (BP) NC, (CMTS) 1860 Census
Cox, Louisa: (B) 1848, (CO) Pulaski, (A) 12, (BP) NC, (CMTS) 1860 Census
Cox, M.: (B) 1826, (CO) Pulaski, (A) 34, (BP) KY, (CMTS) 1860 Census
Cox, Margaret M.: (B) 1852, (CO) Pulaski, (A) 8, (BP) MO, (CMTS) 1860 Census
Cox, Mary: (B) 1854, (CO) Pulaski, (A) 6, (BP) NC, (CMTS) 1860 Census
Cox, Mary A.: (B) 1828, (CO) Pulaski, (A) 32, (BP) VA, (CMTS) 1860 Census
Cox, Mary E.: (B) 1829, (CO) Stone, (A) 21, (BP) KY, (CMTS) 1870 Census
Cox, Mary F: (B) 1846, (CO) Stone, (A) 4, (BP) MO, (CMTS) 1870 Census
Cox, Mary F.: (B) 1849, (CO) Pulaski, (A) 11, (BP) MO, (CMTS) 1860 Census

Cox, Mary J.: (B) 1828, (CO) Stone, (A) 22, (BP) MS, (CMTS) 1870 Census
Cox, Matilda: (B) 1851, (CO) Pulaski, (A) 9, (BP) MO, (CMTS) 1860 Census
Cox, Missouri E.: (B) 1845, (CO) Pulaski, (A) 15, (BP) MO, (CMTS) 1860 Census
Cox, Missouri F: (B) 1849, (CO) Stone, (A) 1, (BP) MO, (CMTS) 1870 Census
Cox, N.: (B) 1820, (CO) Pulaski, (A) 40, (BP) NC, (CMTS) 1860 Census
Cox, Nancy E.: (B) 1847, (CO) Stone, (A) 3, (BP) MO, (CMTS) 1870 Census
Cox, Nathan: (B) 1829, (CO) Stone, (A) 21, (BP) MO, (CMTS) 1870 Census
Cox, Nisa: (B) 1821, (CO) Pulaski, (A) 39, (BP) MO, (CMTS) 1860 Census
Cox, Rachael: (B) 1853, (CO) Pulaski, (A) 7, (BP) TN, (CMTS) 1860 Census
Cox, Rebecca E.: (B) 1847, (CO) Pulaski, (A) 13, (BP) MO, (CMTS) 1860 Census
Cox, Ruth: (B) 1829, (CO) Pulaski, (A) 31, (BP) TN, (CMTS) 1860 Census
Cox, Samuel: (B) 1795, (CO) Pulaski, (A) 65, (BP) NC, (CMTS) 1860 Census
Cox, Sarah: (B) 1840, (CO) Pulaski, (A) 20, (BP) MO, (CMTS) 1860 Census
Cox, Sarah J.: (B) 1856, (CO) Pulaski, (A) 4, (BP) MO, (CMTS) 1860 Census
Cox, Thomas: (B) 1849, (CO) Pulaski, (A) 11, (BP) MO, (CMTS) 1860 Census
Cox, Walter Wayne: (D) Jul. 9, 2000, (CO) Jackson, (NWS) *Kansas City, Missouri Star*, July 12, 2000
Cox, William B.: (B) 1817, (CO) Stone, (A) 33, (BP) TX, (CMTS) 1870 Census
Cox, William R.: (B) 1849, (CO) Stone, (A) 1, (BP) MO, (CMTS) 1870 Census
Craddock, Asa: (B) 1829, (CO) Pulaski, (A) 31, (BP) VA, (CMTS) 1860 Census
Craddock, Berry: (B) 1835, (CO) Pulaski, (A) 25, (BP) TN, (CMTS) 1860 Census
Craddock, Caroline: (B) 1835, (CO) Pulaski, (A) 25, (BP) MO, (CMTS) 1860 Census
Craddock, Elijah: (B) 1858, (CO) Pulaski, (A) 2, (BP) MO, (CMTS)

1860 Census
Craddock, Elizabeth: (B) 1854, (CO) Pulaski, (A) 6, (BP) MO, (CMTS) 1860 Census
Craddock, Lucy: (B) 1856, (CO) Pulaski, (A) 4, (BP) MO, (CMTS) 1860 Census
Craft, John F.: (D) Apr. 20, 1889, (CO) St. Louis, (C) Calvary Cemetery, (A) 33
Craig, Grace C.: (B) 1921, (D) 1953, (CO) St. Louis, (C) Calvary Cemetery
Cramer, Gussie Anne: (B) Apr. 18, 1919, (CO) St. Louis, (PRTS) Gustave A. Cramer and Mary A. Kornmeser, (SPOUSE) June H. Cramer, (MIL) Tech Sgt., U.S. Signal Corps, China, Burma, India, 1943-1945, Bronze Battle Star, Rifle Expert Citation, China, Burma, India Theator Citation.
Crammer, Mary: (B) Dec. 16, 1819, (D) Oct. 12, 1851, (CO) Barry, (C) Cassville Cemetery
Crawford, Henry C.: (D) Dec. 31, 1929, (CO) Grundy, (CMTS) A. F. & A. M. Trenton Lodge 111
Crawley, James T.: (B) 1877, (D) 1898, (CO) St. Louis, (C) Calvary Cemetery
Crawley, Marie: (B) 1872, (D) 1898, (CO) St. Louis, (C) Calvary Cemetery
Creery, Patrick: (D) 1886, (CO) St. Louis, (C) Calvary Cemetery
Creger, James A.: (B) 1827, (CO) Stone, (A) 23, (BP) VA, (CMTS) 1870 Census
Creger, Sely: (B) 1847, (CO) Stone, (A) 3, (BP) MO, (CMTS) 1870 Census
Creger, Susan: (B) 1831, (CO) Stone, (A) 19, (BP) TN, (CMTS) 1870 Census
Crews, James C.: (B) 1822, (D) 1869, (CO) Audrain, (C) Pisgah Cemetery
Crockett, William R.: (D) Mar. 23, 1930, (CO) Grundy, (CMTS) A. F. & A. M. Trenton Lodge 111
Crofa, Elijah M.: (B) 1845, (CO) Pulaski, (A) 15, (BP) TN, (CMTS) 1860 Census
Crofa, Henderson M.: (B) 1851, (CO) Pulaski, (A) 9, (BP) TN, (CMTS) 1860 Census
Crofa, James M.: (B) 1842, (CO) Pulaski, (A) 18, (BP) TN, (CMTS) 1860 Census
Crofa, Josiah L.: (B) 1849, (CO) Pulaski, (A) 11, (BP) TN, (CMTS) 1860 Census
Crofa, Nancy: (B) 1837, (CO) Pulaski, (A) 23, (BP) TN, (CMTS) 1860 Census
Crofa, Robert G.: (B) 1847, (CO) Pulaski, (A) 13, (BP) TN, (CMTS)

1860 Census
Crooks, H.: (D) Jan. 18, 1875, (CO) Audrain, (C) Old Village Cemetery, (A) 61Y 3M 19D
Crooks, William H.: (D) Mar. 12, 1926, (CO) Grundy, (CMTS) A. F. & A. M. Trenton Lodge 111
Cropland, David: (B) 1839, (CO) Pulaski, (A) 21, (BP) TN, (CMTS) 1860 Census
Cropland, Elijah: (B) 1839, (CO) Pulaski, (A) 21, (BP) TN, (CMTS) 1860 Census
Cropland, Jefferson F.: (B) 1849, (CO) Pulaski, (A) 11, (BP) TN, (CMTS) 1860 Census
Cropland, Mary Ann: (B) 1845, (CO) Pulaski, (A) 15, (BP) TN, (CMTS) 1860 Census
Cropland, Samuel: (B) 1794, (CO) Pulaski, (A) 66, (BP) SC, (CMTS) 1860 Census
Cropland, Samuel F.: (B) 1847, (CO) Pulaski, (A) 13, (BP) TN, (CMTS) 1860 Census
Cropland, William: (B) 1854, (CO) Pulaski, (A) 6, (BP) TN, (CMTS) 1860 Census
Crowley, Rosie A.: (B) 1908, (D) 1988, (CO) St. Louis, (C) Calvary Cemetery
Crumley, Catharine: (B) 1823, (CO) Pulaski, (A) 37, (BP) TN, (CMTS) 1860 Census
Crumley, George: (B) 1844, (CO) Pulaski, (A) 16, (BP) TN, (CMTS) 1860 Census
Crumley, James: (B) 1849, (CO) Pulaski, (A) 11, (BP) TN, (CMTS) 1860 Census
Crumley, Martha: (B) 1856, (CO) Pulaski, (A) 4, (BP) TN, (CMTS) 1860 Census
Crumley, Mary E.: (B) 1846, (CO) Pulaski, (A) 14, (BP) TN, (CMTS) 1860 Census
Crumley, Nancy: (B) 1848, (CO) Pulaski, (A) 12, (BP) TN, (CMTS) 1860 Census
Crumley, Samuel: (B) 1842, (CO) Pulaski, (A) 18, (BP) TN, (CMTS) 1860 Census
Crumpley, John S.: (B) 1853, (CO) Stone, (A) 17, (BP) MO, (CMTS) 1870 Census
Crumpley, John W.: (B) 1833, (CO) Stone, (A) 37, (BP) TN, (CMTS) 1870 Census
Crumpley, Mary E.: (B) 1846, (CO) Stone, (A) 24, (BP) MO, (CMTS) 1870 Census
Crumpley, Sarah S.: (B) 1827, (CO) Stone, (A) 43, (BP) TN, (CMTS) 1870 Census

Crumpley, William A.: (B) 1855, (CO) Stone, (A) 15, (BP) MO, (CMTS) 1870 Census
Crumply, Ely: (B) 1837, (CO) Stone, (A) 33, (BP) TN, (CMTS) 1870 Census
Crumply, Mary: (B) 1842, (CO) Stone, (A) 28, (BP) TN, (CMTS) 1870 Census
Csolak, Shirley M.: (D) Aug. 20, 2000, (CO) Cole, (NWS) *Jefferson City, Missouri News-Tribune*, Aug. 22, 2000, (RES) Eldon
Culders, Havins: (B) 1848, (CO) Pulaski, (A) 12, (BP) KY, (CMTS) 1860 Census
Culders, Louisa: (B) 1828, (CO) Pulaski, (A) 32, (BP) KY, (CMTS) 1860 Census
Culders, Mary: (B) 1855, (CO) Pulaski, (A) 5, (BP) KY, (CMTS) 1860 Census
Culders, Nancy: (B) 1850, (CO) Pulaski, (A) 10, (BP) KY, (CMTS) 1860 Census
Culders, William P.: (B) 1828, (CO) Pulaski, (A) 32, (BP) KY, (CMTS) 1860 Census
Cullers, John A.: (D) Jun. 18, 1869, (CO) Grundy, (CMTS) A. F. & A. M. Trenton Lodge 111
Cundiff, Isaac: (B) 1834, (CO) Pulaski, (A) 26, (BP) VA, (CMTS) 1860 Census
Cundiff, Mary: (B) 1833, (CO) Pulaski, (A) 27, (BP) TN, (CMTS) 1860 Census
Cunningham, Elizabeth: (B) 1854, (CO) Stone, (A) 16, (BP) MO, (CMTS) 1870 Census
Cunningham, Frances: (B) May 18, 1863, (D) Apr. 21, 1945, (CO) St. Louis, (C) Calvary Cemetery
Cunningham, James: (B) 1835, (CO) Pulaski, (A) 25, (BP) Ireland, (CMTS) 1860 Census
Cunningham, Jennie: (B) 1820, (CO) Stone, (A) 50, (BP) NC, (CMTS) 1870 Census
Cunningham, Lorraine: (D) Aug. 20, 2000, (CO) Cole, (NWS) *Jefferson City, Missouri News-Tribune*, Aug. 22, 2000, (RES) Hartsburg
Cunningham, Martha: (B) 1848, (CO) Stone, (A) 22, (BP) TN, (CMTS) 1870 Census
Cunningham, Nancy: (B) 1845, (CO) Stone, (A) 25, (BP) TN, (CMTS) 1870 Census
Curtis, Jesse M.: (B) 1853, (CO) Pulaski, (A) 7, (BP) MO, (CMTS) 1860 Census
Curtis, Mary J.: (B) 1844, (CO) Pulaski, (A) 16, (BP) TN, (CMTS) 1860 Census
Curtis, Samuel F.: (B) 1848, (CO) Pulaski, (A) 12, (BP) MO, (CMTS)

1860 Census
Curtis, Sarah E.: (B) 1846, (CO) Pulaski, (A) 14, (BP) MO, (CMTS) 1860 Census
Custer, M.: (B) Apr.15, 1825, (D) Jan. 25, 1913, (CO) Oregon, (C) Cave Springs Cemetery
Cutbeard, Elizabeth: (B) 1845, (CO) Pulaski, (A) 15, (BP) MO, (CMTS) 1860 Census
Cyphers, Raymond: (D) Jan. 20, 1937, (CO) Grundy, (CMTS) A. F. & A. M. Trenton Lodge 111
Dake, Lydia L.: (B) 1829, (CO) Pulaski, (A) 31, (BP) TN, (CMTS) 1860 Census
Dake, Melissa: (B) 1851, (CO) Pulaski, (A) 9, (BP) MO, (CMTS) 1860 Census
Dake, Washington: (B) 1850, (CO) Pulaski, (A) 10, (BP) MO, (CMTS) 1860 Census
Dalton, Gregory: (B) Aug. 23, 1969, (D) Apr. 19, 1999, (CO) Barry, (PRTS) Edward Ray Dalton and Margie Irene Edmonson, (C) Roller Cemetery, near Washburn, (BP) Stockton, CA
Dalton, Julia: (B) Nov. 25, 1882, (D) 6, 18, 1947, (CO) St. Louis, (C) Calvary Cemetery
Dancy, W.: (B) Feb. 12, 1819, (D) Sep. 7, 1871, (CO) Barry, (C) Old Corsicana Cemetery
Dandy, Victor E.: (D) Apr. 25, 1936, (CO) Grundy, (CMTS) A. F. & A. M. Trenton Lodge 111
Daniel, John F.: (D) Dec. 27, 1928, (CO) Grundy, (CMTS) A. F. & A. M. Trenton Lodge 111
Daniel, Leander R.: (B) 1848, (D) 1923, (CO) Cedar, (C) Brashear Cemetery
Daniel, Sarah H.: (B) 1849, (D) 1941, (CO) Cedar, (C) Brashear Cemetery
Daniels, Cartousy A.: (B) 1848, (CO) Stone, (A) 2, (BP) AR, (CMTS) 1870 Census
Daniels, Isaac: (B) 1831, (CO) Stone, (A) 39, (BP) TN, (CMTS) 1870 Census
Daniels, James: (B) 1818, (CO) Stone, (A) 32, (BP) TN, (CMTS) 1870 Census
Daniels, Margarett: (B) 1840, (CO) Stone, (A) 10, (BP) AR, (CMTS) 1870 Census
Daniels, Margarett A.: (B) 1842, (CO) Stone, (A) 28, (BP) TN, (CMTS) 1870 Census
Daniels, Mary Jane: (B) 1826, (CO) Stone, (A) 24, (BP) IL, (CMTS) 1870 Census
Daniels, Missouri L.: (B) 1845, (CO) Stone, (A) 5, (BP) KS, (CMTS) 1870 Census

D'Arcambal, Louis F.: (B) 1823, (D) 1893, (CO) St. Louis, (C) Calvary Cemetery
Darrell, Anna J.: (B) 1823, (CO) Stone, (A) 27, (BP) TN, (CMTS) 1870 Census
Darrell, Hulda: (B) 1849, (CO) Stone, (A) 1, (BP) MO, (CMTS) 1870 Census
Darrell, James M.: (B) 1827, (CO) Stone, (A) 23, (BP) MO, (CMTS) 1870 Census
Darrell, Lorenzo J.: (B) 1847, (CO) Stone, (A) 3, (BP) MO, (CMTS) 1870 Census
Darrell, Martha C.: (B) 1840, (CO) Stone, (A) 10, (BP) MO, (CMTS) 1870 Census
Darrell, Mary: (B) 1828, (CO) Stone, (A) 22, (BP) AR, (CMTS) 1870 Census
Darrell, Thomas J.: (B) 1825, (CO) Stone, (A) 25, (BP) MO, (CMTS) 1870 Census
Dashman, Anna: (B) 1872, (D) 1899, (CO) St. Louis, (C) Calvary Cemetery
Dashman, George: (B) 1863, (D) 1911, (CO) St. Louis, (C) Calvary Cemetery
Dauphin, Jr., Raymond G.: (D) Jul., 1962, (CO) St. Louis, (C) Calvary Cemetery
Dauwalter, Conrad: (B) 1844, (D) 1924, (CO) Henry, (C) Knights of Pythias Cemetery, Deepwater, MO
Dauwalter, Martha: (B) 1851, (D) 1935, (CO) Henry, (C) Knights of Pythias Cemetery, Deepwater, MO
Davenport, John: (B) 1841, (CO) Pulaski, (A) 19, (BP) TN, (CMTS) 1860 Census
Davenport, Marguerite P.: (B) Mar. 3, 1895, (D) Oct. 15, 1967, (CO) St. Louis, (C) Calvary Cemetery
Davenport,William F.: (D) Dec. 27, 1928, (CO) Grundy, (CMTS) A. F. & A. M. Trenton Lodge 111
David, Almisena: (B) 1849, (CO) Pulaski, (A) 11, (BP) MO, (CMTS) 1860 Census
David, Hiram M.: (B) 1853, (CO) Pulaski, (A) 7, (BP) MO, (CMTS) 1860 Census
David, Jane: (B) 1829, (CO) Pulaski, (A) 31, (BP) TN, (CMTS) 1860 Census
David, Lycurgus: (B) 1846, (CO) Pulaski, (A) 14, (BP) TN, (CMTS) 1860 Census
David, Nancy O.: (B) 1851, (CO) Pulaski, (A) 9, (BP) MO, (CMTS) 1860 Census
David, Ruth J.: (B) 1856, (CO) Pulaski, (A) 4, (BP) MO, (CMTS)

1860 Census

Davidson, Horace: (D) Dec. 2, 1928, (CO) Grundy, (CMTS) A. F. & A. M. Trenton Lodge 111

Davidson, James R.: (D) Apr. 6, 1941, (CO) Grundy, (CMTS) A. F. & A. M. Trenton Lodge 111

Davis, Alcie C.: (B) 1833, (CO) Stone, (A) 17, (BP) MO, (CMTS) 1870 Census

Davis, Betsy Ann: (B) 1832, (CO) Stone, (A) 18, (BP) AR, (CMTS) 1870 Census

Davis, Clara J.: (B) 1839, (CO) Stone, (A) 11, (BP) MO, (CMTS) 1870 Census

Davis, Dennis: (B) 1821, (CO) Pulaski, (A) 39, (BP) IL, (CMTS) 1860 Census

Davis, Elizabeth: (B) 1850, (CO) Pulaski, (A) 10, (BP) MO, (CMTS) 1860 Census

Davis, Esther: (B) Mar. 19, 1914, (D) Apr., 1993, (CO) Pulaski, (DP) Dixon, MO

Davis, Francis M.: (B) 1847, (CO) Pulaski, (A) 13, (BP) IL, (CMTS) 1860 Census

Davis, George M.: (B) 1852, (CO) Pulaski, (A) 8, (BP) MO, (CMTS) 1860 Census

Davis, George V.: (D) Aug. 20, 2000, (CO) Jackson, (NWS) *Kansas City, Missouri Star*, Aug. 22, 2000 (C) Brookings Cemetery

Davis, Harden: (B) 1840, (CO) Stone, (A) 10, (BP) MO, (CMTS) 1870 Census

Davis, Jackson: (B) 1834, (CO) Stone, (A) 16, (BP) MO, (CMTS) 1870 Census

Davis, James: (B) 1822, (CO) Stone, (A) 28, (BP) MO, (CMTS) 1870 Census

Davis, James: (B) 1841, (CO) Pulaski, (A) 19, (BP) MO, (CMTS) 1860 Census

Davis, James: (B) 1849, (CO) Stone, (A) 1, (BP) MO, (CMTS) 1870 Census

Davis, James A.: (B) 1856, (CO) Pulaski, (A) 4, (BP) MO, (CMTS) 1860 Census

Davis, John H.: (B) 1830, (CO) Stone, (A) 20, (BP) AR, (CMTS) 1870 Census

Davis, John M.: (B) 1840, (CO) Pulaski, (A) 20, (BP) MO, (CMTS) 1860 Census

Davis, John T.: (B) 1835, (CO) Pulaski, (A) 25, (BP) IL, (CMTS) 1860 Census

Davis, John T.: (B) 1854, (CO) Pulaski, (A) 6, (BP) MO, (CMTS) 1860 Census

Davis, John W.: (B) 1823, (CO) Pulaski, (A) 37, (BP) MO, (CMTS) 1860 Census
Davis, Joshua: (B) 1847, (CO) Stone, (A) 3, (BP) MO, (CMTS) 1870 Census
Davis, Joshua S.: (B) 1838, (CO) Stone, (A) 12, (BP) MO, (CMTS) 1870 Census
Davis, Julia: (B) 1856, (CO) Pulaski, (A) 4, (BP) MO, (CMTS) 1860 Census
Davis, L.: (B) 1818, (CO) Pulaski, (A) 42, (BP) NY, (CMTS) 1860 Census
Davis, Louisa: (B) 1831, (CO) Pulaski, (A) 29, (BP) MO, (CMTS) 1860 Census
Davis, Lucinda H.: (B) Mar. 17, 1826, (D) Jul. 12, 1907, (CO) Wright, (Maiden) Pybus
Davis, Malinda: (D) Apr. 6, 1865, (CO) Audrain, (C) Old Village Cemetery, (A) 75Y. 9M. 6D
Davis, Margaret: (B) 1832, (CO) Stone, (A) 18, (BP) MO, (CMTS) 1870 Census
Davis, Martha: (B) 1836, (CO) Stone, (A) 14, (BP) MO, (CMTS) 1870 Census
Davis, Martha: (B) 1850, (CO) Pulaski, (A) 10, (BP) MO, (CMTS) 1860 Census
Davis, Martha J.: (B) 1831, (CO) Stone, (A) 19, (BP) AR, (CMTS) 1870 Census
Davis, Martha J. C.: (B) May 1, 1834, (D) Feb. 27, 1896, (CO) Barry, (C) Cassville Cemetery
Davis, Mary: (B) 1834, (CO) Pulaski, (A) 26, (BP) TN, (CMTS) 1860 Census
Davis, Mary: (B) 1836, (CO) Pulaski, (A) 24, (BP) IN, (CMTS) 1860 Census
Davis, Mary: (B) 1852, (CO) Pulaski, (A) 8, (BP) MO, (CMTS) 1860 Census
Davis, Mary E.: (B) 1845, (CO) Stone, (A) 5, (BP) MO, (CMTS) 1870 Census
Davis, Mary J.: (B) 1848, (CO) Stone, (A) 2, (BP) MO, (CMTS) 1870 Census
Davis, Matilda: (B) 1839, (CO) Pulaski, (A) 21, (BP) MO, (CMTS) 1860 Census
Davis, Nancy: (B) 1827, (CO) Stone, (A) 23, (BP) MO, (CMTS) 1870 Census
Davis, Nancy: (B) 1838, (CO) Pulaski, (A) 22, (BP) MO, (CMTS) 1860 Census
Davis, Nancy: (B) 1846, (CO) Pulaski, (A) 14, (BP) MO, (CMTS)

1860 Census
Davis, Nancy J.: (B) 1817, (CO) Stone, (A) 33, (BP) MO, (CMTS) 1870 Census
Davis, Nancy J.: (B) 1847, (CO) Stone, (A) 3, (BP) MO, (CMTS) 1870 Census
Davis, Parlina: (B) 1855, (CO) Pulaski, (A) 5, (BP) MO, (CMTS) 1860 Census
Davis, Rachael: (B) 1842, (CO) Pulaski, (A) 18, (BP) MO, (CMTS) 1860 Census
Davis, Rhoda: (B) 1840, (CO) Pulaski, (A) 20, (BP) IL, (CMTS) 1860 Census
Davis, Sarah A.: (B) 1855, (CO) Pulaski, (A) 5, (BP) MO, (CMTS) 1860 Census
Davis, Sarah B.: (B) 1848, (CO) Pulaski, (A) 12, (BP) IL, (CMTS) 1860 Census
Davis, Sarah C.: (B) 1855, (D) 1938, (CO) St. Louis, (C) Calvary Cemetery
Davis, Thomas B.: (B) 1856, (CO) Pulaski, (A) 4, (BP) MO, (CMTS) 1860 Census
Davis, Thos J.: (B) 1842, (CO) Stone, (A) 8, (BP) MO, (CMTS) 1870 Census
Davis, Thomas K.: (B) 1819, (CO) Pulaski, (A) 41, (BP) IL, (CMTS) 1860 Census
Davis, Thomas: (B) 1837, (CO) Pulaski, (A) 23, (BP) TN, (CMTS) 1860 Census
Davis, William H.: (B) 1845, (CO) Pulaski, (A) 15, (BP) IL, (CMTS) 1860 Census
Davis, William M.: (B) 1844, (CO) Pulaski, (A) 16, (BP) MO, (CMTS) 1860 Census
Davis, William M.: (B) 1848, (CO) Pulaski, (A) 12, (BP) MO, (CMTS) 1860 Census
Dawbin, Elizabeth: (B) 1830, (CO) Pulaski, (A) 30, (BP) TN, (CMTS) 1860 Census
Dawbin, William D.: (B) 1853, (CO) Pulaski, (A) 7, (BP) MO, (CMTS) 1860 Census
Dawbin, Zach: (B) 1834, (CO) Pulaski, (A) 26, (BP) MO, (CMTS) 1860 Census
Day, James: (B) 1854, (CO) Pulaski, (A) 6, (BP) MO, (CMTS) 1860 Census
Day, Malvina: (B) 1832, (CO) Pulaski, (A) 28, (BP) TN, (CMTS) 1860 Census
Day, Sarah: (B) 1856, (CO) Pulaski, (A) 4, (BP) MO, (CMTS) 1860 Census

Day, Thomas: (B) 1832, (CO) Pulaski, (A) 28, (BP) TN, (CMTS) 1860 Census
Dayl, Mariah: (B) 1820, (CO) Stone, (A) 30, (BP) KY, (CMTS) 1870 Census
Dayl, Nancy P: (B) 1840, (CO) Stone, (A) 10, (BP) MO, (CMTS) 1870 Census
Dayl, Sarah E.: (B) 1844, (CO) Stone, (A) 6, (BP) AR, (CMTS) 1870 Census
Dayl, Thomas C.: (B) 1838, (CO) Stone, (A) 12, (BP) MO, (CMTS) 1870 Census
Dean, Capt James: (D) 1830, (CO) St. Louis, (C) Calvary Cemetery
Dean, Harriet M.: (B) 1809, (D) 1881, (CO) St. Louis, (C) Calvary Cemetery
Dean, Jane: (B) 1830, (CO) Pulaski, (A) 30, (BP) TN, (CMTS) 1860 Census
Deary, Daniel: (B) 1830, (CO) Pulaski, (A) 30, (BP) Ireland, (CMTS) 1860 Census
Deckard, Norman: (B) Dec. 9, 1918, (D) Nov. 3, 1921, (CO) Oregon, (C) Falling Springs Cemetery
Decker, Azariah: (B) 1837, (CO) Pulaski, (A) 23, (BP) KY, (CMTS) 1860 Census
Decker, George: (B) 1858, (CO) Pulaski, (A) 2, (BP) MO, (CMTS) 1860 Census
Decker, Harriet: (B) 1848, (CO) Pulaski, (A) 12, (BP) KY, (CMTS) 1860 Census
Decker, Henry: (B) 1838, (CO) Pulaski, (A) 22, (BP) MO, (CMTS) 1860 Census
Decker, Henry: (B) 1838, (CO) Pulaski, (A) 22, (BP) KY, (CMTS) 1860 Census
Decker, Henry S.: (B) 1852, (CO) Pulaski, (A) 8, (BP) MO, (CMTS) 1860 Census
Decker, Jane: (B) 1844, (CO) Pulaski, (A) 16, (BP) TN, (CMTS) 1860 Census
Decker, Martha: (B) 1842, (CO) Pulaski, (A) 18, (BP) KY, (CMTS) 1860 Census
Decker, Molly: (B) 1856, (CO) Pulaski, (A) 4, (BP) MO, (CMTS) 1860 Census
Decker, Nancy: (B) 1851, (CO) Pulaski, (A) 9, (BP) KY, (CMTS) 1860 Census
Decker, Samantha: (B) 1835, (CO) Pulaski, (A) 25, (BP) KY, (CMTS) 1860 Census
Decker, Sarah: (B) 1844, (CO) Pulaski, (A) 16, (BP) KY, (CMTS) 1860 Census

Decker, Sinah: (B) 1840, (CO) Pulaski, (A) 20, (BP) TN, (CMTS) 1860 Census
Decker, Wilkins: (B) 1839, (CO) Pulaski, (A) 21, (BP) KY, (CMTS) 1860 Census
Deer, Aliza E.: (B) 1831, (CO) Pulaski, (A) 29, (BP) PA, (CMTS) 1860 Census
Deer, Eli: (B) 1847, (CO) Pulaski, (A) 13, (BP) MO, (CMTS) 1860 Census
Deer, Felix: (B) 1839, (CO) Pulaski, (A) 21, (BP) MO, (CMTS) 1860 Census
Deer, Felix: (B) 1843, (CO) Pulaski, (A) 17, (BP) MO, (CMTS) 1860 Census
Deer, Florinda: (B) 1820, (CO) Pulaski, (A) 40, (BP) KY, (CMTS) 1860 Census
Deer, Isaac: (B) 1854, (CO) Pulaski, (A) 6, (BP) MO, (CMTS) 1860 Census
Deer, J.: (B) 1832, (CO) Pulaski, (A) 28, (BP) MO, (CMTS) 1860 Census
Deer, James A.: (B) 1850, (CO) Pulaski, (A) 10, (BP) MO, (CMTS) 1860 Census
Deer, Jasper: (B) 1836, (CO) Pulaski, (A) 24, (BP) MO, (CMTS) 1860 Census
Deer, John: (B) 1845, (CO) Pulaski, (A) 15, (BP) MO, (CMTS) 1860 Census
Deer, Martha A.: (B) 1855, (CO) Pulaski, (A) 5, (BP) MO, (CMTS) 1860 Census
Deer, Nancy J.: (B) 1841, (CO) Pulaski, (A) 19, (BP) MO, (CMTS) 1860 Census
Deer, Rebecca J.: (B) 1852, (CO) Pulaski, (A) 8, (BP) MO, (CMTS) 1860 Census
Deer, William: (B) 1853, (CO) Pulaski, (A) 7, (BP) MO, (CMTS) 1860 Census
DeGiverille, Vingina K.: (B) 1831, (D) 1913, (CO) St. Louis, (C) Calvary Cemetery
Delargy, Charles: (B) 1896, (D) 1955, (CO) St. Louis, (C) Calvary Cemetery
Delargy, Leo: (B) 1894, (D) 1928, (CO) St. Louis, (C) Calvary Cemetery
Delargy, Mary: (B) 1856, (D) 1930, (CO) St. Louis, (C) Calvary Cemetery
Dell, B. H.: (B) 1854, (CO) Pulaski, (A) 6, (BP) MO, (CMTS) 1860 Census
Dell, Johnathan: (B) 1845, (CO) Pulaski, (A) 15, (BP) IL, (CMTS) 1860 Census
Dell, Lucinda: (B) 1856, (CO) Pulaski, (A) 4, (BP) MO, (CMTS)

1860 Census
Dell, Nancy: (B) 1830, (CO) Pulaski, (A) 30, (BP) IL, (CMTS) 1860 Census
Dell, Robert H.: (B) 1852, (CO) Pulaski, (A) 8, (BP) MO, (CMTS) 1860 Census
Deneuville, Adolphe: (D) Nov. 9, 1929, (CO) St. Louis, (C) Calvary Cemetery
Dennis, Elias: (B) 1830, (CO) Stone, (A) 20, (BP) MO, (CMTS) 1870 Census
Dennis, John G: (B) 1831, (CO) Stone, (A) 19, (BP) MO, (CMTS) 1870 Census
Dennis, Linda: (B) 1855, (CO) Stone, (A) 15, (BP) MO, (CMTS) 1870 Census
Dennis, Sarah: (B) 1832, (CO) Stone, (A) 18, (BP) MO, (CMTS) 1870 Census
Denton, Alice: (B) 1852, (CO) Pulaski, (A) 8, (BP) IL, (CMTS) 1860 Census
Denton, Elizabeth: (B) 1823, (CO) Pulaski, (A) 37, (BP) IL, (CMTS) 1860 Census
Denton, James: (B) 1840, (CO) Pulaski, (A) 20, (BP) IL, (CMTS) 1860 Census
Denton, James: (B) 1854, (CO) Pulaski, (A) 6, (BP) KY, (CMTS) 1860 Census
Denton, Joseph: (B) 1844, (CO) Pulaski, (A) 16, (BP) KY, (CMTS) 1860 Census
Denton, Lucinda: (B) 1856, (CO) Pulaski, (A) 4, (BP) MO, (CMTS) 1860 Census
Denton, Marion: (B) 1851, (CO) Pulaski, (A) 9, (BP) KY, (CMTS) 1860 Census
Denton, Mary: (B) 1832, (CO) Pulaski, (A) 28, (BP) KY, (CMTS) 1860 Census
Denton, Mary: (B) 1844, (CO) Pulaski, (A) 16, (BP) IL, (CMTS) 1860 Census
Denton, Matilda: (B) 1850, (CO) Pulaski, (A) 10, (BP) KY, (CMTS) 1860 Census
Denton, Matilda: (B) 1854, (CO) Pulaski, (A) 6, (BP) IL, (CMTS) 1860 Census
Denton, Nancy: (B) 1856, (CO) Pulaski, (A) 4, (BP) KY, (CMTS) 1860 Census
Denton, Thomas: (B) 1828, (CO) Pulaski, (A) 32, (BP) KY, (CMTS) 1860 Census
Denton, Thomas: (B) 1857, (CO) Pulaski, (A) 3, (BP) KY, (CMTS) 1860 Census

Denton, William: (B) 1847, (CO) Pulaski, (A) 13, (BP) LA, (CMTS) 1860 Census
DeRita, Antonio: (B) Nov. 28, 1829, (D) 1903, (CO) St. Louis, (C) Calvary Cemetery
Desbonne, Rudolph: (B) May 22, 1833, (D) Jul. 27, 1872, (CO) St. Louis, (C) Calvary Cemetery
Desmoulin, Augustus: (D) Jan. 21, 1877, (CO) St. Louis, (C) Calvary Cemetery, (A) 37
Devlin, Bernard: (B) 1838, (D) 1885, (CO) St. Louis, (C) Calvary Cemetery
Devlin, Daniel: (B) 1836, (D) 1894, (CO) St. Louis, (C) Calvary Cemetery
Devlin, George: (B) 1871, (D) 1876, (CO) St. Louis, (C) Calvary Cemetery
Devota, Rosie: (D) Jul. 1, 1909, (CO) St. Louis, (C) Calvary Cemetery
DeWard, Charles: (B) Nov. 11, 1801, (D) Oct. 27, 1841, (CO) St. Louis, (C) Calvary Cemetery
Dickson, H.: (B) 1835, (CO) Pulaski, (A) 25, (BP) Ireland, (CMTS) 1860 Census
Dickson, Lucy Ann: (B) 1822, (D) 1899, (CO) St. Louis,
Die, Hannah: (B) 1818, (CO) Pulaski, (A) 42, (BP) NC, (CMTS) 1860 Census
Die, James: (B) 1822, (CO) Pulaski, (A) 38, (BP) KY, (CMTS) 1860 Census
Die, Mary: (B) 1846, (CO) Pulaski, (A) 14, (BP) MO, (CMTS) 1860 Census
Diehl, Maria: (B) Sep. 17, 1813, (D) Dec. 28, 1896, (CO) Jefferson, (C) Old St. John's Catholic Cemetery
Diehla, Jacob: (B) Oct. 5, 1837, (D) Nov. 5, 1893, (CO) Jefferson, (C) Old St. John's Catholic Cemetery
Dillinger, Anna E.: (B) 1878, (D) 1969, (CO) St. Louis, (C) Calvary Cemetery
Dillinger, Daniel J.: (B) 1876, (D) 1959, (CO) St. Louis, (C) Calvary Cemetery
Dillinger, Lillian: (B) 1899, (D) 1910, (CO) St. Louis, (C) Calvary Cemetery
Dillon, John: (B) 1843, (D) 1902, (CO) St. Louis, (C) Calvary Cemetery
Dillon, John A.: (B) 1853, (CO) Pulaski, (A) 7, (BP) MO, (CMTS) 1860 Census
Dillon, John R.: (B) 1831, (CO) Pulaski, (A) 29, (BP) AL, (CMTS) 1860 Census
Dillon, Sarah H.: (B) 1830, (CO) Pulaski, (A) 30, (BP) VA, (CMTS) 1860 Census
Dinnan, Patrick: (B) 1832, (CO) Pulaski, (A) 28, (BP) Ireland, (CMTS)

1860 Census

Dixon, Martha E.: (B) 1855, (D) 1927, (CO) Henry, (C) Knights of Pythias Cemetery, Deepwater, MO

Dobbs, Clarnido: (B) 1828, (CO) Pulaski, (A) 32, (BP) KY, (CMTS) 1860 Census

Dobbs, George W.: (B) 1854, (CO) Pulaski, (A) 6, (BP) MO, (CMTS) 1860 Census

Dobbs, Margaret E.: (B) 1851, (CO) Pulaski, (A) 9, (BP) TN, (CMTS) 1860 Census

Dobbs, Maryann: (B) 1854, (CO) Pulaski, (A) 6, (BP) MO, (CMTS) 1860 Census

Dobbs, Nancy: (B) 1856, (CO) Pulaski, (A) 4, (BP) MO, (CMTS) 1860 Census

Dobbs, Polly: (B) 1852, (CO) Pulaski, (A) 8, (BP) MO, (CMTS) 1860 Census

Dobbs, Sarah J.: (B) 1848, (CO) Pulaski, (A) 12, (BP) TN, (CMTS) 1860 Census

Dobbs, W.: (B) 1821, (CO) Pulaski, (A) 39, (BP) TN, (CMTS) 1860 Census

Dobbs, William: (B) 1829, (CO) Pulaski, (A) 31, (BP) KY, (CMTS) 1860 Census

Dodd, Hugh: (B) 1834, (CO) Pulaski, (A) 26, (BP) TN, (CMTS) 1860 Census

Dodd, James W.: (B) 1843, (CO) Pulaski, (A) 17, (BP) MO, (CMTS) 1860 Census

Dodd, John: (B) 1856, (CO) Pulaski, (A) 4, (BP) MO, (CMTS) 1860 Census

Dodd, Martha: (B) 1836, (CO) Pulaski, (A) 24, (BP) TN, (CMTS) 1860 Census

Dodd, Milton: (B) 1818, (CO) Pulaski, (A) 42, (BP) TN, (CMTS) 1860 Census

Dodd, Milton C.: (B) 1848, (CO) Pulaski, (A) 12, (BP) MO, (CMTS) 1860 Census

Dodd, Nilly: (B) 1854, (CO) Pulaski, (A) 6, (BP) MO, (CMTS) 1860 Census

Dodd, Winnie C.: (B) 1848, (CO) Pulaski, (A) 12, (BP) MO, (CMTS) 1860 Census

Dodge, Mary: (B) 1846, (CO) Pulaski, (A) 14, (BP) MO, (CMTS) 1860 Census

Dodson, Claiborn: (B) 1833, (CO) Stone, (A) 17, (BP) MO, (CMTS) 1870 Census

Dodson, Thomas: (B) 1831, (CO) Stone, (A) 19, (BP) MO, (CMTS) 1870 Census

Dodson, William Leon: (D) Jul. 11, 2000, (CO) Jackson, (NWS) *Kansas City, Missouri Star*, July 12, 2000
Dohrmann, Carl H.: (B) Dec. 5, 1919, (D) Aug. 21, 2000, (CO) Jackson, (NWS) *Kansas City, Missouri Star*, Aug. 22, 2000, (BP) Bremen, Germany
Dolan, Edward S.: (B) 1885, (D) 1974, (CO) St. Louis, (C) Calvary Cemetery
Dolan, Leonie A.: (B) 1861, (D) 1935, (CO) St. Louis, (C) Calvary Cemetery
Dolan, Timothy S.: (B) 1861, (D) 1942, (CO) St. Louis, (C) Calvary Cemetery
Donegan, John J.: (B) 1899, (D) 1975, (CO) St. Louis, (C) Calvary Cemetery
Donegan, Margarett: (B) 1911, (D) 1994, (CO) St. Louis, (C) Calvary Cemetery
Donnellan, Johanna: (D) Apr. 28, 1855, (CO) St. Louis, (C) Calvary Cemetery, (A) 59
Donnellan, John: (D) Sep. 24, 1849, (CO) St. Louis, (C) Calvary Cemetery, (A) 80
Donnellan, John: (D) May 22, 1869, (CO) St. Louis, (C) Calvary Cemetery, (A) 69
Donnellan, Patrick: (D) Jan. 25, 1851, (CO) St. Louis, (C) Calvary Cemetery, (A) 2
Donovan, Charlotte: (B) Sep. 6, 1846, (D) Sep. 17, 1902, (CO) St. Louis, (C) Calvary Cemetery
Dooley, William: (B) 1849, (CO) Pulaski, (A) 11, (BP) KY, (CMTS) 1860 Census
Dorsey, James J.: (D) Sep. 18, 1894, (CO) St. Louis, (C) Calvary Cemetery
Dorsey, Mary J.: (D) Aug. 13, 1908, (CO) St. Louis, (C) Calvary Cemetery
Dotson, David: (B) 1844, (CO) Stone, (A) 6, (BP) MO, (CMTS) 1870 Census
Dotson, John A.: (B) 1838, (CO) Stone, (A) 12, (BP) TN, (CMTS) 1870 Census
Dotson, Squire B.: (B) 1832, (CO) Stone, (A) 18, (BP) TN, (CMTS) 1870 Census
Dotson, Thomas: (B) 1843, (CO) Stone, (A) 7, (BP) MO, (CMTS) 1870 Census
Dottson, Archibald: (B) 1838, (CO) Stone, (A) 12, (BP) AR, (CMTS) 1870 Census
Dottson, James: (B) 1841, (CO) Stone, (A) 9, (BP) AR, (CMTS) 1870 Census

Dottson, Nancy: (B) 1839, (CO) Stone, (A) 11, (BP) AR, (CMTS) 1870 Census

Dougherty, Edward: (B) Nov. 9, 1866, (D) Oct. 30, 1896, (CO) St. Louis, (C) Calvary Cemetery

Dougherty, James C.: (B) Oct. 3, 1811, (D) Mar. 8, 1882, (CO) St. Louis, (C) Calvary Cemetery

Dougherty, Ruth Mary: (B) 1907, (D) 1958, (CO) St. Louis, (C) Calvary Cemetery

Dougherty, Winifred Walsh: (B) 1887, (D) 1944, (CO) St. Louis, (C) Calvary Cemetery

Douglas, John Madison 1858: (B) 1904, (CO) Oregon, (C) Falling Springs Cemetery

Douglass, Flora A.: (B) Jun. 20, 1891, (D) Aug. 1, 1953, (CO) Oregon, (C) Falling Springs Cemetery

Douglass, Glenna Grace: (B) May 4, 1914, (CO) Oregon, (C) Falling Springs Cemetery

Douglass, Melia Jane (B) Sep. 3, 1860: (D) Dec. 28, 1941, (CO) Oregon, (C) Falling Springs Cemetery

Douglass, Roua: (B) Feb. 15, 1885, (D) Oct. 23, 1968, (CO) Oregon, (C) Falling Springs Cemetery

Douglass, Verel Irene: (B) Mar. 18, 1918, (CO) Oregon, (C) Falling Springs Cemetery

Downing, Dyan V.: (B) Jul. 14, 1968, (D) Jul. 19, 1968, (CO) Henry, (C) Knights of Pythias Cemetery, Deepwater, MO

Doyle, John: (D) Mar. 29, 1907, (CO) St. Louis, (C) Calvary Cemetery, (A) 60

Doyle, John: (D) Feb. 28, 1873, (CO) St. Louis, (C) Calvary Cemetery, (A) 7

Drake, Sr., Vent T.: (D) Jul. 10, 2000, (CO) Jackson, (NWS) *Kansas City, Missouri Star*, July 12, 2000, (RES) Fortuna, MO, (C) Moreau Cemetery, near Tipton, MO.

Dreckhans, Anthony: (D) Feb. 8, 1919, (CO) St. Louis, (C) Calvary Cemetery

Dreckhans, Franciska: (B) 1848, (D) 1917, (CO) St. Louis, (C) Calvary Cemetery

Dreckhans, Herman: (B) 1847, (D) 1903, (CO) St. Louis, (C) Calvary Cemetery

Dreckhans, Myrtle: (D) Aug. 25, 1968, (CO) St. Louis, (C) Calvary Cemetery

Drew, Jessie: (B) 1816, (CO) Stone, (A) 54, (BP) TN, (CMTS) 1870 Census

Drew, Mary: (B) 1815, (CO) Stone, (A) 55, (BP) TN, (CMTS) 1870 Census

Driskill, Thomas: (B) Dec. 7, 1852, (D) Dec. 2, 1931, (CO) Henry, (C) Knights of Pythias Cemetery, Deepwater, MO
Drummock, Hallan: (B) 1852, (CO) Pulaski, (A) 8, (BP) MO, (CMTS) 1860 Census
Drummock, Nancy J.: (B) 1833, (CO) Pulaski, (A) 27, (BP) MO, (CMTS) 1860 Census
Duffy, James C.: (D) Feb. 17, 1895, (CO) St. Louis, (C) Calvary Cemetery, (A) 15
Duffy, Mrs. Rosana: (D) Jan., 1874, (CO) St. Louis, (C) Calvary Cemetery, (A) 80
Dufoid, John: (B) 1827, (CO) Pulaski, (A) 33, (BP) Ireland, (CMTS) 1860 Census
Dugger, Franklin: (B) 1834, (CO) Stone, (A) 16, (BP) MO, (CMTS) 1870 Census
Dugger, Martha J.: (B) 1828, (CO) Stone, (A) 22, (BP) PA, (CMTS) 1870 Census
Dugger, Thomas J.: (B) 1838, (CO) Stone, (A) 12, (BP) MO, (CMTS) 1870 Census
Dugger, William: (B) 1830, (CO) Stone, (A) 20, (BP) TN, (CMTS) 1870 Census
Dumont, Mary J.: (D) Apr. 12, 1921, (CO) St. Louis, (C) Calvary Cemetery
Duncan, Araminta: (B) 1836, (CO) Pulaski, (A) 24, (BP) MO, (CMTS) 1860 Census
Duncan, Benjamin: (B) 1858, (CO) Pulaski, (A) 2, (BP) MO, (CMTS) 1860 Census
Duncan, Benton: (B) 1840, (CO) Pulaski, (A) 20, (BP) MO, (CMTS) 1860 Census
Duncan, Clarissa: (B) 1820, (CO) Pulaski, (A) 40, (BP) OH, (CMTS) 1860 Census
Duncan, Clark: (B) 1836, (CO) Pulaski, (A) 24, (BP) MO, (CMTS) 1860 Census
Duncan, Hannah: (B) 1843, (CO) Pulaski, (A) 17, (BP) MO, (CMTS) 1860 Census
Duncan, Jackson: (B) 1839, (CO) Pulaski, (A) 21, (BP) MO, (CMTS) 1860 Census
Duncan, James A.: (B) 1835, (CO) Pulaski, (A) 25, (BP) MO, (CMTS) 1860 Census
Duncan, James L.: (B) 1849, (CO) Pulaski, (A) 11, (BP) MO, (CMTS) 1860 Census
Duncan, Jemima: (B) 1842, (CO) Pulaski, (A) 18, (BP) TN, (CMTS) 1860 Census
Duncan, Kilsa: (B) 1836, (CO) Pulaski, (A) 24, (BP) IL, (CMTS)

1860 Census
Duncan, Polly: (B) 1815, (CO) Pulaski, (A) 45, (BP) TN, (CMTS) 1860 Census
Duncan, Ponda: (B) 1839, (CO) Pulaski, (A) 21, (BP) MO, (CMTS) 1860 Census
Duncan, William: (B) 1820, (CO) Pulaski, (A) 40, (BP) Hanover, (CMTS) 1860 Census
Duncan, William B.: (B) 1856, (CO) Pulaski, (A) 4, (BP) MO, (CMTS) 1860 Census
Duncan, William H.: (B) 1821, (CO) Pulaski, (A) 39, (BP) MO, (CMTS) 1860 Census
Duncan, William R.: (B) 1846, (CO) Pulaski, (A) 14, (BP) MO, (CMTS) 1860 Census
Dunegan, Joseph W.: (B) 1840, (CO) Stone, (A) 10, (BP) MO, (CMTS) 1870 Census
Dunegan, Lucy A.: (B) 1849, (CO) Stone, (A) 1, (BP) KS, (CMTS) 1870 Census
Dunegan, Millie B.: (B) 1843, (CO) Stone, (A) 7, (BP) MO, (CMTS) 1870 Census
Dunegan, Susan A.: (B) 1831, (CO) Stone, (A) 19, (BP) MO, (CMTS) 1870 Census
Dunfield, Charles: (B) 1836, (CO) Stone, (A) 14, (BP) MO, (CMTS) 1870 Census
Dunlap, Mary E.: (D) Jul. 10, 2000, (CO) Jackson, (NWS) *Kansas City, Missouri Star*, July 12, 2000
Durtschy, Francis J.: (D) Jun. 18, 1999, (CO), (DP) Fredericktown, MO, (SPOUSE) Frieda Reichel, (REL) Catholic, (NWS) *Allentown, Pennslyvania Morning Call*, Jun. 24, 1999
Dusas, Jack: (B) 1839, (CO) Pulaski, (A) 21, (BP) Ireland, (CMTS) 1860 Census
Dutton, Carrie L.: (D) Aug. 28, 1894, (CO) St. Louis, (C) Calvary Cemetery, (A) 26
Eads, Eliza: (B) 1849, (D) 1879, (CO) St. Louis, (C) Calvary Cemetery
Eads, Sarah Ann: (B) 1821, (D) 1882, (CO) St. Louis, (C) Calvary Cemetery
Eads, Vincent: (D) Oct. 15, 1918, (CO) Livingston, (PRTS) J.E and Tempa Eads, (MIL) WWI
Earls, Jesse: (B) 1835, (CO) Pulaski, (A) 25, (BP) KY, (CMTS) 1860 Census
Earls, Mary: (B) 1842, (CO) Pulaski, (A) 18, (BP) IN, (CMTS) 1860 Census
Easter, John: (B) 1826, (CO) Pulaski, (A) 34, (BP) IN, (CMTS) 1860 Census

Eaton, Deborah: (B) 1849, (CO) Stone, (A) 21, (BP) AR, (CMTS) 1870 Census
Eaton, John: (B) 1851, (CO) Stone, (A) 19, (BP) AR, (CMTS) 1870 Census
Eaton, Martha: (B) 1825, (CO) Stone, (A) 45, (BP) AL, (CMTS) 1870 Census
Eaton, Thomas: (B) 1854, (CO) Stone, (A) 16, (BP) AR, (CMTS) 1870 Census
Eaton, William: (B) 1819, (CO) Stone, (A) 51, (BP) TN, (CMTS) 1870 Census
Ebbert, Jack B.: (D) Feb. 13, 2000, (CO) Jackson, (NWS) *Allentown, Pennsylvania Morning Call*, Feb. 15, 2000.
Eckert, Rita: (B) 1889, (D) 1957, (CO) St. Louis, (C) Calvary Cemetery
Edwards, Annise: (B) 1834, (CO) Stone, (A) 36, (BP) TN, (CMTS) 1870 Census
Edwards, Claiborn: (B) 1835, (CO) Stone, (A) 35, (BP) TN, (CMTS) 1870 Census
Edwards, Crownover: (B) 1831, (CO) Stone, (A) 39, (BP) TN, (CMTS) 1870 Census
Edwards, Elisha: (B) 1826, (CO) Stone, (A) 44, (BP) TN, (CMTS) 1870 Census
Edwards, Henry: (B) Sep. 26, 1859, (D) Jun. 18, 1860, (CO) St. Louis, (C) Calvary Cemetery
Edwards, James: (B) 1830, (CO) Stone, (A) 40, (BP) TN, (CMTS) 1870 Census
Edwards, James: (B) Nov. 8, 1863, (D) Feb. 7, 1866, (CO) St. Louis, (C) Calvary Cemetery
Edwards, John: (B) 1851, (CO) Stone, (A) 19, (BP) AL, (CMTS) 1870 Census
Edwards, John A.: (B) 1836, (CO) Stone, (A) 34, (BP) AL, (CMTS) 1870 Census
Edwards, Jonas: (B) 1850, (CO) Stone, (A) 20, (BP) TN, (CMTS) 1870 Census
Edwards, Logan: (B) 1865, (D) 1947, (CO) Henry, (C) Knights of Pythias Cemetery, Deepwater, MO
Edwards, Marion: (B) 1849, (CO) Stone, (A) 21, (BP) AL, (CMTS) 1870 Census
Edwards, Martha: (B) 1852, (CO) Stone, (A) 18, (BP) MO, (CMTS) 1870 Census
Edwards, Mary: (B) 1840, (CO) Stone, (A) 30, (BP) TN, (CMTS) 1870 Census
Edwards, Mary E.: (B) 1849, (CO) Stone, (A) 21, (BP) MO, (CMTS) 1870 Census

Edwards, Nancy: (B) 1854, (CO) Stone, (A) 16, (BP) MO, (CMTS) 1870 Census
Edwards, Nancy A.: (B) 1848, (CO) Stone, (A) 22, (BP) AR, (CMTS) 1870 Census
Edwards, Peter: (B) 1834, (CO) Pulaski, (A) 26, (BP) KY, (CMTS) 1860 Census
Edwards, Phebe: (B) 1815, (CO) Stone, (A) 55, (BP) TN, (CMTS) 1870 Census
Edwards, Samuel: (B) 1834, (CO) Stone, (A) 36, (BP) TN, (CMTS) 1870 Census
Edwards, Sarah: (B) 1853, (CO) Stone, (A) 17, (BP) AL, (CMTS) 1870 Census
Edwards, Susannah: (B) 1833, (CO) Stone, (A) 37, (BP) TN, (CMTS) 1870 Census
Edwards, Tyresia: (B) 1835, (CO) Stone, (A) 35, (BP) TN, (CMTS) 1870 Census
Edwards, William: (B) 1820, (CO) Stone, (A) 50, (BP) TN, (CMTS) 1870 Census
Egan, Catherine: (D) 1854, (CO) St. Louis, (C) Calvary Cemetery, (A) 25
Egan, Patrick: (D) Nov. 12, 1853, (CO) St. Louis, (C) Calvary Cemetery, (A) 50
Eiman, Catherina: (B) Nov. 27, 1825, (D) Oct. 31, 1859, (CO) Andrew, (C) Oak Ridge Cemetery
Eiman, Peter: (D) Sep. 7, 1885, (CO) Andrew, (C) Oak Ridge Cemetery, (A) 65Y.
Elam, Delilah: (B) 1822, (CO) Pulaski, (A) 38, (BP) TN, (CMTS) 1860 Census
Elam, Emily: (B) 1852, (CO) Pulaski, (A) 8, (BP) MO, (CMTS) 1860 Census
Elam, James: (B) 1851, (CO) Pulaski, (A) 9, (BP) MO, (CMTS) 1860 Census
Elam, Locky: (B) 1843, (CO) Pulaski, (A) 17, (BP) MO, (CMTS) 1860 Census
Elam, Sylvester: (B) 1848, (CO) Pulaski, (A) 12, (BP) MO, (CMTS) 1860 Census
Ellens, Columbus: (B) 1845, (CO) Pulaski, (A) 15, (BP) KY, (CMTS) 1860 Census
Ellens, Elizabeth: (B) 1816, (CO) Pulaski, (A) 44, (BP) KY, (CMTS) 1860 Census
Ellens, John H.: (B) 1851, (CO) Pulaski, (A) 9, (BP) KY, (CMTS) 1860 Census
Ellens, Sarah M.: (B) 1846, (CO) Pulaski, (A) 14, (BP) KY, (CMTS) 1860 Census

Elliott, Elizabeth: (B) 1845, (CO) Pulaski, (A) 15, (BP) MO, (CMTS) 1860 Census
Elliott, James M.: (B) 1840, (CO) Pulaski, (A) 20, (BP) IL, (CMTS) 1860 Census
Ellis, Chester: (B) 1881, (D) 1965, (CO) St. Louis, (C) Calvary Cemetery
Ellis, Elizabeth: (B) 1845, (CO) Stone, (A) 25, (BP) MO, (CMTS) 1870 Census
Ellis, Frances: (B) 1853, (CO) Pulaski, (A) 7, (BP) TN, (CMTS) 1860 Census
Ellis, G. B.: (B) 1855, (CO) Pulaski, (A) 5, (BP) MO, (CMTS) 1860 Census
Ellis, James F: (B) 1833, (CO) Stone, (A) 37, (BP) MO, (CMTS) 1870 Census
Ellis, Lottie Score: (B) 1880, (D) 1952, (CO) St. Louis, (C) Calvary Cemetery
Ellis, Sophonia: (B) 1855, (CO) Pulaski, (A) 5, (BP) TN, (CMTS) 1860 Census
Ellison, Lucinda: (B) 1820, (CO) Pulaski, (A) 40, (BP) TN, (CMTS) 1860 Census
Ellison, Nancy M.: (B) 1850, (CO) Pulaski, (A) 10, (BP) TN, (CMTS) 1860 Census
Ellison, Rebecca: (B) 1846, (CO) Pulaski, (A) 14, (BP) NC, (CMTS) 1860 Census
Ellison, Thomas: (B) 1818, (CO) Pulaski, (A) 42, (BP) NC, (CMTS) 1860 Census
Elpin, Elvira C.: (B) 1855, (CO) Pulaski, (A) 5, (BP) MO, (CMTS) 1860 Census
Elpin, Martha: (B) 1830, (CO) Pulaski, (A) 30, (BP) TN, (CMTS) 1860 Census
Elpin, Samuel: (B) 1826, (CO) Pulaski, (A) 34, (BP) TN, (CMTS) 1860 Census
Elpin, Samuel: (B) 1852, (CO) Pulaski, (A) 8, (BP) MO, (CMTS) 1860 Census
Elpin, William: (B) 1850, (CO) Pulaski, (A) 10, (BP) TN, (CMTS) 1860 Census
Elsey, Roy A.: (B) 1885, (D) 1980, (CO) St. Louis, (C) Calvary Cemetery
Elston, George W.: (B) Feb. 29, 1864, (D) Dec. 5, 1951, (CO) Henry, (C) Knights of Pythias Cemetery, Deepwater, MO
Emerson, Cyrus C.: (B) Apr. 21, 1816, (D) Oct. 2, 1888, (CO) Barry, (C) Cassville Cemetery
Emerson, Elizabeth: (B) 1820, (CO) Stone, (A) 30, (BP) OH, (CMTS) 1870 Census
Emerson, Emma J.: (B) 1834, (CO) Stone, (A) 16, (BP) OH, (CMTS)

1870 Census
Emerson, Henry E.: (B) 1832, (CO) Stone, (A) 18, (BP) OH, (CMTS) 1870 Census
Emerson, Lyman S.: (B) 1830, (CO) Stone, (A) 20, (BP) OH, (CMTS) 1870 Census
Endler, Maruerite: (B) 1895, (D) 1963, (CO) St. Louis, (C) Calvary Cemetery
Engle, Henry: (B) Aug. 4, 1819, (D) Aug. 18, 1907, (CO) Henry, (C) Knights of Pythias Cemetery, Deepwater, MO
English, Albert L.: (B) 1849, (CO) Stone, (A) 1, (BP) MO, (CMTS) 1870 Census
English, Catherine R.: (B) 1902, (D) 1976, (CO) St. Louis, (C) Calvary Cemetery
English, Francis M.: (B) 1848, (CO) Stone, (A) 2, (BP) MO, (CMTS) 1870 Census
English, James C.: (B) 1902, (D) 1960, (CO) St. Louis, (C) Calvary Cemetery
English, Mary: (B) 1830, (CO) Stone, (A) 20, (BP) OH, (CMTS) 1870 Census
Erbs, Harry George: (B) Mar. 6, 1906, (CO) St. Louis, (PRTS) Joseph A. and Mary Erbs, (CMTS) Knights of Columbus, 4th Degree
Eschmann, Bertha W.: (D) Mar.,1951, (CO) St. Louis, (C) Calvary Cemetery
Eschmann, Emil F.: (D) Feb., 1936, (CO) St. Louis, (C) Calvary Cemetery
Essary, Isham: (B) 1846, (CO) Stone, (A) 24, (BP) IL, (CMTS) 1870 Census
Essary, James H.: (B) 1853, (CO) Stone, (A) 17, (BP) TN, (CMTS) 1870 Census
Essary, Sarah A.: (B) 1849, (CO) Stone, (A) 21, (BP) MO, (CMTS) 1870 Census
Ester, Cynthia: (B) 1827, (CO) Pulaski, (A) 33, (BP) IN, (CMTS) 1860 Census
Ester, Isaac: (B) 1851, (CO) Pulaski, (A) 9, (BP) IN, (CMTS) 1860 Census
Ester, Jesse: (B) 1845, (CO) Pulaski, (A) 15, (BP) IN, (CMTS) 1860 Census
Ester, Sarah A.: (B) 1854, (CO) Pulaski, (A) 6, (BP) IN, (CMTS) 1860 Census
Ester, Seaburn: (B) 1850, (CO) Pulaski, (A) 10, (BP) IN, (CMTS) 1860 Census
Ester, Thos: (B) 1847, (CO) Pulaski, (A) 13, (BP) IN, (CMTS) 1860 Census
Estes, Amanda: (B) 1845, (CO) Stone, (A) 25, (BP) MO, (CMTS)

1870 Census

Estes, Gussie Anne: (B) Sep. 27, 1885, (CO) Callaway,

Estes, Herman P.: (B) Oct. 28, 1892, (CO) Callaway,

Estes, Ida M.: (B) May 10, 1891, (CO) Callaway,

Estes, James A.: (B) May 26, 1899, (CO) Callaway,

Estes, John: (B) 1797, (CO) Stone, (A) 73, (BP) VA, (CMTS) 1870 Census

Estes, John H.: (B) 1841, (CO) Stone, (A) 29, (BP) TN, (CMTS) 1870 Census

Estes, John T.: (B) May 7, 1856, (D) Jul. 28, 1947, (CO) Callaway, (DP) Hatton, MO

Estes, John W.: (B) 1851, (CO) Stone, (A) 19, (BP) MO, (CMTS) 1870 Census

Estes, Mary E.: (B) 1818, (CO) Stone, (A) 32, (BP) TN, (CMTS) 1870 Census

Estes, Palina: (B) 1827, (CO) Stone, (A) 43, (BP) TN, (CMTS) 1870 Census

Estes, Paul: (B) 1827, (CO) Stone, (A) 43, (BP) TN, (CMTS) 1870 Census

Estes, Robert C.: (B) Jan., 1888, (CO) Callaway,

Estes, Sarah E.: (B) 1854, (CO) Stone, (A) 16, (BP) MO, (CMTS) 1870 Census

Estes,Thomas L.: (B) Mar. 28, 1896, (CO) Callaway,

Etcherson, Jessie T.: (B) 1842, (CO) Stone, (A) 8, (BP) NC, (CMTS) 1870 Census

Eubanks, Cyrena: (B) 1818, (CO) Stone, (A) 32, (BP) KY, (CMTS) 1870 Census

Eubanks, Elizabeth: (B) 1832, (CO) Stone, (A) 18, (BP) MO, (CMTS) 1870 Census

Eubanks, Martha A.: (B) 1837, (CO) Stone, (A) 13, (BP) MO, (CMTS) 1870 Census

Eubanks, Melvina: (B) 1841, (CO) Stone, (A) 9, (BP) MO, (CMTS) 1870 Census

Eubanks, Nancy J.: (B) 1835, (CO) Stone, (A) 15, (BP) MO, (CMTS) 1870 Census

Eubanks, Sarah E.: (B) 1836, (CO) Stone, (A) 14, (BP) MO, (CMTS) 1870 Census

Euchler, Jacob: (B) 1831, (CO) Stone, (A) 19, (BP) MO, (CMTS) 1870 Census

Euchler, John: (B) 1833, (CO) Stone, (A) 17, (BP) MO, (CMTS) 1870 Census

Euchler, Margaret: (B) 1828, (CO) Stone, (A) 22, (BP) MO, (CMTS) 1870 Census

Euchler, Martha: (B) 1815, (CO) Stone, (A) 35, (BP) MO, (CMTS) 1870 Census
Evans, Bernadine: (B) 1922, (D) 1922, (CO) St. Louis, (C) Calvary Cemetery
Evans, John S.: (B) 1844, (CO) Stone, (A) 6, (BP) MO, (CMTS) 1870 Census
Evans, Leonard A.: (B) 1848, (CO) Stone, (A) 2, (BP) MO, (CMTS) 1870 Census
Evans, Mary: (B) 1841, (CO) Stone, (A) 9, (BP) MO, (CMTS) 1870 Census
Evans, Nancy: (B) 1822, (CO) Stone, (A) 28, (BP) TN, (CMTS) 1870 Census
Even, Lena: (B) 1861, (D) 1948, (CO) St. Louis, (C) Calvary Cemetery
Even, Nicholas: (B) 1861, (D) 1933, (CO) St. Louis, (C) Calvary Cemetery
Fagin, Thomas J.: (B) 1852, (D) 1918, (CO) St. Louis, (C) Calvary Cemetery
Fair, Hulda: (B) 1840, (CO) Stone, (A) 10, (BP) AR, (CMTS) 1870 Census
Fair, Nicholas N: (B) 1815, (CO) Stone, (A) 35, (BP) TN, (CMTS) 1870 Census
Faisley, Delilah J.: (B) 1841, (CO) Pulaski, (A) 19, (BP) IL, (CMTS) 1860 Census
Faisley, Emily: (B) 1844, (CO) Pulaski, (A) 16, (BP) IL, (CMTS) 1860 Census
Faisley, John: (B) 1844, (CO) Pulaski, (A) 16, (BP) IL, (CMTS) 1860 Census
Faisley, Nancy: (B) 1821, (CO) Pulaski, (A) 39, (BP) TN, (CMTS) 1860 Census
Faisley, Nancy: (B) 1852, (CO) Pulaski, (A) 8, (BP) MO, (CMTS) 1860 Census
Fanning, Mrs. Mary: (D) Jan. 30, 1877, (CO) St. Louis, (C) Calvary Cemetery, (A) 72
Farmer, Fred: (B) Feb. 8, 1914, (D) Apr. 19, 1999, (CO) Barry, (PRTS) William Farmer and Maggie Weidner, (DP) Carthage, MO
Farmer, George: (B) 1850, (CO) Stone, (A) 20, (BP) AR, (CMTS) 1870 Census
Farmer, Isaac: (B) 1854, (CO) Stone, (A) 16, (BP) AR, (CMTS) 1870 Census
Farmer, Isabell: (B) 1840, (CO) Stone, (A) 30, (BP) AR, (CMTS) 1870 Census
Farris, Sheldon G.: (B) 1834, (CO) Pulaski, (A) 26, (BP) IL, (CMTS) 1860 Census

Febleman, Bertha: (B) 1836, (CO) Pulaski, (A) 24, (BP) Bavaria, (CMTS) 1860 Census
Febleman, Joseph: (B) 1834, (CO) Pulaski, (A) 26, (BP) Hamburg, (CMTS) 1860 Census
Feeney, Mark K.: (B) 1870, (D) 1929, (CO) St. Louis, (C) Calvary Cemetery
Feeney, Martin: (B) 1848, (D) 1910, (CO) St. Louis, (C) Calvary Cemetery
Feeney, Sarah T.: (B) 1849, (D) 1936, (CO) St. Louis, (C) Calvary Cemetery
Ferguson, John: (B) Sep. 23, 1810, (CO) Barry, (C) Old Corsicana Cemetery, (A) 76 Y
Ferguson, John D.: (B) Jul. 18, 1832, (D) Jan. 28, 1896, (CO) Barry, (C) Old Corsicana Cemetery
Ferguson, Nancy P.: (B) Jun. 26, 1836, (D) Jun. 15, 1892, (CO) Barry, (C) Old Corsicana Cemetery
Fields, Francis: (B) 1848, (CO) Pulaski, (A) 12, (BP) IL, (CMTS) 1860 Census
Fields, George: (B) 1844, (CO) Pulaski, (A) 16, (BP) IL, (CMTS) 1860 Census
Fields, James: (B) 1831, (CO) Pulaski, (A) 29, (BP) TN, (CMTS) 1860 Census
Fields, Jeremiah: (B) 1853, (CO) Pulaski, (A) 7, (BP) IL, (CMTS) 1860 Census
Fields, John: (B) 1846, (CO) Pulaski, (A) 14, (BP) IL, (CMTS) 1860 Census
Fields, Louisa: (B) 1854, (CO) Pulaski, (A) 6, (BP) MO, (CMTS) 1860 Census
Fields, Martha H.: (B) 1852, (CO) Pulaski, (A) 8, (BP) IL, (CMTS) 1860 Census
Fields, Nancy: (B) 1850, (CO) Pulaski, (A) 10, (BP) IL, (CMTS) 1860 Census
Fields, Sally: (B) 1820, (CO) Pulaski, (A) 40, (BP) AL, (CMTS) 1860 Census
Figgemeier, Anna E.: (B) 1874, (D) 1955, (CO) St. Louis, (C) Calvary Cemetery
Figgemeier, Frank: (B) 1840, (D) 1893, (CO) St. Louis, (C) Calvary Cemetery
Figgemeier, Frank: (B) 1886, (D) 1910, (CO) St. Louis, (C) Calvary Cemetery
Figgemeier, Henry: (B) 1876, (D) 1908, (CO) St. Louis, (C) Calvary Cemetery
Figgemeier, Mary A.: (B) 1852, (D) 1927, (CO) St. Louis, (C) Calvary

Cemetery
Finch, Coral: (B) 1931, (D) 1990, (CO) St. Louis, (C) Calvary Cemetery
Finch, William H.: (B) 1931, (D) 1989, (CO) St. Louis, (C) Calvary Cemetery
Finley, Caleb: (B) 1854, (CO) Pulaski, (A) 6, (BP) MO, (CMTS) 1860 Census
Finley, Eliza J.: (B) 1855, (CO) Pulaski, (A) 5, (BP) MO, (CMTS) 1860 Census
Finley, Elizabeth: (B) 1839, (CO) Pulaski, (A) 21, (BP) MO, (CMTS) 1860 Census
Finley, Evaline: (B) 1843, (CO) Pulaski, (A) 17, (BP) MO, (CMTS) 1860 Census
Finley, Franklin: (B) 1850, (CO) Pulaski, (A) 10, (BP) MO, (CMTS) 1860 Census
Finley, James H.: (B) 1848, (CO) Pulaski, (A) 12, (BP) MO, (CMTS) 1860 Census
Finley, Jesse: (B) 1842, (CO) Pulaski, (A) 18, (BP) MO, (CMTS) 1860 Census
Finley, Jesse N.: (B) 1845, (CO) Pulaski, (A) 15, (BP) MO, (CMTS) 1860 Census
Finley, Mary: (B) 1845, (CO) Pulaski, (A) 15, (BP) MO, (CMTS) 1860 Census
Finley, N.: (B) 1815, (CO) Pulaski, (A) 45, (BP) NC, (CMTS) 1860 Census
Finley, Robert: (B) 1839, (CO) Pulaski, (A) 21, (BP) TN, (CMTS) 1860 Census
Finley, Sarah: (B) 1834, (CO) Pulaski, (A) 26, (BP) MO, (CMTS) 1860 Census
Finley, Sarah: (B) 1841, (CO) Pulaski, (A) 19, (BP) MO, (CMTS) 1860 Census
Finley, Thomas: (B) 1850, (CO) Pulaski, (A) 10, (BP) MO, (CMTS) 1860 Census
Finley, Tiatina: (B) 1818, (CO) Pulaski, (A) 42, (BP) NC, (CMTS) 1860 Census
Finley, William: (B) 1848, (CO) Pulaski, (A) 12, (BP) MO, (CMTS) 1860 Census
Finley, William: (B) 1857, (CO) Pulaski, (A) 3, (BP) MO, (CMTS) 1860 Census
Fisher, Henry: (B) 1830, (CO) Pulaski, (A) 30, (BP) Prussia, (CMTS) 1860 Census
Fitch, Mary E.: (B) 1837, (CO) Pulaski, (A) 23, (BP) MO, (CMTS) 1860 Census
Fitch, Samuel: (B) 1834, (CO) Pulaski, (A) 26, (BP) TN, (CMTS)

1860 Census
Fitch, William M.: (B) 1853, (CO) Pulaski, (A) 7, (BP) MO, (CMTS) 1860 Census
Fitzgerald, Anna: (B) 1869, (D) 1940, (CO) St. Louis, (C) Calvary Cemetery
Fitzgerald, Charles W.: (B) 1885, (D) 1958, (CO) St. Louis, (C) Calvary Cemetery
Fitzgerald, Charles W.: (B) 1915, (D) 1993, (CO) St. Louis, (C) Calvary Cemetery
Fitzgerald, Claude A.: (B) 1886, (D) 1970, (CO) St. Louis, (C) Calvary Cemetery
Fitzgerald, Claude J.: (B) 1914, (D) 1985, (CO) St. Louis, (C) Calvary Cemetery
Fitzgerald, Gladys M.: (B) 1888, (D) 1967, (CO) St. Louis, (C) Calvary Cemetery
Fitzgerald, Josephine M.: (B) 1918, (CO) St. Louis, (C) Calvary Cemetery
Fitzgerald, Mary M.: (D) Jan. 1, 1964, (CO) St. Louis, (C) Calvary Cemetery
Fitzgerald, Robert J.: (B) 1931, (D) 1952, (CO) St. Louis, (C) Calvary Cemetery
Fitzgerald, Ronald J.: (B) 1932, (D) 1988, (CO) St. Louis, (C) Calvary Cemetery
Fitzgerald, Thomas: (B) 1840, (D) 1917, (CO) St. Louis, (C) Calvary Cemetery
Fitzgerald, Thomas L.: (B) 1922, (D) 1955, (CO) St. Louis, (C) Calvary Cemetery
Fitzsimmons, Ann: (D) Jan. 22, 1877, (CO) St. Louis, (C) Calvary Cemetery, (A) 38
Flemings, Mrs. Julia: (D) Jan. 20, 1873, (CO) St. Louis, (C) Calvary Cemetery, (A) 67
Fletcher, Elizabeth: (B) 1839, (CO) Pulaski, (A) 21, (BP) MO, (CMTS) 1860 Census
Fletcher, Thomas J.: (B) Feb. 9, 1840, (D) Dec. 9, 1878, (CO) Henry, (C) Knights of Pythias Cemetery, Deepwater, MO
Flood, Frances: (B) 1842, (CO) Stone, (A) 28, (BP) AL, (CMTS) 1870 Census
Flood, James: (B) 1835, (CO) Stone, (A) 35, (BP) IRE, (CMTS) 1870 Census
Flood, John: (B) 1877, (D) 1937, (CO) St. Louis, (C) Calvary Cemetery
Flood, Nell: (B) 1877, (D) 1926, (CO) St. Louis, (C) Calvary Cemetery
Flood, Nell M.: (B) 1905, (D) 1976, (CO) St. Louis, (C) Calvary Cemetery
Flowerree, Mary: (B) Aug., 1829, (D) Mar., 1908, (CO) Ralls, (C)

Hydesburg Cemetery
Fly, Marillay: (B) Dec. 18, 1801, (D) May 25, 1860, (CO) Barry, (C) Old Corsicana Cemetery
Fly, Marion: (D) Sept. 18, 1849, (CO) Barry, (C) Old Corsicana Cemetery, (A) 49Y 4M 20D
Fly, Naomia: (B) Aug. 21, 1829, (D) Oct. 6, 1864, (CO) Barry, (C) Old Corsicana Cemetery
Flynn, Clara M.: (B) May 30, 1895, (D) Sep. 6, 1965, (CO) St. Louis, (C) Calvary Cemetery
Flynn, Madeline K.: (B) 1903, (D) 1987, (CO) St. Louis, (C) Calvary Cemetery
Flynn, Marietta Muckerman: (B) Mar. Mar. 1918, (D) Aug. 11, 1993, (CO) St. Louis, (C) Calvary Cemetery
Foley, Kansada: (B) 1837, (CO) Pulaski, (A) 23, (BP) MO, (CMTS) 1860 Census
Foley, Louisa J.: (B) 1851, (CO) Pulaski, (A) 9, (BP) MO, (CMTS) 1860 Census
Foley, Mary A.: (B) 1828, (CO) Pulaski, (A) 32, (BP) TN, (CMTS) 1860 Census
Foley, Mary M.: (B) 1856, (CO) Pulaski, (A) 4, (BP) MO, (CMTS) 1860 Census
Foster, Deborah Kaye: (B) Dec. 8, 1962, (D) Apr. 10, 1973, (CO) Henry, (C) Knights of Pythias Cemetery, Deepwater, MO
Foster, Eli: (B) 1820, (CO) Stone, (A) 50, (BP) TN, (CMTS) 1870 Census
Foster, Elizabeth: (D) Oct. 7, 1855, (CO) Audrain, (C) Old Village Cemetery, (A) 20 Y
Foster, Frances J.: (B) 1848, (CO) Stone, (A) 22, (BP) TN, (CMTS) 1870 Census
Foster, Isham: (B) 1849, (CO) Stone, (A) 21, (BP) MO, (CMTS) 1870 Census
Foster, Perry: (B) 1851, (CO) Stone, (A) 19, (BP) MO, (CMTS) 1870 Census
Foster, Rebecca: (B) 1823, (CO) Stone, (A) 47, (BP) MO, (CMTS) 1870 Census
Foster, Rebecca E.: (B) 1855, (CO) Stone, (A) 15, (BP) MO, (CMTS) 1870 Census
Foster, William: (B) 1848, (CO) Stone, (A) 22, (BP) MO, (CMTS) 1870 Census
Fox, Ervy: (B) 1849, (CO) Stone, (A) 1, (BP) MO, (CMTS) 1870 Census
Fox, Lawrence: (B) 1847, (CO) Stone, (A) 3, (BP) MO, (CMTS) 1870 Census
Fox, Thomas D: (B) 1815, (CO) Stone, (A) 35, (BP) KS, (CMTS) 1870 Census

Francis, Sarah E.: (D) Jan. 12, 1883, (CO) St. Louis, (C) Calvary Cemetery, (A) 29

Franke, Charles H.: (B) May 22, 1833, (D) Mar. 15, 1906, (CO) St. Louis, (C) Calvary Cemetery

Frasier, Charles: (D) Aug. 20, 2000, (CO) Cole, (NWS) *Jefferson City, Missouri News-Tribune*, Aug. 22, 2000, (RES) Camdenton

Frazier, Curran: (B) 1818, (CO) Stone, (A) 32, (BP) MO, (CMTS) 1870 Census

Frazier, Ellen: (B) 1845, (CO) Stone, (A) 5, (BP) MO, (CMTS) 1870 Census

Frazier, Kizzie: (B) 1847, (CO) Stone, (A) 3, (BP) MO, (CMTS) 1870 Census

Frazier, Mary: (B) 1837, (CO) Stone, (A) 13, (BP) MO, (CMTS) 1870 Census

Frazier, Sarah: (B) 1820, (CO) Stone, (A) 30, (BP) MO, (CMTS) 1870 Census

Frederick, Benjamin F.: (B) 1814, (D) 1899, (CO) Henry, (C) Knights of Pythias Cemetery, Deepwater, MO

Frederick, Elizabeth: (B) 1832, (D) 1913, (CO) Henry, (C) Knights of Pythias Cemetery, Deepwater, MO

Freeman, Angeline: (B) 1850, (D) 1940, (CO) Cedar, (C) Brashear Cemetery

Freeman, Isaiah: (B) 1835, (D) 1913, (CO) Cedar, (C) Brashear Cemetery

Freibery, Frederick A.: (B) 1902, (D) 1978, (CO) St. Louis, (C) Calvary Cemetery

Freibery, Mildred G.: (B) 1911, (D) 1986, (CO) St. Louis, (C) Calvary Cemetery

French, Mary J.: (B) 1831, (D) 1900, (CO) Cedar, (C) Brashear Cemetery

French, William C.: (B) 1831, (D) 1912, (CO) Cedar, (C) Brashear Cemetery

Friend, Elizabeth: (B) 1828, (CO) Stone, (A) 22, (BP) MO, (CMTS) 1870 Census

Friend, Matilda: (B) 1848, (CO) Stone, (A) 2, (BP) MO, (CMTS) 1870 Census

Frisbee, Josiah: (B) 1829, (CO) Pulaski, (A) 31, (BP) TN, (CMTS) 1860 Census

Frisbee, Lilphia Ann: (B) 1834, (CO) Pulaski, (A) 26, (BP) TN, (CMTS) 1860 Census

Frisbey, Arthur Wesley: (B) Jul. 23, 1912, (D) Jan. 26, 1972, (CO) Jackson, (DP) Independence, MO

Fritze, Melinde C.: (B) Nov. 4, 1880, (D) May 16, 1961, (CO) St. Louis, (C) Calvary Cemetery

Frost, John: (B) 1840, (CO) Pulaski, (A) 20, (BP) TN, (CMTS)

1860 Census
Frost, J.: (B) Nov. 27, 1816, (D) Dec. 24, 1862, (CO) Barry, (C) Cassville Cemetery
Fry, Deborah: (B) 1843, (CO) Stone, (A) 7, (BP) IN, (CMTS) 1870 Census
Fry, Elizabeth: (B) 1840, (CO) Stone, (A) 10, (BP) IN, (CMTS) 1870 Census
Fry, Epraim: (B) 1793, (CO) Stone, (A) 57, (BP) NC, (CMTS) 1870 Census
Fry, John J.: (B) 1838, (CO) Stone, (A) 12, (BP) IN, (CMTS) 1870 Census
Fry, Martha: (B) 1797, (CO) Stone, (A) 53, (BP) IN, (CMTS) 1870 Census
Fugh, Cynthia S.: (B) 1852, (CO) Pulaski, (A) 8, (BP) TN, (CMTS) 1860 Census
Fugh, George A.: (B) 1843, (CO) Pulaski, (A) 17, (BP) TN, (CMTS) 1860 Census
Fugh, Joseph: (B) 1816, (CO) Pulaski, (A) 44, (BP) TN, (CMTS) 1860 Census
Fuqua, Anna: (B) 1852, (D) 1919, (CO) Cedar, (C) Brashear Cemetery
Furlong, Bridget: (B) 1848, (D) 1908, (CO) St. Louis, (C) Calvary Cemetery
Furlong, Frank J.: (B) 1886, (D) 1962, (CO) St. Louis, (C) Calvary Cemetery
Furlong, Helen M.: (B) 1885, (D) 1952, (CO) St. Louis, (C) Calvary Cemetery
Furlong, Michael: (B) 1838, (D) 1919, (CO) St. Louis, (C) Calvary Cemetery
Gaddy, Emily: (B) 1836, (CO) Stone, (A) 14, (BP) AR, (CMTS) 1870 Census
Gaddy, Lydia: (B) 1795, (CO) Stone, (A) 55, (BP) AR, (CMTS) 1870 Census
Gaddy, Martin: (B) 1832, (CO) Stone, (A) 18, (BP) AR, (CMTS) 1870 Census
Gaddy, Sarah: (B) 1830, (CO) Stone, (A) 20, (BP) AR, (CMTS) 1870 Census
Gaffney, Adell V.: (B) 1887, (D) 1967, (CO) St. Louis, (C) Calvary Cemetery
Gaffney, Harry F.: (B) 1878, (D) 1918, (CO) St. Louis, (C) Calvary Cemetery
Gaffney, Harry F.: (B) 1878, (D) 1913, (CO) St. Louis, (C) Calvary Cemetery
Gaffney, John: (B) 1832, (D) 1914, (CO) St. Louis, (C) Calvary Cemetery

Gaffney, John J.: (B) 1876, (D) 1910, (CO) St. Louis, (C) Calvary Cemetery
Gaffney, Joseph F.: (B) 1882, (D) 1914, (CO) St. Louis, (C) Calvary Cemetery
Gaffney, Thomas F.: (B) 1869, (D) 1913, (CO) St. Louis, (C) Calvary Cemetery
Gaffney, William P.: (B) 1871, (D) 1928, (CO) St. Louis, (C) Calvary Cemetery
Gahn, Mary F: (B) 1836, (CO) Stone, (A) 14, (BP) MO, (CMTS) 1870 Census
Gahn, Samuel: (B) 1845, (CO) Stone, (A) 5, (BP) MO, (CMTS) 1870 Census
Gahn, Thomas: (B) 1831, (CO) Stone, (A) 19, (BP) MO, (CMTS) 1870 Census
Gainey, Jeremiah: (D) Jun. 11, 1880, (CO) St. Louis, (C) Calvary Cemetery
Galion, William J.: (B) 1835, (CO) Stone, (A) 15, (BP) AR, (CMTS) 1870 Census
Gallaher, Lucinda: (B) 1850, (CO) Stone, (A) 20, (BP) MO, (CMTS) 1870 Census
Galloway, Alex: (B) 1835, (CO) Stone, (A) 35, (BP) IN, (CMTS) 1870 Census
Galloway, Charles: (B) 1835, (CO) Stone, (A) 35, (BP) TN, (CMTS) 1870 Census
Galloway, Elender: (B) 1792, (CO) Stone, (A) 78, (BP) NC, (CMTS) 1870 Census
Galloway, Ellen: (B) 1832, (CO) Stone, (A) 38, (BP) TN, (CMTS) 1870 Census
Galloway, Essary: (B) 1844, (CO) Stone, (A) 26, (BP) IL, (CMTS) 1870 Census
Galloway, F. M.: (B) 1845, (CO) Stone, (A) 25, (BP) MO, (CMTS) 1870 Census
Galloway, Melvina: (B) 1849, (CO) Stone, (A) 21, (BP) MO, (CMTS) 1870 Census
Galloway, Susan E.: (B) 1845, (CO) Stone, (A) 25, (BP) TN, (CMTS) 1870 Census
Galvin, Dennis E.: (B) 1862, (D) 1927, (CO) St. Louis, (C) Calvary Cemetery
Gambrino, Rosa: (B) 1819, (D) 1889, (CO) St. Louis, (C) Calvary Cemetery
Ganahl, Mary Petronella: (D) Dec. 25, 1880, (CO) St. Louis, (C) Calvary Cemetery, (A) 39
Gann, Charles: (B) 1851, (CO) Pulaski, (A) 9, (BP) TN, (CMTS)

1860 Census
Gann, Elbert S.: (B) Apr. 24, 1849, (D) Dec. 5, 1911, (CO) Lafayette,
Gann, Elizabeth: (B) 1856, (CO) Pulaski, (A) 4, (BP) TN, (CMTS)
1860 Census
Gann, Henry: (B) 1834, (CO) Pulaski, (A) 26, (BP) TN, (CMTS)
1860 Census
Gann, J.: (B) 1850, (CO) Pulaski, (A) 10, (BP) TN, (CMTS)
1860 Census
Gann, John: (B) 1816, (CO) Pulaski, (A) 44, (BP) TN, (CMTS)
1860 Census
Gann, Margaret S.: (B) 1847, (CO) Pulaski, (A) 13, (BP) TN, (CMTS)
1860 Census
Gann, Mary Catherine: (B) Oct. 21, 1805, (D) Dec. 29, 1885, (CO)
Lafayette
Gann, Mary M.: (B) 1840, (CO) Pulaski, (A) 20, (BP) TN, (CMTS)
1860 Census
Gann, Rebecca: (B) 1834, (CO) Pulaski, (A) 26, (BP) SC, (CMTS)
1860 Census
Gann, Sarah A.: (B) 1821, (CO) Pulaski, (A) 39, (BP) TN, (CMTS)
1860 Census
Gann, William R.: (B) 1842, (CO) Pulaski, (A) 18, (BP) TN, (CMTS)
1860 Census
Garbour,: (B) 1838, (CO) Pulaski, (A) 22, (BP) VA, (CMTS)
1860 Census
Gardner, John: (B) 1842, (CO) Stone, (A) 28, (BP) TN, (CMTS)
1870 Census
Gardner, Julia A.: (B) 1852, (CO) Stone, (A) 18, (BP) IL, (CMTS)
1870 Census
Gardner, Nancy O: (B) 1842, (CO) Stone, (A) 28, (BP) MO, (CMTS)
1870 Census
Garrett, Ruth Frances: (B) Sep. 16, 1864, (D) Dec. 2, 1899, (CO) Wright,
(Maiden) Young
Garrison, Caroline: (B) 1818, (CO) Stone, (A) 32, (BP) MO, (CMTS)
1870 Census
Garrison, Caroline: (B) 1827, (CO) Stone, (A) 23, (BP) MO, (CMTS)
1870 Census
Garrison, Daniel: (B) 1849, (CO) Stone, (A) 1, (BP) MO, (CMTS)
1870 Census
Garrison, Francis M.: (B) 1839, (CO) Stone, (A) 11, (BP) MO, (CMTS)
1870 Census
Garrison, Isham: (B) 1820, (CO) Stone, (A) 30, (BP) IL, (CMTS)
1870 Census
Garrison, James L.: (B) 1849, (CO) Stone, (A) 1, (BP) MO, (CMTS)

1870 Census
Garrison, James M.: (B) 1849, (CO) Stone, (A) 1, (BP) MO, (CMTS) 1870 Census
Garrison, Jane B.: (B) 1792, (CO) Stone, (A) 58, (BP) VA, (CMTS) 1870 Census
Garrison, Jeff: (B) 1833, (CO) Stone, (A) 37, (BP) TN, (CMTS) 1870 Census
Garrison, Joseph A.: (B) 1843, (CO) Stone, (A) 7, (BP) TX, (CMTS) 1870 Census
Garrison, Josephine: (B) 1847, (CO) Stone, (A) 3, (BP) MO, (CMTS) 1870 Census
Garrison, Leonard C.: (B) 1835, (CO) Stone, (A) 15, (BP) MO, (CMTS) 1870 Census
Garrison, Lewis G: (B) 1848, (CO) Stone, (A) 2, (BP) MO, (CMTS) 1870 Census
Garrison, Lydia A.: (B) 1822, (CO) Stone, (A) 28, (BP) MO, (CMTS) 1870 Census
Garrison, Margarete C.: (B) 1831, (CO) Stone, (A) 19, (BP) MO, (CMTS) 1870 Census
Garrison, Martha T.: (B) 1846, (CO) Stone, (A) 4, (BP) TX, (CMTS) 1870 Census
Garrison, Mary: (B) 1834, (CO) Stone, (A) 36, (BP) TN, (CMTS) 1870 Census
Garrison, Mary: (B) 1840, (CO) Stone, (A) 30, (BP) MO, (CMTS) 1870 Census
Garrison, Mary L.: (B) 1829, (CO) Stone, (A) 21, (BP) MO, (CMTS) 1870 Census
Garrison, Sylvester: (B) 1827, (CO) Stone, (A) 23, (BP) MO, (CMTS) 1870 Census
Garrison, Nancy J.: (B) 1832, (CO) Stone, (A) 18, (BP) IL, (CMTS) 1870 Census
Garrison, Sarah: (B) 1847, (CO) Stone, (A) 3, (BP) MO, (CMTS) 1870 Census
Garrison, Sarah Jane: (B) 1845, (CO) Stone, (A) 5, (BP) MO, (CMTS) 1870 Census
Garrison, Sarah L.: (B) 1842, (CO) Stone, (A) 8, (BP) TX, (CMTS) 1870 Census
Garrison, William: (B) 1845, (CO) Stone, (A) 5, (BP) MO, (CMTS) 1870 Census
Garrison, William T.: (B) 1840, (CO) Stone, (A) 10, (BP) MO, (CMTS) 1870 Census
Gates, George W.: (D) Oct. 2, 1862, (CO) St. Louis, (CMTS) From Bremer, IA

Gavan, Louise (Murphy): (B) 1904, (D) 1964, (CO) St. Louis, (C) Calvary Cemetery
Gavigan, John: (D) Sep. 28, 1890, (CO) St. Louis, (C) Calvary Cemetery, (A) 49
Gawein, William: (B) 1862, (D) 1895, (CO) St. Louis, (C) Calvary Cemetery
Geany, Margaret C.: (B) 1862, (D) 1929, (CO) St. Louis, (C) Calvary Cemetery
Geisz, Jr., George: (B) 1876, (D) 1954, (CO) St. Louis, (C) Calvary Cemetery
Gentry, Allen W.: (B) 1827, (CO) Stone, (A) 23, (BP) MO, (CMTS) 1870 Census
Gentry, Benejah: (B) 1811, (D) 1894, (CO) Barry, (C) Old Corsicana Cemetery
Gentry, Eliaza: (B) 1814, (D) 1876, (CO) Barry, (C) Old Corsicana Cemetery
Gentry, Isabella M. E.: (B) 1821, (CO) Stone, (A) 29, (BP) MO, (CMTS) 1870 Census
Gentry, Leonidus C.: (B) 1845, (CO) Stone, (A) 5, (BP) MO, (CMTS) 1870 Census
Gentry, Lizzie A.: (B) 1834, (CO) Stone, (A) 16, (BP) MO, (CMTS) 1870 Census
Gentry, Nancy M.: (B) 1849, (CO) Stone, (A) 1, (BP) MO, (CMTS) 1870 Census
Gentry, Samuel W.: (B) 1847, (CO) Stone, (A) 3, (BP) MO, (CMTS) 1870 Census
Gentry, Sarah E.: (B) 1848, (CO) Stone, (A) 2, (BP) MO, (CMTS) 1870 Census
Gentry, William T.: (B) 1837, (CO) Stone, (A) 13, (BP) MO, (CMTS) 1870 Census
Gentry,: (B) Jan. 12, 1816, (D) Dec. 25, 1894, (CO) Barry, (C) Old Corsicana Cemetery
Gerard, Hannah: (B) 1848, (CO) Pulaski, (A) 12, (BP) TN, (CMTS) 1860 Census
Gerard, John H.: (B) 1849, (CO) Pulaski, (A) 11, (BP) MO, (CMTS) 1860 Census
Gerard, Nancy: (B) 1819, (CO) Pulaski, (A) 41, (BP) TN, (CMTS) 1860 Census
Getsviller, Peter: (B) 1841, (CO) Stone, (A) 29, (BP) ILL, (CMTS) 1870 Census
Ghiglione, Ivo: (D) Jul. 4, 1909, (CO) St. Louis, (C) Calvary Cemetery
Ghio, Anthony J.: (B) 1877, (D) 1963, (CO) St. Louis, (C) Calvary Cemetery

Ghio, Carlotta M.: (B) 1857, (D) 1934, (CO) St. Louis, (C) Calvary Cemetery
Ghio, Delia M.: (B) 1883, (D) 1960, (CO) St. Louis, (C) Calvary Cemetery
Ghio, Elsie: (B) 1892, (D) 1941, (CO) St. Louis, (C) Calvary Cemetery
Ghio, Joseph Q.: (B) 1850, (D) 1927, (CO) St. Louis, (C) Calvary Cemetery
Ghio, Violet K.: (B) 1894, (D) 1981, (CO) St. Louis, (C) Calvary Cemetery
Ghio, William C.: (B) 1893, (D) 1935, (CO) St. Louis, (C) Calvary Cemetery
Giamalva, Jr., Frank: (B) May 3, 1921, (D) Jul. 10, 2000, (CO) Jackson, (NWS) *Kansas City, Missouri Star*, July 12, 2000, (C)
Gibson, Charlotte: (B) 1816, (CO) Pulaski, (A) 44, (BP) MO, (CMTS) 1860 Census
Gideon, Caroline: (B) 1837, (CO) Pulaski, (A) 23, (BP) MO, (CMTS) 1860 Census
Gideon, Elizabeth: (B) 1852, (CO) Pulaski, (A) 8, (BP) MO, (CMTS) 1860 Census
Gideon, John: (B) 1854, (CO) Pulaski, (A) 6, (BP) MO, (CMTS) 1860 Census
Gideon, Mary: (B) 1856, (CO) Pulaski, (A) 4, (BP) MO, (CMTS) 1860 Census
Gilbert, David Becker: (D) Aug. 20, 2000, (CO) Cole, (NWS) *Jefferson City, Missouri News-Tribune*, Aug. 22, 2000, (RES) Chamois
Gilbert, Martha J.: (B) 1834, (CO) Stone, (A) 16, (BP) AR, (CMTS) 1870 Census
Gilbert, Thomas: (B) 1825, (CO) Stone, (A) 25, (BP) MO, (CMTS) 1870 Census
Gillespie, Caroline: (B) 1837, (CO) Pulaski, (A) 23, (BP) MO, (CMTS) 1860 Census
Gillespie, Elizabeth: (B) 1840, (CO) Pulaski, (A) 20, (BP) MO, (CMTS) 1860 Census
Gillespie, Harriet: (B) 1854, (CO) Pulaski, (A) 6, (BP) MO, (CMTS) 1860 Census
Gillespie, Jesse: (B) 1826, (CO) Pulaski, (A) 34, (BP) MO, (CMTS) 1860 Census
Gillespie, William S.: (B) 1850, (CO) Pulaski, (A) 10, (BP) MO, (CMTS) 1860 Census
Gillis, Lafayette: (B) 1829, (CO) Pulaski, (A) 31, (BP) TN, (CMTS) 1860 Census
Gillis, Martha: (B) 1834, (CO) Pulaski, (A) 26, (BP) TN, (CMTS) 1860 Census

Gillis, Moses J.: (B) 1831, (CO) Pulaski, (A) 29, (BP) TN, (CMTS) 1860 Census
Gillis, Susannah: (B) 1840, (CO) Pulaski, (A) 20, (BP) TN, (CMTS) 1860 Census
Gipperich, Felix J.: (D) Aug. 13, 1862, (CO) St. Louis, (C) Calvary Cemetery
Gipperich, Raymond: (D) 1925, (CO) St. Louis, (C) Calvary Cemetery
Gipperich, Thomas A.: (B) 1901, (D) 1952, (CO) St. Louis, (C) Calvary Cemetery
Gippert, Eva: (D) 11, 1915, (CO) St. Louis, (C) Calvary Cemetery, (A) 53
Gipprich, Bessie: (D) Jul., 1906, (CO) St. Louis, (C) Calvary Cemetery, (A) 19
Gipson, Barbara Ann: (D) Dec., 1993, (CO) St. Louis, (C) Calvary Cemetery, (A) 1
Gipson, Evelyn Jean: (D) Dec., 1993, (CO) St. Louis, (C) Calvary Cemetery, (A) 4
Gipson, Geraldine: (D) Jun., 1955, (CO) St. Louis, (C) Calvary Cemetery
Girmore, Emily Quinn: (B) Sep. 13, 1874, (D) Aug. 10, 1966, (CO) St. Louis, (C) Calvary Cemetery
Girmore, John: (B) Mar. 7, 1872, (D) May 6, 1945, (CO) St. Louis, (C) Calvary Cemetery
Glenn, Mrs. Dora: (D) Jul. 28, 1964, (CO) Caroll, (NWS) *Carrollton Daily Democrat*, Jul. 28, 1964, (A) 83
Glossop, Joel: (B) 1849, (CO) Stone, (A) 21, (BP) AL, (CMTS) 1870 Census
Glossop, Martha: (B) 1855, (CO) Stone, (A) 15, (BP) AL, (CMTS) 1870 Census
Glossop, Mary: (B) 1847, (CO) Stone, (A) 23, (BP) AL, (CMTS) 1870 Census
Glossop, Sarah: (B) 1851, (CO) Stone, (A) 19, (BP) AL, (CMTS) 1870 Census
Glover, C.: (B) 1837, (CO) Pulaski, (A) 23, (BP) TN, (CMTS) 1860 Census
Glover, Charles S.: (B) May 19, 1890, (D) May 30, 1970, (CO) Dunklin,
Glover, Martha: (B) 1833, (CO) Pulaski, (A) 27, (BP) TN, (CMTS) 1860 Census
Goald, James: (B) 1849, (CO) Stone, (A) 21, (BP) TN, (CMTS) 1870 Census
Goald, Perilee: (B) 1847, (CO) Stone, (A) 23, (BP) TN, (CMTS) 1870 Census
Goff, Emma Jane: (B) 1836, (CO) Stone, (A) 14, (BP) NY, (CMTS) 1870 Census
Goff, Maggie: (B) 1846, (CO) Stone, (A) 4, (BP) MO, (CMTS)

1870 Census
Goff, William G: (B) 1847, (CO) Stone, (A) 23, (BP) MO, (CMTS) 1870 Census
Goforth, James: (B) 1844, (CO) Stone, (A) 26, (BP) AR, (CMTS) 1870 Census
Goforth, Lucy E.: (B) 1850, (CO) Stone, (A) 20, (BP) AR, (CMTS) 1870 Census
Goforth, William: (B) 1850, (CO) Stone, (A) 20, (BP) AR, (CMTS) 1870 Census
Gold, Elizabeth: (B) 1854, (CO) Stone, (A) 16, (BP) MO, (CMTS) 1870 Census
Gold, Martha A.: (B) 1855, (CO) Stone, (A) 15, (BP) MO, (CMTS) 1870 Census
Gold, Mary A.: (B) 1855, (CO) Stone, (A) 15, (BP) MO, (CMTS) 1870 Census
Gold, Mary J.: (B) 1830, (CO) Stone, (A) 40, (BP) TN, (CMTS) 1870 Census
Gold, Sarah P: (B) 1832, (CO) Stone, (A) 38, (BP) TN, (CMTS) 1870 Census
Gold, William: (B) 1851, (CO) Stone, (A) 19, (BP) TN, (CMTS) 1870 Census
Gold, William C.: (B) 1830, (CO) Stone, (A) 40, (BP) TN, (CMTS) 1870 Census
Golden, Lucinda: (B) 1826, (CO) Pulaski, (A) 34, (BP) TN, (CMTS) 1860 Census
Golden, Nancy J.: (B) 1856, (CO) Pulaski, (A) 4, (BP) IL, (CMTS) 1860 Census
Golden, Rosanna: (B) 1848, (CO) Pulaski, (A) 12, (BP) IL, (CMTS) 1860 Census
Golden, Vina: (B) 1848, (CO) Pulaski, (A) 12, (BP) IL, (CMTS) 1860 Census
Gooblee, Catherine: (B) 1848, (CO) Stone, (A) 22, (BP) NC, (CMTS) 1870 Census
Gooblee, John: (B) 1848, (CO) Stone, (A) 22, (BP) NC, (CMTS) 1870 Census
Good, Berry: (B) 1818, (D) 1870, (CO) Adair, (A) 52, (CMTS) 1870 Mortality Schedule
Goodman, Alfred: (B) 1838, (CO) Pulaski, (A) 22, (BP) TN, (CMTS) 1860 Census
Goodman, Allie: (B) 1844, (CO) Pulaski, (A) 16, (BP) TN, (CMTS) 1860 Census
Goodman, Benjamin L.: (B) 1858, (CO) Pulaski, (A) 2, (BP) IN, (CMTS) 1860 Census

Goodman, Calahan: (B) 1840, (CO) Pulaski, (A) 20, (BP) TN, (CMTS) 1860 Census
Goodman, Hannah: (B) 1821, (CO) Pulaski, (A) 39, (BP) TN, (CMTS) 1860 Census
Goodman, Hester: (B) 1854, (CO) Pulaski, (A) 6, (BP) IN, (CMTS) 1860 Census
Goodman, Isaac: (B) 1837, (CO) Pulaski, (A) 23, (BP) TN, (CMTS) 1860 Census
Goodman, James: (B) 1821, (CO) Pulaski, (A) 39, (BP) TN, (CMTS) 1860 Census
Goodman, Jameson: (B) 1846, (CO) Pulaski, (A) 14, (BP) TN, (CMTS) 1860 Census
Goodman, Jesse: (B) 1848, (CO) Pulaski, (A) 12, (BP) IN, (CMTS) 1860 Census
Goodman, John: (B) 1842, (CO) Pulaski, (A) 18, (BP) TN, (CMTS) 1860 Census
Goodman, Margaret: (B) 1855, (CO) Pulaski, (A) 5, (BP) IN, (CMTS) 1860 Census
Goodman, Martha: (B) 1855, (CO) Pulaski, (A) 5, (BP) MO, (CMTS) 1860 Census
Goodman, Martha J.: (B) 1855, (CO) Pulaski, (A) 5, (BP) IN, (CMTS) 1860 Census
Goodman, Paralee F.: (B) 1842, (CO) Pulaski, (A) 18, (BP) MO, (CMTS) 1860 Census
Goodman, Rebecca: (B) 1833, (CO) Pulaski, (A) 27, (BP) NC, (CMTS) 1860 Census
Goodman, Sarah: (B) 1837, (CO) Pulaski, (A) 23, (BP) IN, (CMTS) 1860 Census
Goodman, Sarah: (B) 1853, (CO) Pulaski, (A) 7, (BP) IN, (CMTS) 1860 Census
Goodman, William: (B) 1833, (CO) Pulaski, (A) 27, (BP) TN, (CMTS) 1860 Census
Gore, Isome: (B) 1831, (CO) Stone, (A) 19, (BP) MO, (CMTS) 1870 Census
Gore, James: (B) 1827, (CO) Stone, (A) 23, (BP) TN, (CMTS) 1870 Census
Gore, Leean: (B) 1855, (CO) Stone, (A) 15, (BP) AR, (CMTS) 1870 Census
Gore, Mexico: (B) 1847, (CO) Stone, (A) 3, (BP) MO, (CMTS) 1870 Census
Gosey, Jane: (B) 1840, (CO) Pulaski, (A) 20, (BP) MO, (CMTS) 1860 Census
Gosey, Lavanda: (B) 1848, (CO) Pulaski, (A) 12, (BP) MO, (CMTS)

1860 Census
Gosey, Lewis: (B) 1828, (CO) Pulaski, (A) 32, (BP) MO, (CMTS) 1860 Census
Gosey, Sarah: (B) 1846, (CO) Pulaski, (A) 14, (BP) MO, (CMTS) 1860 Census
Gosey, William: (B) 1843, (CO) Pulaski, (A) 17, (BP) MO, (CMTS) 1860 Census
Goss, Mahala: (B) 1838, (CO) Pulaski, (A) 22, (BP) TN, (CMTS) 1860 Census
Goss, Rebecca: (B) 1854, (CO) Pulaski, (A) 6, (BP) MO, (CMTS) 1860 Census
Graham, Robert: (B) Mar. 4, 1930, (D) Apri. 14, 1999, (CO) Barry, (RES) Shell Knob, (BP) Evanston, IL, (PRTS) Gordon Graham and Edith Cloyes
Graves, James W.: (B) 1864, (CO) Missouri, (RES) Graves Co., TX, (CMTS) 1920 Census, p. 100
Gray, Edmond: (B) 1851, (CO) Pulaski, (A) 9, (BP) MO, (CMTS) 1860 Census
Gray, Franklin: (B) 1845, (CO) Pulaski, (A) 15, (BP) MO, (CMTS) 1860 Census
Gray, James E.: (B) 1841, (CO) Stone, (A) 29, (BP) NC, (CMTS) 1870 Census
Gray, Martha: (B) 1849, (CO) Pulaski, (A) 11, (BP) MO, (CMTS) 1860 Census
Gray, Mary E.: (B) 1847, (CO) Stone, (A) 23, (BP) TN, (CMTS) 1870 Census
Gray, Richard: (B) 1855, (CO) Pulaski, (A) 5, (BP) MO, (CMTS) 1860 Census
Gray, Robert: (B) 1843, (CO) Pulaski, (A) 17, (BP) KY, (CMTS) 1860 Census
Gray, Shelby: (B) 1847, (CO) Pulaski, (A) 13, (BP) MO, (CMTS) 1860 Census
Green, Elizabeth: (B) 1833, (CO) Pulaski, (A) 27, (BP) AL, (CMTS) 1860 Census
Green, Harriet: (B) 1853, (CO) Pulaski, (A) 7, (BP) MO, (CMTS) 1860 Census
Green, James A.: (B) 1838, (D) 1902, (CO) Cedar, (C) Brashear Cemetery
Green, John: (B) 1838, (CO) Pulaski, (A) 22, (BP) IL, (CMTS) 1860 Census
Green, Martha: (B) 1830, (CO) Pulaski, (A) 30, (BP) TN, (CMTS) 1860 Census
Green, Nettie J.: (B) 1841, (CO) Cedar, (C) Brashear Cemetery
Green, Tolbert: (B) 1857, (CO) Pulaski, (A) 3, (BP) MO, (CMTS)

1860 Census
Greene, Priscilla: (B) 1837, (CO) Pulaski, (A) 23, (BP) MO, (CMTS) 1860 Census
Greene, Thomas: (B) 1837, (CO) Pulaski, (A) 23, (BP) IL, (CMTS) 1860 Census
Greensbut, Ervin: (B) 1838, (CO) Pulaski, (A) 22, (BP) MO, (CMTS) 1860 Census
Greensbut, Susan: (B) 1840, (CO) Pulaski, (A) 20, (BP) MO, (CMTS) 1860 Census
Greensteed, Allen M.: (B) 1847, (CO) Pulaski, (A) 13, (BP) MO, (CMTS) 1860 Census
Greensteed, David: (B) 1858, (CO) Pulaski, (A) 2, (BP) MO, (CMTS) 1860 Census
Greensteed, John D.: (B) 1843, (CO) Pulaski, (A) 17, (BP) MO, (CMTS) 1860 Census
Greensteed, Martin V.: (B) 1842, (CO) Pulaski, (A) 18, (BP) MO, (CMTS) 1860 Census
Greensteed, Mary E.: (B) 1845, (CO) Pulaski, (A) 15, (BP) MO, (CMTS) 1860 Census
Greensteed, Nellie: (B) 1820, (CO) Pulaski, (A) 40, (BP) MO, (CMTS) 1860 Census
Greensteed, Zach: (B) 1818, (CO) Pulaski, (A) 42, (BP) MO, (CMTS) 1860 Census
Greensteed, Zach M.: (B) 1850, (CO) Pulaski, (A) 10, (BP) MO, (CMTS) 1860 Census
Greer, Susan: (B) 1849, (CO) Pulaski, (A) 11, (BP) VA, (CMTS) 1860 Census
Gregg, Martha A.: (B) 1841, (CO) Stone, (A) 9, (BP) MO, (CMTS) 1870 Census
Gregg, Mary A.: (B) 1819, (CO) Stone, (A) 31, (BP) MO, (CMTS) 1870 Census
Greig, Isaac: (B) 1832, (CO) Stone, (A) 38, (BP) OH, (CMTS) 1870 Census
Griffin, Bryan B.: (B) 1839, (CO) Stone, (A) 11, (BP) MO, (CMTS) 1870 Census
Griffin, Emiline: (B) 1820, (CO) Stone, (A) 30, (BP) MO, (CMTS) 1870 Census
Griffin, Joseph: (B) 1794, (CO) Stone, (A) 56, (BP) IL, (CMTS) 1870 Census
Griffin, Louisa: (B) 1841, (CO) Pulaski, (A) 19, (BP) MO, (CMTS) 1860 Census
Griffin, Lucinda: (B) 1841, (CO) Stone, (A) 9, (BP) MO, (CMTS) 1870 Census

Griffin, William: (B) 1836, (CO) Pulaski, (A) 24, (BP) IL, (CMTS) 1860 Census
Griffin, William P.: (B) 1836, (CO) Pulaski, (A) 24, (BP) IL, (CMTS) 1860 Census
Griffis, Harriet A.: (B) 1821, (CO) Stone, (A) 49, (BP) TN, (CMTS) 1870 Census
Griffis, Mary A.: (B) 1848, (CO) Stone, (A) 22, (BP) MO, (CMTS) 1870 Census
Griffis, Nancy C.: (B) 1854, (CO) Stone, (A) 16, (BP) MO, (CMTS) 1870 Census
Griffis, Susan: (B) 1853, (CO) Stone, (A) 17, (BP) MO, (CMTS) 1870 Census
Griffis, William G: (B) 1825, (CO) Stone, (A) 45, (BP) TN, (CMTS) 1870 Census
Grisham, Mary: (B) 1831, (CO) Stone, (A) 39, (BP) VA, (CMTS) 1870 Census
Grisham, Susan: (B) 1851, (CO) Stone, (A) 19, (BP) MO, (CMTS) 1870 Census
Grob, Anna: (B) Aug. 8, 1865, (D) Jul. 2, 1910, (CO) Henry, (C) Knights of Pythias Cemetery, Deepwater, MO
Grob, John A.: (B) 1862, (D) 1933, (CO) Henry, (C) Knights of Pythias Cemetery, Deepwater, MO
Grogan, Mary: (B) 1835, (D) 1870, (CO) Adair, (A) 35, (CMTS) 1870 Mortality Schedule
Groom, Jefferson: (B) 1861, (D) 1948, (CO) Henry, (C) Knights of Pythias Cemetery, Deepwater, MO
Guest, James: (B) 1829, (CO) Stone, (A) 41, (BP) TN, (CMTS) 1870 Census
Guest, Margaret: (B) 1856, (CO) Stone, (A) 14, (BP) MO, (CMTS) 1870 Census
Guest, Martha: (B) 1834, (CO) Stone, (A) 36, (BP) TN, (CMTS) 1870 Census
Guest, Mary A.: (B) 1851, (CO) Stone, (A) 19, (BP) MO, (CMTS) 1870 Census
Guest, William M.: (B) 1854, (CO) Stone, (A) 16, (BP) MO, (CMTS) 1870 Census
Gullett, Matilda M.: (B) 1837, (CO) Pulaski, (A) 23, (BP) TN, (CMTS) 1860 Census
Gullett, William: (B) 1834, (CO) Pulaski, (A) 26, (BP) TN, (CMTS) 1860 Census
Gustur, James: (B) 1845, (CO) Pulaski, (A) 15, (BP) OH, (CMTS) 1860 Census
Gustur, Rachel: (B) 1847, (CO) Pulaski, (A) 13, (BP) OH, (CMTS)

1860 Census
Haefer, Raymond G.: (B) May 20, 1898, (D) Mar. 21, 1989, (CO) St. Francois,
Hager, Martha M.: (B) 1851, (D) 1937, (CO) Cedar, (C) Brashear Cemetery
Hager, William Theo: (B) 1848, (D) 1919, (CO) Cedar, (C) Brashear Cemetery
Haggerty, Lucinda: (B) 1846, (CO) Stone, (A) 24, (BP) GA, (CMTS) 1870 Census
Haggerty, William: (B) 1828, (CO) Stone, (A) 42, (BP) MA, (CMTS) 1870 Census
Hale, Elias J.: (B) 1819, (CO) Stone, (A) 31, (BP) TN, (CMTS) 1870 Census
Hale, Huldy P: (B) 1828, (CO) Stone, (A) 22, (BP) AR, (CMTS) 1870 Census
Hale, James A.: (B) 1854, (CO) Pulaski, (A) 6, (BP) MO, (CMTS) 1860 Census
Hale, Joseph H.: (B) 1852, (CO) Pulaski, (A) 8, (BP) MO, (CMTS) 1860 Census
Hale, Mary A.: (B) 1830, (CO) Pulaski, (A) 30, (BP) MO, (CMTS) 1860 Census
Hale, Mary E.: (B) 1846, (CO) Stone, (A) 4, (BP) MO, (CMTS) 1870 Census
Hale, Sarah E.: (B) 1841, (CO) Stone, (A) 9, (BP) MO, (CMTS) 1870 Census
Hale, Sarah J.: (B) 1818, (CO) Stone, (A) 32, (BP) AR, (CMTS) 1870 Census
Hale, Sarah J.: (B) 1848, (CO) Stone, (A) 2, (BP) AR, (CMTS) 1870 Census
Hale, Thomas W.: (B) 1827, (CO) Stone, (A) 23, (BP) TN, (CMTS) 1870 Census
Hale, Thomas J.: (B) 1856, (CO) Pulaski, (A) 4, (BP) MO, (CMTS) 1860 Census
Hale, Vina L.: (B) 1849, (CO) Stone, (A) 1, (BP) MO, (CMTS) 1870 Census
Hale, William T.: (B) 1839, (CO) Stone, (A) 11, (BP) AR, (CMTS) 1870 Census
Hall, Amanda: (B) 1849, (D) 1932, (CO) Cedar, (C) Brashear Cemetery
Hall, Andy: (B) 1835, (CO) Pulaski, (A) 25, (BP) TN, (CMTS) 1860 Census
Hall, Charlotte: (B) 1838, (D) 1870, (CO) Adair, (A) 32, (CMTS) 1870 Mortality Schedule
Hall, Elizabeth: (B) 1855, (CO) Pulaski, (A) 5, (BP) MO, (CMTS)

1860 Census
Hall, Emeline: (B) 1854, (CO) Pulaski, (A) 6, (BP) MO, (CMTS) 1860 Census
Hall, James: (B) 1845, (CO) Stone, (A) 25, (BP) TN, (CMTS) 1870 Census
Hall, Jane: (B) 1839, (CO) Pulaski, (A) 21, (BP) IN, (CMTS) 1860 Census
Hall, Jane: (B) 1843, (CO) Stone, (A) 27, (BP) MO, (CMTS) 1870 Census
Hall, John W.: (B) 1847, (CO) Stone, (A) 3, (BP) MO, (CMTS) 1870 Census
Hall, Mary C.: (B) 1830, (CO) Stone, (A) 20, (BP) MO, (CMTS) 1870 Census
Hall, Mary J.: (B) 1853, (CO) Stone, (A) 17, (BP) MO, (CMTS) 1870 Census
Hall, Robert W.: (B) 1842, (D) 1920, (CO) Cedar, (C) Brashear Cemetery
Halpin, Mrs . Ann: (D) Jan. 26, 1877, (CO) St. Louis, (C) Calvary Cemetery
Halton, Elish: (B) 1852, (CO) Pulaski, (A) 8, (BP) VA, (CMTS) 1860 Census
Halton, Emily: (B) 1858, (CO) Pulaski, (A) 2, (BP) VA, (CMTS) 1860 Census
Halton, Harmon: (B) 1829, (CO) Pulaski, (A) 31, (BP) VA, (CMTS) 1860 Census
Halton, John: (B) 1855, (CO) Pulaski, (A) 5, (BP) VA, (CMTS) 1860 Census
Halton, Nancy: (B) 1850, (CO) Pulaski, (A) 10, (BP) VA, (CMTS) 1860 Census
Halton, Tabitha: (B) 1835, (CO) Pulaski, (A) 25, (BP) VA, (CMTS) 1860 Census
Hamer, Allen: (B) 1821, (CO) Pulaski, (A) 39, (BP) PA, (CMTS) 1860 Census
Hamer, Joseph H.: (B) 1848, (CO) Pulaski, (A) 12, (BP) MO, (CMTS) 1860 Census
Hamer, Louis C.: (B) 1846, (CO) Pulaski, (A) 14, (BP) MO, (CMTS) 1860 Census
Hamer, Margaret: (B) 1822, (CO) Pulaski, (A) 38, (BP) PA, (CMTS) 1860 Census
Hamilton, Angeline: (B) 1850, (CO) Pulaski, (A) 10, (BP) KY, (CMTS) 1860 Census
Hamilton, Gabrilla: (B) 1851, (CO) Pulaski, (A) 9, (BP) MO, (CMTS) 1860 Census
Hamilton, George W.: (B) 1848, (CO) Pulaski, (A) 12, (BP) MO, (CMTS) 1860 Census

Hamilton, Isabella V.: (B) 1856, (CO) Pulaski, (A) 4, (BP) MO, (CMTS) 1860 Census
Hamilton, Jackson: (B) 1851, (CO) Pulaski, (A) 9, (BP) KY, (CMTS) 1860 Census
Hamilton, James E.: (B) 1848, (CO) Pulaski, (A) 12, (BP) MO, (CMTS) 1860 Census
Hamilton, Levi: (B) 1846, (CO) Pulaski, (A) 14, (BP) KY, (CMTS) 1860 Census
Hamilton, Mary: (B) 1823, (CO) Pulaski, (A) 37, (BP) AL, (CMTS) 1860 Census
Hamilton, Mary: (B) 1830, (CO) Pulaski, (A) 30, (BP) AL, (CMTS) 1860 Census
Hamilton, Mary: (B) 1854, (CO) Pulaski, (A) 6, (BP) KY, (CMTS) 1860 Census
Hamilton, Mary A.: (B) 1854, (CO) Pulaski, (A) 6, (BP) MO, (CMTS) 1860 Census
Hamilton, Nancy J.: (B) 1845, (CO) Pulaski, (A) 15, (BP) MO, (CMTS) 1860 Census
Hamilton, Nancy J.: (B) 1850, (CO) Pulaski, (A) 10, (BP) MO, (CMTS) 1860 Census
Hamilton, Robert: (B) 1836, (CO) Pulaski, (A) 24, (BP) MO, (CMTS) 1860 Census
Hamilton, Samuel: (B) 1820, (CO) Pulaski, (A) 40, (BP) PA, (CMTS) 1860 Census
Hamilton, Samuel: (B) 1852, (CO) Pulaski, (A) 8, (BP) MO, (CMTS) 1860 Census
Hamilton, Sarah J.: (B) 1855, (CO) Pulaski, (A) 5, (BP) MO, (CMTS) 1860 Census
Hamilton, Sophronia: (B) 1839, (CO) Pulaski, (A) 21, (BP) MO, (CMTS) 1860 Census
Hamilton, Thomas: (B) 1834, (CO) Pulaski, (A) 26, (BP) MO, (CMTS) 1860 Census
Hamilton, Wade M.: (B) 1857, (CO) Pulaski, (A) 3, (BP) MO, (CMTS) 1860 Census
Hamilton, Wallace: (B) 1848, (CO) Pulaski, (A) 12, (BP) KY, (CMTS) 1860 Census
Hamilton, Washington: (B) 1851, (CO) Pulaski, (A) 9, (BP) KY, (CMTS) 1860 Census
Hamilton, William A.: (B) 1835, (CO) Pulaski, (A) 25, (BP) MO, (CMTS) 1860 Census
Hammock, Damis: (B) 1847, (CO) Pulaski, (A) 13, (BP) MO, (CMTS) 1860 Census
Hammock, Melissa: (B) 1856, (CO) Pulaski, (A) 4, (BP) MO, (CMTS)

1860 Census
Hammock, Samantha: (B) 1827, (CO) Pulaski, (A) 33, (BP) MO, (CMTS) 1860 Census
Hammock, William: (B) 1825, (CO) Pulaski, (A) 35, (BP) TN, (CMTS) 1860 Census
Hammock, William J.: (B) 1849, (CO) Pulaski, (A) 11, (BP) MO, (CMTS) 1860 Census
Hammond, Eliza: (B) 1847, (CO) Pulaski, (A) 13, (BP) MO, (CMTS) 1860 Census
Hammond, Francis: (B) 1838, (CO) Pulaski, (A) 22, (BP) MO, (CMTS) 1860 Census
Hammond, Jacob: (B) 1851, (CO) Pulaski, (A) 9, (BP) MO, (CMTS) 1860 Census
Hammond, James: (B) 1838, (CO) Pulaski, (A) 22, (BP) MO, (CMTS) 1860 Census
Hammond, John: (B) 1848, (CO) Pulaski, (A) 12, (BP) MO, (CMTS) 1860 Census
Hammond, Rebecca J.: (B) 1844, (CO) Pulaski, (A) 16, (BP) MO, (CMTS) 1860 Census
Hammond, Rebecca J.: (B) 1844, (CO) Pulaski, (A) 16, (BP) MO, (CMTS) 1860 Census
Hammond, Sarah: (B) 1835, (CO) Pulaski, (A) 25, (BP) TN, (CMTS) 1860 Census
Hampton, Jane: (B) 1827, (CO) Stone, (A) 23, (BP) IN, (CMTS) 1870 Census
Hampton, Willis T.: (B) 1820, (CO) Stone, (A) 30, (BP) IN, (CMTS) 1870 Census
Hance, Berry: (B) 1837, (CO) Pulaski, (A) 23, (BP) TN, (CMTS) 1860 Census
Hancock, David: (B) 1829, (CO) Pulaski, (A) 31, (BP) MO, (CMTS) 1860 Census
Hancock, Jamesper: (B) 1833, (CO) Pulaski, (A) 27, (BP) AL, (CMTS) 1860 Census
Hancock, Margaret: (B) Dec. 1, 1835, (D) Feb 28, 1899, (CO) Audrain, (C) Pisgah Cemetery
Hancock, Melissa: (B) 1840, (CO) Pulaski, (A) 20, (BP) KY, (CMTS) 1860 Census
Handley, Thomas: (D) Jan. 30, 1873, (CO) St. Louis, (C) Calvary Cemetery, (A) 29
Hankins,Thomas. R.: (B) Jan. 17, 1838, (D) Dec. 6, 1892, (CO) Barry, (C) Cassville Cemetery
Hanks, B.: (B) 1835, (CO) Pulaski, (A) 25, (BP) TN, (CMTS) 1860 Census

Hanks, Laura V: (B) 1855, (CO) Pulaski, (A) 5, (BP) MO, (CMTS) 1860 Census
Hanlady, Catharine: (B) 1833, (CO) Pulaski, (A) 27, (BP) Ireland, (CMTS) 1860 Census
Hanlady, Cordelia: (B) 1856, (CO) Pulaski, (A) 4, (BP) MO, (CMTS) 1860 Census
Hanlon, Maud: (B) Sep. 27, 1895, (D) Nov. 22, 1981, (CO) St. Louis, (C) Calvary Cemetery
Hannan, Paul R.: (B) Dec. 6, 1900, (D) Sep. 21, 1906, (CO) Henry, (C) Knights of Pythias Cemetery, Deepwater, MO
Hannerty, Catherine: (B) 1858, (D) 1934, (CO) St. Louis, (C) Calvary Cemetery
Hannerty, Mary: (B) 1848, (D) 1906, (CO) St. Louis, (C) Calvary Cemetery
Hannon,: (B) 1856, (CO) Pulaski, (A) 4, (BP) MO, (CMTS) 1860 Census
Hansell, Elizabeth S.: (B) 1827, (CO) Stone, (A) 23, (BP) IL, (CMTS) 1870 Census
Hansell, Jessie W.: (B) 1819, (CO) Stone, (A) 31, (BP) OH, (CMTS) 1870 Census
Harbart, M.: (B) 1838, (D) 1894, (CO) Barry, (C) Cassville Cemetery
Hardison, Armstrong: (B) 1856, (CO) Pulaski, (A) 4, (BP) MO, (CMTS) 1860 Census
Hardison, Edward: (B) 1850, (CO) Pulaski, (A) 10, (BP) MO, (CMTS) 1860 Census
Hardison, Lucinda: (B) 1853, (CO) Pulaski, (A) 7, (BP) MO, (CMTS) 1860 Census
Hardison, Mary: (B) 1842, (CO) Pulaski, (A) 18, (BP) MO, (CMTS) 1860 Census
Hardison, Nancy: (B) 1844, (CO) Pulaski, (A) 16, (BP) MO, (CMTS) 1860 Census
Hardison, Noah: (B) 1848, (CO) Pulaski, (A) 12, (BP) MO, (CMTS) 1860 Census
Hardister, John: (B) 1838, (CO) Pulaski, (A) 22, (BP) MO, (CMTS) 1860 Census
Hare, Mary: (B) 1821, (CO) Stone, (A) 49, (BP) TN, (CMTS) 1870 Census
Hare, Mary: (B) 1836, (CO) Stone, (A) 34, (BP) TN, (CMTS) 1870 Census
Hare, Zackariah: (B) 1835, (CO) Stone, (A) 35, (BP) TN, (CMTS) 1870 Census
Harland,Nancy Ann: (B) 1837, (D) Jun. 30, 1890, (CO) Callaway, (C) Old Salem Cemetery, Reform, MO

Harley, Ellen: (B) 1870, (D) 1906, (CO) St. Louis, (C) Calvary Cemetery
Harley, Patrick: (B) 1845, (D) 1934, (CO) St. Louis, (C) Calvary Cemetery
Harman, Mary: (B) 1840, (CO) Pulaski, (A) 20, (BP) TN, (CMTS) 1860 Census
Harper, Daniel: (B) 1833, (CO) Pulaski, (A) 27, (BP) IN, (CMTS) 1860 Census
Harper, Hannah: (B) Jun. 23, 1817, (D) Dec. 27, 1882, (CO) Barry, (C) Old Corsicana Cemetery
Harper, Harriet: (B) 1827, (CO) Pulaski, (A) 33, (BP) OH, (CMTS) 1860 Census
Harper, Harriet: (B) 1842, (CO) Stone, (A) 28, (BP) AR, (CMTS) 1870 Census
Harper, Henry: (B) Mar. 16, 1813, (D) Sep. 4, 1886, (CO) Barry, (C) Old Corsicana Cemetery
Harper, John: (B) 1845, (CO) Stone, (A) 25, (BP) GA, (CMTS) 1870 Census
Harper, Mary: (B) 1825, (CO) Stone, (A) 45, (BP) AR, (CMTS) 1870 Census
Harris, Alfred: (B) 1863, (D) 1948, (CO) Henry, (C) Knights of Pythias Cemetery, Deepwater, MO
Harris, Caleb: (B) 1816, (CO) Pulaski, (A) 44, (BP) KY, (CMTS) 1860 Census
Harris, Caleb: (B) 1849, (CO) Pulaski, (A) 11, (BP) MO, (CMTS) 1860 Census
Harris, Celia: (B) 1834, (CO) Pulaski, (A) 26, (BP) IN, (CMTS) 1860 Census
Harris, Charity: (B) 1833, (CO) Pulaski, (A) 27, (BP) IL, (CMTS) 1860 Census
Harris, Clara: (B) 1829, (CO) Pulaski, (A) 31, (BP) Bavaria, (CMTS) 1860 Census
Harris, Elijah: (B) 1833, (CO) Pulaski, (A) 27, (BP) IN, (CMTS) 1860 Census
Harris, Helena: (B) 1854, (CO) Pulaski, (A) 6, (BP) MO, (CMTS) 1860 Census
Harris, James D.: (B) 1856, (CO) Pulaski, (A) 4, (BP) MO, (CMTS) 1860 Census
Harris, James T.: (B) 1852, (CO) Pulaski, (A) 8, (BP) MO, (CMTS) 1860 Census
Harris, James W.: (B) 1852, (CO) Pulaski, (A) 8, (BP) IN, (CMTS) 1860 Census
Harris, John A.: (B) 1855, (CO) Pulaski, (A) 5, (BP) MO, (CMTS) 1860 Census

Harris, Lemuel R.: (B) 1840, (CO) Pulaski, (A) 20, (BP) MO, (CMTS) 1860 Census
Harris, Nancy E.: (B) 1846, (CO) Pulaski, (A) 14, (BP) MO, (CMTS) 1860 Census
Harris, Nancy J.: (B) 1835, (CO) Pulaski, (A) 25, (BP) TN, (CMTS) 1860 Census
Harris, Robert: (B) 1855, (CO) Pulaski, (A) 5, (BP) MO, (CMTS) 1860 Census
Harris, Samuel: (B) 1849, (CO) Pulaski, (A) 11, (BP) MO, (CMTS) 1860 Census
Harris, Sarah A.: (B) 1842, (CO) Pulaski, (A) 18, (BP) MO, (CMTS) 1860 Census
Harris, Simon: (B) 1831, (CO) Pulaski, (A) 29, (BP) Hessie, (CMTS) 1860 Census
Harris, Susan: (B) 1854, (CO) Stone, (A) 16, (BP) MO, (CMTS) 1870 Census
Harris, William: (B) 1833, (CO) Pulaski, (A) 27, (BP) KY, (CMTS) 1860 Census
Harris, William J.: (B) 1843, (CO) Pulaski, (A) 17, (BP) MO, (CMTS) 1860 Census
Harris, Rebecca: (B) Jan. 10, 1827, (D) Jan. 10, 1899, (CO) Barry, (C) Cassville Cemetery, (A) 72
Harrison, Eddy: (B) 1845, (CO) Stone, (A) 5, (BP) WI, (CMTS) 1870 Census
Harrison, Edward B.: (B) 1848, (CO) Stone, (A) 2, (BP) MO, (CMTS) 1870 Census
Harrison, Eliza Ann: (B) 1840, (CO) Pulaski, (A) 20, (BP) MO, (CMTS) 1860 Census
Harrison, Emma: (B) 1849, (CO) Stone, (A) 1, (BP) WI, (CMTS) 1870 Census
Harrison, Francis M.: (B) 1833, (CO) Stone, (A) 17, (BP) WI, (CMTS) 1870 Census
Harrison, G.: (B) 1835, (CO) Pulaski, (A) 25, (BP) MO, (CMTS) 1860 Census
Harrison, Ida: (B) 1847, (CO) Stone, (A) 3, (BP) WI, (CMTS) 1870 Census
Harrison, John: (B) 1794, (CO) Stone, (A) 56, (BP) IL, (CMTS) 1870 Census
Harrison, John W.: (B) 1836, (CO) Stone, (A) 14, (BP) MO, (CMTS) 1870 Census
Harrison, Joshua M.: (B) 1834, (CO) Stone, (A) 16, (BP) MO, (CMTS) 1870 Census
Harrison, Julia A.: (B) 1844, (CO) Stone, (A) 6, (BP) MO, (CMTS) 1870

Census
Harrison, Mary E.: (B) 1837, (CO) Stone, (A) 13, (BP) WI, (CMTS) 1870 Census
Harrison, Mary L.: (B) 1842, (CO) Stone, (A) 8, (BP) MO, (CMTS) 1870 Census
Harrison, Susan: (B) 1831, (CO) Stone, (A) 19, (BP) OH, (CMTS) 1870 Census
Harrison, William B.: (B) 1831, (CO) Stone, (A) 19, (BP) MO, (CMTS) 1870 Census
Hart, James W.: (D) Aug. 11, 1869, (CO) Barry, (C) Old Corsicana Cemetery, (A) 40
Hart, Laura Taylor: (B) 1911, (CO) St. Louis, (C) Calvary Cemetery
Hart, Paul E.: (B) 1915, (D) 1976, (CO) St. Louis, (C) Calvary Cemetery
Hart, Rachael D.: (B) Jun. 13, 1828, (D) Sep. 17, 1876, (CO) Barry, (C) Old Corsicana Cemetery
Harte, William A.: (D) May 6, 1895, (CO) St. Louis, (C) Calvary Cemetery, (A) 9
Hartman, Charles W.: (D) Oct.20, 1888, (CO) Andrew, (C) Oak Ridge Cemetery, (A) 68Y. 2D
Hartman, Ellen: (D) Jun. 3, 1895, (CO) Andrew, (C) Oak Ridge Cemetery, (A) 67Y 7M 14D
Hartnett, Joseph J.: (B) 1898, (D) 1982, (CO) St. Louis, (C) Calvary Cemetery
Harttman, Daniel I.: (B) Jul. 4, 1833, (D) Nov. 20, 1833, (CO) Andrew, (C) Oak Ridge Cemetery
Harty, Edmond: (D) Jan. 13, 1883, (CO) St. Louis, (C) Calvary Cemetery
Harvey, David A.: (D) Jan. 13, 1877, (CO) St. Louis, (C) Calvary Cemetery, (A) 69
Harvey, Paterick: (B) 1828, (CO) Pulaski, (A) 32, (BP) Ireland, (CMTS) 1860 Census
Haskins, Harley: (B) 1855, (CO) Stone, (A) 15, (BP) WI, (CMTS) 1870 Census
Haskins, Horace B.: (B) 1823, (CO) Stone, (A) 27, (BP) MO, (CMTS) 1870 Census
Haskins, Martha W.: (B) 1848, (CO) Stone, (A) 2, (BP) MO, (CMTS) 1870 Census
Haskins, Mary E.: (B) 1849, (CO) Stone, (A) 1, (BP) MO, (CMTS) 1870 Census
Haskins, Sarah: (B) 1827, (CO) Stone, (A) 23, (BP) CAN, (CMTS) 1870 Census
Haskins, Susan: (B) 1821, (CO) Stone, (A) 49, (BP) NY, (CMTS) 1870 Census
Hastins, Daniel: (B) 1858, (CO) Pulaski, (A) 2, (BP) MO, (CMTS)

1860 Census
Hastins, Missouri: (B) 1856, (CO) Pulaski, (A) 4, (BP) MO, (CMTS) 1860 Census
Hastins, Permelia: (B) 1840, (CO) Pulaski, (A) 20, (BP) TN, (CMTS) 1860 Census
Hastins, William: (B) 1828, (CO) Pulaski, (A) 32, (BP) TN, (CMTS) 1860 Census
Haven, Mary: (B) 1834, (CO) Pulaski, (A) 26, (BP) MO, (CMTS) 1860 Census
Havens, Dicy Ann: (B) 1839, (CO) Pulaski, (A) 21, (BP) TN, (CMTS) 1860 Census
Havens, Eliza: (B) 1839, (CO) Pulaski, (A) 21, (BP) TN, (CMTS) 1860 Census
Havens, Henry: (B) 1838, (CO) Pulaski, (A) 22, (BP) TN, (CMTS) 1860 Census
Havens, Jame R.: (B) 1851, (CO) Pulaski, (A) 9, (BP) IL, (CMTS) 1860 Census
Havens, Mary A.: (B) 1848, (CO) Pulaski, (A) 12, (BP) IL, (CMTS) 1860 Census
Havens, Naomi: (B) 1845, (CO) Pulaski, (A) 15, (BP) IL, (CMTS) 1860 Census
Hawkins, B. H.: (B) Feb. 17, 1833, (D) May 4, 1877, (CO) Barry, (C) Old Corsicana Cemetery
Hawkins, George E.: (B) 1854, (CO) Stone, (A) 16, (BP) MO, (CMTS) 1870 Census
Hawkins, Mary M.: (B) 1842, (CO) Stone, (A) 28, (BP) IN, (CMTS) 1870 Census
Hawkins, Susannah: (B) 1820, (D) 1870, (CO) Adair, (A) 50, (CMTS) 1870 Mortality Schedule
Hawkins, Thomas K: (B) 1818, (CO) Stone, (A) 52, (BP) TN, (CMTS) 1870 Census
Hawkins, Virginia E.: (B) 1849, (CO) Stone, (A) 21, (BP) MO, (CMTS) 1870 Census
Hawkins,: (B) Jan. 30, 1811, (D) Jan. 30 1874, (CO) Barry, (C) Old Corsicana Cemetery
Hayes, Agnes: (B) 1793, (CO) Stone, (A) 57, (BP) TN, (CMTS) 1870 Census
Hayes, Levi: (B) 1838, (D) 1917, (CO) Henry, (C) Knights of Pythias Cemetery, Deepwater, MO
Haynes, Allen C.: (B) Feb. 20, 1869, (D) Jun. 1, 1968, (CO) Oregon, (C) Falling Springs Cemetery
Haynes, Cleo: (B) 1922, (CO) Oregon, (C) Falling Springs Cemetery
Haynes, Clyde Jackson: (B) May 2, 1897, (D) Mar. 2, 1963, (CO) Oregon,

(C) Falling Springs Cemetery
Haynes, Eliza M.: (B) Aug. 8, 1871, (CO) Barry,
Haynes, Frances: (B) Dec. 26, 1876, (D) Mar. 20, 1942, (CO) Oregon, (C) Falling Springs Cemetery
Haynes, George: (B) 1848, (CO) Stone, (A) 22, (BP) TN, (CMTS) 1870 Census
Haynes, Hannah M.: (B) 1844, (CO) Stone, (A) 26, (BP) TN, (CMTS) 1870 Census
Haynes, Homer: (B) Nov. 7, 1899, (D) Jul. 12, 1975, (CO) Oregon, (C) Falling Springs Cemetery
Haynes, Lazarus: (B) 1839, (CO) Stone, (A) 31, (BP) TN, (CMTS) 1870 Census
Haynes, Martha Ann: (B) Apr. 22, 1829, (D) Sep. 14, 1892, (CO) Barry, (C) Eugene Gates Cemetery, Purdy, MO
Haynes, Martin L.: (B) Aug. 31, 1828, (D) Feb. 18, 1883, (CO) Barry, (C) Eugene Gates Cemetery, Purdy, MO
Haynes, Vetura: (B) 1851, (CO) Stone, (A) 19, (BP) MO, (CMTS) 1870 Census
Haynes, Virginia E.: (B) Jan. 21, 1894, (D) Jan. 28, 1972, (CO) Oregon, (C) Falling Springs Cemetery
Haynes, Virgle: (B) 1903, (D) 1941, (CO) Oregon, (C) Falling Springs Cemetery
Haynes, William: (B) 1846, (CO) Stone, (A) 24, (BP) TN, (CMTS) 1870 Census
Haynes, William C.: (B) 1859, (D) 1902, (CO) Oregon, (C) Falling Springs Cemetery
Haynes, Willis: (B) 1885, (D) 1965, (CO) Oregon, (C) Falling Springs Cemetery
Hays, James: (B) 1837, (CO) Pulaski, (A) 23, (BP) Ireland, (CMTS) 1860 Census
Hays, Michael: (B) 1828, (CO) Pulaski, (A) 32, (BP) Ireland, (CMTS) 1860 Census
Hays, Morris: (B) 1844, (CO) Pulaski, (A) 16, (BP) Ireland, (CMTS) 1860 Census
Hazett, Elizabeth Leahy: (B) Mar. 7, 1847, (D) Jan. 29, 1929, (CO) St. Louis, (C) Calvary Cemetery
Heade, Bridget: (D) Aug. 30, 1890, (CO) St. Louis, (C) Calvary Cemetery, (A) 51
Heade, Catherine: (B) 1877, (D) 1950, (CO) St. Louis, (C) Calvary Cemetery
Heade, Nellie M.: (D) Jan. 5, 1887, (CO) St. Louis, (C) Calvary Cemetery, (A) 16
Heade, Richard: (B) 1872, (D) 1927, (CO) St. Louis, (C) Calvary

Cemetery
Heade, Richard: (D) Feb. 21, 1895, (CO) St. Louis, (C) Calvary Cemetery, (A) 63
Heade, William M.: (B) 1876, (D) 1909, (CO) St. Louis, (C) Calvary Cemetery
Heath, Clarissa: (B) 1844, (CO) Pulaski, (A) 16, (BP) MO, (CMTS) 1860 Census
Heath, Polly: (B) 1840, (CO) Pulaski, (A) 20, (BP) KY, (CMTS) 1860 Census
Heideman, Alexander J.: (B) 1909, (D) 1988, (CO) St. Louis, (C) Calvary Cemetery
Heideman, Margaret C.: (B) 1907, (D) 1989, (CO) St. Louis, (C) Calvary Cemetery
Heidenreich, George H.: (B) 1900, (D) 1954, (CO) St. Louis, (C) Calvary Cemetery
Heidenrich, Genevieve M.: (B) 1900, (D) 1949, (CO) St. Louis, (C) Calvary Cemetery
Hein, Arthur: (B) 1895, (CO) St. Louis, (C) Calvary Cemetery
Hein, Michael: (B) 1870, (D) 1903, (CO) St. Louis, (C) Calvary Cemetery
Heinbecker, Mary T.: (D) Jul. 15, 1979, (CO) St. Louis, (C) Calvary Cemetery
Heinz, John: (B) 1820, (CO) Pulaski, (A) 40, (BP) Hanover, (CMTS) 1860 Census
Heitkamp, Eugene A.: (B) Sep. 26, 1889, (D) Oct. 21, 1973, (CO) St. Louis, (C) Calvary Cemetery
Heitkamp, Lena E.: (B) Oct. 3, 1879, (D) Oct. 17, 1950, (CO) St. Louis, (C) Calvary Cemetery
Helms, James: (B) 1854, (CO) Pulaski, (A) 6, (BP) MO, (CMTS) 1860 Census
Helms, Joshua: (B) 1844, (CO) Pulaski, (A) 16, (BP) MO, (CMTS) 1860 Census
Helms, Leonard: (B) 1856, (CO) Pulaski, (A) 4, (BP) MO, (CMTS) 1860 Census
Helms, Lucinda: (B) 1820, (CO) Pulaski, (A) 40, (BP) KY, (CMTS) 1860 Census
Helms, Margaret: (B) 1845, (CO) Pulaski, (A) 15, (BP) MO, (CMTS) 1860 Census
Helms, Martha: (B) 1850, (CO) Pulaski, (A) 10, (BP) AR, (CMTS) 1860 Census
Helms, Mary: (B) 1820, (CO) Pulaski, (A) 40, (BP) PA, (CMTS) 1860 Census
Helms, Miranda: (B) 1850, (CO) Pulaski, (A) 10, (BP) MO, (CMTS) 1860 Census

Helms, Sarah J.: (B) 1850, (CO) Pulaski, (A) 10, (BP) MO, (CMTS) 1860 Census
Helms, William: (B) 1841, (CO) Pulaski, (A) 19, (BP) MO, (CMTS) 1860 Census
Helton, Andrew: (B) 1858, (CO) Pulaski, (A) 2, (BP) MO, (CMTS) 1860 Census
Helton, Elizabeth: (B) 1842, (CO) Pulaski, (A) 18, (BP) TN, (CMTS) 1860 Census
Helton, John: (B) 1850, (CO) Pulaski, (A) 10, (BP) TN, (CMTS) 1860 Census
Helton, Levi: (B) 1853, (CO) Pulaski, (A) 7, (BP) TN, (CMTS) 1860 Census
Helton, Mariam: (B) 1840, (CO) Pulaski, (A) 20, (BP) MO, (CMTS) 1860 Census
Helton, Narcissa A.: (B) 1845, (CO) Pulaski, (A) 15, (BP) TN, (CMTS) 1860 Census
Helton, Walter: (B) 1837, (CO) Pulaski, (A) 23, (BP) TN, (CMTS) 1860 Census
Hembree, Cyntha A.: (B) 1842, (CO) Stone, (A) 8, (BP) MO, (CMTS) 1870 Census
Hembree, Dorathe: (B) 1842, (CO) Stone, (A) 28, (BP) MO, (CMTS) 1870 Census
Hembree, Lewis: (B) 1840, (CO) Stone, (A) 30, (BP) MO, (CMTS) 1870 Census
Hembree, Mary E.: (B) 1846, (CO) Stone, (A) 4, (BP) MO, (CMTS) 1870 Census
Hembree, Nancy Ann: (B) 1820, (CO) Stone, (A) 30, (BP) IN, (CMTS) 1870 Census
Hembree, Peggy Jane: (B) 1838, (CO) Stone, (A) 12, (BP) MO, (CMTS) 1870 Census
Hembree, Peggy Jane: (B) 1840, (CO) Stone, (A) 10, (BP) MO, (CMTS) 1870 Census
Hembree, Simon M.: (B) 1834, (CO) Stone, (A) 16, (BP) MO, (CMTS) 1870 Census
Hembree, William: (B) 1796, (CO) Stone, (A) 54, (BP) IN, (CMTS) 1870 Census
Hembree, William A.: (B) 1848, (CO) Stone, (A) 2, (BP) MO, (CMTS) 1870 Census
Hendrick, sJames W.: (B) 1855, (CO) Stone, (A) 15, (BP) MO, (CMTS) 1870 Census
Hendrick, Mary: (B) 1854, (CO) Stone, (A) 16, (BP) MO, (CMTS) 1870 Census
Hendricks, Annie M.: (B) 1851, (CO) Pulaski, (A) 9, (BP) MO, (CMTS)

1860 Census
Hendricks, Elmira: (B) 1845, (CO) Pulaski, (A) 15, (BP) MO, (CMTS) 1860 Census
Hendricks, John: (B) 1836, (CO) Pulaski, (A) 24, (BP) KY, (CMTS) 1860 Census
Hendricks, Joseph R.: (B) 1840, (CO) Stone, (A) 30, (BP) TN, (CMTS) 1870 Census
Hendricks, Margaret: (B) 1845, (CO) Pulaski, (A) 15, (BP) MO, (CMTS) 1860 Census
Hendricks, Polly: (B) 1843, (CO) Pulaski, (A) 17, (BP) KY, (CMTS) 1860 Census
Hendricks, Polly Ann: (B) 1844, (CO) Stone, (A) 26, (BP) TN, (CMTS) 1870 Census
Hendricks, Robert A.: (B) 1843, (CO) Pulaski, (A) 17, (BP) MO, (CMTS) 1860 Census
Hendricks, Robert H.: (B) 1837, (CO) Pulaski, (A) 23, (BP) KY, (CMTS) 1860 Census
Hendricks, Sally: (B) 1818, (CO) Pulaski, (A) 42, (BP) KY, (CMTS) 1860 Census
Hendricks, Sarah: (B) 1843, (CO) Pulaski, (A) 17, (BP) MO, (CMTS) 1860 Census
Hendricks, Sarah A.: (B) 1840, (CO) Pulaski, (A) 20, (BP) KY, (CMTS) 1860 Census
Hendricks, Sarah E.: (B) 1841, (CO) Pulaski, (A) 19, (BP) KY, (CMTS) 1860 Census
Hendricks, Sophia: (B) 1857, (CO) Pulaski, (A) 3, (BP) KY, (CMTS) 1860 Census
Hendricks, Virginia F.: (B) 1847, (CO) Pulaski, (A) 13, (BP) MO, (CMTS) 1860 Census
Heneley, Augustus: (B) 1849, (CO) Pulaski, (A) 11, (BP) MO, (CMTS) 1860 Census
Heneley, Mary: (B) 1820, (CO) Pulaski, (A) 40, (BP) MO, (CMTS) 1860 Census
Heneley, Zachariah: (B) 1847, (CO) Pulaski, (A) 13, (BP) MO, (CMTS) 1860 Census
Henna, John: (B) 1834, (CO) Pulaski, (A) 26, (BP) Ireland, (CMTS) 1860 Census
Hennessy, William: (B) 1883, (D) 1932, (CO) St. Louis, (C) Calvary Cemetery
Hennesy, Pat.: (B) 1828, (CO) Pulaski, (A) 32, (BP) Ireland, (CMTS) 1860 Census
Henry, Amanda: (B) 1846, (CO) Pulaski, (A) 14, (BP) AR, (CMTS) 1860 Census

Henry, Elizabeth: (B) 1839, (CO) Pulaski, (A) 21, (BP) IN, (CMTS) 1860 Census
Henry, Emalene: (B) 1848, (CO) Pulaski, (A) 12, (BP) W, (CMTS) 1860 Census
Henry, Harriet: (B) 1840, (CO) Pulaski, (A) 20, (BP) IN, (CMTS) 1860 Census
Henry, Harrison: (B) 1852, (CO) Pulaski, (A) 8, (BP) MO, (CMTS) 1860 Census
Henry, Joseph: (B) 1834, (CO) Stone, (A) 36, (BP) TN, (CMTS) 1870 Census
Henry, Julia A.: (B) 1836, (CO) Pulaski, (A) 24, (BP) IN, (CMTS) 1860 Census
Henry, Martha: (B) 1840, (CO) Stone, (A) 30, (BP) TN, (CMTS) 1870 Census
Henry, Mary J.: (B) 1838, (CO) Pulaski, (A) 22, (BP) KY, (CMTS) 1860 Census
Henry, Nancy: (B) 1855, (CO) Pulaski, (A) 5, (BP) MO, (CMTS) 1860 Census
Henry, Sarah: (B) 1842, (CO) Pulaski, (A) 18, (BP) AR, (CMTS) 1860 Census
Henry, Sarah J.: (B) 1853, (CO) Stone, (A) 17, (BP) MO, (CMTS) 1870 Census
Henry, Susan: (B) 1855, (CO) Stone, (A) 15, (BP) MO, (CMTS) 1870 Census
Henry, Thomas: (B) 1854, (CO) Pulaski, (A) 6, (BP) MO, (CMTS) 1860 Census
Henshaw, Elizabeth: (B) 1846, (CO) Pulaski, (A) 14, (BP) PA, (CMTS) 1860 Census
Henshaw, Levi: (B) 1821, (CO) Pulaski, (A) 39, (BP) TN, (CMTS) 1860 Census
Henshaw, Levi: (B) 1821, (CO) Pulaski, (A) 39, (BP) TN, (CMTS) 1860 Census
Henshaw, Parmelia: (B) 1826, (CO) Pulaski, (A) 34, (BP) KY, (CMTS) 1860 Census
Henshaw, Parmelia: (B) 1826, (CO) Pulaski, (A) 34, (BP) KY, (CMTS) 1860 Census
Henshaw, Susan: (B) 1844, (CO) Pulaski, (A) 16, (BP) TN, (CMTS) 1860 Census
Henshaw, Susan: (B) 1844, (CO) Pulaski, (A) 16, (BP) PA, (CMTS) 1860 Census
Henshaw, Walker P.: (B) 1857, (CO) Pulaski, (A) 3, (BP) MO, (CMTS) 1860 Census
Hensley, Billy Dee: (B) Mar. 1, 1942, (D) Oct. 16, 1947, (CO) Worth,

Hensley, L.: (B) Feb. 22, 1941, (D) Feb. 22, 1941, (CO) Worth,
Hensley, Verl Wilson: (B) Oct. 15, 1917, (D) May 15, 1969, (CO) Worth,
Henson, Arinola: (B) 1819, (CO) Stone, (A) 51, (BP) KY, (CMTS) 1870 Census
Henson, Charity: (B) 1854, (CO) Pulaski, (A) 6, (BP) MO, (CMTS) 1860 Census
Henson, Charllotta: (B) 1845, (CO) Stone, (A) 25, (BP) OH, (CMTS) 1870 Census
Henson, Cornelius: (B) 1838, (CO) Pulaski, (A) 22, (BP) IN, (CMTS) 1860 Census
Henson, Dillie: (B) 1854, (CO) Stone, (A) 16, (BP) AR, (CMTS) 1870 Census
Henson, Elisha: (B) 1849, (CO) Stone, (A) 21, (BP) MO, (CMTS) 1870 Census
Henson, F Marion: (B) 1854, (CO) Stone, (A) 16, (BP) MO, (CMTS) 1870 Census
Henson, James: (B) 1845, (CO) Pulaski, (A) 15, (BP) MO, (CMTS) 1860 Census
Henson, Lucretia: (B) 1839, (CO) Stone, (A) 31, (BP) MO, (CMTS) 1870 Census
Henson, Malinda: (B) 1836, (CO) Pulaski, (A) 24, (BP) MO, (CMTS) 1860 Census
Henson, Margaret: (B) Jan.1, 1851, (D) Jul. 21, 1932, (CO) Polk, (C) Turkey Creek Cemetery
Henson, Nancy: (B) 1840, (CO) Pulaski, (A) 20, (BP) MO, (CMTS) 1860 Census
Henson, Susan: (B) 1847, (CO) Pulaski, (A) 13, (BP) MO, (CMTS) 1860 Census
Henson, Susan: (B) 1856, (CO) Stone, (A) 14, (BP) MO, (CMTS) 1870 Census
Henson, William: (B) 1847, (CO) Stone, (A) 23, (BP) MO, (CMTS) 1870 Census
Hermann, Chris: (D) Dec. 1874, (CO) St. Louis, (C) Calvary Cemetery
Hermann, Christian: (D) May 1934, (CO) St. Louis, (C) Calvary Cemetery
Hermann, Mathias: (D) 11, 1908, (CO) St. Louis, (C) Calvary Cemetery
Hermann, Otto H.: (D) Apr. 1885, (CO) St. Louis, (C) Calvary Cemetery
Hermann, Pauline: (D) 11, 1923, (CO) St. Louis, (C) Calvary Cemetery
Herndon, John D: (B) 1849, (CO) Stone, (A) 21, (BP) KY, (CMTS) 1870 Census
Herndon, Julia: (B) 1856, (CO) Stone, (A) 14, (BP) MO, (CMTS) 1870 Census
Herndon, Martha J.: (B) 1832, (CO) Stone, (A) 38, (BP) MI, (CMTS) 1870 Census

Herndon, William H.: (B) 1818, (CO) Stone, (A) 52, (BP) VA, (CMTS) 1870 Census
Herner, Moses: (B) 1839, (D) 1897, (CO) Cedar, (C) Brashear Cemetery
Herod, Idille: (B) 1838, (CO) Stone, (A) 12, (BP) AR, (CMTS) 1870 Census
Herod, John W.: (B) 1854, (CO) Pulaski, (A) 6, (BP) TN, (CMTS) 1860 Census
Herod, Joseph: (B) 1815, (CO) Stone, (A) 35, (BP) AR, (CMTS) 1870 Census
Herod, Joseph: (B) 1842, (CO) Stone, (A) 8, (BP) MO, (CMTS) 1870 Census
Herod, Josephus: (B) 1844, (CO) Stone, (A) 6, (BP) MO, (CMTS) 1870 Census
Herod, Thomas: (B) 1846, (CO) Stone, (A) 4, (BP) MO, (CMTS) 1870 Census
Hess, Martha: (B) 1911, (D) 1966, (CO) St. Louis, (C) Calvary Cemetery
Hibbs, Campbell: (B) 1822, (CO) Pulaski, (A) 38, (BP) KY, (CMTS) 1860 Census
Hibbs, Elsa: (B) 1822, (CO) Pulaski, (A) 38, (BP) KY, (CMTS) 1860 Census
Hibbs, Francis: (B) 1855, (CO) Pulaski, (A) 5, (BP) MO, (CMTS) 1860 Census
Hibbs, James: (B) 1853, (CO) Pulaski, (A) 7, (BP) MO, (CMTS) 1860 Census
Hibbs, James: (B) 1853, (CO) Pulaski, (A) 7, (BP) MO, (CMTS) 1860 Census
Hibbs, Julia A.: (B) 1830, (CO) Pulaski, (A) 30, (BP) IL, (CMTS) 1860 Census
Hibbs, Keziah: (B) 1853, (CO) Pulaski, (A) 7, (BP) MO, (CMTS) 1860 Census
Hibbs, Milton: (B) 1836, (CO) Pulaski, (A) 24, (BP) IN, (CMTS) 1860 Census
Hibbs, Nancy: (B) 1856, (CO) Pulaski, (A) 4, (BP) MO, (CMTS) 1860 Census
Hibbs, Nancy J.: (B) 1841, (CO) Pulaski, (A) 19, (BP) MO, (CMTS) 1860 Census
Hibbs, Polly: (B) 1820, (CO) Pulaski, (A) 40, (BP) KY, (CMTS) 1860 Census
Hibbs, Polly: (B) 1832, (CO) Pulaski, (A) 28, (BP) KY, (CMTS) 1860 Census
Hibbs, Sarah: (B) 1846, (CO) Pulaski, (A) 14, (BP) KY, (CMTS) 1860 Census
Hick, C.: (B) 1838, (CO) Pulaski, (A) 22, (BP) IL, (CMTS)

1860 Census
Hickey, Denis: (D) May 23, 1916, (CO) St. Louis, (C) Calvary Cemetery
Hickey, Elizabeth: (D) Jan. 3, 1922, (CO) St. Louis, (C) Calvary Cemetery
Hickey, George: (B) 1830, (CO) Pulaski, (A) 30, (BP) Ireland, (CMTS) 1860 Census
Hicks, Commodore: (B) 1852, (CO) Pulaski, (A) 8, (BP) MO, (CMTS) 1860 Census
Hicks, D.: (B) 1823, (CO) Pulaski, (A) 37, (BP) TN, (CMTS) 1860 Census
Hicks, George J.: (B) 1851, (CO) Pulaski, (A) 9, (BP) TN, (CMTS) 1860 Census
Hicks, James W.: (B) 1856, (CO) Pulaski, (A) 4, (BP) MO, (CMTS) 1860 Census
Hicks, Jane: (B) 1837, (CO) Pulaski, (A) 23, (BP) MO, (CMTS) 1860 Census
Hicks, L.: (B) 1823, (CO) Pulaski, (A) 37, (BP) TN, (CMTS) 1860 Census
Hicks, Martha J.: (B) 1830, (CO) Pulaski, (A) 30, (BP) TN, (CMTS) 1860 Census
Hicks, Oliver P.: (B) 1855, (CO) Pulaski, (A) 5, (BP) MO, (CMTS) 1860 Census
Hicks, Rebecca: (B) 1827, (CO) Pulaski, (A) 33, (BP) TN, (CMTS) 1860 Census
Hicks, T.: (B) 1828, (CO) Pulaski, (A) 32, (BP) TN, (CMTS) 1860 Census
Hicks, W. T.: (B) 1855, (D) 1938, (CO) Cedar, (C) Brashear Cemetery
Hicks, Waterman: (B) 1837, (CO) Pulaski, (A) 23, (BP) TN, (CMTS) 1860 Census
Hiemenz, Arthur Charles Jr.: (B) 1924, (D) 1982, (CO) St. Louis, (C) Calvary Cemetery
Hiemenz, Henry: (B) 1857, (D) 1928, (CO) St. Louis, (C) Calvary Cemetery
Hiemenz, Clara Volm: (B) 1865, (D) 1955, (CO) St. Louis, (C) Calvary Cemetery
Hiemenz, Infant: (D) Apr. 25, 1928, (CO) St. Louis, (C) Calvary Cemetery
Hieronymus, Samantha E.: (B) 1861, (D) 1936, (CO) Henry, (C) Knights of Pythias Cemetery, Deepwater, MO
Hieronymus, Stephen R.: (B) 1846, (D) 1931, (CO) Henry, (C) Knights of Pythias Cemetery, Deepwater, MO
Higgins, Benjamin: (B) 1856, (CO) Pulaski, (A) 4, (BP) MO, (CMTS) 1860 Census

Higgins, Christopher: (B) 1839, (CO) Pulaski, (A) 21, (BP) MO, (CMTS) 1860 Census
Higgins, Dasha Ann: (B) 1837, (CO) Pulaski, (A) 23, (BP) MO, (CMTS) 1860 Census
Higgins, Marion: (B) 1842, (CO) Pulaski, (A) 18, (BP) MO, (CMTS) 1860 Census
Higgins, Mary M.: (B) 1847, (D) 1908, (CO) Cedar, (C) Brashear Cemetery
High, Barbary E.: (B) 1849, (CO) Stone, (A) 1, (BP) MO, (CMTS) 1870 Census
High, Elisabeth: (B) 1826, (CO) Stone, (A) 24, (BP) AR, (CMTS) 1870 Census
High, George W.: (B) 1826, (CO) Stone, (A) 24, (BP) AR, (CMTS) 1870 Census
High, John M.: (B) 1832, (CO) Stone, (A) 18, (BP) AR, (CMTS) 1870 Census
High, Louisa A.: (B) 1847, (CO) Stone, (A) 3, (BP) AR, (CMTS) 1870 Census
High, Mary C.: (B) 1834, (CO) Stone, (A) 16, (BP) MO, (CMTS) 1870 Census
High, Mary E.: (B) 1849, (CO) Stone, (A) 1, (BP) MO, (CMTS) 1870 Census
High, Sarah L.: (B) 1852, (CO) Stone, (A) 18, (BP) AR, (CMTS) 1870 Census
Hildebrand, John: (B) 1827, (CO) Pulaski, (A) 33, (BP) Germany, (CMTS) 1860 Census
Hilgert, John: (B) May 10, 1823, (D) Jun. 29, 1868, (CO) Jefferson, (C) Old St. John's Catholic Cemetery
Hill, B.: (B) 1828, (CO) Pulaski, (A) 32, (BP) KY, (CMTS) 1860 Census
Hill, Elizabeth M.: (B) 1844, (CO) Stone, (A) 26, (BP) IL, (CMTS) 1870 Census
Hill, Nancy: (B) 1833, (CO) Pulaski, (A) 27, (BP) MO, (CMTS) 1860 Census
Hill, Samuel B.: (B) 1823, (CO) Stone, (A) 47, (BP) TN, (CMTS) 1870 Census
Hillhouse, George Stephens: (B) Feb. 14, 1840, (D) Sep. 14, 1902, (CO) Lawrence,
Hillhouse, Lenna Gertrude: (B) Jan. 8, 1876, (D) Jan. 21, 1901, (CO) Lawrence, (PRTS) James William Hillhouse and Nancy Adaline Maxwell
Hillhouse, Michael Clay: (B) Oct. 26, 1952, (CO) Wright, (PRTS) Edward Dale Hillhouse and Elizabeth Jane Patterson

Hillman, Matilda: (B) 1831, (CO) Pulaski, (A) 29, (BP) TN, (CMTS) 1860 Census
Hillman, Phebe T.: (B) 1791, (CO) Pulaski, (A) 69, (BP) NC, (CMTS) 1860 Census
Hillman, Robert P.: (B) 1856, (CO) Pulaski, (A) 4, (BP) TN, (CMTS) 1860 Census
Hillman, Thomas: (B) 1833, (CO) Pulaski, (A) 27, (BP) TN, (CMTS) 1860 Census
Hillman, William H.: (B) 1854, (CO) Pulaski, (A) 6, (BP) TN, (CMTS) 1860 Census
Hills, John Frederick: (B) Dec. 29, 1919, (D) Apr. 21, 1984, (CO) Henry, (C) Knights of Pythias Cemetery, Deepwater, MO
Hills, John Steven: (B) Dec. 23, 1949, (D) Nov. 1, 1977, (CO) Henry, (C) Knights of Pythias Cemetery, Deepwater, MO
Hillwig, Mary T.: (B) 1920, (CO) St. Louis, (C) Calvary Cemetery
Hillwig, William G.: (B) 1913, (D) 1990, (CO) St. Louis, (C) Calvary Cemetery
Hilpert, Grace: (B) 1892, (D) 1973, (CO) St. Louis, (C) Calvary Cemetery
Hilpert, Otto: (B) 1884, (D) 1928, (CO) St. Louis, (C) Calvary Cemetery
Hinds, Rizy M.: (B) 1832, (CO) Stone, (A) 38, (BP) TN, (CMTS) 1870 Census
Hobbs, Caroline: (B) 1823, (CO) Pulaski, (A) 37, (BP) TN, (CMTS) 1860 Census
Hobbs, Caroline: (B) 1850, (CO) Pulaski, (A) 10, (BP) MO, (CMTS) 1860 Census
Hobbs, James: (B) 1826, (CO) Stone, (A) 24, (BP) MO, (CMTS) 1870 Census
Hobbs, John: (B) 1844, (CO) Pulaski, (A) 16, (BP) MO, (CMTS) 1860 Census
Hobbs, Joseph: (B) 1841, (CO) Pulaski, (A) 19, (BP) MO, (CMTS) 1860 Census
Hobbs, Margaret: (B) 1841, (CO) Pulaski, (A) 19, (BP) MO, (CMTS) 1860 Census
Hobbs, Nathan: (B) 1843, (CO) Stone, (A) 7, (BP) MO, (CMTS) 1870 Census
Hobbs, Philemon: (B) 1849, (CO) Stone, (A) 1, (BP) MO, (CMTS) 1870 Census
Hobbs, Rebecca: (B) 1829, (CO) Stone, (A) 21, (BP) AL, (CMTS) 1870 Census
Hobbs, Tabitha: (B) 1854, (CO) Pulaski, (A) 6, (BP) MO, (CMTS) 1860 Census
Hobbs, Vincent: (B) 1847, (CO) Pulaski, (A) 13, (BP) MO, (CMTS) 1860 Census

Hober, Anthony: (B) 1820, (CO) Pulaski, (A) 40, (BP) PA, (CMTS) 1860 Census
Hodgens, William: (D) May 7, 1903, (CO) St. Louis, (C) Calvary Cemetery, (A) 57
Hoffman, Alonza: (B) 1850, (CO) Stone, (A) 20, (BP) IN, (CMTS) 1870 Census
Hoffman, Israel: (B) 1819, (CO) Stone, (A) 51, (BP) KY, (CMTS) 1870 Census
Hoffman, Jemima: (B) 1854, (CO) Stone, (A) 16, (BP) IL, (CMTS) 1870 Census
Hoffman, Susan: (B) 1829, (CO) Stone, (A) 41, (BP) IN, (CMTS) 1870 Census
Hogan, Patrick: (B) 1830, (CO) Pulaski, (A) 30, (BP) Ireland, (CMTS) 1860 Census
Hollesby, Mary Jane: (B) 1841, (CO) Stone, (A) 9, (BP) IL, (CMTS) 1870 Census
Hollesby, Robert: (B) 1848, (CO) Stone, (A) 2, (BP) MO, (CMTS) 1870 Census
Hollesby, Sylvia: (B) 1827, (CO) Stone, (A) 23, (BP) IL, (CMTS) 1870 Census
Hollis, Jacob: (B) Aug. 10, 1835, (D) Feb. 14, 1863, (CO) Barry, (C) Old Corsicana Cemetery
Holmes, Elizabeth A.: (B) 1874, (D) 1929, (CO) St. Louis, (C) Calvary Cemetery
Holmes, Hanora: (B) 1842, (D) 1903, (CO) St. Louis, (C) Calvary Cemetery
Holmes, James J.: (B) 1871, (D) 1901, (CO) St. Louis, (C) Calvary Cemetery
Holmes, James L.: (B) 1844, (D) 1917, (CO) St. Louis, (C) Calvary Cemetery
Holmes, John M.: (B) 1866, (D) 1884, (CO) St. Louis, (C) Calvary Cemetery
Holsey, Imogene: (B) 1867, (CO) Missouri, (RES) Graves Co., TX, (CMTS) 1920 Census, p. 113
Holt, James: (B) Dec. 14, 1822, (D) Oct. 11, 1892, (CO) Barry, (C) Cassville Cemetery
Holt, Jeremiah: (B) 1854, (CO) Stone, (A) 16, (BP) MO, (CMTS) 1870 Census
Holt, Martha: (B) 1856, (CO) Stone, (A) 14, (BP) MO, (CMTS) 1870 Census
Holt, Martha: (B) Jan. 14, 1825, (D) Jun. 11, 1864, (CO) Barry, (C) Cassville Cemetery
Holt, Mary: (B) 1834, (CO) Stone, (A) 36, (BP) MO, (CMTS) 1870

Census
Holt, Mary L.: (B) 1840, (CO) Stone, (A) 10, (BP) AR, (CMTS) 1870 Census
Holt, Wade H.: (B) 1838, (CO) Stone, (A) 12, (BP) IO, (CMTS) 1870 Census
Holt, William: (B) 1835, (CO) Stone, (A) 15, (BP) IO, (CMTS) 1870 Census
Holzapfel, WilliamHenry: (B) 1859, (D) 1924, (CO) Henry, (C) Knights of Pythias Cemetery, Deepwater, MO
Hood, Alex: (B) 1832, (CO) Stone, (A) 38, (BP) TN, (CMTS) 1870 Census
Hood, Eli: (B) 1820, (CO) Pulaski, (A) 40, (BP) KY, (CMTS) 1860 Census
Hood, Rachel C.: (B) 1837, (CO) Stone, (A) 33, (BP) TN, (CMTS) 1870 Census
Hood, Sarah E.: (B) 1856, (CO) Stone, (A) 14, (BP) AR, (CMTS) 1870 Census
Hooten, Benjamin: (B) 1831, (CO) Stone, (A) 39, (BP) IN, (CMTS) 1870 Census
Hooten, Benjamin: (B) 1858, (CO) Stone, (A) 12, (BP) MO, (CMTS) 1870 Census
Hooten, Martha J.: (B) 1844, (CO) Stone, (A) 26, (BP) MO, (CMTS) 1870 Census
Hooten, Matilda: (B) 1842, (CO) Stone, (A) 28, (BP) TN, (CMTS) 1870 Census
Hooten, Thomas: (B) 1857, (CO) Stone, (A) 13, (BP) MO, (CMTS) 1870 Census
Hooten, William: (B) 1839, (CO) Stone, (A) 31, (BP) IN, (CMTS) 1870 Census
Hoover, Katherine: (D) Aug. 20, 2000, (CO) Cole, (NWS) *Jefferson City, Missouri News-Tribune*, Aug. 22, 2000, (RES) Jefferson City
Hopkins, James: (B) 1838, (CO) Pulaski, (A) 22, (BP) MO, (CMTS) 1860 Census
Horan, William: (D) Nov. 27, 1918, (CO) St. Louis, (C) Calvary Cemetery
Horn, Auguste: (B) 1858, (CO) Stone, (A) 12, (BP) MO, (CMTS) 1870 Census
Horn, Gideon: (B) 1842, (CO) Stone, (A) 28, (BP) TN, (CMTS) 1870 Census
Horn, Jacob: (B) 1830, (CO) Stone, (A) 40, (BP) TN, (CMTS) 1870 Census
Horn, Jefferson: (B) 1854, (CO) Stone, (A) 16, (BP) MO, (CMTS) 1870 Census

Horn, John: (B) 1848, (CO) Stone, (A) 22, (BP) TN, (CMTS) 1870 Census
Horn, Lizah: (B) 1839, (CO) Stone, (A) 31, (BP) MO, (CMTS) 1870 Census
Horn, Malinda: (B) 1826, (CO) Stone, (A) 44, (BP) TN, (CMTS) 1870 Census
Horn, Mary: (B) 1853, (CO) Stone, (A) 17, (BP) MO, (CMTS) 1870 Census
Horn, Roberson Saml: (B) 1849, (CO) Stone, (A) 21, (BP) TN, (CMTS) 1870 Census
Horzt, Jane: (D) Feb. 22, 1888, (CO) Andrew, (C) Oak Ridge Cemetery, (A) 65Y 1M 2D
Hosman, RachelC.: (B) 1851, (D) 1925, (CO) Henry, (C) Knights of Pythias Cemetery, Deepwater, MO
Hosman, William S.: (B) 1850, (D) 1921, (CO) Henry, (C) Knights of Pythias Cemetery, Deepwater, MO
Houser, David Malott: (B) 1834, (D) 1915, (CO) St. Louis,
Houser, James M.: (B) 1847, (CO) Stone, (A) 23, (BP) TN, (CMTS) 1870 Census
Houser, Martha: (B) 1848, (CO) Stone, (A) 22, (BP) MO, (CMTS) 1870 Census
Howard, Corwin F. Dr.: (B) 1856, (D) 1932, (CO) Henry, (C) Knights of Pythias Cemetery, Deepwater, MO
Howard, Flora J.: (B) 1855, (CO) Stone, (A) 15, (BP) MO, (CMTS) 1870 Census
Howard, Martha E.: (B) 1838, (CO) Stone, (A) 32, (BP) MO, (CMTS) 1870 Census
Howard, Mary J.: (B) 1846, (CO) Stone, (A) 24, (BP) MO, (CMTS) 1870 Census
Howard, Thos: (B) 1825, (CO) Stone, (A) 45, (BP) KY, (CMTS) 1870 Census
Howard, Virgil Cyrus: (B) 1836, (CO) Stone, (A) 34, (BP) KY, (CMTS) 1870 Census
Howe, Alfred S,: (B) Oct. 17, 1817, (D) Sep. 6, 1851, (CO) Audrain, (C) Old Village Cemetery
Howell, Mary E.: (B) 1853, (CO) Stone, (A) 17, (BP) TN, (CMTS) 1870 Census
Howell, Medline F: (B) 1855, (CO) Stone, (A) 15, (BP) MO, (CMTS) 1870 Census
Howell, Sarah: (B) 1831, (CO) Stone, (A) 39, (BP) TN, (CMTS) 1870 Census
Howerton, Rufus: (B) Jun. 1, 1824, (D) Aug. 16, 1896, (CO) Barry, (C) Old Corsicana Cemetery

Hoyle, George W.: (B) 1837, (CO) Stone, (A) 33, (BP) TN, (CMTS) 1870 Census
Hoyle, Phebe: (B) 1844, (CO) Stone, (A) 26, (BP) AL, (CMTS) 1870 Census
Hubble, Ira: (B) 1827, (CO) Pulaski, (A) 33, (BP) NY, (CMTS) 1860 Census
Hubble, Sarah: (B) 1840, (CO) Pulaski, (A) 20, (BP) PA, (CMTS) 1860 Census
Huddleson, Elisha: (B) 1830, (CO) Pulaski, (A) 30, (BP) MO, (CMTS) 1860 Census
Huddleson, Nancy: (B) 1834, (CO) Pulaski, (A) 26, (BP) MO, (CMTS) 1860 Census
Huddleson, Sarah: (B) 1857, (CO) Pulaski, (A) 3, (BP) MO, (CMTS) 1860 Census
Hudgens, Olen Gale "Corkey": (B) Dec. 7, 1929, (D) Jul. 11, 1998, (CO)
Hudgins, Dabner T.: (B) 1850, (CO) Pulaski, (A) 10, (BP) MO, (CMTS) 1860 Census
Hudgins, Florinda: (B) 1844, (CO) Pulaski, (A) 16, (BP) MO, (CMTS) 1860 Census
Hudgins, James: (B) 1840, (CO) Pulaski, (A) 20, (BP) MO, (CMTS) 1860 Census
Hudgins, King D.: (B) 1848, (CO) Pulaski, (A) 12, (BP) MO, (CMTS) 1860 Census
Hudgins, Mahala: (B) 1823, (CO) Pulaski, (A) 37, (BP) TN, (CMTS) 1860 Census
Hudgins, Robert: (B) 1816, (CO) Pulaski, (A) 44, (BP) KY, (CMTS) 1860 Census
Hudgins, Robert: (B) 1853, (CO) Pulaski, (A) 7, (BP) MO, (CMTS) 1860 Census
Hudgins, Stephen A. D.: (B) 1855, (CO) Pulaski, (A) 5, (BP) MO, (CMTS) 1860 Census
Hudgins, Tally A.: (B) 1857, (CO) Pulaski, (A) 3, (BP) MO, (CMTS) 1860 Census
Hudson, Hulda E.: (B) 1846, (CO) Stone, (A) 24, (BP) MO, (CMTS) 1870 Census
Hudson, Maggie: (B) 1841, (D) 1920, (CO) Cedar, (C) Brashear Cemetery
Hudson, Polly A.: (B) 1865, (D) 1953, (CO) Henry, (C) Knights of Pythias Cemetery, Deepwater, MO
Huff, James: (B) 1855, (CO) Pulaski, (A) 5, (BP) MO, (CMTS) 1860 Census
Huff, John: (B) 1851, (CO) Pulaski, (A) 9, (BP) MO, (CMTS) 1860 Census
Huff, Mary: (B) 1829, (CO) Pulaski, (A) 31, (BP) MO, (CMTS)

1860 Census
Huff, William: (B) 1817, (CO) Pulaski, (A) 43, (BP) KY, (CMTS) 1860 Census
Huff, William W.: (B) 1853, (CO) Pulaski, (A) 7, (BP) MO, (CMTS) 1860 Census
Huffman, James V.: (B) 1903, (D) 1962, (CO) St. Louis, (C) Calvary Cemetery
Hughes, Anna: (B) 1878, (D) 1957, (CO) St. Louis, (C) Calvary Cemetery
Hughes, Eliza A.: (B) 1858, (CO) Stone, (A) 12, (BP) MO, (CMTS) 1870 Census
Hughes, Martin: (B) 1872, (D) 1929, (CO) St. Louis, (C) Calvary Cemetery
Hughes, Sarah: (B) 1830, (CO) Stone, (A) 40, (BP) AL, (CMTS) 1870 Census
Hughs, Bettie: (B) 1843, (D) 1918, (CO) Henry, (C) Knights of Pythias Cemetery, Deepwater, MO
Hughs, John: (B) 1843, (D) 1904, (CO) Henry, (C) Knights of Pythias Cemetery, Deepwater, MO
Hulick, George: (B) 1840, (D) 1887, (CO) Cedar, (C) Brashear Cemetery
Hunter, Hiram: (B) 1835, (CO) Pulaski, (A) 25, (BP) KY, (CMTS) 1860 Census
Hunter, Hiram: (B) 1837, (CO) Pulaski, (A) 23, (BP) NC, (CMTS) 1860 Census
Hunter, John E.: (B) 1856, (CO) Pulaski, (A) 4, (BP) MO, (CMTS) 1860 Census
Hunter, Nancy: (B) 1835, (CO) Pulaski, (A) 25, (BP) VA, (CMTS) 1860 Census
Hunter, Narcissa: (B) 1846, (CO) Pulaski, (A) 14, (BP) MO, (CMTS) 1860 Census
Hunter, William: (B) 1820, (CO) Pulaski, (A) 40, (BP) KY, (CMTS) 1860 Census
Hunter, William: (B) 1820, (CO) Pulaski, (A) 40, (BP) KY, (CMTS) 1860 Census
Hunter, William F.: (B) 1848, (CO) Pulaski, (A) 12, (BP) MO, (CMTS) 1860 Census
Huntsman, J.: (B) 1827, (CO) Pulaski, (A) 33, (BP) IL, (CMTS) 1860 Census
Hurley, Patrick: (B) 1830, (CO) Pulaski, (A) 30, (BP) Ireland, (CMTS) 1860 Census
Hurst, Elizabeth: (B) 1839, (CO) Stone, (A) 31, (BP) KY, (CMTS) 1870 Census
Hurst, Hardy: (B) 1838, (CO) Stone, (A) 32, (BP) TN, (CMTS) 1870 Census

Hurst, Harrison: (B) 1838, (CO) Stone, (A) 32, (BP) TN, (CMTS) 1870 Census
Hurst, James: (B) 1842, (CO) Pulaski, (A) 18, (BP) IN, (CMTS) 1860 Census
Hurst, Jordon: (B) 1852, (CO) Stone, (A) 18, (BP) TN, (CMTS) 1870 Census
Hurst, Margaretta: (B) 1849, (CO) Stone, (A) 21, (BP) TN, (CMTS) 1870 Census
Hurst, Mary: (B) 1839, (CO) Stone, (A) 31, (BP) TN, (CMTS) 1870 Census
Hurst, Rufus: (B) 1854, (CO) Stone, (A) 16, (BP) MO, (CMTS) 1870 Census
Hurst, Samuel W.: (B) Mar. 19, 1889, (D) Oct. 10, 1918, (CO) Oregon, (C) Falling Springs Cemetery
Hurst, Tillman: (B) 1845, (CO) Pulaski, (A) 15, (BP) IN, (CMTS) 1860 Census
Hurst, William: (B) 1815, (CO) Pulaski, (A) 45, (BP) IN, (CMTS) 1860 Census
Hurst, William A.: (B) 1849, (CO) Pulaski, (A) 11, (BP) MO, (CMTS) 1860 Census
Hurst, William C.: (B) Dec. 15, 1884, (D) Dec. 12, 1934, (CO) Henry, (C) Knights of Pythias Cemetery, Deepwater, MO
Huston, Martha A.: (B) 1849, (D) 1924, (CO) Henry, (C) Knights of Pythias Cemetery, Deepwater, MO
Huston, William Calvin: (B) 1844, (D) 1914, (CO) Henry, (C) Knights of Pythias Cemetery, Deepwater, MO
Hutchinson, Cyrus E.: (B) 1852, (D) 1906, (CO) Cedar, (C) Brashear Cemetery
Hyland, Dorothy: (B) Nov. 4, 1891, (D) Aug. 25, 1964, (CO) St. Louis, (C) Calvary Cemetery
Hymer, Elizabeth E.: (B) 1839, (CO) Pulaski, (A) 21, (BP) IN, (CMTS) 1860 Census
Hynes, Mrs . Maria: (D) Jan. 4, 1881, (CO) St. Louis, (C) Calvary Cemetery, (A) 58
Ickler, George: (B) 1816, (D) 1870, (CO) Adair, (A) 54, (CMTS) 1870 Mortality Schedule
Iller, Martha: (B) 1836, (D) 1870, (CO) Adair, (A) 34, (CMTS) 1870 Mortality Schedule
Ingraham, David: (B) 1851, (CO) Pulaski, (A) 9, (BP) MO, (CMTS) 1860 Census
Ingraham, Jane: (B) 1828, (CO) Pulaski, (A) 32, (BP) TN, (CMTS) 1860 Census
Ingraham, Jane: (B) 1854, (CO) Pulaski, (A) 6, (BP) AR, (CMTS)

1860 Census
Ingraham, John: (B) 1854, (CO) Pulaski, (A) 6, (BP) TX, (CMTS) 1860 Census
Ingraham, Tennessee: (B) 1846, (CO) Pulaski, (A) 14, (BP) IL, (CMTS) 1860 Census
Ingraham, William: (B) 1829, (CO) Pulaski, (A) 31, (BP) IL, (CMTS) 1860 Census
Ingram, Charles: (B) 1833, (D) 1890, (CO) Cedar, (C) Brashear Cemetery
Ingram, JaneC: (B) 1836, (D) 1918, (CO) Cedar, (C) Brashear Cemetery
Ingram, Laura Leann FIFe: (B) Dec. 6, 1972, (D) Jan. 1, 1997 (CO) Henry, (C) Knights of Pythias Cemetery, Deepwater, MO
Ingram, Nancy J.: (B) 1834, (D) 1908, (CO) Cedar, (C) Brashear Cemetery
Inmon, Elizabeth: (B) 1821, (CO) Pulaski, (A) 39, (BP) TN, (CMTS) 1860 Census
Inmon, John W.: (B) 1844, (CO) Pulaski, (A) 16, (BP) MO, (CMTS) 1860 Census
Inmon, Mary C.: (B) 1847, (CO) Pulaski, (A) 13, (BP) MO, (CMTS) 1860 Census
Inmon, S.: (B) 1818, (CO) Pulaski, (A) 42, (BP) TN, (CMTS) 1860 Census
Inmon, Sarah Jane: (B) 1843, (CO) Pulaski, (A) 17, (BP) MO, (CMTS) 1860 Census
Inmon, Jane: (B) 1836, (CO) Stone, (A) 34, (BP) TN, (CMTS) 1870 Census
Inmon?, John: (B) 1831, (CO) Stone, (A) 39, (BP) KY, (CMTS) 1870 Census
Irving, Caroline: (B) 1849, (CO) Pulaski, (A) 11, (BP) IL, (CMTS) 1860 Census
Irving, Elizabeth: (B) 1846, (CO) Pulaski, (A) 14, (BP) IL, (CMTS) 1860 Census
Irving, Hethelda: (B) 1842, (CO) Pulaski, (A) 18, (BP) IL, (CMTS) 1860 Census
Irving, Hiram: (B) 1837, (CO) Pulaski, (A) 23, (BP) IL, (CMTS) 1860 Census
Irving, James: (B) 1853, (CO) Pulaski, (A) 7, (BP) IL, (CMTS) 1860 Census
Irving, Rachael: (B) 1844, (CO) Pulaski, (A) 16, (BP) IL, (CMTS) 1860 Census
Jackson, Andrew: (B) 1858, (CO) Stone, (A) 12, (BP) MO, (CMTS) 1870 Census
Jackson, Dicy: (B) 1838, (CO) Stone, (A) 32, (BP) AR, (CMTS) 1870 Census

Jackson, Elijah: (B) 1852, (CO) Stone, (A) 18, (BP) MO, (CMTS) 1870 Census

Jackson, Elizabeth: (B) 1856, (CO) Pulaski, (A) 4, (BP) MO, (CMTS) 1860 Census

Jackson, Elizabeth: (B) 1856, (CO) Pulaski, (A) 4, (BP) MO, (CMTS) 1860 Census

Jackson, George: (B) 1837, (CO) Pulaski, (A) 23, (BP) TN, (CMTS) 1860 Census

Jackson, Gilbert: (B) 1826, (CO) Stone, (A) 44, (BP) TN, (CMTS) 1870 Census

Jackson, Goodwin: (B) 1845, (CO) Stone, (A) 25, (BP) MO, (CMTS) 1870 Census

Jackson, Henry: (B) 1852, (CO) Pulaski, (A) 8, (BP) MO, (CMTS) 1860 Census

Jackson, Jacob: (B) 1820, (CO) Pulaski, (A) 40, (BP) PA, (CMTS) 1860 Census

Jackson, Jane: (B) 1835, (CO) Pulaski, (A) 25, (BP) TN, (CMTS) 1860 Census

Jackson, Jane: (B) 1835, (CO) Pulaski, (A) 25, (BP) TN, (CMTS) 1860 Census

Jackson, Malinda: (B) 1854, (CO) Stone, (A) 16, (BP) MO, (CMTS) 1870 Census

Jackson, Martha: (B) 1836, (CO) Stone, (A) 34, (BP) TN, (CMTS) 1870 Census

Jackson, Mary: (B) 1852, (CO) Pulaski, (A) 8, (BP) MO, (CMTS) 1860 Census

Jackson, Matilda: (B) 1856, (CO) Stone, (A) 14, (BP) MO, (CMTS) 1870 Census

Jackson, Parolee: (B) 1850, (CO) Stone, (A) 20, (BP) MO, (CMTS) 1870 Census

Jackson, Robert: (B) 1835, (CO) Pulaski, (A) 25, (BP) MO, (CMTS) 1860 Census

Jackson, Sarah: (B) 1854, (CO) Stone, (A) 16, (BP) MO, (CMTS) 1870 Census

Jackson, Susannah: (B) 1856, (CO) Stone, (A) 14, (BP) MO, (CMTS) 1870 Census

Jackson, Thos: (B) 1840, (CO) Pulaski, (A) 20, (BP) TN, (CMTS) 1860 Census

Jackson, Winona Elizabeth: (B) Dec. 16, 1915, (D) Dec. 23, 1992, (CO) Henry, (C) Knights of Pythias Cemetery, Deepwater, MO

James, Catherine: (B) 1837, (CO) Stone, (A) 33, (BP) IO, (CMTS) 1870 Census

James, Charlotta: (B) 1858, (CO) Stone, (A) 12, (BP) MO, (CMTS)

1870 Census
James, George W.: (B) 1856, (CO) Stone, (A) 14, (BP) MO, (CMTS) 1870 Census
James, Sophia: (B) 1826, (CO) Stone, (A) 44, (BP) TN, (CMTS) 1870 Census
James, Susan: (B) 1854, (CO) Stone, (A) 16, (BP) MO, (CMTS) 1870 Census
James, William I: (B) 1833, (CO) Stone, (A) 37, (BP) KY, (CMTS) 1870 Census
Janes, John M.: (B) Nov. 20, 1850, (D) Jul. 18, 1938, (CO) St. Louis, (C) Calvary Cemetery
Jefferies, Clary: (B) Dec. 1, 1812, (D) Feb. 12, 1897, (CO) Barry, (C) Old Corsicana Cemetery
Jefferies, R.: (B) Jan. 8, 1813, (D) Sep. 4, 1869, (CO) Barry, (C) Old Corsicana Cemetery
Jeffers, John A.: (B) Nov. 25, 1885, (D) 6, 19, 1962, (CO) St. Louis, (C) Calvary Cemetery
Jeneten, James: (B) 1856, (CO) Pulaski, (A) 4, (BP) TN, (CMTS) 1860 Census
Jeneten, Mary J.: (B) 1849, (CO) Pulaski, (A) 11, (BP) KY, (CMTS) 1860 Census
Jeneten, Phebe: (B) 1833, (CO) Pulaski, (A) 27, (BP) KY, (CMTS) 1860 Census
Jeneten, William: (B) 1832, (CO) Pulaski, (A) 28, (BP) TN, (CMTS) 1860 Census
Jeneten, William: (B) 1850, (CO) Pulaski, (A) 10, (BP) MO, (CMTS) 1860 Census
Jenkins, Alfred: (B) 1794, (CO) Stone, (A) 56, (BP) VA, (CMTS) 1870 Census
Jenkins, Chatherine: (B) 1794, (CO) Stone, (A) 56, (BP) TN, (CMTS) 1870 Census
Jenkins, Eli: (B) 1833, (CO) Stone, (A) 17, (BP) TN, (CMTS) 1870 Census
Jenkins, Elizabeth: (B) 1839, (CO) Stone, (A) 11, (BP) MO, (CMTS) 1870 Census
Jenkins, Felix: (B) 1832, (CO) Stone, (A) 18, (BP) TN, (CMTS) 1870 Census
Jenkins, George W.: (B) 1828, (CO) Stone, (A) 22, (BP) TN, (CMTS) 1870 Census
Jenkins, Henry P: (B) 1830, (CO) Stone, (A) 20, (BP) TN, (CMTS) 1870 Census
Jenkins, Isaac: (B) 1833, (CO) Stone, (A) 17, (BP) MO, (CMTS) 1870 Census

Jenkins, Joseph: (B) 1835, (CO) Stone, (A) 15, (BP) MO, (CMTS) 1870 Census
Jenkins, Mary: (B) 1841, (CO) Stone, (A) 9, (BP) MO, (CMTS) 1870 Census
Jenkins, Sarah: (B) 1827, (CO) Stone, (A) 23, (BP) TN, (CMTS) 1870 Census
Jennings, Emeline: (B) 1844, (CO) Pulaski, (A) 16, (BP) MO, (CMTS) 1860 Census
Jennings, Malinda: (B) 1852, (CO) Pulaski, (A) 8, (BP) MO, (CMTS) 1860 Census
Jennings, Mary A.: (B) 1845, (CO) Pulaski, (A) 15, (BP) MO, (CMTS) 1860 Census
Jennings, Nancy: (B) 1850, (CO) Pulaski, (A) 10, (BP) MO, (CMTS) 1860 Census
Jennings, Silas: (B) 1820, (CO) Pulaski, (A) 40, (BP) VA, (CMTS) 1860 Census
Jett, George Washington: (B) Jan. 10, 1883, (CO) Missouri
Jewell, Catharine: (B) 1842, (CO) Pulaski, (A) 18, (BP) TN, (CMTS) 1860 Census
Jewell, David S.: (B) Mar. 1, 1834, (D) Feb. 28, 1900, (CO) Butler,
Jewell, Elizabeth: (B) 1847, (CO) Pulaski, (A) 13, (BP) TN, (CMTS) 1860 Census
Jewell, George W.: (B) 1848, (CO) Pulaski, (A) 12, (BP) MO, (CMTS) 1860 Census
Jewell, Marion: (B) 1844, (CO) Pulaski, (A) 16, (BP) MO, (CMTS) 1860 Census
Jewell, Marion: (B) 1844, (CO) Pulaski, (A) 16, (BP) TN, (CMTS) 1860 Census
Jewell, Milly: (B) 1855, (CO) Pulaski, (A) 5, (BP) MO, (CMTS) 1860 Census
Jewell, Reubein: (B) 1850, (CO) Pulaski, (A) 10, (BP) MO, (CMTS) 1860 Census
Jewell, Victoria: (B) Jan. 8, 1841, (D) Apr. 17, 1917, (CO) Butler,
John, James: (B) 1833, (CO) Stone, (A) 17, (BP) AR, (CMTS) 1870 Census
John, Martha: (B) 1839, (CO) Stone, (A) 11, (BP) AR, (CMTS) 1870 Census
Johnson, Charles L.: (B) 1844, (CO) Pulaski, (A) 16, (BP) MO, (CMTS) 1860 Census
Johnson, David: (B) 1849, (CO) Pulaski, (A) 11, (BP) MO, (CMTS) 1860 Census
Johnson, Delina: (B) 1833, (CO) Stone, (A) 37, (BP) TN, (CMTS) 1870 Census

Johnson, Dewitt: (B) 1828, (CO) Stone, (A) 22, (BP) MO, (CMTS) 1870 Census
Johnson, Elizabeth: (B) 1818, (CO) Pulaski, (A) 42, (BP) KY, (CMTS) 1860 Census
Johnson, Emaline: (B) 1848, (CO) Pulaski, (A) 12, (BP) KY, (CMTS) 1860 Census
Johnson, Francis: (B) Jan. 7, 1856, (D) May 6, 1923, (CO) Pettis, (C) Black Baptist Cemetery, Prairie Township
Johnson, Frederick: (B) May 18, 1919, (D) Feb. 18, 1929, (CO) Pettis, (C) Black Baptist Cemetery, Prairie Township
Johnson, George: (B) 1851, (CO) Pulaski, (A) 9, (BP) MO, (CMTS) 1860 Census
Johnson, Hester: (B) 1849, (CO) Pulaski, (A) 11, (BP) KY, (CMTS) 1860 Census
Johnson, Hiram: (B) 1822, (CO) Pulaski, (A) 38, (BP) IN, (CMTS) 1860 Census
Johnson, James: (B) 1823, (CO) Stone, (A) 47, (BP) TN, (CMTS) 1870 Census
Johnson, James: (B) 1844, (CO) Pulaski, (A) 16, (BP) KY, (CMTS) 1860 Census
Johnson, James: (B) 1853, (CO) Pulaski, (A) 7, (BP) MO, (CMTS) 1860 Census
Johnson, James H.: (B) 1846, (CO) Pulaski, (A) 14, (BP) MO, (CMTS) 1860 Census
Johnson, James L.: (B) 1854, (CO) Pulaski, (A) 6, (BP) MO, (CMTS) 1860 Census
Johnson, John: (B) 1855, (CO) Pulaski, (A) 5, (BP) KY, (CMTS) 1860 Census
Johnson, John E.: (B) 1856, (CO) Pulaski, (A) 4, (BP) MO, (CMTS) 1860 Census
Johnson, John H.: (B) 1844, (CO) Pulaski, (A) 16, (BP) MO, (CMTS) 1860 Census
Johnson, Johnathan D.: (B) 1856, (CO) Pulaski, (A) 4, (BP) MO, (CMTS) 1860 Census
Johnson, Joseph B.: (B) Mar. 28, 1850, (CO) Greene,
Johnson, Julia A.: (B) 1855, (CO) Pulaski, (A) 5, (BP) MO, (CMTS) 1860 Census
Johnson, Laura: (B) Apr. 19, 1882, (D) Sep. 7, 1927, (CO) Pettis, (C) Black Baptist Cemetery, Prairie Township
Johnson, Leander A.: (B) 1853, (CO) Stone, (A) 17, (BP) MO, (CMTS) 1870 Census
Johnson, Llewellen: (B) 1820, (CO) Pulaski, (A) 40, (BP) MO, (CMTS) 1860 Census

Johnson, Ludolphus: (B) 1855, (CO) Pulaski, (A) 5, (BP) MO, (CMTS) 1860 Census
Johnson, Luther: (B) 1883, (D) 1966, (CO) Pettis, (C) Black Baptist Cemetery, Prairie Township
Johnson, Marion: (B) 1842, (CO) Pulaski, (A) 18, (BP) MO, (CMTS) 1860 Census
Johnson, Martha J.: (B) 1847, (CO) Stone, (A) 3, (BP) AR, (CMTS) 1870 Census
Johnson, Mary: (B) 1847, (CO) Pulaski, (A) 13, (BP) KY, (CMTS) 1860 Census
Johnson, Moses: (B) 1823, (CO) Pulaski, (A) 37, (BP) TN, (CMTS) 1860 Census
Johnson, Nancy: (B) 1825, (CO) Pulaski, (A) 35, (BP) KY, (CMTS) 1860 Census
Johnson, Nancy: (B) 1851, (CO) Pulaski, (A) 9, (BP) MO, (CMTS) 1860 Census
Johnson, Polly: (B) 1831, (CO) Pulaski, (A) 29, (BP) TN, (CMTS) 1860 Census
Johnson, Rebecca: (B) 1826, (CO) Pulaski, (A) 34, (BP) KY, (CMTS) 1860 Census
Johnson, Rubin: (B) 1856, (CO) Pulaski, (A) 4, (BP) MO, (CMTS) 1860 Census
Johnson, Rubin: (B) 1857, (CO) Pulaski, (A) 3, (BP) MO, (CMTS) 1860 Census
Johnson, Ruffus: (B) Dec. 3, 1914, (D) Apr., 1932, (CO) Pettis, (C) Black Baptist Cemetery, Prairie Township
Johnson, Sally: (B) 1856, (CO) Pulaski, (A) 4, (BP) MO, (CMTS) 1860 Census
Johnson, Samuel: (B) 1839, (CO) Pulaski, (A) 21, (BP) MO, (CMTS) 1860 Census
Johnson, Sarah C.: (B) 1829, (CO) Pulaski, (A) 31, (BP) KY, (CMTS) 1860 Census
Johnson, Sarah J.: (B) 1834, (CO) Stone, (A) 16, (BP) IN, (CMTS) 1870 Census
Johnson, Sarah K.: (B) 1849, (CO) Pulaski, (A) 11, (BP) MO, (CMTS) 1860 Census
Johnson, Taylor: (B) 1828, (CO) Stone, (A) 22, (BP) AR, (CMTS) 1870 Census
Johnson, Temple?: (B) 1826, (CO) Stone, (A) 24, (BP) AR, (CMTS) 1870 Census
Johnson, William: (B) 1829, (D) 1870, (CO) Adair, (A) 41, (CMTS) 1870 Mortality Schedule
Johnson, William: (B) 1844, (CO) Pulaski, (A) 16, (BP) KY, (CMTS)

1860 Census
Johnson, William: (B) 1850, (CO) Pulaski, (A) 10, (BP) MO, (CMTS) 1860 Census
Johnson, William P: (B) 1848, (CO) Stone, (A) 2, (BP) AR, (CMTS) 1870 Census
Johnson, Willis: (B) 1841, (CO) Pulaski, (A) 19, (BP) KY, (CMTS) 1860 Census
Johnson, Wilson: (B) 1844, (CO) Pulaski, (A) 16, (BP) MO, (CMTS) 1860 Census
Jones, Asa G: (B) 1838, (CO) Stone, (A) 12, (BP) MO, (CMTS) 1870 Census
Jones, Celia J.: (B) 1855, (CO) Pulaski, (A) 5, (BP) TN, (CMTS) 1860 Census
Jones, Clara: (B) 1835, (CO) Pulaski, (A) 25, (BP) TN, (CMTS) 1860 Census
Jones, Crishington S.: (B) Feb. 20, 1832, (D) Oct. 21, 1907, (CO) Henry, (C) Knights of Pythias Cemetery, Deepwater, MO
Jones, Cynthia: (B) 1832, (CO) Pulaski, (A) 28, (BP) MO, (CMTS) 1860 Census
Jones, Edward: (B) Dec. 2, 1884, (D) Mar. 21, 1922, (CO) Henry, (C) Knights of Pythias Cemetery, Deepwater, MO
Jones, Elizabeth: (B) 1849, (CO) Stone, (A) 1, (BP) MO, (CMTS) 1870 Census
Jones, Emaline: (B) 1853, (CO) Pulaski, (A) 7, (BP) IL, (CMTS) 1860 Census
Jones, Ester: (B) 1849, (CO) Pulaski, (A) 11, (BP) TN, (CMTS) 1860 Census
Jones, Frances: (B) 1830, (CO) Stone, (A) 20, (BP) AR, (CMTS) 1870 Census
Jones, Henry M.: (B) 1850, (D) 1935, (CO) Cedar, (C) Brashear Cemetery
Jones, Hezekiah: (B) 1793, (CO) Stone, (A) 57, (BP) NC, (CMTS) 1870 Census
Jones, Hiram S.: (B) 1855, (CO) Pulaski, (A) 5, (BP) MO, (CMTS) 1860 Census
Jones, Jabez: (B) 1793, (CO) Stone, (A) 57, (BP) MO, (CMTS) 1870 Census
Jones, Jackson: (B) 1840, (CO) Pulaski, (A) 20, (BP) MO, (CMTS) 1860 Census
Jones, John: (B) 1835, (CO) Pulaski, (A) 25, (BP) TN, (CMTS) 1860 Census
Jones, John T.: (B) 1847, (CO) Stone, (A) 3, (BP) MO, (CMTS) 1870 Census
Jones, Joseph H.: (B) 1841, (CO) Stone, (A) 29, (BP) MO, (CMTS) 1870

Census
Jones, Manville: (B) 1856, (CO) Pulaski, (A) 4, (BP) MO, (CMTS) 1860 Census
Jones, Margarett: (B) 1835, (CO) Stone, (A) 15, (BP) MO, (CMTS) 1870 Census
Jones, Martin: (B) 1825, (CO) Stone, (A) 25, (BP) AR, (CMTS) 1870 Census
Jones, Mary J.: (B) 1846, (CO) Pulaski, (A) 14, (BP) TN, (CMTS) 1860 Census
Jones, Matilda: (B) 1820, (CO) Pulaski, (A) 40, (BP) TN, (CMTS) 1860 Census
Jones, Matilda A.: (B) 1826, (CO) Stone, (A) 24, (BP) MO, (CMTS) 1870 Census
Jones, Nancy: (B) 1845, (CO) Pulaski, (A) 15, (BP) MO, (CMTS) 1860 Census
Jones, Parmelia: (B) 1839, (CO) Pulaski, (A) 21, (BP) IL, (CMTS) 1860 Census
Jones, Parmelia A.: (B) 1849, (CO) Stone, (A) 1, (BP) MO, (CMTS) 1870 Census
Jones, Polly: (B) 1831, (CO) Pulaski, (A) 29, (BP) TN, (CMTS) 1860 Census
Jones, Rachael: (B) 1822, (CO) Pulaski, (A) 38, (BP) MO, (CMTS) 1860 Census
Jones, Richard: (B) 1842, (CO) Pulaski, (A) 18, (BP) MO, (CMTS) 1860 Census
Jones, Samuel H. Dr.: (B) 1837, (D) 1898, (CO) Henry, (C) Knights of Pythias Cemetery, Deepwater, MO
Jones, Sarah: (B) 1848, (CO) Pulaski, (A) 12, (BP) KY, (CMTS) 1860 Census
Jones, Sarah E.: (B) 1827, (CO) Stone, (A) 23, (BP) MO, (CMTS) 1870 Census
Jones, Sarah E.: (B) 1840, (CO) Stone, (A) 10, (BP) MO, (CMTS) 1870 Census
Jones, Sarah J.: (B) 1850, (CO) Pulaski, (A) 10, (BP) MO, (CMTS) 1860 Census
Jones, Sue Elvira: (B) 1856, (D) 1931, (CO) Henry, (C) Knights of Pythias Cemetery, Deepwater, MO
Jones, Theodore: (B) 1845, (CO) Stone, (A) 5, (BP) AR, (CMTS) 1870 Census
Jones, Thomas: (B) 1839, (CO) Pulaski, (A) 21, (BP) IN, (CMTS) 1860 Census
Jones, W.: (B) 1820, (CO) Pulaski, (A) 40, (BP) TN, (CMTS) 1860 Census

Jones, W.: (B) 1857, (CO) Pulaski, (A) 3, (BP) IL, (CMTS) 1860 Census
Jones, William: (B) 1851, (CO) Pulaski, (A) 9, (BP) MO, (CMTS) 1860 Census
Jones, William D: (B) 1848, (CO) Stone, (A) 2, (BP) MO, (CMTS) 1870 Census
Jones, William J.: (B) 1840, (CO) Pulaski, (A) 20, (BP) TN, (CMTS) 1860 Census
Jones, William J.: (B) 1853, (CO) Pulaski, (A) 7, (BP) MO, (CMTS) 1860 Census
Jones, William R.: (B) 1835, (CO) Stone, (A) 15, (BP) MO, (CMTS) 1870 Census
Jordan, Lloyd: (B) May 27, 1921, (D) Apr. 10, 1999, (CO) Barry, (RES) Cassville, (BP) Cherokee, KS, (C) St. George Cemetery, next to Lake Michigan, MI, (F) Bruch Funeral Home, Kenosha, WI
Jordan, Martin: (B) 1840, (CO) Pulaski, (A) 20, (BP) MO, (CMTS) 1860 Census
Jourdan, Daniel: (B) 1823, (CO) Pulaski, (A) 37, (BP) PA, (CMTS) 1860 Census
Jourdan, Isabella: (B) 1851, (CO) Pulaski, (A) 9, (BP) MO, (CMTS) 1860 Census
Jourdan, Nancy: (B) 1830, (CO) Pulaski, (A) 30, (BP) KY, (CMTS) 1860 Census
Joyce, Sarah: (B) 1864, (D) 1939, (CO) St. Louis, (C) Calvary Cemetery
Juddy, Jane: (B) 1834, (CO) Stone, (A) 16, (BP) AR, (CMTS) 1870 Census
Judkins, John: (B) 1843, (CO) Pulaski, (A) 17, (BP) MO, (CMTS) 1860 Census
Kadled, Anton: (B) May 26, 1831, (D) Mar. --, 1878, (CO) Jefferson, (C) Old St. John's Catholic Cemetery
Kaemmerer, John: (D) Dec., 1904, (CO) St. Louis, (C) Calvary Cemetery
Kaemmerer, Pauline: (D) Jul., 1985, (CO) St. Louis, (C) Calvary Cemetery
Kaemmerer, Theresa: (D) Sep., 1955, (CO) St. Louis, (C) Calvary Cemetery
Kallenbach, Mary Ann: (B) Oct. 11, 1855, (D) Jan. 16, 1889, (CO) Cole,
Kanatags, Calvin: (B) 1832, (CO) Pulaski, (A) 28, (BP) TN, (CMTS) 1860 Census
Kanatags, Rebecca: (B) 1834, (CO) Pulaski, (A) 26, (BP) MO, (CMTS) 1860 Census
Kaune, Antoinette: (B) 1860, (D) 1934, (CO) St. Louis, (C) Calvary Cemetery
Kaune, Cecelia E.: (B) 1871, (D) 1925, (CO) St. Louis, (C) Calvary

Cemetery
Kaune, Frank: (B) 1857, (D) 1916, (CO) St. Louis, (C) Calvary Cemetery
Kaune, Henry: (B) 1820, (D) 1878, (CO) St. Louis, (C) Calvary Cemetery
Kaune, Henry F.: (B) 1854, (D) 1925, (CO) St. Louis, (C) Calvary Cemetery
Kaune, Mary: (B) 1824, (D) 1899, (CO) St. Louis, (C) Calvary Cemetery
Kavanaugh, Phil J.: (B) 1876, (D) 1951, (CO) St. Louis, (C) Calvary Cemetery
Keane, Catherine: (D) 1950, (CO) St. Louis, (C) Calvary Cemetery
Keane, Mary: (B) 1842, (D) 1918, (CO) St. Louis, (C) Calvary Cemetery
Keane, Peter J.: (B) 1880, (D) 1890, (CO) St. Louis, (C) Calvary Cemetery
Keane, William: (B) 1842, (D) 1913, (CO) St. Louis, (C) Calvary Cemetery
Kearney, Daniel: (B) 1900, (D) 1957, (CO) St. Louis, (C) Calvary Cemetery
Kearney, Maric M.: (B) 1903, (D) 1995, (CO) St. Louis, (C) Calvary Cemetery
Kearns, Jerry Allen: (B) Jul. 8, 1944, (CO) Clark, (PRTS) Virgil Alonzo and Catherine Minnie Kearns, (SPOUSE) Diane C. Kearns, (MIL) U.S. Airforce, Greenland, 1965-1968.
Keech, Betty: (B) 1846, (CO) Stone, (A) 24, (BP) AR, (CMTS) 1870 Census
Keech, John M.: (B) 1845, (CO) Stone, (A) 25, (BP) AR, (CMTS) 1870 Census
Keenan, John: (D) Jan. 8, 1883, (CO) St. Louis, (C) Calvary Cemetery, (A) 41
Keeton, IvanC.: (B) Dec. 6, 1903, (D) Mar. 25, 1904, (CO) Henry, (C) Knights of Pythias Cemetery, Deepwater, MO
Keiflein, Edward J.: (B) 1882, (D) 1958, (CO) St. Louis, (C) Calvary Cemetery
Keiflein, Mary A.: (B) 1883, (D) 1977, (CO) St. Louis, (C) Calvary Cemetery
Keller, David Myron: (B) Nov. 11, 1958, (CO) Linn,
Keller, Samuel: (B) 1827, (D) 1870, (CO) Adair, (A) 43, (CMTS) 1870 Mortality Schedule
Kelley, Decater: (B) 1855, (CO) Pulaski, (A) 5, (BP) TN, (CMTS) 1860 Census
Kelley, Frances: (B) 1854, (CO) Pulaski, (A) 6, (BP) TN, (CMTS) 1860 Census
Kelley, John: (B) 1838, (CO) Pulaski, (A) 22, (BP) PA, (CMTS) 1860 Census
Kelley, John: (B) 1851, (CO) Pulaski, (A) 9, (BP) TN, (CMTS)

1860 Census
Kelley, Levi: (B) 1842, (CO) Pulaski, (A) 18, (BP) TN, (CMTS) 1860 Census
Kelley, Lewis: (B) 1844, (CO) Pulaski, (A) 16, (BP) TN, (CMTS) 1860 Census
Kelley, Sarah: (B) 1821, (CO) Pulaski, (A) 39, (BP) TN, (CMTS) 1860 Census
Kelley, William: (B) 1840, (CO) Pulaski, (A) 20, (BP) TN, (CMTS) 1860 Census
Kelly, Bridget: (B) 1854, (CO) Pulaski, (A) 6, (BP) KY, (CMTS) 1860 Census
Kelly, Bridget J.: (D) Jan. 10, 1883, (CO) St. Louis, (C) Calvary Cemetery
Kelly, James W.: (D) Oct. 30, 1906, (CO) St. Louis, (C) Calvary Cemetery, (A) 34
Kelly, Julia: (B) 1852, (CO) Pulaski, (A) 8, (BP) KY, (CMTS) 1860 Census
Kelly, Marie M.: (B) 1917, (D) 1995, (CO) St. Louis, (C) Calvary Cemetery
Kelly, Mary: (B) 1820, (CO) Pulaski, (A) 40, (BP) Ireland, (CMTS) 1860 Census
Kelly, Michael: (B) 1843, (CO) Pulaski, (A) 17, (BP) Ireland, (CMTS) 1860 Census
Kelly, Nicklas: (B) 1844, (CO) Pulaski, (A) 16, (BP) Ireland, (CMTS) 1860 Census
Kelly, Sadie: (B) 1848, (CO) Pulaski, (A) 12, (BP) Ireland, (CMTS) 1860 Census
Kendrick, John T.: (B) 1832, (CO) Pulaski, (A) 28, (BP) KY, (CMTS) 1860 Census
Kendrick, Nancy J.: (B) 1835, (CO) Pulaski, (A) 25, (BP) KY, (CMTS) 1860 Census
Kennedy, Andrew: (D) May 13, 1941, (CO) St. Louis, (C) Calvary Cemetery
Kennedy, David: (D) Aug. 28, 1867, (CO) Audrain, (C) Old Village Cemetery, (A) 62Y. 1M
Kennedy, David R.: (B) 1834, (CO) Pulaski, (A) 26, (BP) MS, (CMTS) 1860 Census
Kennedy, Elizabeth: (B) 1833, (CO) Pulaski, (A) 27, (BP) KY, (CMTS) 1860 Census
Kennedy, Helen C.: (D) Dec. 24, 1996, (CO) St. Louis, (C) Calvary Cemetery
Kennedy, Mary A.: (B) 1857, (D) 1928, (CO) St. Louis, (C) Calvary Cemetery
Kennedy, Rebecca: (B) 1839, (CO) Pulaski, (A) 21, (BP) VA, (CMTS)

1860 Census
Kenny, Jr., Daniel R.: (B) 1924, (D) 1944, (CO) St. Louis, (C) Calvary Cemetery
Kenny, Sr., Daniel R.: (B) 1898, (D) 1946, (CO) St. Louis, (C) Calvary Cemetery
Kenny, Stella M.: (B) 1890, (D) 1940, (CO) St. Louis, (C) Calvary Cemetery
Kerber, Michael: (D) Jul. 3, 1909, (CO) St. Louis, (C) Calvary Cemetery, (A) 78
Kercher, George Anton: (B) 1902, (D) 1990, (CO) St. Louis, (C) Calvary Cemetery
Kercher, Olive Merry: (B) 1904, (CO) St. Louis, (C) Calvary Cemetery
Kerney, Hannah: (B) 1818, (CO) Pulaski, (A) 42, (BP) Ireland, (CMTS) 1860 Census
Kerr, L. Smith: (B) 1845, (CO) Stone, (A) 25, (BP) TN, (CMTS) 1870 Census
Kerr, Sarah F: (B) 1850, (CO) Stone, (A) 20, (BP) MO, (CMTS) 1870 Census
Kessler, Adeline: (B) 1870, (D) 1933, (CO) St. Louis, (C) Calvary Cemetery
Kessler, Antoinette K.: (B) 1906, (D) 1986, (CO) St. Louis, (C) Calvary Cemetery
Kessler, Joseph: (B) 1872, (D) 1938, (CO) St. Louis, (C) Calvary Cemetery
Kessler, Julius: (B) 1860, (D) 1928, (CO) St. Louis, (C) Calvary Cemetery
Keth, Daniel: (B) 1835, (CO) Pulaski, (A) 25, (BP) KY, (CMTS) 1860 Census
Keth, Susan: (B) 1837, (CO) Pulaski, (A) 23, (BP) KY, (CMTS) 1860 Census
Kettner, Marion: (B) 1846, (CO) Stone, (A) 24, (BP) MO, (CMTS) 1870 Census
Kettner, Mary A.: (B) 1847, (CO) Stone, (A) 23, (BP) KY, (CMTS) 1870 Census
Kilcullen, Bernard J.: (D) May 8, 1967, (CO) St. Louis, (C) Calvary Cemetery
Killer, Henry: (B) 1835, (CO) Pulaski, (A) 25, (BP) Baden, (CMTS) 1860 Census
Killman, Grandmother: (B) 1839, (D) 1917, (CO) Henry, (C) Knights of Pythias Cemetery, Deepwater, MO
Killman, Harold C.: (B) Feb. 1, 1910, (D) Mar. 28, 1910, (CO) Henry, (C) Knights of Pythias Cemetery, Deepwater, MO
Kimball, Elizabeth: (B) 1834, (CO) Pulaski, (A) 26, (BP) MO, (CMTS) 1860 Census

Kimball, William: (B) 1838, (CO) Pulaski, (A) 22, (BP) MO, (CMTS) 1860 Census
Kimberlin, David: (B) 1821, (CO) Stone, (A) 49, (BP) MO, (CMTS) 1870 Census
Kimberlin, Elisabeth: (B) 1844, (CO) Stone, (A) 26, (BP) AR, (CMTS) 1870 Census
Kimberlin, James: (B) 1846, (CO) Stone, (A) 24, (BP) MO, (CMTS) 1870 Census
Kimberlin, John: (B) 1848, (CO) Stone, (A) 2, (BP) MO, (CMTS) 1870 Census
Kimberlin, Margarett: (B) 1847, (CO) Stone, (A) 23, (BP) TN, (CMTS) 1870 Census
Kimberlin, Rebecca: (B) 1820, (CO) Stone, (A) 50, (BP) IL, (CMTS) 1870 Census
Kimberlin, William W.: (B) 1822, (CO) Stone, (A) 28, (BP) MO, (CMTS) 1870 Census
Kimberling, Farney: (B) 1833, (CO) Stone, (A) 17, (BP) MO, (CMTS) 1870 Census
Kimberling, Nancy: (B) 1847, (CO) Stone, (A) 3, (BP) MO, (CMTS) 1870 Census
Kimberling, Perry: (B) 1816, (CO) Stone, (A) 34, (BP) KS, (CMTS) 1870 Census
Kimberling, Peter: (B) 1825, (CO) Stone, (A) 25, (BP) MO, (CMTS) 1870 Census
Kimberling, Rachel: (B) 1821, (CO) Stone, (A) 29, (BP) MO, (CMTS) 1870 Census
Kimberling, Rebecca J.: (B) 1840, (CO) Stone, (A) 10, (BP) MO, (CMTS) 1870 Census
Kimberling, Sarah: (B) 1825, (CO) Stone, (A) 25, (BP) IL, (CMTS) 1870 Census
Kindall, Eliza Jane: (B) 1827, (CO) Stone, (A) 23, (BP) IN, (CMTS) 1870 Census
Kindall, James: (B) 1833, (CO) Stone, (A) 17, (BP) IO, (CMTS) 1870 Census
Kindall, John W.: (B) 1826, (CO) Stone, (A) 24, (BP) MO, (CMTS) 1870 Census
Kindall, Mary: (B) 1826, (CO) Stone, (A) 24, (BP) KY, (CMTS) 1870 Census
Kindall, May Jane: (B) 1847, (CO) Stone, (A) 3, (BP) MO, (CMTS) 1870 Census
Kindall, William R.: (B) 1844, (CO) Stone, (A) 6, (BP) MO, (CMTS) 1870 Census
Kinder, Alice: (B) Jun. 18, 1908, (D) Feb. 1977, (CO), (DP)

Whitewater, MO
Kinder, Alma: (B) Oct. 5, 1903, (D) Jan. 1983, (CO) Cape Girardeau,
Kindred, Zeck: (B) 1848, (D) 1913, (CO) Cedar, (C) Brashear Cemetery
King, Alphred: (B) 1847, (CO) Pulaski, (A) 13, (BP) TN, (CMTS) 1860 Census
King, Catharine: (B) 1839, (CO) Pulaski, (A) 21, (BP) MO, (CMTS) 1860 Census
King, Cyrus L.: (B) 1855, (CO) Stone, (A) 15, (BP) MO, (CMTS) 1870 Census
King, Desdemonia: (B) Feb. 17, 1826, (D) Dec. 18, 1891, (CO) Andrew, (C) Oak Ridge Cemetery
King, Eva R.: (B) 1832, (CO) Pulaski, (A) 28, (BP) TN, (CMTS) 1860 Census
King, Francis M.: (B) 1835, (CO) Pulaski, (A) 25, (BP) MO, (CMTS) 1860 Census
King, George: (B) 1840, (CO) Pulaski, (A) 20, (BP) MO, (CMTS) 1860 Census
King, Hiram: (D) February 2, 1862, (CO) New Madrid, (CMTS) From Bremer, IA
King, Hiram W.: (B) 1834, (CO) Pulaski, (A) 26, (BP) MO, (CMTS) 1860 Census
King, James W.: (B) 1850, (CO) Pulaski, (A) 10, (BP) TN, (CMTS) 1860 Census
King, Jinsey: (B) 1848, (CO) Pulaski, (A) 12, (BP) TN, (CMTS) 1860 Census
King, John: (B) 1849, (CO) Stone, (A) 21, (BP) MO, (CMTS) 1870 Census
King, John H.: (B) 1836, (CO) Pulaski, (A) 24, (BP) MO, (CMTS) 1860 Census
King, Johnson: (D) Ju. 12, 1867, (CO) Andrew, (C) Oak Ridge Cemetery, (A) 70Y 4M 5D
King, Joseph M.: (B) 1837, (CO) Stone, (A) 33, (BP) OH, (CMTS) 1870 Census
King, Lutitia: (B) 1818, (CO) Pulaski, (A) 42, (BP) TN, (CMTS) 1860 Census
King, Lutitia O.: (B) 1850, (CO) Pulaski, (A) 10, (BP) TN, (CMTS) 1860 Census
King, Malinda: (B) 1827, (CO) Stone, (A) 43, (BP) OH, (CMTS) 1870 Census
King, Margaret: (B) 1852, (CO) Pulaski, (A) 8, (BP) TN, (CMTS) 1860 Census
King, Martha C: (B) 1844, (CO) Stone, (A) 26, (BP) MO, (CMTS) 1870 Census

King, Martin: (B) 1815, (CO) Pulaski, (A) 45, (BP) KY, (CMTS) 1860 Census
King, Mary: (D) Feb. 2, 1877, (CO) Andrew, (C) Oak Ridge Cemetery, (A) 73Y 11M 19D
King, Mary F.: (B) 1853, (CO) Pulaski, (A) 7, (BP) TN, (CMTS) 1860 Census
King, Newton: (B) 1846, (CO) Pulaski, (A) 14, (BP) KY, (CMTS) 1860 Census
King, Phebe: (B) 1848, (CO) Pulaski, (A) 12, (BP) TN, (CMTS) 1860 Census
King, Rebecca: (B) 1820, (CO) Pulaski, (A) 40, (BP) VA, (CMTS) 1860 Census
King, Vanburen: (B) 1841, (CO) Pulaski, (A) 19, (BP) TN, (CMTS) 1860 Census
King, William W.: (B) 1853, (CO) Stone, (A) 17, (BP) MO, (CMTS) 1870 Census
King, William W.: (B) 1855, (CO) Pulaski, (A) 5, (BP) TN, (CMTS) 1860 Census
Kirby, James J.: (D) Nov. 22, 1906, (CO) St. Louis, (C) Calvary Cemetery
Kirk, Caroline: (B) 1840, (CO) Stone, (A) 30, (BP) TN, (CMTS) 1870 Census
Kirk, James W.: (B) 1840, (CO) Stone, (A) 30, (BP) AL, (CMTS) 1870 Census
Klaus, Bernard: (D) Mar. 13,. 1939, (CO) St. Louis, (C) Calvary Cemetery
Klaus, Caroline: (D) Jan. 26, 1941, (CO) St. Louis, (C) Calvary Cemetery
Klaus, Dora F.: (D) Jan. 12, 1953, (CO) St. Louis, (C) Calvary Cemetery
Klaus, William: (D) Apr. 13, 1933, (CO) St. Louis, (C) Calvary Cemetery
Kleekamp, John C.: (B) Nov. 7, 1816, (D) Mar. 14, 1887, (CO) St. Louis, (C) Calvary Cemetery
Kleekamp, Mary E.: (B) Mar. 3, 1814, (D) Jan. 12, 1884, (CO) St. Louis, (C) Calvary Cemetery
Kleekamp, Thomas: (B) 1891, (D) 1910, (CO) St. Louis, (C) Calvary Cemetery
Kleepkamp, Joseph: (B) 1860, (D) 1907, (CO) St. Louis, (C) Calvary Cemetery
Kleine, Anna: (B) 1875, (D) 1902, (CO) St. Louis, (C) Calvary Cemetery
Kleine, Joseph: (B) 1848, (D) 1878, (CO) St. Louis, (C) Calvary Cemetery
Kleine, Mary: (B) 1849, (D) 1931, (CO) St. Louis, (C) Calvary Cemetery
Kline, George R.: (B) Oct. 5, 1849, (D) Oct. 26, 1903, (CO) St. Louis, (C) Calvary Cemetery
Klum, Jacob: (B) 1832, (CO) Pulaski, (A) 28, (BP) Hessie, (CMTS)

1860 Census
Knapp, Francis: (B) 1849, (CO) Pulaski, (A) 11, (BP) MO, (CMTS) 1860 Census
Knapp, Joshua T.: (B) 1855, (CO) Pulaski, (A) 5, (BP) MO, (CMTS) 1860 Census
Knapp, Margaret: (B) 1836, (CO) Pulaski, (A) 24, (BP) MO, (CMTS) 1860 Census
Knapp, Sarah J.: (B) 1856, (CO) Pulaski, (A) 4, (BP) MO, (CMTS) 1860 Census
Knecht, Louis R.: (B) Aug. 24, 1920, (CO) St. Louis, (PRTS) Louis B. and Charlotte Knecht, (SPOUSE) Marjorie Knecht, (MIL) Capt., U. S. Army Signal Corps and USAF.
Knox, George: (B) 1844, (CO) Pulaski, (A) 16, (BP) TN, (CMTS) 1860 Census
Knox, George W.: (B) 1847, (CO) Pulaski, (A) 13, (BP) MO, (CMTS) 1860 Census
Knox, Mary W.: (B) 1844, (CO) Pulaski, (A) 16, (BP) TN, (CMTS) 1860 Census
Knox, William: (B) 1794, (CO) Pulaski, (A) 66, (BP) SC, (CMTS) 1860 Census
Koehler, Casper: (B) 1833, (D) 1896, (CO) Audrain, (C) St. Joseph Catholic Cemetery
Kosark, Albert J.: (B) Sep. 5, 1833, (D) Sep. 6, 1919, (CO) Gasconade, (DP) Owensville
Kosark, Chatherine: (D) Nov. 25, 1912, (CO) St. Louis,
Kranz, Catherine: (D) 1951, (CO) St. Louis, (C) Calvary Cemetery
Kranz, Sr., Charles L.: (B) 1865, (D) 1942, (CO) St. Louis, (C) Calvary Cemetery
Kranz, Dorothy: (D) 1922, (CO) St. Louis, (C) Calvary Cemetery
Kranz, George: (D) 1941, (CO) St. Louis, (C) Calvary Cemetery
Kranz, George: (D) 1917, (CO) St. Louis, (C) Calvary Cemetery
Kranz, Jr., Charles L.: (B) May 14, 1891, (D) May 23, 1959, (CO) St. Louis, (C) Calvary Cemetery
Kraus, Charlotte: (B) 1831, (CO) Pulaski, (A) 29, (BP) Prussia, (CMTS) 1860 Census
Kraus, Jn.: (B) 1829, (CO) Pulaski, (A) 31, (BP) Baden, (CMTS) 1860 Census
Kreft, Matilda: (B) 1868, (D) 1953, (CO) St. Louis, (C) Calvary Cemetery
Krekeler, Rose: (D) Jul. 2, 1945, (CO) St. Louis, (C) Calvary Cemetery
Krekwood, Lutitia: (B) 1850, (CO) Pulaski, (A) 10, (BP) MO, (CMTS) 1860 Census
Krekwood, Phebe A.: (B) 1847, (CO) Pulaski, (A) 13, (BP) MO, (CMTS) 1860 Census

Krekwood, Robert: (B) 1849, (CO) Pulaski, (A) 11, (BP) MO, (CMTS) 1860 Census
Kricke, John: (B) 1834, (CO) Pulaski, (A) 26, (BP) Prussia, (CMTS) 1860 Census
Krimmens, John: (B) 1832, (CO) Pulaski, (A) 28, (BP) Ireland, (CMTS) 1860 Census
Kuchta, John W.: (B) Jul. 11, 1929, (D) May, 1991, (CO) Henry, (C) Knights of Pythias Cemetery, Deepwater, MO
Lackay, Prudence C.: (D) Apr. 7, 1877, (CO) St. Louis, (C) Calvary Cemetery, (A) 71
Lackey, Elisa: (B) 1838, (CO) Pulaski, (A) 22, (BP) MO, (CMTS) 1860 Census
Lackey, Henry: (B) 1839, (CO) Pulaski, (A) 21, (BP) MO, (CMTS) 1860 Census
Lackey, Phebe: (B) 1838, (CO) Pulaski, (A) 22, (BP) MO, (CMTS) 1860 Census
Lacy, Harriett: (B) 1848, (CO) Stone, (A) 22, (BP) AR, (CMTS) 1870 Census
Lacy, John: (B) 1845, (D) 1870, (CO) Cedar, (C) Brashear Cemetery
Laguay, Enerdee: (B) 1853, (CO) Pulaski, (A) 7, (BP) MO, (CMTS) 1860 Census
Laguay, Joseph: (B) 1849, (CO) Pulaski, (A) 11, (BP) MO, (CMTS) 1860 Census
Laguay, Martha: (B) 1856, (CO) Pulaski, (A) 4, (BP) MO, (CMTS) 1860 Census
Laguay, Nancy: (B) 1815, (CO) Pulaski, (A) 45, (BP) MO, (CMTS) 1860 Census
Laguay, Nichodemus: (B) 1845, (CO) Pulaski, (A) 15, (BP) MO, (CMTS) 1860 Census
Laguay, Silas: (B) 1843, (CO) Pulaski, (A) 17, (BP) MO, (CMTS) 1860 Census
Lamey, Alfred: (B) 1838, (CO) Pulaski, (A) 22, (BP) IL, (CMTS) 1860 Census
LaMore, France E.: (B) 1929, (D) 1985, (CO) St. Louis, (C) Calvary Cemetery
Lane, Amanda: (B) 1841, (CO) Stone, (A) 29, (BP) AR, (CMTS) 1870 Census
Lane, Chals M.: (B) 1841, (CO) Stone, (A) 29, (BP) MO, (CMTS) 1870 Census
Lane, Custon G.: (B) 1849, (CO) Pulaski, (A) 11, (BP) MO, (CMTS) 1860 Census
Lane, Elizabeth: (B) 1835, (CO) Pulaski, (A) 25, (BP) IN, (CMTS) 1860 Census

Lane, Elizabeth M.: (B) 1832, (CO) Stone, (A) 38, (BP) MO, (CMTS) 1870 Census
Lane, Francis M.: (B) 1845, (CO) Pulaski, (A) 15, (BP) MO, (CMTS) 1860 Census
Lane, Jesse J.: (B) 1832, (CO) Pulaski, (A) 28, (BP) MO, (CMTS) 1860 Census
Lane, John J.: (B) 1846, (D) 1928, (CO) Henry, (C) Knights of Pythias Cemetery, Deepwater, MO
Lane, Joseph: (B) Jul. 23, 1888, (D) Apr. 21, 1961, (CO) Henry, (C) Knights of Pythias Cemetery, Deepwater, MO
Lane, Louisa: (B) 1848, (CO) Pulaski, (A) 12, (BP) MO, (CMTS) 1860 Census
Lane, Miles: (B) Aug. 5, 1836, (D) Aug. 12, 1910, (CO) Henry, (C) Knights of Pythias Cemetery, Deepwater, MO
Lane, Nancy J.: (B) 1855, (CO) Pulaski, (A) 5, (BP) MO, (CMTS) 1860 Census
Lane, Sophia A.: (B) 1854, (D) 1912, (CO) Henry, (C) Knights of Pythias Cemetery, Deepwater, MO
Lane, Zechariah T.: (B) 1846, (CO) Pulaski, (A) 14, (BP) MO, (CMTS) 1860 Census
Laney, Malvina: (B) 1846, (CO) Pulaski, (A) 14, (BP) KY, (CMTS) 1860 Census
Langa, John: (B) 1884, (D) 1938, (CO) St. Louis, (C) Calvary Cemetery
Langa, Rose: (B) 1885, (D) 1964, (CO) St. Louis, (C) Calvary Cemetery
Langford, Edward: (B) Mar. 1, 1838, (CO) Washington, (PRTS) Philip Langford and Francis Smith, negroes, (MD) Jul. 31, 1865, (CMTS) Former Slaves
Langford, Francis Maria: (B) Feb. 2, 1863, (CO) Washington, (PRTS) Anderson Langford and Nancy Johnson, negroes, (MD) Jul. 31, 1865, (CMTS) Former Slaves.
Langford, Hilliard: (B) Mar. 15, 1839, (CO) Washington, (PRTS) Philip Langford and Francis Smith, negroes, (MD) Jul. 31, 1865, (CMTS) Former Slaves
Langford, Philip: (B) Aug. 12, 1860, (CO) Washington, (PRTS) Anderson Langford and Nancy Johnson, negroes, (MD) Jul. 31, 1865, (CMTS) Former Slaves.
Langford, Sarah Ellano: (B) Feb. 2, 1863, (CO) Washington, (PRTS) Anderson Langford and Nancy Johnson, negroes, (MD) Jul. 31, 1865, (CMTS) Former Slaves.
Langley, Granville: (B) 1849, (CO) Stone, (A) 21, (BP) MO, (CMTS) 1870 Census
Langley, Louisa: (B) 1844, (CO) Stone, (A) 26, (BP) MO, (CMTS) 1870 Census

Langley, Nancy E.: (B) 1850, (CO) Stone, (A) 20, (BP) MO, (CMTS) 1870 Census
Langley, Robert B.: (B) 1844, (CO) Stone, (A) 26, (BP) MO, (CMTS) 1870 Census
Langston, Andrew J.: (B) 1834, (CO) Stone, (A) 16, (BP) MO, (CMTS) 1870 Census
Langston, James W.: (B) 1841, (CO) Stone, (A) 9, (BP) MO, (CMTS) 1870 Census
Langston, Lavina A.: (B) 1825, (CO) Stone, (A) 25, (BP) MO, (CMTS) 1870 Census
Langston, William H.: (B) 1831, (CO) Stone, (A) 19, (BP) MO, (CMTS) 1870 Census
Lansdow, Vera: (B) Apr. 3, 1923, (D) Apr. 15, 1999, (CO) Barry, (DP) Cassville, MO, (C) Williams Cemetery, Berryville, AR, (BP) Neodesha, KS.
Lanul, Denacia: (B) 1828, (CO) Pulaski, (A) 32, (BP) MO, (CMTS) 1860 Census
Lanul, Emaline: (B) 1850, (CO) Pulaski, (A) 10, (BP) MO, (CMTS) 1860 Census
Lanul, Lilly: (B) 1852, (CO) Pulaski, (A) 8, (BP) MO, (CMTS) 1860 Census
Lanul, Mary A.: (B) 1847, (CO) Pulaski, (A) 13, (BP) MO, (CMTS) 1860 Census
Lanul, Nancy: (B) 1848, (CO) Pulaski, (A) 12, (BP) MO, (CMTS) 1860 Census
LaPresto, Frank: (B) 1856, (D) 1939, (CO) St. Louis, (C) Calvary Cemetery
LaPresto, Josephine: (B) 1898, (D) 1982, (CO) St. Louis, (C) Calvary Cemetery
LaPresto, Louis: (B) 1878, (D) 1958, (CO) St. Louis, (C) Calvary Cemetery
LaPresto, Louis: (B) 1895, (D) 1965, (CO) St. Louis, (C) Calvary Cemetery
LaPresto, Margherita: (B) 1882, (D) 1961, (CO) St. Louis, (C) Calvary Cemetery
LaPresto, Rosie: (B) 1860, (D) 1942, (CO) St. Louis, (C) Calvary Cemetery
Largin, Elizabeth: (B) 1844, (CO) Pulaski, (A) 16, (BP) NC, (CMTS) 1860 Census
Largin, Jane: (B) 1849, (CO) Pulaski, (A) 11, (BP) NC, (CMTS) 1860 Census
Largin, Orra: (B) 1846, (CO) Pulaski, (A) 14, (BP) NC, (CMTS) 1860 Census

Largin, Preston: (B) 1847, (CO) Pulaski, (A) 13, (BP) NC, (CMTS) 1860 Census
Largin, William: (B) 1855, (CO) Pulaski, (A) 5, (BP) MO, (CMTS) 1860 Census
LaRocca, Vincenza: (B) Sep. 12, 1884, (D) Mar. 10, 1972, (CO) St. Louis, (C) Calvary Cemetery
Laster, Elizabeth R.: (B) 1837, (CO) Pulaski, (A) 23, (BP) SC, (CMTS) 1860 Census
Laster, Robert: (B) 1836, (CO) Pulaski, (A) 24, (BP) SC, (CMTS) 1860 Census
Laughlin, Catherine: (B) 1832, (CO) Pulaski, (A) 28, (BP) IN, (CMTS) 1860 Census
Laughlin, Charles N.: (B) 1852, (CO) Pulaski, (A) 8, (BP) MO, (CMTS) 1860 Census
Laughlin, John J.: (B) 1820, (CO) Pulaski, (A) 40, (BP) MO, (CMTS) 1860 Census
Laughlin, Margaret L.: (B) 1850, (CO) Pulaski, (A) 10, (BP) MO, (CMTS) 1860 Census
Laughlin, Patrick: (D) Mar. 24, 1906, (CO) St. Louis, (C) Calvary Cemetery, (A) 73
Laughlin, Samuel H. G.: (B) 1854, (CO) Pulaski, (A) 6, (BP) MO, (CMTS) 1860 Census
Law, Robert: (B) 1839, (CO) Pulaski, (A) 21, (BP) IN, (CMTS) 1860 Census
Lawler, William F.: (D) Jan. 4, 1883, (CO) St. Louis, (C) Calvary Cemetery, (A) 27
Lawrence, Bridget: (D) 11, 18, 1905, (CO) St. Louis, (C) Calvary Cemetery, (A) 66
Lawrence, Patrick: (D) Oct. 15, 1905, (CO) St. Louis, (C) Calvary Cemetery, (A) 38
Laws, Elizabeth J.: (B) 1845, (CO) Stone, (A) 5, (BP) IL, (CMTS) 1870 Census
Laws, Joseph W.: (B) 1843, (CO) Stone, (A) 7, (BP) IL, (CMTS) 1870 Census
Laws, Perry: (B) 1820, (CO) Stone, (A) 30, (BP) IL, (CMTS) 1870 Census
Laws, Rosetta C.: (B) 1848, (CO) Stone, (A) 2, (BP) IL, (CMTS) 1870 Census
Laws, Sarah: (B) 1820, (CO) Stone, (A) 30, (BP) TN, (CMTS) 1870 Census
Lawson, Eda: (B) 1829, (CO) Pulaski, (A) 31, (BP) TN, (CMTS) 1860 Census
Lawson, Ener J.: (B) 1856, (CO) Pulaski, (A) 4, (BP) MO, (CMTS)

1860 Census
Lawson, John L.: (B) 1849, (CO) Pulaski, (A) 11, (BP) MO, (CMTS) 1860 Census
Lawson, Julia A.: (B) 1828, (CO) Pulaski, (A) 32, (BP) MO, (CMTS) 1860 Census
Lawson, William: (B) 1854, (CO) Pulaski, (A) 6, (BP) MO, (CMTS) 1860 Census
Leach, Elizabeth: (B) 1849, (CO) Pulaski, (A) 11, (BP) IL, (CMTS) 1860 Census
Leach, James: (B) 1853, (CO) Pulaski, (A) 7, (BP) MO, (CMTS) 1860 Census
Leach, Sarah Elizabeth: (B) Jun. 30, 1853, (D) Dec. 15,1934, (CO) MO, Carls Junction, MO.
Leach, William: (B) 1851, (CO) Pulaski, (A) 9, (BP) MO, (CMTS) 1860 Census
Leadbetter, Amanda: (B) 1845, (CO) Stone, (A) 25, (BP) IL, (CMTS) 1870 Census
Leadbetter, Lewis: (B) 1836, (CO) Stone, (A) 34, (BP) TN, (CMTS) 1870 Census
Leahy, Delia: (B) 1859, (D) 1951, (CO) St. Louis, (C) Calvary Cemetery
Leahy, Lawrence: (B) 1865, (D) 1929, (CO) St. Louis, (C) Calvary Cemetery
Leahy, Lester L.: (B) 1898, (D) 1948, (CO) St. Louis, (C) Calvary Cemetery
Leahy, Magverite W.: (B) 1894, (D) 1943, (CO) St. Louis, (C) Calvary Cemetery
Leahy, Veronica M.: (B) 1902, (D) 1964, (CO) St. Louis, (C) Calvary Cemetery
Leahy, Sr., Virgil P.: (B) 1896, (D) 1976, (CO) St. Louis, (C) Calvary Cemetery
LeBee, Frank A.: (B) 1866, (D) 1935, (CO) St. Louis, (C) Calvary Cemetery
LeBee, Theresa A.: (B) 1875, (D) 1967, (CO) St. Louis, (C) Calvary Cemetery
Leber, Julius: (B) 1874, (D) 1931, (CO) St. Louis, (C) Calvary Cemetery
Lecan, Joseph: (B) 1816, (CO) Pulaski, (A) 44, (BP) England, (CMTS) 1860 Census
LeDuc, Mimi Chauvin: (B) Mar. 3, 1845, (D) Nov. 19, 1895, (CO) St. Louis, (C) Calvary Cemetery
Lee, Candase: (B) 1842, (CO) Stone, (A) 28, (BP) IL, (CMTS) 1870 Census
Lee, Charlotta C.: (B) 1837, (CO) Stone, (A) 33, (BP) IL, (CMTS) 1870 Census

Lee, James W.: (B) 1854, (CO) Stone, (A) 16, (BP) MO, (CMTS) 1870 Census
Lee, Jane: (D) May 24, 1861, (CO) Audrain, (C) Old Village Cemetery, (A) 71 Y
Lee, Lawrence W.: (B) 1855, (D) 1911, (CO) Cedar, (C) Brashear Cemetery
Lee, Mary: (B) 1865, (D) 1945, (CO) St. Louis, (C) Calvary Cemetery
Lee, Mary Ellen: (B) Mar. 18,1829, (D) May 20, 1857, (CO) Audrain, (C) Old Village Cemetery
Lee, Michael: (B) 1869, (D) 1891, (CO) St. Louis, (C) Calvary Cemetery
Lee, Pattie H.: (B) Jun. 3, 1825, (D) Jan. 11, 1859, (CO) Audrain, (C) Old Village Cemetery
Lee, Phebe: (B) 1832, (CO) Stone, (A) 38, (BP) VA, (CMTS) 1870 Census
Lee, Richard E.: (B) Sep. 15, 1789, (D) Sep. 3, 1845, (CO) Audrain, (C) Old Village Cemetery
Leek, Amanda: (B) 1838, (CO) Pulaski, (A) 22, (BP) MO, (CMTS) 1860 Census
Leek, Cynthia: (B) 1856, (CO) Pulaski, (A) 4, (BP) MO, (CMTS) 1860 Census
Leek, Hannah: (B) 1845, (CO) Pulaski, (A) 15, (BP) MO, (CMTS) 1860 Census
Leek, Jane: (B) 1826, (CO) Pulaski, (A) 34, (BP) KY, (CMTS) 1860 Census
Leek, John: (B) 1820, (CO) Pulaski, (A) 40, (BP) TN, (CMTS) 1860 Census
Leek, John W.: (B) 1856, (CO) Pulaski, (A) 4, (BP) MO, (CMTS) 1860 Census
Leek, Martha J.: (B) 1853, (CO) Pulaski, (A) 7, (BP) MO, (CMTS) 1860 Census
Leek, Maryet: (B) 1847, (CO) Pulaski, (A) 13, (BP) MO, (CMTS) 1860 Census
Leek, Nancy: (B) 1851, (CO) Pulaski, (A) 9, (BP) MO, (CMTS) 1860 Census
Leek, Richard: (B) 1842, (CO) Pulaski, (A) 18, (BP) MO, (CMTS) 1860 Census
Leek, William: (B) 1837, (CO) Pulaski, (A) 23, (BP) MO, (CMTS) 1860 Census
Leek, William M.: (B) 1854, (CO) Pulaski, (A) 6, (BP) MO, (CMTS) 1860 Census
Legg, William: (B) Aug. 25, 1782, (D) Jul. 25, 1889, (CO) Lewis, (DP) Canton, (SPOUSE) Susanne Frans, (MIL) War of 1812
Lemon, Cynthia: (B) 1855, (CO) Pulaski, (A) 5, (BP) TX, (CMTS)

1860 Census
Lemon, Mary E.: (B) 1838, (CO) Pulaski, (A) 22, (BP) KY, (CMTS) 1860 Census
Lemon, Willis P.: (B) 1828, (CO) Pulaski, (A) 32, (BP) KY, (CMTS) 1860 Census
Lemons, Artamesa: (B) 1846, (CO) Pulaski, (A) 14, (BP) KY, (CMTS) 1860 Census
Lemons, Buck: (B) 1828, (CO) Pulaski, (A) 32, (BP) KY, (CMTS) 1860 Census
Lemons, Charles W.: (B) 1842, (CO) Pulaski, (A) 18, (BP) KY, (CMTS) 1860 Census
Lemons, Elizabeth: (B) 1838, (CO) Pulaski, (A) 22, (BP) MO, (CMTS) 1860 Census
Lemons, Elizabeth: (B) 1842, (CO) Pulaski, (A) 18, (BP) TN, (CMTS) 1860 Census
Lemons, George W.: (B) 1831, (CO) Pulaski, (A) 29, (BP) KY, (CMTS) 1860 Census
Lemons, Jacob: (B) 1854, (CO) Pulaski, (A) 6, (BP) KY, (CMTS) 1860 Census
Lemons, James: (B) 1835, (CO) Pulaski, (A) 25, (BP) KY, (CMTS) 1860 Census
Lemons, James F.: (B) 1839, (CO) Pulaski, (A) 21, (BP) KY, (CMTS) 1860 Census
Lemons, John: (B) 1832, (CO) Pulaski, (A) 28, (BP) KY, (CMTS) 1860 Census
Lemons, John W.: (B) 1840, (CO) Pulaski, (A) 20, (BP) KY, (CMTS) 1860 Census
Lemons, Melissa K.: (B) 1841, (CO) Pulaski, (A) 19, (BP) KY, (CMTS) 1860 Census
Lemons, Samantha: (B) 1843, (CO) Pulaski, (A) 17, (BP) MO, (CMTS) 1860 Census
Lemons, Sarah J.: (B) 1839, (CO) Pulaski, (A) 21, (BP) MO, (CMTS) 1860 Census
Lemons, Solomon C.: (B) 1850, (CO) Pulaski, (A) 10, (BP) KY, (CMTS) 1860 Census
Lemons, William H.: (B) 1838, (CO) Pulaski, (A) 22, (BP) KY, (CMTS) 1860 Census
Lemons, Winfield: (B) 1855, (CO) Pulaski, (A) 5, (BP) MO, (CMTS) 1860 Census
Lemons, Winfield S.: (B) 1848, (CO) Pulaski, (A) 12, (BP) KY, (CMTS) 1860 Census
Lemons, Woodford: (B) 1844, (CO) Pulaski, (A) 16, (BP) KY, (CMTS) 1860 Census

Lemons, Zachariah T.: (B) 1848, (CO) Pulaski, (A) 12, (BP) KY, (CMTS) 1860 Census
Lenigow, Alice V.: (B) 1847, (CO) Pulaski, (A) 13, (BP) MO, (CMTS) 1860 Census
Lenigow, Endora E.: (B) 1853, (CO) Pulaski, (A) 7, (BP) MO, (CMTS) 1860 Census
Lenigow, G.: (B) 1820, (CO) Pulaski, (A) 40, (BP) VA, (CMTS) 1860 Census
Lenigow, Jr., G.: (B) 1851, (CO) Pulaski, (A) 9, (BP) AR, (CMTS) 1860 Census
Lenigow, Laura Belle: (B) 1843, (CO) Pulaski, (A) 17, (BP) KY, (CMTS) 1860 Census
Lenigow, Mary J.: (B) 1820, (CO) Pulaski, (A) 40, (BP) VA, (CMTS) 1860 Census
Lenigow, Mary J.: (B) 1849, (CO) Pulaski, (A) 11, (BP) MO, (CMTS) 1860 Census
Lenigow, Ninnie: (B) 1856, (CO) Pulaski, (A) 4, (BP) MO, (CMTS) 1860 Census
Lenigow, Susan M.: (B) 1845, (CO) Pulaski, (A) 15, (BP) MO, (CMTS) 1860 Census
Lenigow, William K.: (B) 1841, (CO) Pulaski, (A) 19, (BP) KY, (CMTS) 1860 Census
Leonard, James H.: (B) Aug. 28, 1896, (D) Apr. 8, 1972, (CO) Henry, (C) Knights of Pythias Cemetery, Deepwater, MO
Leonard, John W.: (B) 1848, (CO) Stone, (A) 2, (BP) MO, (CMTS) 1870 Census
Leonard, Terry: (B) 1863, (D) 1968, (CO) Henry, (C) Knights of Pythias Cemetery, Deepwater, MO
Lepscomb, Amanda: (B) 1854, (CO) Pulaski, (A) 6, (BP) MO, (CMTS) 1860 Census
Lepscomb, Harriet: (B) 1858, (CO) Pulaski, (A) 2, (BP) MO, (CMTS) 1860 Census
Lepscomb, Julia A.: (B) 1856, (CO) Pulaski, (A) 4, (BP) MO, (CMTS) 1860 Census
Lepscomb, Nancy: (B) 1846, (CO) Pulaski, (A) 14, (BP) MO, (CMTS) 1860 Census
Lepscomb, Polly: (B) 1817, (CO) Pulaski, (A) 43, (BP) TN, (CMTS) 1860 Census
Lepscomb, Sally: (B) 1843, (CO) Pulaski, (A) 17, (BP) MO, (CMTS) 1860 Census
Lepscomb, Susannah: (B) 1850, (CO) Pulaski, (A) 10, (BP) MO, (CMTS) 1860 Census
Leslie, Eliza: (B) Mar. 1, 1880, (D) Jul. 3, 1948, (CO) Oregon, (C) Falling

Springs Cemetery
Leslie, Ervin Eugene: (B) 1930, (D) 1931, (CO) Oregon, (C) Falling Springs Cemetery
Leslie, John P.: (B) 1907, (D) 1955, (CO) Oregon, (C) Falling Springs Cemetery
Leslie,: (B) Feb. 25, 1869, (D) Apr. 4, 1940, (CO) Oregon, (C) Falling Springs Cemetery
Lett, Theo O.: (B) Dec. 28, 1907, (D) Aug. 6, 1909, (CO) Henry, (C) Knights of Pythias Cemetery, Deepwater, MO
Letterell, Cynthia: (B) 1834, (CO) Pulaski, (A) 26, (BP) AL, (CMTS) 1860 Census
Letterell, Shelton: (B) 1836, (CO) Pulaski, (A) 24, (BP) IL, (CMTS) 1860 Census
Levah, James R.: (B) 1848, (CO) Stone, (A) 22, (BP) KY, (CMTS) 1870 Census
Levah, Mary Eliza: (B) 1850, (CO) Stone, (A) 20, (BP) TN, (CMTS) 1870 Census
Lever, Ellen: (D) Nov. 9, 1909, (CO) St. Louis, (C) Calvary Cemetery
Lever, Thomas: (D) Jan. 4, 1910, (CO) St. Louis, (C) Calvary Cemetery
Lever, William: (D) Jan. 15, 1942, (CO) St. Louis, (C) Calvary Cemetery
Lewis, Arthur E.: (B) 1861, (D) 1905, (CO) St. Louis, (C) Calvary Cemetery
Lewis, Diona: (B) 1848, (CO) Pulaski, (A) 12, (BP) MO, (CMTS) 1860 Census
Lewis, Ellen: (B) 1856, (CO) Pulaski, (A) 4, (BP) MO, (CMTS) 1860 Census
Lewis, George: (B) 1848, (CO) Pulaski, (A) 12, (BP) MO, (CMTS) 1860 Census
Lewis, J.: (B) 1834, (CO) Pulaski, (A) 26, (BP) MO, (CMTS) 1860 Census
Lewis, James: (B) 1854, (CO) Pulaski, (A) 6, (BP) MO, (CMTS) 1860 Census
Lewis, Joanna: (B) 1840, (CO) Pulaski, (A) 20, (BP) MO, (CMTS) 1860 Census
Lewis, John: (B) 1830, (CO) Pulaski, (A) 30, (BP) TN, (CMTS) 1860 Census
Lewis, John: (B) 1830, (CO) Pulaski, (A) 30, (BP) PA, (CMTS) 1860 Census
Lewis, Martha A.: (B) 1835, (CO) Pulaski, (A) 25, (BP) MO, (CMTS) 1860 Census
Lewis, Mary: (B) 1855, (CO) Pulaski, (A) 5, (BP) MO, (CMTS) 1860 Census
Lewis, Mildred: (B) Feb. 15, 1909, (D) Nov. 5, 1909, (CO) Henry, (C)

Knights of Pythias Cemetery, Deepwater, MO
Lewis, Mildred Augusta: (B) Dec. 11, 1881, (D) Apr. 14, 1963, (CO) Henry, (C) Knights of Pythias Cemetery, Deepwater, MO
Lewis, N.: (B) 1836, (CO) Pulaski, (A) 24, (BP) MO, (CMTS) 1860 Census
Lewis, Sarah J.: (B) 1829, (CO) Pulaski, (A) 31, (BP) KY, (CMTS) 1860 Census
Lewis, William: (B) 1835, (CO) Pulaski, (A) 25, (BP) MO, (CMTS) 1860 Census
Lewis, William L.: (B) 1855, (CO) Pulaski, (A) 5, (BP) MO, (CMTS) 1860 Census
Licklider, Thomas R.: (B) 1892, (D) 1959, (CO) St. Louis, (C) Calvary Cemetery
Liedes, Nancy M.: (B) 1840, (CO) Pulaski, (A) 20, (BP) MO, (CMTS) 1860 Census
Liedes, Peter: (B) 1833, (CO) Pulaski, (A) 27, (BP) MO, (CMTS) 1860 Census
Lilley, Joseph: (B) Dec. 23, 1875, (D) Jan. 31, 1902, (CO) Henry, (C) Knights of Pythias Cemetery, Deepwater, MO
Lillie, Lura A.: (B) Jun. 15, 1826, (D) Jan. 26, 1868, (CO) Audrain, (C) Old Village Cemetery
Linsey, James S.: (D) June 25, 1862, (CO) Greene, (CMTS) From Bremer, IA, (DP) Springfield
Linus, Martha: (D) Feb. 7,1851, (CO) Andrew, (C) Oak Ridge Cemetery, (A) 22Y 5M
Litterell, George W.: (B) 1847, (CO) Pulaski, (A) 13, (BP) IL, (CMTS) 1860 Census
Litterell, James: (B) 1837, (CO) Pulaski, (A) 23, (BP) TN, (CMTS) 1860 Census
Litterell, Mahala: (B) 1815, (CO) Pulaski, (A) 45, (BP) TN, (CMTS) 1860 Census
Litterell, Polly Ann: (B) 1849, (CO) Pulaski, (A) 11, (BP) IL, (CMTS) 1860 Census
Litterell, Sarah: (B) 1840, (CO) Pulaski, (A) 20, (BP) IL, (CMTS) 1860 Census
Little, Eligha L.: (B) Jun. 28, 1880, (D) Nov. 1, 1918, (CO) Oregon, (C) Falling Springs Cemetery
Lloyd, Rebecca: (B) 1841, (D) 1914, (CO) Cedar, (C) Brashear Cemetery
Lloyd, William: (B) 1842, (CO) Cedar, (C) Brashear Cemetery
Logan, Anthony M.: (B) 1855, (CO) Pulaski, (A) 5, (BP) MO, (CMTS) 1860 Census
Logan, Elizabeth: (B) 1852, (CO) Pulaski, (A) 8, (BP) TN, (CMTS) 1860 Census

Logan, Gelina: (B) 1842, (CO) Pulaski, (A) 18, (BP) AR, (CMTS) 1860 Census
Logan, George: (B) 1819, (CO) Pulaski, (A) 41, (BP) VA, (CMTS) 1860 Census
Logan, George L.: (B) 1844, (CO) Pulaski, (A) 16, (BP) TN, (CMTS) 1860 Census
Logan, Jacob H.: (B) 1831, (CO) Pulaski, (A) 29, (BP) VA, (CMTS) 1860 Census
Logan, James W.: (B) 1835, (CO) Pulaski, (A) 25, (BP) VA, (CMTS) 1860 Census
Logan, John: (B) Jul. 30, 1810, (D) Jan. 15, 1819, (CO) Barry, (C) Cassville Cemetery
Logan, John A.: (B) 1848, (CO) Pulaski, (A) 12, (BP) TN, (CMTS) 1860 Census
Logan, John H.: (B) 1843, (CO) Pulaski, (A) 17, (BP) MO, (CMTS) 1860 Census
Logan, Margaret: (B) 1836, (CO) Pulaski, (A) 24, (BP) TN, (CMTS) 1860 Census
Logan, Mary C.: (B) 1842, (CO) Pulaski, (A) 18, (BP) TN, (CMTS) 1860 Census
Logan, Matilda C.: (B) 1822, (CO) Pulaski, (A) 38, (BP) TN, (CMTS) 1860 Census
Logan, Rhoda E.: (B) 1856, (CO) Pulaski, (A) 4, (BP) MO, (CMTS) 1860 Census
Logan, Sarah: (B) 1820, (CO) Pulaski, (A) 40, (BP) VA, (CMTS) 1860 Census
Logan, Sarah A.: (B) 1846, (CO) Pulaski, (A) 14, (BP) TN, (CMTS) 1860 Census
Logan, Sarah J.: (B) 1855, (CO) Pulaski, (A) 5, (BP) MO, (CMTS) 1860 Census
Logan, Thomas R.: (B) 1865, (D) 1946, (CO) Henry, (C) Knights of Pythias Cemetery, Deepwater, MO
Logeson, Isaac A.: (B) 1846, (CO) Pulaski, (A) 14, (BP) MO, (CMTS) 1860 Census
Logeson, James R.: (B) 1849, (CO) Pulaski, (A) 11, (BP) MO, (CMTS) 1860 Census
Logeson, Phillip A.: (B) 1848, (CO) Pulaski, (A) 12, (BP) MO, (CMTS) 1860 Census
Logeson, Sarah: (B) 1823, (CO) Pulaski, (A) 37, (BP) MO, (CMTS) 1860 Census
Logeson, Sarah J.: (B) 1854, (CO) Pulaski, (A) 6, (BP) MO, (CMTS) 1860 Census
Logeson, Silence N.: (B) 1853, (CO) Pulaski, (A) 7, (BP) MO, (CMTS)

1860 Census
Long, Donald Wayne: (B) Dec. 12, 1957, (D) Jul. 5, 1994, (CO) Henry, (C) Knights of Pythias Cemetery, Deepwater, MO
Long, Isaac H.: (B) 1850, (CO) Stone, (A) 20, (BP) AR, (CMTS) 1870 Census
Long, Isabella: (B) 1844, (CO) Pulaski, (A) 16, (BP) MO, (CMTS) 1860 Census
Long, J. Abner: (B) 1848, (CO) Stone, (A) 22, (BP) MO, (CMTS) 1870 Census
Long, Martha: (D) Jan. 14, 1881, (CO) Barry, (C) Old Corsicana Cemetery, (A) 75
Long, Mary E.: (B) Sep. 9, 1874, (D) Jul. 12, 1943, (CO) St. Louis, (C) Calvary Cemetery
Long, Philip: (B) Nov. 10, 1810, (D) Apr. 8, 1887, (CO) Barry, (C) Old Corsicana Cemetery
Long, Polly: (B) 1852, (CO) Stone, (A) 18, (BP) MO, (CMTS) 1870 Census
Long, Sallie: (B) 1854, (CO) Stone, (A) 16, (BP) MO, (CMTS) 1870 Census
Long, Sarah: (B) 1841, (CO) Pulaski, (A) 19, (BP) VA, (CMTS) 1860 Census
Long, Viana: (B) 1844, (CO) Stone, (A) 26, (BP) MO, (CMTS) 1870 Census
Long, William: (B) 1838, (CO) Pulaski, (A) 22, (BP) IL, (CMTS) 1860 Census
Long, William: (B) 1846, (CO) Stone, (A) 24, (BP) MO, (CMTS) 1870 Census
Long,George W.: (B) 1851, (CO) Stone, (A) 19, (BP) AR, (CMTS) 1870 Census
Long,Sarah E.: (B) 1833, (CO) Stone, (A) 37, (BP) TN, (CMTS) 1870 Census
Longbrake, Lydia: (B) 1830, (D) 1896, (CO) Cedar, (C) Brashear Cemetery
Longinotti, Anthony: (B) 1877, (D) 1941, (CO) St. Louis, (C) Calvary Cemetery
Longinotti, Augustas J.: (B) 1837, (D) 1911, (CO) St. Louis, (C) Calvary Cemetery
Longinotti, Augustus: (B) 1873, (D) 1920, (CO) St. Louis, (C) Calvary Cemetery
Longinotti, Catherine: (B) 1843, (D) 1941, (CO) St. Louis, (C) Calvary Cemetery
Longinotti, Lillian: (B) 1874, (D) 1961, (CO) St. Louis, (C) Calvary Cemetery

Longinotti, Vada L.: (B) 1897, (D) 1905, (CO) St. Louis, (C) Calvary Cemetery
Lord, Asa D.: (B) 1833, (D) 1922, (CO) Henry, (C) Knights of Pythias Cemetery, Deepwater, MO
Lord, Mary A.: (B) 1830, (D) 1916, (CO) Henry, (C) Knights of Pythias Cemetery, Deepwater, MO
Lossden, George F.: (B) 1858, (CO) Pulaski, (A) 2, (BP) MO, (CMTS) 1860 Census
Lossden, James: (B) 1826, (CO) Pulaski, (A) 34, (BP) KY, (CMTS) 1860 Census
Lossden, Martha E.: (B) 1848, (CO) Pulaski, (A) 12, (BP) MO, (CMTS) 1860 Census
Lossden, Mourning: (B) 1856, (CO) Pulaski, (A) 4, (BP) TX, (CMTS) 1860 Census
Lossden, Sarah E.: (B) 1829, (CO) Pulaski, (A) 31, (BP) KY, (CMTS) 1860 Census
Louthman, Jemima: (B) 1840, (CO) Pulaski, (A) 20, (BP) MO, (CMTS) 1860 Census
Louthman, Peter: (B) 1837, (CO) Pulaski, (A) 23, (BP) KY, (CMTS) 1860 Census
Lovell, James: (B) 1852, (CO) Pulaski, (A) 8, (BP) TN, (CMTS) 1860 Census
Lovell, Mary: (B) 1827, (CO) Pulaski, (A) 33, (BP) TN, (CMTS) 1860 Census
Lovell, Selina: (B) 1856, (CO) Pulaski, (A) 4, (BP) MO, (CMTS) 1860 Census
Lovell, Thomas: (B) 1855, (CO) Pulaski, (A) 5, (BP) TN, (CMTS) 1860 Census
Lovell, William: (B) 1854, (CO) Pulaski, (A) 6, (BP) TN, (CMTS) 1860 Census
Lowder, Eliza: (B) 1850, (CO) Pulaski, (A) 10, (BP) MO, (CMTS) 1860 Census
Lowder, Elvira: (B) 1841, (CO) Pulaski, (A) 19, (BP) MO, (CMTS) 1860 Census
Lowder, William C.: (B) 1833, (CO) Pulaski, (A) 27, (BP) TN, (CMTS) 1860 Census
Lowry, Louisa P.: (B) 1832, (CO) Pulaski, (A) 28, (BP) NC, (CMTS) 1860 Census
Loyd, John: (B) 1805, (D) Sep. 30, 1875, (CO) Henry, (C) Knights of Pythias Cemetery, Deepwater, MO
Lucker, James F.: (B) 1847, (CO) Pulaski, (A) 13, (BP) MO, (CMTS) 1860 Census
Lucker, Sarah E.: (B) 1850, (CO) Pulaski, (A) 10, (BP) MO, (CMTS)

1860 Census
Luke, George: (B) 1841, (CO) Pulaski, (A) 19, (BP) MO, (CMTS) 1860 Census
Lukes, Jefferson M.: (B) 1853, (CO) Pulaski, (A) 7, (BP) MO, (CMTS) 1860 Census
Lukes, John W.: (B) 1855, (CO) Pulaski, (A) 5, (BP) MO, (CMTS) 1860 Census
Lukes, Jolene: (B) 1851, (CO) Pulaski, (A) 9, (BP) TN, (CMTS) 1860 Census
Lukes, Lucinda: (B) 1837, (CO) Pulaski, (A) 23, (BP) TN, (CMTS) 1860 Census
Lukes, Mary M.: (B) 1823, (CO) Pulaski, (A) 37, (BP) TN, (CMTS) 1860 Census
Lukes, Nancy J.: (B) 1849, (CO) Pulaski, (A) 11, (BP) TN, (CMTS) 1860 Census
Lukes, Reuben C.: (B) 1857, (CO) Pulaski, (A) 3, (BP) MO, (CMTS) 1860 Census
Lukes, William: (B) 1822, (CO) Pulaski, (A) 38, (BP) MO, (CMTS) 1860 Census
Lumcati, Christopher: (B) 1834, (CO) Pulaski, (A) 26, (BP) MO, (CMTS) 1860 Census
Lumcati, Nancy: (B) 1838, (CO) Pulaski, (A) 22, (BP) MO, (CMTS) 1860 Census
Lumcati, William H.: (B) 1857, (CO) Pulaski, (A) 3, (BP) MO, (CMTS) 1860 Census
Lunt, Harry: (B) Oct. 7, 1878, (D) Feb. 27, 1937, (CO) St. Louis, (C) Calvary Cemetery
Lunt, Ralph F.: (B) 1911, (D) 1968, (CO) St. Louis, (C) Calvary Cemetery
Lykins, Archibald: (B) Oct. 15, 1831, (D) Jun. 6, 1898, (CO) Andrew, (C) Oak Ridge Cemetery
Lykins, Elizabeth: (B) Mar. 29, 1804, (D) Aug 23, 1864, (CO) Andrew, (C) Oak Ridge Cemetery
Lykins, Sr, Andrew: (B) Feb. 14, 1801, (D) Nov. 18, 1881, (CO) Andrew, (C) Oak Ridge Cemetery
Lynam, Ellen Donowan: (B) 1855, (D) 1913, (CO) St. Louis, (C) Calvary Cemetery
Lynam, Jesse F.: (B) Mar. 5, 1879, (D) Jan. 7, 1904, (CO) St. Louis, (C) Calvary Cemetery
Lynch, James J.: (D) Feb. 14, 1920, (CO) St. Louis, (C) Calvary Cemetery
Lynch, James J.: (D) Jan. 2, 1970, (CO) St. Louis, (C) Calvary Cemetery
Lynch, Mary L.: (D) Jan. 28, 1930, (CO) St. Louis, (C) Calvary Cemetery
Lytle, Henry: (B) 1826, (CO) Stone, (A) 24, (BP) OH, (CMTS) 1870 Census

Lytle, Malinda: (B) 1848, (CO) Stone, (A) 2, (BP) MO, (CMTS) 1870 Census
Lytle, Nancy: (B) 1828, (CO) Stone, (A) 22, (BP) KY, (CMTS) 1870 Census
Mack, John: (B) 1837, (CO) Pulaski, (A) 23, (BP) NY, (CMTS) 1860 Census
Mackay, Archos X.: (D) Dec. 25, 1934, (CO) St. Louis, (C) Calvary Cemetery
Mackay, Susan D.: (D) Aug. 13, 1894, (CO) St. Louis, (C) Calvary Cemetery
Mackin, Sr., Daniel P.: (D) Sep., 1966, (CO) St. Louis, (C) Calvary Cemetery
Magee, John Joseph: (B) Sep. 7, 1932, (CO) St. Louis, (SPOUSE) Jane
Magee, (MIL) 1st Lt., USAF, 1954-1958.
Mahan, Bridgett: (B) 1830, (CO) Pulaski, (A) 30, (BP) Ireland, (CMTS) 1860 Census
Mahan, John: (B) 1855, (CO) Pulaski, (A) 5, (BP) MO, (CMTS) 1860 Census
Mahan, Patrick: (B) 1820, (CO) Pulaski, (A) 40, (BP) Ireland, (CMTS) 1860 Census
Mahana, Daniel: (B) 1833, (CO) Pulaski, (A) 27, (BP) MO, (CMTS) 1860 Census
Mahana, Elizabeth: (B) 1841, (CO) Pulaski, (A) 19, (BP) TN, (CMTS) 1860 Census
Mahana, Henry: (B) 1844, (CO) Pulaski, (A) 16, (BP) TN, (CMTS) 1860 Census
Mahana, Jane: (B) 1848, (CO) Pulaski, (A) 12, (BP) TN, (CMTS) 1860 Census
Mahana, Jamesper: (B) 1845, (CO) Pulaski, (A) 15, (BP) TN, (CMTS) 1860 Census
Mahana, Jesse M.: (B) 1839, (CO) Pulaski, (A) 21, (BP) TN, (CMTS) 1860 Census
Mahana, ThoMAs B.: (B) 1850, (CO) Pulaski, (A) 10, (BP) TN, (CMTS) 1860 Census
Maher, Catherine: (B) 1847, (D) 1925, (CO) St. Louis, (C) Calvary Cemetery
Maher, Joseph: (B) 1883, (D) 1903, (CO) St. Louis, (C) Calvary Cemetery
Maher, Jr., Joseph: (B) 1874, (D) 1954, (CO) St. Louis, (C) Calvary Cemetery
Maher, Rose: (B) 1874, (D) 1937, (CO) St. Louis, (C) Calvary Cemetery
Malay, Benjamin: (B) 1843, (CO) Pulaski, (A) 17, (BP) MO, (CMTS) 1860 Census
Malay, James: (B) 1846, (CO) Pulaski, (A) 14, (BP) MO, (CMTS)

1860 Census
Malay, John Anthony: (B) 1840, (CO) Pulaski, (A) 20, (BP) MO, (CMTS) 1860 Census
Malay, Lucy: (B) 1842, (CO) Pulaski, (A) 18, (BP) MO, (CMTS) 1860 Census
Mallmann, Anton: (B) Dec. 14, 1860, (D) Mar. 26, 1905, (CO) Henry, (C) Knights of Pythias Cemetery, Deepwater, MO
Malloy, Bridget: (D) Jul. 2, 1909, (CO) St. Louis, (C) Calvary Cemetery, (A) 73
Malon, Elkancy: (B) 1845, (CO) Pulaski, (A) 15, (BP) MO, (CMTS) 1860 Census
Malon, Lovina: (B) 1836, (CO) Pulaski, (A) 24, (BP) MO, (CMTS) 1860 Census
Malon, Lydia: (B) 1849, (CO) Pulaski, (A) 11, (BP) MO, (CMTS) 1860 Census
Malon, Martha: (B) 1852, (CO) Pulaski, (A) 8, (BP) MO, (CMTS) 1860 Census
Malon, Shelton: (B) 1840, (CO) Pulaski, (A) 20, (BP) MO, (CMTS) 1860 Census
Malon, William: (B) 1849, (CO) Pulaski, (A) 11, (BP) MO, (CMTS) 1860 Census
Malone, Andy: (B) 1852, (CO) Pulaski, (A) 8, (BP) MO, (CMTS) 1860 Census
Malone, Isaac: (B) 1852, (CO) Pulaski, (A) 8, (BP) MO, (CMTS) 1860 Census
Malone, Narcissa: (B) 1847, (CO) Pulaski, (A) 13, (BP) MO, (CMTS) 1860 Census
Malone, Robert: (B) 1825, (CO) Pulaski, (A) 35, (BP) MO, (CMTS) 1860 Census
Malone, Rosanna: (B) 1825, (CO) Pulaski, (A) 35, (BP) MO, (CMTS) 1860 Census
Malone, William: (B) 1850, (CO) Pulaski, (A) 10, (BP) MO, (CMTS) 1860 Census
Maloney, Bridget: (B) 1835, (CO) Pulaski, (A) 25, (BP) Ireland, (CMTS) 1860 Census
Maloney, William: (B) 1835, (CO) Pulaski, (A) 25, (BP) Ireland, (CMTS) 1860 Census
Maniaci, Angeline: (B) 1908, (D) 1985, (CO) St. Louis, (C) Calvary Cemetery
Maniaci, Josephine: (B) 1881, (D) 1959, (CO) St. Louis, (C) Calvary Cemetery
Maniaci, Salvatore: (B) 1900, (D) 1972, (CO) St. Louis, (C) Calvary Cemetery

Maniaci, Sebastiano Liuzza: (B) 1911, (D) 1972, (CO) St. Louis, (C) Calvary Cemetery
Manns, Albert: (B) 1829, (CO) Pulaski, (A) 31, (BP) TN, (CMTS) 1860 Census
Manns, C.: (B) 1840, (CO) Pulaski, (A) 20, (BP) MO, (CMTS) 1860 Census
Manns, Calaway: (B) 1848, (CO) Pulaski, (A) 12, (BP) MO, (CMTS) 1860 Census
Manns, Columbus: (B) 1843, (CO) Pulaski, (A) 17, (BP) MO, (CMTS) 1860 Census
Manns, Daniel: (B) 1850, (CO) Pulaski, (A) 10, (BP) TN, (CMTS) 1860 Census
Manns, Harrison: (B) 1846, (CO) Pulaski, (A) 14, (BP) MO, (CMTS) 1860 Census
Manns, John: (B) 1848, (CO) Pulaski, (A) 12, (BP) TN, (CMTS) 1860 Census
Manns, Mahala: (B) 1849, (CO) Pulaski, (A) 11, (BP) TN, (CMTS) 1860 Census
Manns, Marion: (B) 1842, (CO) Pulaski, (A) 18, (BP) TN, (CMTS) 1860 Census
Manns, Matilda: (B) 1853, (CO) Pulaski, (A) 7, (BP) TN, (CMTS) 1860 Census
Manns, Miranda: (B) 1831, (CO) Pulaski, (A) 29, (BP) KY, (CMTS) 1860 Census
Manns, Nancy: (B) 1840, (CO) Pulaski, (A) 20, (BP) MO, (CMTS) 1860 Census
Manns, Newton: (B) 1844, (CO) Pulaski, (A) 16, (BP) TN, (CMTS) 1860 Census
Manns, Sarah: (B) 1845, (CO) Pulaski, (A) 15, (BP) TN, (CMTS) 1860 Census
Manns, Seth: (B) 1852, (CO) Pulaski, (A) 8, (BP) MO, (CMTS) 1860 Census
Manns, Simeon: (B) 1846, (CO) Pulaski, (A) 14, (BP) TN, (CMTS) 1860 Census
Manns, William: (B) 1842, (CO) Pulaski, (A) 18, (BP) MO, (CMTS) 1860 Census
Mansfield, Leo N.: (B) 1898, (D) 1967, (CO) St. Louis, (C) Calvary Cemetery
Maoek, Johan Nepomus: (B) May 17, 1757, (D) Feb. 10, 1865, (CO) Jefferson, (C) Old St. John's Catholic Cemetery
Maphies, Joseph: (B) 1850, (D) 1928, (CO) Cedar, (C) Brashear Cemetery
Maphies, Martha J.: (B) 1854, (D) 1928, (CO) Cedar, (C) Brashear Cemetery

Maples, Catherine: (B) 1840, (CO) Stone, (A) 30, (BP) TN, (CMTS) 1870 Census
Maples, Eliza C.: (B) 1851, (CO) Stone, (A) 19, (BP) TN, (CMTS) 1870 Census
Maples, Gillien: (B) 1855, (CO) Stone, (A) 15, (BP) MO, (CMTS) 1870 Census
Maples, James: (B) 1844, (CO) Stone, (A) 26, (BP) TN, (CMTS) 1870 Census
Maples, Josiah: (B) 1855, (CO) Stone, (A) 15, (BP) TN, (CMTS) 1870 Census
Maples, Leon: (B) 1846, (CO) Stone, (A) 24, (BP) TN, (CMTS) 1870 Census
Maples, Martha A.: (B) 1849, (CO) Stone, (A) 21, (BP) TN, (CMTS) 1870 Census
Maples, Mary: (B) 1849, (CO) Stone, (A) 21, (BP) TN, (CMTS) 1870 Census
Maples, Nancy A.: (B) 1855, (CO) Stone, (A) 15, (BP) MO, (CMTS) 1870 Census
Maples, Perry: (B) 1817, (CO) Stone, (A) 53, (BP) TN, (CMTS) 1870 Census
Maples, Rhoda A.: (B) 1856, (CO) Stone, (A) 14, (BP) MO, (CMTS) 1870 Census
Maples, Sarah: (B) 1854, (CO) Stone, (A) 16, (BP) TN, (CMTS) 1870 Census
Maples, Simon: (B) 1843, (CO) Stone, (A) 27, (BP) TN, (CMTS) 1870 Census
Mapleton, Elizabeth: (B) 1822, (CO) Stone, (A) 28, (BP) AR, (CMTS) 1870 Census
Mapleton, Richard: (B) 1849, (CO) Stone, (A) 1, (BP) MO, (CMTS) 1870 Census
Marony, Catherine: (B) 1871, (D) 1941, (CO) St. Louis, (C) Calvary Cemetery
Martin, Arleigh H.: (B) Jul. 17, 1918, (D) May 14, 1991, (CO) Henry, (C) Knights of Pythias Cemetery, Deepwater, MO
Martin, Elizabeth C.: (B) 1848, (D) 1942, (CO) Cedar, (C) Brashear Cemetery
Martin, Elizabeth C.: (B) Aug. 7, 1928, (D) May 11, 1984, (CO) Henry, (C) Knights of Pythias Cemetery, Deepwater, MO
Martin, George: (B) 1838, (CO) Pulaski, (A) 22, (BP) VA, (CMTS) 1860 Census
Martin, Hannah E.: (B) 1843, (CO) Pulaski, (A) 17, (BP) VA, (CMTS) 1860 Census
Martin, John N.: (B) 1852, (CO) Pulaski, (A) 8, (BP) TN, (CMTS)

1860 Census
Martin, Katrina Lynn: (B) Oct. 28, 1958, (D) Dec. 10, 1976, (CO) Oregon, (C) Falling Springs Cemetery
Martin, Walter: (B) 1837, (D) 1905, (CO) Cedar, (C) Brashear Cemetery
Marx, Jr., Arthur W.: (B) Sep. 3, 1927, (D) Oct. 19, 1953, (CO) St. Louis, (C) Calvary Cemetery
Mashburn, John J.: (B) 1854, (CO) Pulaski, (A) 6, (BP) MO, (CMTS) 1860 Census
Mashburn, Louisa: (B) 1840, (CO) Pulaski, (A) 20, (BP) KY, (CMTS) 1860 Census
Mashburn, Peter: (B) 1833, (CO) Pulaski, (A) 27, (BP) TN, (CMTS) 1860 Census
Mason, Littlebury: (B) 1789, (D) Jul. 3, 1852, (CO) Barry, (C) Cassville Cemetery
Massengale, David: (B) 1834, (CO) Stone, (A) 16, (BP) MO, (CMTS) 1870 Census
Massengale, George W.: (B) 1832, (CO) Stone, (A) 18, (BP) MO, (CMTS) 1870 Census
Massengale, Jessie: (B) 1836, (CO) Stone, (A) 14, (BP) MO, (CMTS) 1870 Census
Massengale, John: (B) 1829, (CO) Stone, (A) 21, (BP) MO, (CMTS) 1870 Census
Massengale, Mary L.: (B) 1847, (CO) Stone, (A) 3, (BP) MO, (CMTS) 1870 Census
Massengale, Nathaniel: (B) 1841, (CO) Stone, (A) 9, (BP) AR, (CMTS) 1870 Census
Massengale, William: (B) 1839, (CO) Stone, (A) 11, (BP) AR, (CMTS) 1870 Census
Massing, Phillip: (D) Jul. 25, 1923, (CO) St. Louis, (C) Calvary Cemetery
Massing, Phillip A.: (D) Mar. 24, 1952, (CO) St. Louis, (C) Calvary Cemetery
Mast, Frank: (D) Jul. 1, 1909, (CO) St. Louis, (C) Calvary Cemetery, (A) 24
Mathews, Araminta: (B) 1856, (CO) Pulaski, (A) 4, (BP) MO, (CMTS) 1860 Census
Mathews, Elizabeth: (B) 1851, (CO) Pulaski, (A) 9, (BP) MO, (CMTS) 1860 Census
Mathews, George D.: (B) 1845, (CO) Pulaski, (A) 15, (BP) MO, (CMTS) 1860 Census
Mathews, James: (B) 1834, (CO) Pulaski, (A) 26, (BP) TN, (CMTS) 1860 Census
Mathews, John D.: (B) 1853, (CO) Pulaski, (A) 7, (BP) MO, (CMTS) 1860 Census

Mathews, John W.: (B) 1827, (CO) Pulaski, (A) 33, (BP) KY, (CMTS) 1860 Census
Mathews, Louisa J.: (B) 1849, (CO) Pulaski, (A) 11, (BP) MO, (CMTS) 1860 Census
Mathews, Maron: (B) 1835, (CO) Pulaski, (A) 25, (BP) MO, (CMTS) 1860 Census
Mathews, Martha: (B) 1830, (CO) Pulaski, (A) 30, (BP) TN, (CMTS) 1860 Census
Mathews, Mary: (B) 1839, (CO) Pulaski, (A) 21, (BP) TN, (CMTS) 1860 Census
Mathews, Nancy L.: (B) 1855, (CO) Pulaski, (A) 5, (BP) MO, (CMTS) 1860 Census
Mathews, Polly: (B) 1835, (CO) Pulaski, (A) 25, (BP) MO, (CMTS) 1860 Census
Mathews, Samuel: (B) 1847, (CO) Pulaski, (A) 13, (BP) MO, (CMTS) 1860 Census
Mathews, Sarah A.: (B) 1857, (CO) Pulaski, (A) 3, (BP) MO, (CMTS) 1860 Census
Mathews, William: (B) 1797, (CO) Pulaski, (A) 63, (BP) VA, (CMTS) 1860 Census
Mathews, William M.: (B) 1853, (CO) Pulaski, (A) 7, (BP) MO, (CMTS) 1860 Census
Mathis, Dorcas: (B) 1818, (CO) Stone, (A) 32, (BP) TN, (CMTS) 1870 Census
Mathis, Elsie C.: (B) 1840, (CO) Stone, (A) 30, (BP) TN, (CMTS) 1870 Census
Mathis, Green: (B) 1820, (CO) Stone, (A) 30, (BP) MO, (CMTS) 1870 Census
Mathis, Joseph: (B) 1841, (CO) Stone, (A) 9, (BP) MO, (CMTS) 1870 Census
Mathis, Josephine: (B) 1835, (CO) Stone, (A) 15, (BP) MO, (CMTS) 1870 Census
Mathis, Mary F: (B) 1844, (CO) Stone, (A) 6, (BP) MO, (CMTS) 1870 Census
Mathis, Nancy E.: (B) 1846, (CO) Stone, (A) 4, (BP) MO, (CMTS) 1870 Census
Mathis, Sigle: (B) 1843, (CO) Stone, (A) 7, (BP) MO, (CMTS) 1870 Census
Mathis, Squire W.: (B) 1836, (CO) Stone, (A) 34, (BP) TN, (CMTS) 1870 Census
Mathis, William D: (B) 1848, (CO) Stone, (A) 2, (BP) MO, (CMTS) 1870 Census
Matlock, Eliza: (B) 1828, (CO) Pulaski, (A) 32, (BP) IL, (CMTS)

1860 Census
Matlock, John B.: (B) 1849, (CO) Pulaski, (A) 11, (BP) IA, (CMTS) 1860 Census
Matney, Isaiah: (B) 1823, (CO) Stone, (A) 47, (BP) IN, (CMTS) 1870 Census
Matney, Jacob: (B) 1854, (CO) Stone, (A) 16, (BP) MO, (CMTS) 1870 Census
Matney, Martha: (B) 1831, (CO) Stone, (A) 39, (BP) IN, (CMTS) 1870 Census
Mattock, Howard: (B) 1839, (CO) Pulaski, (A) 21, (BP) MO, (CMTS) 1860 Census
Maxcy, James: (B) 1829, (CO) Pulaski, (A) 31, (BP) TN, (CMTS) 1860 Census
Maxcy, Margaret: (B) 1831, (CO) Pulaski, (A) 29, (BP) TN, (CMTS) 1860 Census
Maxcy, William H.: (B) 1855, (CO) Pulaski, (A) 5, (BP) MO, (CMTS) 1860 Census
May, Cynthia E.: (B) 1844, (CO) Stone, (A) 6, (BP) MO, (CMTS) 1870 Census
May, David C.: (B) 1840, (CO) Stone, (A) 10, (BP) MO, (CMTS) 1870 Census
May, Jacob: (B) 1842, (CO) Stone, (A) 8, (BP) MO, (CMTS) 1870 Census
May, James R. P: (B) 1828, (CO) Stone, (A) 22, (BP) MO, (CMTS) 1870 Census
May, John: (B) 1820, (CO) Stone, (A) 30, (BP) MO, (CMTS) 1870 Census
May, John: (B) 1828, (CO) Stone, (A) 22, (BP) MO, (CMTS) 1870 Census
May, John C.: (B) 1848, (CO) Stone, (A) 2, (BP) MO, (CMTS) 1870 Census
May, Joseph C.: (B) 1840, (CO) Pulaski, (A) 20, (BP) TN, (CMTS) 1860 Census
May, Margarete: (B) 1837, (CO) Stone, (A) 13, (BP) AR, (CMTS) 1870 Census
May, Martin: (B) 1833, (CO) Stone, (A) 17, (BP) MO, (CMTS) 1870 Census
May, Mary: (B) 1822, (CO) Stone, (A) 28, (BP) MO, (CMTS) 1870 Census
May, Mary E.: (B) 1845, (CO) Stone, (A) 5, (BP) MO, (CMTS) 1870 Census
May, Mary M.: (B) 1839, (CO) Stone, (A) 11, (BP) MO, (CMTS) 1870 Census

May, Melia J.: (B) 1847, (CO) Stone, (A) 3, (BP) MO, (CMTS) 1870 Census
May, Miles: (B) 1835, (CO) Stone, (A) 15, (BP) AR, (CMTS) 1870 Census
May, Nancy Ann: (B) 1818, (CO) Stone, (A) 32, (BP) MO, (CMTS) 1870 Census
May, Rebecca: (B) 1850, (CO) Stone, (A), (BP) 21, (CMTS) 1870 Census
May, William B.: (B) 1842, (CO) Stone, (A) 8, (BP) MO, (CMTS) 1870 Census
May, William H.: (B) 1840, (CO) Stone, (A) 10, (BP) MO, (CMTS) 1870 Census
Mayberry, Reubin: (B) 1820, (CO) Stone, (A) 50, (BP) TN, (CMTS) 1870 Census
Mays, Martha: (B) 1830, (CO) Pulaski, (A) 30, (BP) PA, (CMTS) 1860 Census
Mays, Nancy A.: (B) 1844, (CO) Pulaski, (A) 16, (BP) TN, (CMTS) 1860 Census
Mays, Rebecca: (B) 1846, (CO) Pulaski, (A) 14, (BP) MO, (CMTS) 1860 Census
Mays, Sherrid: (B) 1821, (CO) Pulaski, (A) 39, (BP) TN, (CMTS) 1860 Census
Mays, William F.: (B) 1848, (CO) Pulaski, (A) 12, (BP) MO, (CMTS) 1860 Census
McArtor, James H.: (B) May 23, 1837, (D) Sep. 11, 1880, (CO) Barry, (C) Cassville Cemetery
McBride, James: (D) Jan. 17, 1873, (CO) St. Louis, (C) Calvary Cemetery, (A) 40
McCafferty, Dr. James B.: (B) Sep. 13, 1892, (D) Aug. 7, 1952, (CO) St. Louis, (C) Calvary Cemetery
McCarty, Patrick: (B) 1837, (CO) Pulaski, (A) 23, (BP) PA, (CMTS) 1860 Census
McCluskey, Catherine: (B) 1869, (D) 1923, (CO) St. Louis, (C) Calvary Cemetery
McCluskey, Elizabeth: (B) 1878, (D) 1931, (CO) St. Louis, (C) Calvary Cemetery
McCluskey, John W.: (B) 1866, (D) 1951, (CO) St. Louis, (C) Calvary Cemetery
McCluskey, May: (B) 1896, (D) 1959, (CO) St. Louis, (C) Calvary Cemetery
McConnel, Sylvia E.: (B) 1843, (CO) Stone, (A) 27, (BP) SC, (CMTS) 1870 Census
McConnel, William A.: (B) 1830, (CO) Stone, (A) 40, (BP) TN, (CMTS)

1870 Census
McCorkle, Mahulda: (B) 1844, (CO) Stone, (A) 26, (BP) TN, (CMTS) 1870 Census
McCorkle, Samuel: (B) 1842, (CO) Stone, (A) 28, (BP) MO, (CMTS) 1870 Census
McCormack, Catherine: (B) 1849, (D) 1919, (CO) St. Louis, (C) Calvary Cemetery
McCormack, John: (B) 1841, (D) 1903, (CO) St. Louis, (C) Calvary Cemetery
McCortney, Alexander: (B) 1845, (CO) Pulaski, (A) 15, (BP) MO, (CMTS) 1860 Census
McCortney, Dorcas: (B) 1852, (CO) Pulaski, (A) 8, (BP) MO, (CMTS) 1860 Census
McCortney, James: (B) 1838, (CO) Pulaski, (A) 22, (BP) MO, (CMTS) 1860 Census
McCortney, John: (B) 1844, (CO) Pulaski, (A) 16, (BP) MO, (CMTS) 1860 Census
McCortney, Joshua: (B) 1848, (CO) Pulaski, (A) 12, (BP) MO, (CMTS) 1860 Census
McCortney, Marion: (B) 1846, (CO) Pulaski, (A) 14, (BP) MO, (CMTS) 1860 Census
McCortney, Martin: (B) 1848, (CO) Pulaski, (A) 12, (BP) MO, (CMTS) 1860 Census
McCortney, Sarah: (B) 1837, (CO) Pulaski, (A) 23, (BP) MO, (CMTS) 1860 Census
McCullah, David S.: (B) 1842, (CO) Stone, (A) 8, (BP) MO, (CMTS) 1870 Census
McCullah, George W.: (B) 1840, (CO) Stone, (A) 10, (BP) MO, (CMTS) 1870 Census
McCullah, John A.: (B) 1836, (CO) Stone, (A) 14, (BP) IL, (CMTS) 1870 Census
McCullah, Joseph W.: (B) 1837, (CO) Stone, (A) 13, (BP) IL, (CMTS) 1870 Census
McCullah, Lucinda: (B) 1830, (CO) Stone, (A) 20, (BP) IL, (CMTS) 1870 Census
McCullah, Mary P: (B) 1842, (CO) Stone, (A) 28, (BP) MO, (CMTS) 1870 Census
McCullah, Sarah C.: (B) 1845, (CO) Stone, (A) 5, (BP) MO, (CMTS) 1870 Census
McDaniel, Benjamin A.: (B) 1828, (CO) Stone, (A) 42, (BP) MO, (CMTS) 1870 Census
McDonald, Alexander: (D) Sep. 12, 1852, (CO) Andrew, (C) Oak Ridge Cemetery, (A) 62Y. 9M. 19D

McDonald, Archie A.: (D) Feb. 18, 1911, (CO) St. Louis, (C) Calvary Cemetery
McDonald, Ellen V.: (D) Dec. 16, 1915, (CO) St. Louis, (C) Calvary Cemetery
McDonald, Isabella A.: (B) 1853, (CO) Pulaski, (A) 7, (BP) MO, (CMTS) 1860 Census
McDonald, Lawrence T.: (B) Sep. 23, 1920, (D) Oct. 23, 1979, (CO) St. Louis, (C) Calvary Cemetery
McDonald, Mary J.: (B) 1832, (CO) Pulaski, (A) 28, (BP) MO, (CMTS) 1860 Census
McDonald, Michael: (B) 1833, (CO) Pulaski, (A) 27, (BP) Ireland, (CMTS) 1860 Census
McDonald, Pricilla: (D) Oct. 10, 1876, (CO) Andrew, (C) Oak Ridge Cemetery, (A) 76Y. 6M. 25D
McDonald, W.: (B) 1821, (CO) Pulaski, (A) 39, (BP) MO, (CMTS) 1860 Census
McDonald,: (B) 1832, (CO) Pulaski, (A) 28, (BP) Ireland, (CMTS) 1860 Census
McDowel, Eliza E.: (B) 1841, (CO) Stone, (A) 9, (BP) MO, (CMTS) 1870 Census
McDowel, George W.: (B) 1836, (CO) Stone, (A) 14, (BP) MO, (CMTS) 1870 Census
McDowel, Henry: (B) 1830, (CO) Stone, (A) 20, (BP) MO, (CMTS) 1870 Census
McDowel, Nancy M.: (B) 1844, (CO) Stone, (A) 6, (BP) MO, (CMTS) 1870 Census
McDowel, Rebecca: (B) 1838, (CO) Stone, (A) 12, (BP) MO, (CMTS) 1870 Census
McDowel, Vina: (B) 1834, (CO) Stone, (A) 16, (BP) KY, (CMTS) 1870 Census
McDowel, Wiley: (B) 1794, (CO) Stone, (A) 56, (BP) TN, (CMTS) 1870 Census
McDowell, Charlotta: (B) 1828, (CO) Stone, (A) 22, (BP) AR, (CMTS) 1870 Census
McDowell, George: (B) 1854, (CO) Pulaski, (A) 6, (BP) MO, (CMTS) 1860 Census
McDowell, Henry: (B) 1842, (CO) Pulaski, (A) 18, (BP) MO, (CMTS) 1860 Census
McDowell, Isaac: (B) 1850, (CO) Pulaski, (A) 10, (BP) MO, (CMTS) 1860 Census
McDowell, James: (B) 1846, (CO) Pulaski, (A) 14, (BP) MO, (CMTS) 1860 Census
McDowell, John R.: (B) 1851, (CO) Pulaski, (A) 9, (BP) MO, (CMTS)

1860 Census
McDowell, Margaret B.: (B) 1829, (CO) Stone, (A) 21, (BP) AR, (CMTS) 1870 Census
McDowell, Mathew: (B) 1852, (CO) Pulaski, (A) 8, (BP) MO, (CMTS) 1860 Census
McDowell, Nancy: (B) 1844, (CO) Pulaski, (A) 16, (BP) MO, (CMTS) 1860 Census
McDowell, Polly: (B) 1843, (CO) Pulaski, (A) 17, (BP) MO, (CMTS) 1860 Census
McDowell, Sarah: (B) 1846, (CO) Pulaski, (A) 14, (BP) MO, (CMTS) 1860 Census
McDowell, Thomas: (B) 1848, (CO) Pulaski, (A) 12, (BP) MO, (CMTS) 1860 Census
McDowell, William: (B) 1834, (CO) Pulaski, (A) 26, (BP) TN, (CMTS) 1860 Census
McDowell, William E.: (B) 1821, (CO) Stone, (A) 29, (BP) MO, (CMTS) 1870 Census
McDowell, Zachariah: (B) 1829, (CO) Stone, (A) 21, (BP) MO, (CMTS) 1870 Census
Mcelroy, Alfred: (B) 1796, (CO) Pulaski, (A) 64, (BP) SC, (CMTS) 1860 Census
Mcelroy, Catherine: (B) 1845, (CO) Pulaski, (A) 15, (BP) MO, (CMTS) 1860 Census
Mcelroy, James A.: (B) 1834, (CO) Pulaski, (A) 26, (BP) MO, (CMTS) 1860 Census
Mcelroy, James M.: (B) 1851, (CO) Pulaski, (A) 9, (BP) MO, (CMTS) 1860 Census
Mcelroy, Jane J.: (B) 1845, (CO) Pulaski, (A) 15, (BP) MO, (CMTS) 1860 Census
Mcelroy, Maria: (B) 1854, (CO) Pulaski, (A) 6, (BP) MO, (CMTS) 1860 Census
Mcelroy, Mary J.: (B) 1856, (CO) Pulaski, (A) 4, (BP) MO, (CMTS) 1860 Census
Mcelroy, William A.: (B) 1849, (CO) Pulaski, (A) 11, (BP) MO, (CMTS) 1860 Census
Mcelroy, William R.: (B) 1844, (CO) Pulaski, (A) 16, (BP) MO, (CMTS) 1860 Census
McGee, John: (B) 1854, (CO) Pulaski, (A) 6, (BP) MO, (CMTS) 1860 Census
McGee, Lucretia: (B) 1853, (CO) Pulaski, (A) 7, (BP) MO, (CMTS) 1860 Census
McGee, Robert: (B) 1851, (CO) Pulaski, (A) 9, (BP) MO, (CMTS) 1860 Census

McGee, Sarah: (B) 1847, (CO) Pulaski, (A) 13, (BP) MO, (CMTS) 1860 Census
McGee, Silence: (B) 1845, (CO) Pulaski, (A) 15, (BP) MO, (CMTS) 1860 Census
McGill, James G: (B) 1852, (CO) Stone, (A) 18, (BP) AR, (CMTS) 1870 Census
McGill, Nancy: (B) 1856, (CO) Stone, (A) 14, (BP) AR, (CMTS) 1870 Census
McGinnis, Walter P.: (B) Aug. 9, 1874, (D) Mar. 2, 1960, (CO) Henry, (C) Knights of Pythias Cemetery, Deepwater, MO
McGowen, David: (B) 1837, (CO) Pulaski, (A) 23, (BP) MO, (CMTS) 1860 Census
McGowen, Jane: (B) 1837, (CO) Pulaski, (A) 23, (BP) AR, (CMTS) 1860 Census
McGuire, Robert: (B) 1852, (CO) Pulaski, (A) 8, (BP) MO, (CMTS) 1860 Census
McHale, Mrs . Bridget: (D) Sep. 29,. 1880, (CO) St. Louis, (C) Calvary Cemetery, (A) 35
McIntyre, Caroline: (B) 1830, (CO) Pulaski, (A) 30, (BP) MO, (CMTS) 1860 Census
McIntyre, John S.: (B) 1855, (CO) Pulaski, (A) 5, (BP) MO, (CMTS) 1860 Census
McIntyre, Sarah J.: (B) 1853, (CO) Pulaski, (A) 7, (BP) MO, (CMTS) 1860 Census
McIntyre, William J.: (B) 1854, (CO) Pulaski, (A) 6, (BP) MO, (CMTS) 1860 Census
McKee, Elizabeth: (B) 1828, (CO) Pulaski, (A) 32, (BP) VA, (CMTS) 1860 Census
McKee, H.: (B) 1828, (CO) Pulaski, (A) 32, (BP) MA, (CMTS) 1860 Census
McKee, Louis B.: (B) Dec. 28, 1881, (D) Feb. 19, 1962, (CO) Henry, (C) Knights of Pythias Cemetery, Deepwater, MO
McKinnon, Andrew A.: (B) 1833, (CO) Pulaski, (A) 27, (BP) MO, (CMTS) 1860 Census
McKinnon, Augustus: (B) 1830, (CO) Pulaski, (A) 30, (BP) MO, (CMTS) 1860 Census
McKinnon, Elijah: (B) 1858, (CO) Pulaski, (A) 2, (BP) MO, (CMTS) 1860 Census
McKinnon, Elizabeth: (B) 1831, (CO) Pulaski, (A) 29, (BP) MO, (CMTS) 1860 Census
McKinnon, Elizabeth: (B) 1851, (CO) Pulaski, (A) 9, (BP) MO, (CMTS) 1860 Census
McKinnon, Elizabeth: (B) 1854, (CO) Pulaski, (A) 6, (BP) MO, (CMTS)

1860 Census
McKinnon, Frances: (B) 1856, (CO) Pulaski, (A) 4, (BP) MO, (CMTS) 1860 Census
McKinnon, Holly: (B) 1845, (CO) Pulaski, (A) 15, (BP) MO, (CMTS) 1860 Census
McKinnon, James: (B) 1838, (CO) Pulaski, (A) 22, (BP) MO, (CMTS) 1860 Census
McKinnon, Jane: (B) 1851, (CO) Pulaski, (A) 9, (BP) MO, (CMTS) 1860 Census
McKinnon, Jeremiah: (B) 1842, (CO) Pulaski, (A) 18, (BP) MO, (CMTS) 1860 Census
McKinnon, John T.: (B) 1836, (CO) Pulaski, (A) 24, (BP) MO, (CMTS) 1860 Census
McKinnon, Julia: (B) 1843, (CO) Pulaski, (A) 17, (BP) MO, (CMTS) 1860 Census
McKinnon, Loretta: (B) 1852, (CO) Pulaski, (A) 8, (BP) MO, (CMTS) 1860 Census
McKinnon, Philip: (B) 1840, (CO) Pulaski, (A) 20, (BP) MO, (CMTS) 1860 Census
McMahan, Baptist: (B) 1830, (CO) Pulaski, (A) 30, (BP) TN, (CMTS) 1860 Census
McMahan, Elizabeth J.: (B) 1835, (CO) Pulaski, (A) 25, (BP) MO, (CMTS) 1860 Census
McMahan, John: (B) 1840, (CO) Pulaski, (A) 20, (BP) Ireland, (CMTS) 1860 Census
McMahan, Lucy: (B) 1855, (CO) Pulaski, (A) 5, (BP) MO, (CMTS) 1860 Census
McMillan, Elizabeth: (B) 1830, (CO) Pulaski, (A) 30, (BP) TN, (CMTS) 1860 Census
McMillan, Sarah: (B) 1849, (CO) Pulaski, (A) 11, (BP) TN, (CMTS) 1860 Census
McMillen, Barney: (B) 1854, (CO) Pulaski, (A) 6, (BP) IL, (CMTS) 1860 Census
McMillen, Dianah: (B) 1847, (CO) Pulaski, (A) 13, (BP) IL, (CMTS) 1860 Census
McMillen, George: (B) 1849, (CO) Pulaski, (A) 11, (BP) IL, (CMTS) 1860 Census
McMillen, Jackson: (B) 1856, (CO) Pulaski, (A) 4, (BP) IL, (CMTS) 1860 Census
McMillen, Jacob: (B) 1843, (CO) Pulaski, (A) 17, (BP) IL, (CMTS) 1860 Census
McMillen, James: (B) 1819, (CO) Pulaski, (A) 41, (BP) KY, (CMTS) 1860 Census

McMillen, Mary: (B) 1819, (CO) Pulaski, (A) 41, (BP) TN, (CMTS) 1860 Census
McMillen, Peter: (B) 1850, (CO) Pulaski, (A) 10, (BP) IL, (CMTS) 1860 Census
McMullin, Elizabeth: (B) 1849, (CO) Pulaski, (A) 11, (BP) MO, (CMTS) 1860 Census
McMullin, John: (B) 1847, (CO) Pulaski, (A) 13, (BP) MO, (CMTS) 1860 Census
McMullin, Martha: (B) 1846, (CO) Pulaski, (A) 14, (BP) MO, (CMTS) 1860 Census
McMullin, Mary: (B) 1855, (CO) Pulaski, (A) 5, (BP) MO, (CMTS) 1860 Census
McMullin, Sally: (B) 1853, (CO) Pulaski, (A) 7, (BP) MO, (CMTS) 1860 Census
McNeely, James A.: (B) 1833, (CO) Stone, (A) 37, (BP) KY, (CMTS) 1870 Census
McNeely, Margaret: (B) 1832, (CO) Stone, (A) 38, (BP) KY, (CMTS) 1870 Census
McNeely, Melisa A.: (B) 1854, (CO) Stone, (A) 16, (BP) KY, (CMTS) 1870 Census
McNeill, Lucy: (B) 1836, (D) 1920, (CO) Cedar, (C) Brashear Cemetery
Medearis, Rufus G.: (B) 1886, (D) 1950, (CO) St. Louis, (C) Calvary Cemetery
Meehan, Cilburn J.: (B) 1875, (D) 1958, (CO) St. Louis, (C) Calvary Cemetery
Meehan, Edward L.C.: (B) 1912, (D) 1978, (CO) St. Louis, (C) Calvary Cemetery
Meehan, May Elizabeth: (B) 1886, (D) 1949, (CO) St. Louis, (C) Calvary Cemetery
Meek, Eliza: (B) 1838, (CO) Stone, (A) 12, (BP) TX, (CMTS) 1870 Census
Meek, George: (B) 1838, (CO) Stone, (A) 12, (BP) AR, (CMTS) 1870 Census
Meek, George C.: (B) 1820, (CO) Stone, (A) 50, (BP) TN, (CMTS) 1870 Census
Meek, Harriet: (B) 1837, (CO) Stone, (A) 13, (BP) TX, (CMTS) 1870 Census
Meek, Jack Alma: (B) 1854, (CO) Stone, (A) 16, (BP) TX, (CMTS) 1870 Census
Meek, James H.: (B) 1847, (CO) Stone, (A) 3, (BP) AR, (CMTS) 1870 Census
Meek, Jeremiah: (B) 1849, (CO) Stone, (A) 1, (BP) MO, (CMTS) 1870 Census

Meek, John: (B) 1842, (CO) Stone, (A) 8, (BP) AR, (CMTS) 1870 Census
Meek, Lewis: (B) 1795, (CO) Stone, (A) 55, (BP) TN, (CMTS) 1870 Census
Meek, Lewis: (B) 1840, (CO) Stone, (A) 10, (BP) TX, (CMTS) 1870 Census
Meek, Lewis: (B) 1849, (CO) Stone, (A) 1, (BP) AR, (CMTS) 1870 Census
Meek, Martha: (B) 1820, (CO) Stone, (A) 30, (BP) AR, (CMTS) 1870 Census
Meek, Martha J.: (B) 1851, (CO) Stone, (A) 19, (BP) MO, (CMTS) 1870 Census
Meek, Mary A.: (B) 1847, (CO) Stone, (A) 3, (BP) AR, (CMTS) 1870 Census
Meek, Mary J.: (B) 1851, (CO) Stone, (A) 19, (BP) TX, (CMTS) 1870 Census
Meek, Melissa: (B) 1849, (CO) Stone, (A) 21, (BP) TN, (CMTS) 1870 Census
Meek, Moses: (B) 1825, (CO) Stone, (A) 25, (BP) AR, (CMTS) 1870 Census
Meek, Nancy: (B) 1848, (CO) Stone, (A) 2, (BP) AR, (CMTS) 1870 Census
Meek, Rebecca: (B) 1826, (CO) Stone, (A) 24, (BP) AR, (CMTS) 1870 Census
Meek, Richard: (B) 1834, (CO) Stone, (A) 16, (BP) TX, (CMTS) 1870 Census
Meek, Squire: (B) 1847, (CO) Stone, (A) 23, (BP) AR, (CMTS) 1870 Census
Meek, Thomas J.: (B) 1845, (CO) Stone, (A) 25, (BP) AR, (CMTS) 1870 Census
Meek, William: (B) 1857, (CO) Stone, (A) 13, (BP) TX, (CMTS) 1870 Census
Meek, Willliam: (B) 1832, (CO) Stone, (A) 18, (BP) TX, (CMTS) 1870 Census
Meier, Fred August: (B) 1901, (CO) Camden,
Meier, Lillie Mae: (B) 1905, (CO) Camden,
Meier, Mary Pearl: (B) 1902, , (CO) Camden,
Melton, Alcy A.: (B) 1857, (CO) Stone, (A) 13, (BP) MO, (CMTS) 1870 Census
Melton, Alcy M.: (B) 1849, (CO) Stone, (A) 1, (BP) MO, (CMTS) 1870 Census
Melton, Elisha J.: (B) 1831, (CO) Stone, (A) 39, (BP) TN, (CMTS) 1870 Census

Melton, Elizabeth: (B) 1826, (CO) Stone, (A) 24, (BP) TN, (CMTS) 1870 Census
Melton, George: (B) 1835, (CO) Pulaski, (A) 25, (BP) NY, (CMTS) 1860 Census
Melton, Joel D: (B) 1823, (CO) Stone, (A) 27, (BP) MO, (CMTS) 1870 Census
Melton, Susan: (B) 1840, (CO) Stone, (A) 30, (BP) IL, (CMTS) 1870 Census
Merrill, Dan: (B) 1821, (CO) Pulaski, (A) 39, (BP) NC, (CMTS) 1860 Census
Merrill, Eliza E.: (B) 1854, (CO) Pulaski, (A) 6, (BP) MO, (CMTS) 1860 Census
Merrill, Elizabeth: (B) 1836, (CO) Pulaski, (A) 24, (BP) MO, (CMTS) 1860 Census
Merrill, John: (B) 1832, (CO) Pulaski, (A) 28, (BP) NC, (CMTS) 1860 Census
Merrill, Lucretia: (B) 1848, (CO) Pulaski, (A) 12, (BP) MO, (CMTS) 1860 Census
Merrill, Mary A.: (B) 1827, (CO) Pulaski, (A) 33, (BP) NC, (CMTS) 1860 Census
Merrill, Rebecca: (B) 1823, (CO) Pulaski, (A) 37, (BP) IN, (CMTS) 1860 Census
Merrill, William: (B) 1856, (CO) Pulaski, (A) 4, (BP) MO, (CMTS) 1860 Census
Mesinger, Dan: (B) 1838, (CO) Stone, (A) 32, (BP) OH, (CMTS) 1870 Census
Mesinger, Eliza: (B) 1838, (CO) Stone, (A) 32, (BP) TN, (CMTS) 1870 Census
Messmer, Chris: (D) May 1928, (CO) St. Louis, (C) Calvary Cemetery
Messmer, Elizabeth: (D) Feb. 1876, (CO) St. Louis, (C) Calvary Cemetery
Messmer, Leopold: (B) Nov. 15, 1824, (CO) St. Louis, (C) Calvary Cemetery
Meyer, Bridget: (B) 1855, (D) 1910, (CO) St. Louis, (C) Calvary Cemetery
Miles, Caroline: (B) 1847, (CO) Stone, (A) 23, (BP) MO, (CMTS) 1870 Census
Miles, Carr: (B) 1852, (CO) Stone, (A) 18, (BP) MO, (CMTS) 1870 Census
Miles, John: (B) 1844, (CO) Stone, (A) 26, (BP) MO, (CMTS) 1870 Census
Miles, John: (B) 1856, (CO) Stone, (A) 14, (BP) MO, (CMTS) 1870 Census
Miles, Matilda: (B) 1793, (CO) Stone, (A) 57, (BP) NC, (CMTS) 1870

Census
Miles, Nathaniel: (B) 1834, (CO) Stone, (A) 16, (BP) MO, (CMTS) 1870 Census
Miles, William H.: (B) 1830, (CO) Stone, (A) 20, (BP) MO, (CMTS) 1870 Census
Miller, Elizabeth: (B) 1837, (CO) Pulaski, (A) 23, (BP) MO, (CMTS) 1860 Census
Miller, Elizabeth: (B) 1854, (CO) Pulaski, (A) 6, (BP) IL, (CMTS) 1860 Census
Miller, Fannie: (B) Oct. 23, 1909, (D) Apr. 15, 1999, (CO) Barry, (RES) Marionville, (BP) Marionville, (DP) Russellville, AR, (C) Mars Hill Cemetery, (PRTS) Fines Forester and Lizzie Macaslin
Miller, George W.: (B) 1843, (CO) Pulaski, (A) 17, (BP) MO, (CMTS) 1860 Census
Miller, Henry: (B) 1867, (D) 1934, (CO) St. Louis, (C) Calvary Cemetery
Miller, J. H.: (B) 1844, (D) 1931, (CO) Cedar, (C) Brashear Cemetery
Miller, James: (B) 1852, (CO) Pulaski, (A) 8, (BP) MO, (CMTS) 1860 Census
Miller, Jennie: (B) 1870, (D) 1931, (CO) St. Louis, (C) Calvary Cemetery
Miller, Jessie: (B) 1819, (CO) Stone, (A) 51, (BP) NC, (CMTS) 1870 Census
Miller, John C.: (B) 1850, (CO) Pulaski, (A) 10, (BP) MO, (CMTS) 1860 Census
Miller, John T.: (B) 1846, (CO) Pulaski, (A) 14, (BP) TN, (CMTS) 1860 Census
Miller, Joseph: (B) 1830, (CO) Pulaski, (A) 30, (BP) KY, (CMTS) 1860 Census
Miller, Lucinda: (B) 1849, (CO) Pulaski, (A) 11, (BP) TN, (CMTS) 1860 Census
Miller, M.: (B) 1834, (CO) Pulaski, (A) 26, (BP) TN, (CMTS) 1860 Census
Miller, Marinda C.: (B) 1835, (CO) Pulaski, (A) 25, (BP) MO, (CMTS) 1860 Census
Miller, Mary: (B) 1822, (CO) Pulaski, (A) 38, (BP) TN, (CMTS) 1860 Census
Miller, Mary: (B) 1834, (CO) Stone, (A) 36, (BP) TN, (CMTS) 1870 Census
Miller, P.: (B) 1818, (CO) Pulaski, (A) 42, (BP) TN, (CMTS) 1860 Census
Miller, Pearl: (B) Jul. 18, 1885, (D) Sep. 16, 1903, (CO) Henry, (C) Knights of Pythias Cemetery, Deepwater, MO
Miller, Polly: (B) 1823, (CO) Pulaski, (A) 37, (BP) MO, (CMTS) 1860 Census

Miller, Polly E.: (B) 1857, (CO) Pulaski, (A) 3, (BP) TN, (CMTS) 1860 Census
Miller, Robert M.: (B) 1845, (CO) Pulaski, (A) 15, (BP) TN, (CMTS) 1860 Census
Miller, Samuel: (B) 1855, (CO) Pulaski, (A) 5, (BP) MO, (CMTS) 1860 Census
Miller, Sarah E.: (B) 1855, (CO) Pulaski, (A) 5, (BP) TN, (CMTS) 1860 Census
Miller, Susan: (B) 1820, (CO) Pulaski, (A) 40, (BP) TN, (CMTS) 1860 Census
Miller, Thomas: (B) 1852, (CO) Pulaski, (A) 8, (BP) TN, (CMTS) 1860 Census
Miller, William: (B) 1830, (CO) Pulaski, (A) 30, (BP) TN, (CMTS) 1860 Census
Miller, William: (B) 1834, (CO) Pulaski, (A) 26, (BP) Baden, (CMTS) 1860 Census
Miller, William: (B) 1857, (CO) Pulaski, (A) 3, (BP) MO, (CMTS) 1860 Census
Miller, William: (B) 1850, (D) 1929, (CO) Cedar, (C) Brashear Cemetery
Miller, William H.: (B) 1851, (CO) Pulaski, (A) 9, (BP) TN, (CMTS) 1860 Census
Miller, William M.: (B) 1845, (CO) Pulaski, (A) 15, (BP) TN, (CMTS) 1860 Census
Miller, William P.: (B) 1847, (CO) Pulaski, (A) 13, (BP) MO, (CMTS) 1860 Census
Milliken, John W.: (B) Aprl 14, 1836, (D) Sep. 8, 1888, (CO) Audrain, (C) Pisgah Cemetery
Mills, Hannah: (B) 1846, (CO) Stone, (A) 24, (BP) TN, (CMTS) 1870 Census
Mills, Marvel: (B) 1836, (CO) Stone, (A) 34, (BP) TN, (CMTS) 1870 Census
Mills, William R.: (B) 1857, (CO) Stone, (A) 13, (BP) MO, (CMTS) 1870 Census
Mitchell, Anthony B.: (B) 1820, (CO) Pulaski, (A) 40, (BP) TN, (CMTS) 1860 Census
Mitchell, Eliza Ann: (B) 1854, (D) 1945, (CO) Cedar, (C) Brashear Cemetery
Mitchell, Elizabeth: (B) 1826, (CO) Pulaski, (A) 34, (BP) MO, (CMTS) 1860 Census
Mitchell, Geneva B.: (B) Dec. 25, 1902, (D) Jul. 26, 1983, (CO) Henry, (C) Knights of Pythias Cemetery, Deepwater, MO
Mitchell, George: (B) 1854, (CO) Pulaski, (A) 6, (BP) MO, (CMTS) 1860 Census

Mitchell, Hannah: (B) 1855, (CO) Pulaski, (A) 5, (BP) MO, (CMTS) 1860 Census
Mitchell, Henry: (B) 1827, (CO) Pulaski, (A) 33, (BP) AL, (CMTS) 1860 Census
Mitchell, James: (B) 1844, (CO) Pulaski, (A) 16, (BP) MO, (CMTS) 1860 Census
Mitchell, John T.: (B) 1843, (CO) Pulaski, (A) 17, (BP) MO, (CMTS) 1860 Census
Mitchell, Joseph Y.: (B) 1853, (CO) Pulaski, (A) 7, (BP) MO, (CMTS) 1860 Census
Mitchell, Lorena: (B) 1850, (CO) Pulaski, (A) 10, (BP) MO, (CMTS) 1860 Census
Mitchell, Martin: (B) 1855, (CO) Pulaski, (A) 5, (BP) MO, (CMTS) 1860 Census
Mitchell, Mary: (B) 1832, (CO) Pulaski, (A) 28, (BP) MO, (CMTS) 1860 Census
Mitchell, Mary T.: (B) 1848, (CO) Pulaski, (A) 12, (BP) MO, (CMTS) 1860 Census
Mitchell, Nancy: (B) 1836, (CO) Pulaski, (A) 24, (BP) MO, (CMTS) 1860 Census
Mitchell, Perry: (B) 1826, (CO) Pulaski, (A) 34, (BP) AL, (CMTS) 1860 Census
Mitchell, Rachael: (B) 1834, (CO) Pulaski, (A) 26, (BP) AL, (CMTS) 1860 Census
Mitchell, Sally A.: (B) 1851, (CO) Pulaski, (A) 9, (BP) MO, (CMTS) 1860 Census
Mitchell, Samuel J.: (B) 1848, (CO) Pulaski, (A) 12, (BP) MO, (CMTS) 1860 Census
Mitchell, William: (B) 1825, (CO) Pulaski, (A) 35, (BP) Mecklenburg, (CMTS) 1860 Census
Mitchell, William: (B) 1842, (CO) Pulaski, (A) 18, (BP) MO, (CMTS) 1860 Census
Moldenhon, Fritz: (B) 1832, (CO) Pulaski, (A) 28, (BP) Saxony, (CMTS) 1860 Census
Moles, David: (B) 1850, (CO) Pulaski, (A) 10, (BP) AR, (CMTS) 1860 Census
Moles, Isaac: (B) 1837, (CO) Pulaski, (A) 23, (BP) TN, (CMTS) 1860 Census
Moles, John: (B) 1845, (CO) Pulaski, (A) 15, (BP) AR, (CMTS) 1860 Census
Moles, Mary: (B) 1837, (CO) Pulaski, (A) 23, (BP) IA, (CMTS) 1860 Census
Moles, Mary C.: (B) 1843, (CO) Pulaski, (A) 17, (BP) AR, (CMTS)

1860 Census
Moles, Thomas: (B) 1848, (CO) Pulaski, (A) 12, (BP) AR, (CMTS) 1860 Census
Monroe, Gerritt: (B) 1842, (CO) Stone, (A) 8, (BP) MO, (CMTS) 1870 Census
Monroe, John D: (B) 1843, (CO) Stone, (A) 7, (BP) MO, (CMTS) 1870 Census
Monroe, Manerva E.: (B) 1835, (CO) Stone, (A) 15, (BP) MO, (CMTS) 1870 Census
Monroe, Thomas: (B) 1840, (CO) Stone, (A) 10, (BP) MO, (CMTS) 1870 Census
Monroe, William: (B) 1846, (CO) Stone, (A) 4, (BP) MO, (CMTS) 1870 Census
Monroe, William D: (B) 1849, (CO) Stone, (A) 1, (BP) MO, (CMTS) 1870 Census
Montrief,Frances: (B) Aug. 25, 1814, (D) Aug. 18, 1899, (CO) Audrain, (C) Pisgah Cemetery
Moore, Betty Biggs: (B) 1836, (CO) Stone, (A) 14, (BP) MO, (CMTS) 1870 Census
Moore, Mary A.: (B) 1815, (CO) Stone, (A) 35, (BP) MO, (CMTS) 1870 Census
Moore, Mary E.: (B) 1838, (CO) Stone, (A) 12, (BP) MO, (CMTS) 1870 Census
Moore, Mary Jane: (B) Infant, (CO) Oregon, (C) Falling Springs Cemetery
Moore, Peter: (B) 1852, (CO) Stone, (A) 18, (BP) MO, (CMTS) 1870 Census
Moore, Sarah J.: (B) 1849, (CO) Stone, (A) 1, (BP) MO, (CMTS) 1870 Census
Moore, Vibra: (B) 1847, (CO) Stone, (A) 3, (BP) MO, (CMTS) 1870 Census
Moore, Vina: (B) 1842, (CO) Stone, (A) 8, (BP) MO, (CMTS) 1870 Census
Moore, William M.: (B) Feb. 11, 1864, (D) Oct. 14, 1909, (CO) Henry, (C) Knights of Pythias Cemetery, Deepwater, MO
Morgan, Emeline: (B) 1840, (CO) Pulaski, (A) 20, (BP) KY, (CMTS) 1860 Census
Morgan, George: (B) 1850, (CO) Pulaski, (A) 10, (BP) MO, (CMTS) 1860 Census
Morgan, Hazel M.: (B) Jul. 12, 1908, (D) Sep. 25, 1977, (CO) Henry, (C) Knights of Pythias Cemetery, Deepwater, MO
Morgan, Jane: (B) 1843, (CO) Pulaski, (A) 17, (BP) MO, (CMTS) 1860 Census

Morgan, John: (B) 1818, (CO) Pulaski, (A) 42, (BP) TN, (CMTS) 1860 Census
Morgan, John: (B) 1834, (CO) Pulaski, (A) 26, (BP) KY, (CMTS) 1860 Census
Morgan, Luna: (B) 1852, (CO) Pulaski, (A) 8, (BP) MO, (CMTS) 1860 Census
Morgan, Mary A.: (B) 1828, (CO) Pulaski, (A) 32, (BP) TN, (CMTS) 1860 Census
Morgan, Nellie G.: (B) Dec. 22, 1900, (D) Jan. 23, 1947, (CO) Henry, (C) Knights of Pythias Cemetery, Deepwater, MO
Morgan, Rebecca J.: (B) 1847, (CO) Pulaski, (A) 13, (BP) MO, (CMTS) 1860 Census
Morgan, William: (B) 1839, (CO) Pulaski, (A) 21, (BP) KY, (CMTS) 1860 Census
Morgan, William: (B) 1856, (CO) Pulaski, (A) 4, (BP) MO, (CMTS) 1860 Census
Morphew, James B.: (B) 1821, (CO) Stone, (A) 49, (BP) TN, (CMTS) 1870 Census
Morphew, Louisa J.: (B) 1853, (CO) Stone, (A) 17, (BP) AR, (CMTS) 1870 Census
Morris, Alexander: (B) 1845, (CO) Pulaski, (A) 15, (BP) GA, (CMTS) 1860 Census
Morris, Alexander F.: (B) 1856, (CO) Pulaski, (A) 4, (BP) MO, (CMTS) 1860 Census
Morris, Amanda J.: (B) 1841, (CO) Stone, (A) 9, (BP) AR, (CMTS) 1870 Census
Morris, Andrew J.: (B) 1831, (CO) Stone, (A) 19, (BP) AR, (CMTS) 1870 Census
Morris, Charles: (B) 1858, (CO) Pulaski, (A) 2, (BP) MO, (CMTS) 1860 Census
Morris, Elizabeth: (B) 1839, (CO) Pulaski, (A) 21, (BP) KY, (CMTS) 1860 Census
Morris, Emeline: (B) 1816, (CO) Pulaski, (A) 44, (BP) TN, (CMTS) 1860 Census
Morris, Evaline: (B) 1846, (CO) Pulaski, (A) 14, (BP) MO, (CMTS) 1860 Census
Morris, James A.: (B) 1846, (CO) Pulaski, (A) 14, (BP) MS, (CMTS) 1860 Census
Morris, James F: (B) 1838, (CO) Stone, (A) 12, (BP) AR, (CMTS) 1870 Census
Morris, John: (B) 1833, (CO) Pulaski, (A) 27, (BP) KY, (CMTS) 1860 Census
Morris, John: (B) 1856, (CO) Pulaski, (A) 4, (BP) MO, (CMTS)

1860 Census
Morris, Laura: (B) 1837, (CO) Pulaski, (A) 23, (BP) IN, (CMTS) 1860 Census
Morris, Mellissa: (B) 1844, (CO) Pulaski, (A) 16, (BP) MO, (CMTS) 1860 Census
Morris, Nancy: (B) 1836, (CO) Pulaski, (A) 24, (BP) KY, (CMTS) 1860 Census
Morris, Nancy: (B) 1848, (CO) Pulaski, (A) 12, (BP) MS, (CMTS) 1860 Census
Morris, Parmelia: (B) 1850, (CO) Pulaski, (A) 10, (BP) MS, (CMTS) 1860 Census
Morris, Sarah: (B) 1841, (CO) Pulaski, (A) 19, (BP) MO, (CMTS) 1860 Census
Morris, Sarah C.: (B) 1829, (CO) Stone, (A) 21, (BP) AR, (CMTS) 1870 Census
Morris, Steven: (B) 1835, (CO) Stone, (A) 15, (BP) AR, (CMTS) 1870 Census
Morris, Susan E.: (B) 1854, (CO) Pulaski, (A) 6, (BP) MO, (CMTS) 1860 Census
Morris, William: (B) 1835, (CO) Pulaski, (A) 25, (BP) IL, (CMTS) 1860 Census
Morrison, John H.: (B) 1836, (CO) Pulaski, (A) 24, (BP) MO, (CMTS) 1860 Census
Morrissey, Ida R.: (B) 1900, (D) 1954, (CO) St. Louis, (C) Calvary Cemetery
Morrissey, Joseph *: (B) 1896, (D) 1953, (CO) St. Louis, (C) Calvary Cemetery
Morrissey, Loretta E.: (B) 1904, (D) 1995, (CO) St. Louis, (C) Calvary Cemetery
Morrissey, Thomas J.: (B) 1908, (D) 1972, (CO) St. Louis, (C) Calvary Cemetery
Morrow, Alfred L.: (B) 1851, (CO) Pulaski, (A) 9, (BP) MO, (CMTS) 1860 Census
Morrow, Elizabeth: (B) 1838, (CO) Pulaski, (A) 22, (BP) MO, (CMTS) 1860 Census
Morrow, Hugh: (B) 1830, (CO) Pulaski, (A) 30, (BP) NC, (CMTS) 1860 Census
Morrow, Martha: (B) 1855, (CO) Pulaski, (A) 5, (BP) MO, (CMTS) 1860 Census
Morrow, Rebecca: (B) 1853, (CO) Pulaski, (A) 7, (BP) MO, (CMTS) 1860 Census
Mortly, Susah E.: (B) 1837, (CO) Stone, (A) 33, (BP) MO, (CMTS) 1870 Census

Moschberger, Anna: (B) Oct. 23, 1811, (D) Jan. 4, 1892, (CO) Andrew, (C) Oak Ridge Cemetery
Moseby, Margaret: (B) 1846, (CO) Pulaski, (A) 14, (BP) KY, (CMTS) 1860 Census
Moseby, Mary: (B) 1852, (CO) Pulaski, (A) 8, (BP) KY, (CMTS) 1860 Census
Moseby, Micajah: (B) 1849, (CO) Pulaski, (A) 11, (BP) KY, (CMTS) 1860 Census
Moseby, Nancy: (B) 1855, (CO) Pulaski, (A) 5, (BP) KY, (CMTS) 1860 Census
Mosen, Patrick: (B) 1827, (CO) Pulaski, (A) 33, (BP) Ireland, (CMTS) 1860 Census
Moser, John: (B) Feb. 17, 1817, (D) Mar. 30, 1887, (CO) Andrew, (C) Oak Ridge Cemetery
Mosles, George W.: (B) 1850, (CO) Pulaski, (A) 10, (BP) MO, (CMTS) 1860 Census
Mosles, Lovisa: (B) 1848, (CO) Pulaski, (A) 12, (BP) MO, (CMTS) 1860 Census
Mosles, Mary J.: (B) 1853, (CO) Pulaski, (A) 7, (BP) MO, (CMTS) 1860 Census
Mosles, Nancy E.: (B) 1855, (CO) Pulaski, (A) 5, (BP) MO, (CMTS) 1860 Census
Mosles, William A.: (B) 1849, (CO) Pulaski, (A) 11, (BP) MO, (CMTS) 1860 Census
Moulder, Alice: (B) 1841, (CO) Stone, (A) 9, (BP) AR, (CMTS) 1870 Census
Moulder, Ellen: (B) 1840, (CO) Stone, (A) 10, (BP) AR, (CMTS) 1870 Census
Moulder, Elyza: (B) 1843, (CO) Stone, (A) 7, (BP) MO, (CMTS) 1870 Census
Moulder, Jane: (B) 1832, (CO) Stone, (A) 18, (BP) AR, (CMTS) 1870 Census
Moulder, James: (B) 1820, (CO) Stone, (A) 30, (BP) TN, (CMTS) 1870 Census
Moulder, John: (B) 1838, (CO) Stone, (A) 12, (BP) AR, (CMTS) 1870 Census
Moulder, Julina: (B) 1842, (CO) Stone, (A) 8, (BP) AR, (CMTS) 1870 Census
Moulder, Susan: (B) 1834, (CO) Stone, (A) 16, (BP) AR, (CMTS) 1870 Census
Moulder, Vanstell: (B) 1826, (CO) Stone, (A) 24, (BP) TN, (CMTS) 1870 Census
Mudd, Dayton Henry: (B) Nov. 22, 1878, (D) Mar. 5, 1928, (CO) St.

Louis, (C) Calvary Cemetery
Mullaly, Patrick: (D) Jan. 7, 1881, (CO) St. Louis, (C) Calvary Cemetery, (A) 51
Mullen, Lawrence M.: (B) Nov. 2, 1893, (D) Dec. 4, 1954, (CO) St. Louis, (C) Calvary Cemetery
Mullens, Agnes: (B) 1858, (CO) Pulaski, (A) 2, (BP) MO, (CMTS) 1860 Census
Mullens, Armstrong: (B) 1826, (CO) Pulaski, (A) 34, (BP) KY, (CMTS) 1860 Census
Mullens, Catharine: (B) 1830, (CO) Pulaski, (A) 30, (BP) KY, (CMTS) 1860 Census
Mullens, James: (B) 1850, (CO) Pulaski, (A) 10, (BP) AR, (CMTS) 1860 Census
Mullens, Lucinda: (B) 1853, (CO) Pulaski, (A) 7, (BP) AR, (CMTS) 1860 Census
Mundy, Felix: (D) Feb. 3, 1877, (CO) St. Louis, (C) Calvary Cemetery
Munro, William: (B) 1817, (CO) Pulaski, (A) 43, (BP) NY, (CMTS) 1860 Census
Murphy, Alvens: (B) 1855, (CO) Pulaski, (A) 5, (BP) MO, (CMTS) 1860 Census
Murphy, Charles I.: (B) 1868, (D) 1909, (CO) St. Louis, (C) Calvary Cemetery
Murphy, James: (B) 1851, (CO) Stone, (A) 19, (BP) MO, (CMTS) 1870 Census
Murphy, James J.: (B) Sep. 11, 1914, (D) Jan. 12, 1982, (CO) St. Louis, (C) Calvary Cemetery
Murphy, John: (B) 1829, (CO) Stone, (A) 41, (BP) KY, (CMTS) 1870 Census
Murphy, John: (B) 1843, (CO) Pulaski, (A) 17, (BP) MO, (CMTS) 1860 Census
Murphy, John: (D) Nov. 3, 1901, (CO) St. Louis, (C) Calvary Cemetery
Murphy, John C.: (B) 1868, (D) 1952, (CO) St. Louis, (C) Calvary Cemetery
Murphy, Julius I.: (B) 1884, (D) 1910, (CO) St. Louis, (C) Calvary Cemetery
Murphy, Kate L.: (B) 1870, (D) 1959, (CO) St. Louis, (C) Calvary Cemetery
Murphy, Kesiah: (B) 1827, (CO) Stone, (A) 43, (BP) TN, (CMTS) 1870 Census
Murphy, Lucinda: (B) 1838, (CO) Pulaski, (A) 22, (BP) MO, (CMTS) 1860 Census
Murphy, Mary T.: (B) 1877, (D) 1944, (CO) St. Louis, (C) Calvary Cemetery

Murphy, Nora: (B) 1845, (D) 1906, (CO) St. Louis, (C) Calvary Cemetery
Murphy, Susanna: (D) Jun. 27, 1880, (CO) St. Louis, (C) Calvary Cemetery, (A) 5
Murphy,: (B) 1836, (D) 1912, (CO) St. Louis, (C) Calvary Cemetery
Murray, John: (B) Sep. 1, 1877, (D) Jul. 2, 1944, (CO) St. Louis, (C) Calvary Cemetery
Murray, Patience Hubert: (B) 1796, (D) 1892, (CO) St. Louis, (C) Calvary Cemetery
Murry, Joseph: (B) 1848, (CO) Pulaski, (A) 12, (BP) MO, (CMTS) 1860 Census
Murry, Louisa: (B) 1850, (CO) Pulaski, (A) 10, (BP) MO, (CMTS) 1860 Census
Murry, Nancy: (B) 1833, (CO) Pulaski, (A) 27, (BP) MO, (CMTS) 1860 Census
Murry, William: (B) 1820, (CO) Pulaski, (A) 40, (BP) NC, (CMTS) 1860 Census
Muse, John: (B) 1819, (CO) Stone, (A) 51, (BP) VA, (CMTS) 1870 Census
Muse, Joseph Z: (B) 1851, (CO) Stone, (A) 19, (BP) TN, (CMTS) 1870 Census
Muse, Mary N: (B) 1850, (CO) Stone, (A) 20, (BP) TN, (CMTS) 1870 Census
Muse, Peggie: (B) 1820, (CO) Stone, (A) 50, (BP) TN, (CMTS) 1870 Census
Muse, William: (B) 1853, (CO) Stone, (A) 17, (BP) AR, (CMTS) 1870 Census
Musgrave, Caroline: (B) 1844, (CO) Pulaski, (A) 16, (BP) MO, (CMTS) 1860 Census
Musgrave, Elihu: (B) 1832, (CO) Pulaski, (A) 28, (BP) IL, (CMTS) 1860 Census
Musgrave, Fiat: (B) 1840, (CO) Pulaski, (A) 20, (BP) IL, (CMTS) 1860 Census
Musgrave, George W.: (B) 1845, (CO) Pulaski, (A) 15, (BP) MO, (CMTS) 1860 Census
Musgrave, Harriet: (B) 1851, (CO) Pulaski, (A) 9, (BP) MO, (CMTS) 1860 Census
Musgrave, James C.: (B) 1826, (CO) Pulaski, (A) 34, (BP) TN, (CMTS) 1860 Census
Musgrave, James H.: (B) 1848, (CO) Pulaski, (A) 12, (BP) MO, (CMTS) 1860 Census
Musgrave, John B.: (B) 1855, (CO) Pulaski, (A) 5, (BP) MO, (CMTS) 1860 Census

Musgrave, Marion: (B) 1842, (CO) Pulaski, (A) 18, (BP) MO, (CMTS) 1860 Census
Musgrave, Mellissa: (B) 1847, (CO) Pulaski, (A) 13, (BP) MO, (CMTS) 1860 Census
Musgrave, Nancy: (B) 1838, (CO) Pulaski, (A) 22, (BP) MO, (CMTS) 1860 Census
Musgrave, S.: (B) 1847, (CO) Pulaski, (A) 13, (BP) MO, (CMTS) 1860 Census
Musgrave, Sanford S.: (B) 1848, (CO) Pulaski, (A) 12, (BP) MO, (CMTS) 1860 Census
Musgrave, Susanah: (B) 1839, (CO) Pulaski, (A) 21, (BP) MO, (CMTS) 1860 Census
Musgrave, William H.: (B) 1851, (CO) Pulaski, (A) 9, (BP) MO, (CMTS) 1860 Census
Musicl, Catherine L.: (B) 1851, (D) 1934, (CO) St. Louis, (C) Calvary Cemetery
Nangle, Harriet S.: (B) 1907, (D) 1981, (CO) St. Louis, (C) Calvary Cemetery
Nangle, James F.: (B) 1904, (D) 1991, (CO) St. Louis, (C) Calvary Cemetery
Nangle, John J.: (B) Mar. 28, 1891, (D) Aug. 23, 1960, (CO) St. Louis, (C) Calvary Cemetery
Napier, Mary Ann: (B) 1845, (CO) Stone, (A) 25, (BP) MO, (CMTS) 1870 Census
Napier, William: (B) 1843, (CO) Stone, (A) 27, (BP) AR, (CMTS) 1870 Census
Nave, Angeline: (B) 1840, (D) 1926, (CO) Cedar, (C) Brashear Cemetery
Nave, W. B.: (B) 1836, (D) 1915, (CO) Cedar, (C) Brashear Cemetery
Nelson, Benjamin T.: (B) 1856, (CO) Pulaski, (A) 4, (BP) MO, (CMTS) 1860 Census
Nelson, Frances: (B) 1826, (CO) Stone, (A) 24, (BP) AR, (CMTS) 1870 Census
Nelson, George W.: (B) 1841, (CO) Pulaski, (A) 19, (BP) MO, (CMTS) 1860 Census
Nelson, Henry C.: (B) 1842, (CO) Pulaski, (A) 18, (BP) MO, (CMTS) 1860 Census
Nelson, Jerome: (B) 1826, (CO) Stone, (A) 24, (BP) MO, (CMTS) 1870 Census
Nelson, John: (B) 1836, (CO) Pulaski, (A) 24, (BP) MO, (CMTS) 1860 Census
Nelson, John T.: (B) 1840, (CO) Stone, (A) 30, (BP) MO, (CMTS) 1870 Census
Nelson, Louisa: (B) 1840, (CO) Stone, (A) 30, (BP) MO, (CMTS) 1870

Census
Nelson, Lovissa: (B) 1851, (CO) Pulaski, (A) 9, (BP) MO, (CMTS) 1860 Census
Nelson, Malinda: (B) 1835, (CO) Pulaski, (A) 25, (BP) MO, (CMTS) 1860 Census
Nelson, Martha: (B) 1840, (CO) Pulaski, (A) 20, (BP) NC, (CMTS) 1860 Census
Nelson, Mary E.: (B) 1853, (CO) Pulaski, (A) 7, (BP) MO, (CMTS) 1860 Census
Nelson, Mirissa: (B) 1848, (CO) Pulaski, (A) 12, (BP) MO, (CMTS) 1860 Census
Nelson, Nancy E.: (B) 1846, (CO) Pulaski, (A) 14, (BP) MO, (CMTS) 1860 Census
Nelson, Octavia: (B) 1833, (CO) Stone, (A) 17, (BP) MO, (CMTS) 1870 Census
Nelson, Robert: (B) 1857, (CO) Pulaski, (A) 3, (BP) MO, (CMTS) 1860 Census
Nelson, Sarah Jane: (B) 1839, (CO) Pulaski, (A) 21, (BP) MO, (CMTS) 1860 Census
Nelson, Thomas W.: (B) 1844, (CO) Pulaski, (A) 16, (BP) MO, (CMTS) 1860 Census
Nelson, Uriah C.: (B) 1852, (CO) Pulaski, (A) 8, (BP) MO, (CMTS) 1860 Census
Nesbit, Mary M.: (B) 1942, (D) 1972, (CO) St. Louis, (C) Calvary Cemetery
Newman, Laura A.: (B) 1854, (CO) Stone, (A) 16, (BP) MO, (CMTS) 1870 Census
Newman, Levi: (B) 1849, (CO) Stone, (A) 21, (BP) MO, (CMTS) 1870 Census
Newman, Maria: (B) 1857, (D) 1902, (CO) St. Louis, (C) Calvary Cemetery
Newman, Melinda: (B) 1852, (CO) Stone, (A) 18, (BP) MO, (CMTS) 1870 Census
Newman, Patrick: (B) 1852, (D) 1913, (CO) St. Louis, (C) Calvary Cemetery
Newman, Patrick: (B) 1886, (D) 1890, (CO) St. Louis, (C) Calvary Cemetery
Newman, Rufus: (B) 1856, (CO) Stone, (A) 14, (BP) MO, (CMTS) 1870 Census
Newman, Sarah: (B) 1822, (CO) Stone, (A) 48, (BP) KY, (CMTS) 1870 Census
Newman, Thomas: (B) 1820, (CO) Stone, (A) 50, (BP) KY, (CMTS) 1870 Census

Nobles, Chesley: (B) 1840, (CO) Pulaski, (A) 20, (BP) MO, (CMTS) 1860 Census
Noonan, Thomas: (D) Apr. 30, 1925, (CO) St. Louis, (C) Calvary Cemetery
Norris, J.: (B) 1838, (D) 1912, (CO) Cedar, (C) Brashear Cemetery
Norris, Sophia: (B) 1844, (D) 1902, (CO) Cedar, (C) Brashear Cemetery
Nouse, Anna Catherina: (D) Jul. 3, 1909, (CO) St. Louis, (C) Calvary Cemetery
Nowland, Jacob: (B) 1846, (CO) Pulaski, (A) 14, (BP) IL, (CMTS) 1860 Census
Nowland, John: (B) 1855, (CO) Pulaski, (A) 5, (BP) IL, (CMTS) 1860 Census
Nowland, Mary A.: (B) 1844, (CO) Pulaski, (A) 16, (BP) IL, (CMTS) 1860 Census
Nowland, Nathaniel: (B) 1845, (CO) Pulaski, (A) 15, (BP) IL, (CMTS) 1860 Census
Nowland, Samuel: (B) 1852, (CO) Pulaski, (A) 8, (BP) IL, (CMTS) 1860 Census
Nowland, Sarah J.: (B) 1854, (CO) Pulaski, (A) 6, (BP) IL, (CMTS) 1860 Census
Nowland, William: (B) 1848, (CO) Pulaski, (A) 12, (BP) IL, (CMTS) 1860 Census
Nox, Julia A.: (B) 1823, (CO) Pulaski, (A) 37, (BP) TN, (CMTS) 1860 Census
Nox, Nathaniel: (B) 1823, (CO) Pulaski, (A) 37, (BP) TN, (CMTS) 1860 Census
Nuell, Henry: (B) 1875, (D) 1988, (CO) St. Louis, (C) Calvary Cemetery
Nuell, Irs T.: (B) 1908, (D) 1988, (CO) St. Louis, (C) Calvary Cemetery
Nuell, Laura M. Heidemann: (B) 1876, (D) 1941, (CO) St. Louis, (C) Calvary Cemetery
Nuell, Raymond F.: (B) 1904, (D) 1927, (CO) St. Louis, (C) Calvary Cemetery
Nuell, Theresa M.: (B) 1878, (D) 1963, (CO) St. Louis, (C) Calvary Cemetery
Nutty, William: (B) 1835, (CO) Pulaski, (A) 25, (BP) TN, (CMTS) 1860 Census
Nye, John: (B) Feb. 23, 1849, (D) Sep. 6, 1899, (CO) Henry, (C) Knights of Pythias Cemetery, Deepwater, MO
Obermeier, Edward A.: (B) May 27, 1865, (D) Mar. 10, 1928, (CO) St. Louis, (C) Calvary Cemetery
Obrien, Julia: (B) 1830, (CO) Pulaski, (A) 30, (BP) Ireland, (CMTS) 1860 Census
Obrien, Julia: (B) 1854, (CO) Pulaski, (A) 6, (BP) MO, (CMTS)

1860 Census
O'Brien, Edward J.: (B) 1899, (D) 1969, (CO) St. Louis, (C) Calvary Cemetery
O'Brien, Katherine: (B) 1873, (D) 1960, (CO) St. Louis, (C) Calvary Cemetery
O'Brien, Lucille E.: (B) 1907, (D) 1961, (CO) St. Louis, (C) Calvary Cemetery
O'Brien, Mary: (B) 1863, (D) 1943, (CO) St. Louis, (C) Calvary Cemetery
O'Brien, Mary Rose: (B) 1900, (D) 1989, (CO) St. Louis, (C) Calvary Cemetery
O'Brien, Michael: (B) 1868, (D) 1944, (CO) St. Louis, (C) Calvary Cemetery
O'Brien, Walter W.: (B) 1902, (D) 1986, (CO) St. Louis, (C) Calvary Cemetery
O'Brien, William: (B) 1820, (CO) Pulaski, (A) 40, (BP) Ireland, (CMTS) 1860 Census
O'Connor, Cecelia: (B) 1900, (D) 1903, (CO) St. Louis, (C) Calvary Cemetery
O'Connor, Charles F.: (B) 1893, (D) 1916, (CO) St. Louis, (C) Calvary Cemetery
O'Connor, Ellen: (B) 1864, (D) 1943, (CO) St. Louis, (C) Calvary Cemetery
O'Connor, John J.: (B) 1860, (D) 1926, (CO) St. Louis, (C) Calvary Cemetery
O'Connor, Mary: (B) 1895, (D) 1895, (CO) St. Louis, (C) Calvary Cemetery
O'Connor, Matthew: (D) Feb. 25, 1877, (CO) St. Louis, (C) Calvary Cemetery, (A) 48
O'Day, Marjorie: (B) 1899, (D) 1945, (CO) St. Louis, (C) Calvary Cemetery
O'Day, Neil: (B) 1901, (D) 1946, (CO) St. Louis, (C) Calvary Cemetery
O'Donnell, Frances: (D) Jan. 27, 1921, (CO) St. Louis, (C) Calvary Cemetery
O'Donnell, Gertrude C.: (D) Jun. 22, 1964, (CO) St. Louis, (C) Calvary Cemetery
O'Donnell, William Gerald: (D) Aug. 27, 1950, (CO) St. Louis, (C) Calvary Cemetery
O'Donnell, William L.: (D) Jan. 2, 1974, (CO) St. Louis, (C) Calvary Cemetery
Ogletree, Burrill: (B) 1838, (CO) Pulaski, (A) 22, (BP) TN, (CMTS) 1860 Census
Ogletree, Catharine: (B) 1856, (CO) Pulaski, (A) 4, (BP) TN, (CMTS) 1860 Census

Ogletree, John A.: (B) 1826, (CO) Pulaski, (A) 34, (BP) TN, (CMTS) 1860 Census
Ogletree, Mary A.: (B) 1829, (CO) Pulaski, (A) 31, (BP) TN, (CMTS) 1860 Census
O'Halloran, James: (D) Jan. 1, 1883, (CO) St. Louis, (C) Calvary Cemetery
O'Hearn, James R.: (B) 1877, (D) 1959, (CO) St. Louis, (C) Calvary Cemetery
O'Hearn, Lillian: (B) 1889, (D) 1957, (CO) St. Louis, (C) Calvary Cemetery
O'Keefe, Jr., Daniel J.: (B) 1936, (CO) St. Louis, (C) Calvary Cemetery
O'Keefe, Joan C.: (B) 1937, (D) 1991, (CO) St. Louis, (C) Calvary Cemetery
O'Laughlin, Sr., Daniel Robert: (D) Dec. 12, 1996, (CO) St. Louis, (C) Calvary Cemetery
O'Leary, John: (D) Feb. 5, 1877, (CO) St. Louis, (C) Calvary Cemetery
O'Madigan, Nannie J.: (D) Apr. 7, 1877, (CO) St. Louis, (C) Calvary Cemetery, (A) 27
O'Neill, Thomas: (D) Jan. 10, 1884, (CO) St. Louis, (C) Calvary Cemetery
Oniel, Michael: (B) 1838, (CO) Pulaski, (A) 22, (BP) Ireland, (CMTS) 1860 Census
Orahood, Mary: (B) 1837, (D) 1905, (CO) Cedar, (C) Brashear Cemetery
Osborn, William: (B) 1840, (CO) Pulaski, (A) 20, (BP) MD, (CMTS) 1860 Census
Osburn, NancyC.: (B) 1843, (D) 1902, (CO) Henry, (C) Knights of Pythias Cemetery, Deepwater, MO
Oswald, Stephen: (B) 1832, (CO) Pulaski, (A) 28, (BP) Baden, (CMTS) 1860 Census
Otto, Raymond E.: (D) Dec., 1974, (CO) St. Louis, (C) Calvary Cemetery
Owen, Charlotte: (B) 1854, (CO) Pulaski, (A) 6, (BP) MO, (CMTS) 1860 Census
Owen, Daniel: (B) 1858, (CO) Pulaski, (A) 2, (BP) MO, (CMTS) 1860 Census
Owen, James: (B) 1852, (CO) Pulaski, (A) 8, (BP) MO, (CMTS) 1860 Census
Owen, Margaret: (B) 1850, (CO) Pulaski, (A) 10, (BP) MO, (CMTS) 1860 Census
Owen, Matilda: (B) 1856, (CO) Pulaski, (A) 4, (BP) MO, (CMTS) 1860 Census
Owen, Nancy: (B) 1825, (CO) Pulaski, (A) 35, (BP) IN, (CMTS) 1860 Census
Owen, Thomas: (B) 1847, (CO) Pulaski, (A) 13, (BP) MO, (CMTS)

1860 Census
Owens, DavidC: (B) 1849, (CO) Stone, (A) 21, (BP) MO, (CMTS) 1870 Census
Owens, Elias A.: (B) 1832, (CO) Pulaski, (A) 28, (BP) TN, (CMTS) 1860 Census
Owens, Elizabeth: (B) 1838, (CO) Pulaski, (A) 22, (BP) TN, (CMTS) 1860 Census
Owens, Hugh J.: (B) 1854, (CO) Stone, (A) 16, (BP) MO, (CMTS) 1870 Census
Owens, JamesC: (B) 1852, (CO) Stone, (A) 18, (BP) MO, (CMTS) 1870 Census
Owens, John A.: (B) 1856, (CO) Stone, (A) 14, (BP) MO, (CMTS) 1870 Census
Owens, Malona: (B) 1852, (CO) Stone, (A) 18, (BP) MO, (CMTS) 1870 Census
Owens, Mary A.: (B) 1849, (CO) Stone, (A) 21, (BP) MO, (CMTS) 1870 Census
Owens, Sarah: (B) 1826, (CO) Stone, (A) 44, (BP) GA, (CMTS) 1870 Census
Owens, William: (B) 1815, (CO) Stone, (A) 55, (BP) TN, (CMTS) 1870 Census
Owens, William H.: (B) 1855, (CO) Pulaski, (A) 5, (BP) TN, (CMTS) 1860 Census
Owings, Agnes King: (B) 1872, (D) 1952, (CO) St. Louis, (C) Calvary Cemetery
Owings, Zebulon: (B) 1865, (D) 1948, (CO) St. Louis, (C) Calvary Cemetery
Packwood, Mary: (B) 1829, (CO) Stone, (A) 21, (BP) CA, (CMTS) 1870 Census
Packwood, William S.: (B) 1848, (CO) Stone, (A) 2, (BP) MO, (CMTS) 1870 Census
Painter, George W.: (B) 1822, (CO) Stone, (A) 28, (BP) MO, (CMTS) 1870 Census
Painter, Julia B.: (B) 1827, (CO) Stone, (A) 23, (BP) WI, (CMTS) 1870 Census
Paisley, Samuel: (B) 1838, (CO) Pulaski, (A) 22, (BP) IL, (CMTS) 1860 Census
Palmer, Margaret: (B) 1815, (CO) Stone, (A) 35, (BP) AL, (CMTS) 1870 Census
Parker, David P: (B) 1855, (CO) Stone, (A) 15, (BP) MO, (CMTS) 1870 Census
Parker, Elizabeth A.: (B) 1842, (CO) Stone, (A) 28, (BP) TN, (CMTS) 1870 Census

Parker, Everena: (B) 1818, (CO) Stone, (A) 32, (BP) TN, (CMTS) 1870 Census
Parker, James D: (B) 1838, (CO) Stone, (A) 32, (BP) TN, (CMTS) 1870 Census
Parker, Jefferson: (B) 1838, (CO) Stone, (A) 12, (BP) MO, (CMTS) 1870 Census
Parker, John: (B) 1847, (CO) Stone, (A) 3, (BP) MO, (CMTS) 1870 Census
Parker, Mary C.: (B) 1852, (CO) Stone, (A) 18, (BP) IL, (CMTS) 1870 Census
Parker, Mary E.: (B) 1841, (CO) Stone, (A) 9, (BP) MO, (CMTS) 1870 Census
Parker, Melinda: (B) 1856, (CO) Stone, (A) 14, (BP) MO, (CMTS) 1870 Census
Parker, Polly Ann: (B) 1828, (CO) Stone, (A) 42, (BP) SC, (CMTS) 1870 Census
Parker, William: (B) 1848, (CO) Stone, (A) 22, (BP) MO, (CMTS) 1870 Census
Parks, Cordelia B.: (B) Feb. 22, 1859, (D) Jul. 31, 1904, (CO) Henry, (C) Knights of Pythias Cemetery, Deepwater, MO
Parrott, Lahey T.: (B) 1864, (D) 1944, (CO) Oregon, (C) Falling Springs Cemetery
Parsons, Caledona: (B) 1847, (CO) Stone, (A) 3, (BP) MO, (CMTS) 1870 Census
Parsons, Carolina: (B) 1833, (CO) Stone, (A) 37, (BP) KY, (CMTS) 1870 Census
Parsons, Daisy Lee: (B) Oct. 25, 1906, (D) Dec. 25, 1986, (CO) Butler, (Maiden) Campbell
Parsons, George James Dewey: (B) Nov. 6, 1898, (D) Oct. 22, 1986, (CO) Lincoln, (DP) Butler Co., MO
Parsons, Henry G: (B) 1840, (CO) Stone, (A) 10, (BP) AL, (CMTS) 1870 Census
Parsons, Hiram N: (B) 1838, (CO) Stone, (A) 12, (BP) AR, (CMTS) 1870 Census
Parsons, Jonathan: (B) 1833, (CO) Stone, (A) 37, (BP) MO, (CMTS) 1870 Census
Parsons, Martha: (B) 1841, (CO) Stone, (A) 9, (BP) AR, (CMTS) 1870 Census
Parsons, Mary L.: (B) 1844, (CO) Stone, (A) 26, (BP) AL, (CMTS) 1870 Census
Parsons, Nancy: (B) 1845, (CO) Stone, (A) 5, (BP) MO, (CMTS) 1870 Census
Parsons, Richard G: (B) 1832, (CO) Stone, (A) 18, (BP) MS, (CMTS)

1870 Census
Parsons, Thomas J.: (B) 1829, (CO) Stone, (A) 21, (BP) AL, (CMTS) 1870 Census
Parsons, William: (B) 1840, (CO) Stone, (A) 30, (BP) TN, (CMTS) 1870 Census
Parsons, William C.: (B) 1839, (CO) Stone, (A) 11, (BP) AR, (CMTS) 1870 Census
Partridge, Don R.: (B) 1927, (D) 1971, (CO) Oregon, (C) Falling Springs Cemetery
Partridge, Gladys E.: (B) 1919, (D) 1979, (CO) Oregon, (C) Falling Springs Cemetery
Patton, Charles: (B) 1852, (CO) Pulaski, (A) 8, (BP) MO, (CMTS) 1860 Census
Patton, Hate: (B) 1848, (CO) Pulaski, (A) 12, (BP) MO, (CMTS) 1860 Census
Patton, Jennette: (B) May 1, 1828, (D) Jun. 18, 1896, (CO) Andrew, (C) Oak Ridge Cemetery
Paul, Eliza: (B) 1840, (CO) Pulaski, (A) 20, (BP) MO, (CMTS) 1860 Census
Paul, William: (B) 1840, (CO) Pulaski, (A) 20, (BP) TN, (CMTS) 1860 Census
Payne, James: (B) 1829, (CO) Stone, (A) 41, (BP) TN, (CMTS) 1870 Census
Payne, Sophia J.: (B) 1843, (CO) Stone, (A) 27, (BP) MO, (CMTS) 1870 Census
Payson, Louis B.: (D) March 8, 1862, (CO) Pettis, (CMTS) From Bremer, IA, (DP) Sedalia, MO
Peacher, Anna: (B) 1807, (D) 1896, (CO) Audrain, (C) Pisgah Cemetery
Pearson, Susan E.: (B) Jun. 20, 1837, (D) Apr. 15, 1855, (CO) Audrain, (C) Old Village Cemetery
Peck, George W.: (B) 1852, (CO) Pulaski, (A) 8, (BP) GA, (CMTS) 1860 Census
Peck, Harrison: (B) 1841, (CO) Pulaski, (A) 19, (BP) TN, (CMTS) 1860 Census
Peck, Jacob R.: (B) 1848, (CO) Pulaski, (A) 12, (BP) TN, (CMTS) 1860 Census
Peck, James M.: (B) 1850, (CO) Pulaski, (A) 10, (BP) MO, (CMTS) 1860 Census
Peck, John T.: (B) 1853, (CO) Pulaski, (A) 7, (BP) MO, (CMTS) 1860 Census
Peck, Mary M.: (B) 1854, (CO) Pulaski, (A) 6, (BP) IL, (CMTS) 1860 Census
Peck, Nancy A.: (B) 1843, (CO) Pulaski, (A) 17, (BP) TN, (CMTS)

1860 Census
Peck, William J.: (B) 1856, (CO) Pulaski, (A) 4, (BP) MO, (CMTS) 1860 Census
Peck, William Wethers: (B) 1847, (CO) Pulaski, (A) 13, (BP) MO, (CMTS) 1860 Census
Peck, Winfield Scott: (B) 1846, (CO) Pulaski, (A) 14, (BP) TN, (CMTS) 1860 Census
Peck, Yornig: (B) 1844, (CO) Pulaski, (A) 16, (BP) TN, (CMTS) 1860 Census
Peer, Sarah L.: (B) 1855, (D) 1930, (CO) Cedar, (C) Brashear Cemetery
Peer,: (B) 1845, (D) 1910, (CO) Cedar, (C) Brashear Cemetery
Pegram, Francis: (B) 1829, (CO) Stone, (A) 21, (BP) MO, (CMTS) 1870 Census
Pegram, James S.: (B) 1842, (CO) Stone, (A) 8, (BP) MO, (CMTS) 1870 Census
Pemberton, John J.: (B) 1856, (CO) Pulaski, (A) 4, (BP) MO, (CMTS) 1860 Census
Pemberton, Lucinda: (B) 1829, (CO) Pulaski, (A) 31, (BP) KY, (CMTS) 1860 Census
Pemberton, William: (B) 1832, (CO) Pulaski, (A) 28, (BP) TN, (CMTS) 1860 Census
Pensa, Antonio: (B) 1824, (D) 1904, (CO) St. Louis, (C) Calvary Cemetery
Pensa, Rose Gardella: (B) 1835, (D) 1873, (CO) St. Louis, (C) Calvary Cemetery
Periman, Jessie Lea: (B) Dec. 26, 1917, (D) Nov. 17, 1985, (CO) Henry, (C) Knights of Pythias Cemetery, Deepwater, MO
Peters, Albert F.: (D) Oct. 23, 1905, (CO) St. Louis, (C) Calvary Cemetery, (A) 31
Peters, Rosanah: (B) 1841, (CO) Stone, (A) 29, (BP) TN, (CMTS) 1870 Census
Peters, William: (B) 1841, (CO) Stone, (A) 29, (BP) VA, (CMTS) 1870 Census
Peterson, Eliza: (B) 1833, (CO) Stone, (A) 17, (BP) KY, (CMTS) 1870 Census
Peterson, Eliza: (B) 1846, (CO) Pulaski, (A) 14, (BP) MO, (CMTS) 1860 Census
Peterson, Elizabeth: (B) 1839, (CO) Stone, (A) 11, (BP) IL, (CMTS) 1870 Census
Peterson, Georgeaiana: (B) 1846, (CO) Stone, (A) 4, (BP) IL, (CMTS) 1870 Census
Peterson, Gertrude: (B) 1848, (CO) Stone, (A) 2, (BP) MO, (CMTS) 1870 Census

Peterson, James: (B) 1852, (CO) Pulaski, (A) 8, (BP) MO, (CMTS) 1860 Census
Peterson, Mary: (B) 1830, (CO) Pulaski, (A) 30, (BP) MO, (CMTS) 1860 Census
Peterson, Moses: (B) 1848, (CO) Pulaski, (A) 12, (BP) MO, (CMTS) 1860 Census
Peterson, Thomas: (B) 1794, (CO) Stone, (A) 56, (BP) NJ, (CMTS) 1870 Census
Peterson, Thomas: (B) 1856, (CO) Pulaski, (A) 4, (BP) MO, (CMTS) 1860 Census
Peterson, William: (B) 1828, (CO) Stone, (A) 22, (BP) OH, (CMTS) 1870 Census
Peterson, William: (B) 1850, (CO) Pulaski, (A) 10, (BP) MO, (CMTS) 1860 Census
Pettgen, Mattie G.: (B) 1893, (D) 1949, (CO) St. Louis, (C) Calvary Cemetery
Pettis, James S.: (B) 1837, (CO) Pulaski, (A) 23, (BP) TN, (CMTS) 1860 Census
Pettis, John H.: (B) 1839, (CO) Pulaski, (A) 21, (BP) TN, (CMTS) 1860 Census
Pettit, Andrew: (B) 1856, (CO) Pulaski, (A) 4, (BP) TN, (CMTS) 1860 Census
Pettit, Franklin: (B) 1851, (CO) Pulaski, (A) 9, (BP) TN, (CMTS) 1860 Census
Pettit, Martha: (B) 1853, (CO) Pulaski, (A) 7, (BP) TN, (CMTS) 1860 Census
Pettit, Rebecca: (B) 1830, (CO) Pulaski, (A) 30, (BP) TN, (CMTS) 1860 Census
Pettit, Seymore: (B) 1834, (CO) Pulaski, (A) 26, (BP) TN, (CMTS) 1860 Census
Petty, James: (B) 1849, (D) 1930, (CO) Henry, (C) Knights of Pythias Cemetery, Deepwater, MO
Petty, Leticha K.: (B) 1854, (D) 1919, (CO) Henry, (C) Knights of Pythias Cemetery, Deepwater, MO
Petty, Luther: (B) Feb. 29, 1881, (D) Jan. 20, 1956, (CO) Henry, (C) Knights of Pythias Cemetery, Deepwater, MO
Pharris, B.: (B) 1840, (CO) Pulaski, (A) 20, (BP) MO, (CMTS) 1860 Census
Pharris, Ione: (B) 1854, (CO) Pulaski, (A) 6, (BP) MO, (CMTS) 1860 Census
Pharris, Leonidas: (B) 1841, (CO) Pulaski, (A) 19, (BP) MO, (CMTS) 1860 Census
Pharris, Louis: (B) 1842, (CO) Pulaski, (A) 18, (BP) MO, (CMTS)

1860 Census
Pharris, Lucinda: (B) 1818, (CO) Pulaski, (A) 42, (BP) TN, (CMTS) 1860 Census
Pharris, M.: (B) 1815, (CO) Pulaski, (A) 45, (BP) TN, (CMTS) 1860 Census
Pharris, Remus: (B) 1847, (CO) Pulaski, (A) 13, (BP) GA, (CMTS) 1860 Census
Pharris, Tillman: (B) 1845, (CO) Pulaski, (A) 15, (BP) TN, (CMTS) 1860 Census
Pharris, William: (B) 1849, (CO) Pulaski, (A) 11, (BP) TN, (CMTS) 1860 Census
Phelan, Corneluis: (D) Jul. Jul., 1955, (CO) St. Louis, (C) Calvary Cemetery
Phelps, James L.: (B) Dec. 1, 1875, (D) Aug. 26, 1958, (CO) Henry, (C) Knights of Pythias Cemetery, Deepwater, MO
Philiber, Mary E.: (B) 1816, (CO) Stone, (A) 54, (BP) MO, (CMTS) 1870 Census
Philiber, t Elizabeth: (B) 1830, (CO) Stone, (A) 40, (BP) TN, (CMTS) 1870 Census
Philibert, Adolphus: (B) 1851, (CO) Stone, (A) 19, (BP) MO, (CMTS) 1870 Census
Philibert, Elizabeth: (B) 1846, (CO) Stone, (A) 4, (BP) MO, (CMTS) 1870 Census
Philibert, Elizabeth: (B) 1855, (CO) Stone, (A) 15, (BP) IN, (CMTS) 1870 Census
Philibert, Florence: (B) 1848, (CO) Stone, (A) 2, (BP) MO, (CMTS) 1870 Census
Philibert, James: (B) 1844, (CO) Stone, (A) 6, (BP) MO, (CMTS) 1870 Census
Phillips, Benjamin F.: (B) 1856, (CO) Pulaski, (A) 4, (BP) MO, (CMTS) 1860 Census
Phillips, Caroline: (B) 1828, (CO) Pulaski, (A) 32, (BP) MO, (CMTS) 1860 Census
Phillips, Catharine: (B) 1858, (CO) Pulaski, (A) 2, (BP) MO, (CMTS) 1860 Census
Phillips, Cerxes: (B) 1854, (CO) Pulaski, (A) 6, (BP) MO, (CMTS) 1860 Census
Phillips, Martha O.: (B) 1854, (CO) Pulaski, (A) 6, (BP) MO, (CMTS) 1860 Census
Phillips, R.: (B) 1825, (CO) Pulaski, (A) 35, (BP) IND, (CMTS) 1860 Census
Phillips, Valeria J.: (B) 1848, (CO) Pulaski, (A) 12, (BP) MO, (CMTS) 1860 Census

Phillips, Vetricia J.: (B) 1851, (CO) Pulaski, (A) 9, (BP) MO, (CMTS) 1860 Census
Picasso, Marie Elice: (B) 1896, (D) 1915, (CO) St. Louis, (C) Calvary Cemetery
Pickering, Alfred: (B) 1845, (CO) Pulaski, (A) 15, (BP) MO, (CMTS) 1860 Census
Pickering, Charles D.: (B) 1854, (CO) Pulaski, (A) 6, (BP) MO, (CMTS) 1860 Census
Pickering, Edward C.: (B) 1858, (CO) Pulaski, (A) 2, (BP) MO, (CMTS) 1860 Census
Pickering, James H.: (B) 1841, (CO) Pulaski, (A) 19, (BP) MO, (CMTS) 1860 Census
Pickering, Louisa G.: (B) 1847, (CO) Pulaski, (A) 13, (BP) MO, (CMTS) 1860 Census
Pickering, Rebecca: (B) 1844, (CO) Pulaski, (A) 16, (BP) MO, (CMTS) 1860 Census
Pickering, Thomas A.: (B) 1856, (CO) Pulaski, (A) 4, (BP) MO, (CMTS) 1860 Census
Pickering, William R.: (B) 1849, (CO) Pulaski, (A) 11, (BP) MO, (CMTS) 1860 Census
Picolto, Theresa: (B) 1877, (D) 1958, (CO) St. Louis, (C) Calvary Cemetery
Pierce, John H.: (B) 1847, (CO) Stone, (A) 23, (BP) MO, (CMTS) 1870 Census
Pierce, Melissa: (B) 1841, (CO) Stone, (A) 29, (BP) IL, (CMTS) 1870 Census
Pierson, Douglass: (B) 1840, (CO) Stone, (A) 10, (BP) IL, (CMTS) 1870 Census
Pierson, Harriet: (B) 1848, (CO) Stone, (A) 2, (BP) IL, (CMTS) 1870 Census
Pierson, Joseph A.: (B) 1845, (CO) Stone, (A) 5, (BP) IL, (CMTS) 1870 Census
Pierson, William: (B) 1836, (CO) Stone, (A) 14, (BP) IL, (CMTS) 1870 Census
Pillow, Albert Jefferson: (B) Nov. 27, 1850, (D) Dec. 16, 1915, (CO) Missouri, (DP) Senath, MO
Pinkley, Benjamin F: (B) 1845, (CO) Stone, (A) 5, (BP) MO, (CMTS) 1870 Census
Pinkley, Medalia John A.: (B) 1838, (CO) Stone, (A) 12, (BP) MO, (CMTS) 1870 Census
Pinkley, Rachel: (B) 1820, (CO) Stone, (A) 30, (BP) IN, (CMTS) 1870 Census
Piokik, John: (B) 1904, (D) 1974, (CO) St. Louis, (C) Calvary Cemetery

Piosik, Elizabeth: (B) 1889, (D) 1968, (CO) St. Louis, (C) Calvary Cemetery
Piosik, John: (B) 1860, (D) 1947, (CO) St. Louis, (C) Calvary Cemetery
Piosik, Martha: (B) 1861, (D) 1932, (CO) St. Louis, (C) Calvary Cemetery
Pitman, Angelina: (B) 1834, (CO) Pulaski, (A) 26, (BP) KY, (CMTS) 1860 Census
Pitman, Ann: (B) 1842, (CO) Pulaski, (A) 18, (BP) MO, (CMTS) 1860 Census
Pitman, Henry: (B) 1839, (CO) Pulaski, (A) 21, (BP) KY, (CMTS) 1860 Census
Pitman, Isabella: (B) 1853, (CO) Pulaski, (A) 7, (BP) MO, (CMTS) 1860 Census
Pitman, James: (B) 1850, (CO) Pulaski, (A) 10, (BP) MO, (CMTS) 1860 Census
Pitman, Jonathan: (B) 1856, (CO) Pulaski, (A) 4, (BP) MO, (CMTS) 1860 Census
Pitman, Martha: (B) 1839, (CO) Pulaski, (A) 21, (BP) MO, (CMTS) 1860 Census
Pitman, William: (B) 1830, (CO) Pulaski, (A) 30, (BP) TN, (CMTS) 1860 Census
Pittis, Winsey: (B) 1834, (CO) Stone, (A) 36, (BP) IN, (CMTS) 1870 Census
Pitts, Alfred: (B) 1823, (CO) Stone, (A) 27, (BP) MO, (CMTS) 1870 Census
Pitts, George W.: (B) 1848, (CO) Stone, (A) 2, (BP) MO, (CMTS) 1870 Census
Pitts, Harriett R.: (B) 1846, (CO) Stone, (A) 4, (BP) KS, (CMTS) 1870 Census
Pitts, Martha A.: (B) 1827, (CO) Stone, (A) 23, (BP) MO, (CMTS) 1870 Census
Pitts, Martin V: (B) 1825, (CO) Stone, (A) 25, (BP) KY, (CMTS) 1870 Census
Pitts, Mexico: (B) 1849, (CO) Stone, (A) 1, (BP) MO, (CMTS) 1870 Census
Pitts, Nancy J.: (B) 1844, (CO) Stone, (A) 6, (BP) MO, (CMTS) 1870 Census
Pitts, Rebecca J.: (B) 1845, (CO) Stone, (A) 5, (BP) MO, (CMTS) 1870 Census
Pitts, Robert: (B) Dec. 28, 1927, (D) Apr. 16, 1999, (CO) Barry, (PRTS) Theophelus E Pitts and Mary E Sims, (C) Maplewood Cemetery
Pitts, Sarah: (B) 1827, (CO) Stone, (A) 23, (BP) MO, (CMTS) 1870 Census
Pleasants, Antoinette M.: (B) 1932, (D) 1984, (CO) St. Louis, (C) Calvary

Cemetery
Pleasants, Paul E.: (B) 1931, (CO) St. Louis, (C) Calvary Cemetery
Pollard, Harriett: (B) 1818, (CO) Stone, (A) 52, (BP) MO, (CMTS) 1870 Census
Pollard, Jane C.: (B) 1845, (CO) Stone, (A) 25, (BP) MO, (CMTS) 1870 Census
Poteet, Henry: (B) 1847, (CO) Pulaski, (A) 13, (BP) MO, (CMTS) 1860 Census
Poteet, James H.: (B) 1849, (CO) Pulaski, (A) 11, (BP) MO, (CMTS) 1860 Census
Poteet, Jane: (B) 1846, (CO) Pulaski, (A) 14, (BP) MO, (CMTS) 1860 Census
Poteet, John E.: (B) 1852, (CO) Pulaski, (A) 8, (BP) MO, (CMTS) 1860 Census
Poteet, Martha A.: (B) 1851, (CO) Pulaski, (A) 9, (BP) MO, (CMTS) 1860 Census
Poteet, Mary: (B) 1845, (CO) Pulaski, (A) 15, (BP) MO, (CMTS) 1860 Census
Poteet, Narcissa: (B) 1826, (CO) Pulaski, (A) 34, (BP) MO, (CMTS) 1860 Census
Poteet, William F.: (B) 1856, (CO) Pulaski, (A) 4, (BP) MO, (CMTS) 1860 Census
Potter, David R.: (B) 1858, (CO) Stone, (A) 12, (BP) MO, (CMTS) 1870 Census
Potter, James B.: (B) 1851, (CO) Stone, (A) 19, (BP) MO, (CMTS) 1870 Census
Potter, Orpha: (B) 1825, (CO) Stone, (A) 45, (BP) TN, (CMTS) 1870 Census
Potter, Rebecca E.: (B) 1856, (CO) Stone, (A) 14, (BP) MO, (CMTS) 1870 Census
Pounce, Emily: (B) 1838, (CO) Pulaski, (A) 22, (BP) KY, (CMTS) 1860 Census
Pounce, Martha E.: (B) 1848, (CO) Pulaski, (A) 12, (BP) MO, (CMTS) 1860 Census
Pounce, Sarah J.: (B) 1847, (CO) Pulaski, (A) 13, (BP) MO, (CMTS) 1860 Census
Pounce, Willis: (B) 1821, (CO) Pulaski, (A) 39, (BP) MO, (CMTS) 1860 Census
Powell, Earl Wright: (B) 1894, (D) 1959, (CO) St. Louis, (C) Calvary Cemetery
Powell, James V.: (B) 1929, (D) 1967, (CO) St. Louis, (C) Calvary Cemetery
Powell, Lillian A.: (B) 1898, (D) 1979, (CO) St. Louis, (C) Calvary

Cemetery
Powell, R.: (B) 1832, (CO) Pulaski, (A) 28, (BP) VA, (CMTS) 1860 Census
Powers, Celeste M.: (B) 1902, (D) 1972, (CO) St. Louis, (C) Calvary Cemetery
Powers, James Hugh: (D) May 2, 1951, (CO) St. Louis, (C) Calvary Cemetery
Powers, Mary M.: (B) May 20, 1857, (D) Jun. 13, 1942, (CO) St. Louis, (C) Calvary Cemetery
Powers, Roy: (B) 1893, (D) 1966, (CO) St. Louis, (C) Calvary Cemetery
Prater, Elizabeth: (B) 1850, (CO) Pulaski, (A) 10, (BP) IL, (CMTS) 1860 Census
Prater, George A.: (B) 1847, (CO) Stone, (A) 3, (BP) AR, (CMTS) 1870 Census
Prater, Martha L.: (B) 1849, (CO) Stone, (A) 1, (BP) TX, (CMTS) 1870 Census
Prater, Mary: (B) 1828, (CO) Stone, (A) 22, (BP) IL, (CMTS) 1870 Census
Prebil, Adolph J.: (D) Dec., 1976, (CO) St. Louis, (C) Calvary Cemetery
Price, Joseph H.: (B) Apr. 12, 1835, (D) Nov. 29, 1886, (CO) Barry, (C) Old Corsicana Cemetery
Pricer, Dora: (B) Feb. 24, 1898, (D) Oct. 8, 1900, (CO) Henry, (C) Knights of Pythias Cemetery, Deepwater, MO
Pritchard, Bethane E.: (B) 1842, (CO) Stone, (A) 28, (BP) TN, (CMTS) 1870 Census
Pritchard, Bethena: (B) 1798, (CO) Stone, (A) 72, (BP) TN, (CMTS) 1870 Census
Pritchard, Henry: (B) 1840, (CO) Stone, (A) 30, (BP) TN, (CMTS) 1870 Census
Pritchard, Julia: (B) 1822, (CO) Stone, (A) 48, (BP) TN, (CMTS) 1870 Census
Pritchard, Melvina: (B) 1849, (CO) Stone, (A) 21, (BP) MO, (CMTS) 1870 Census
Pritchard, Melvira: (B) 1850, (CO) Stone, (A) 20, (BP) MO, (CMTS) 1870 Census
Pritchard, Paulina: (B) 1856, (CO) Stone, (A) 14, (BP) MO, (CMTS) 1870 Census
Pritchard, Perlina: (B) 1847, (CO) Stone, (A) 23, (BP) MO, (CMTS) 1870 Census
Pritchard, Steven: (B) 1837, (CO) Stone, (A) 33, (BP) TN, (CMTS) 1870 Census
Pritchard, Susan: (B) 1838, (CO) Stone, (A) 32, (BP) VA, (CMTS) 1870 Census

Pritchard, Susan: (B) 1845, (CO) Stone, (A) 25, (BP) MO, (CMTS) 1870 Census
Pritchard, Thomas: (B) 1836, (CO) Stone, (A) 34, (BP) TN, (CMTS) 1870 Census
Profit, Lucinda: (B) 1833, (CO) Stone, (A) 17, (BP) AR, (CMTS) 1870 Census
Provast, Mrs. Marie Rose: (D) Feb. 3, 1873, (CO) St. Louis, (C) Calvary Cemetery, (A) 74
Pryor, George W.: (B) 1858, (CO) Stone, (A) 12, (BP) MO, (CMTS) 1870 Census
Pryor, Nancy: (B) 1853, (CO) Stone, (A) 17, (BP) MO, (CMTS) 1870 Census
Pryor, Nancy A.: (B) 1853, (CO) Stone, (A) 17, (BP) MO, (CMTS) 1870 Census
Pryor, Sarah: (B) 1815, (CO) Stone, (A) 55, (BP) KY, (CMTS) 1870 Census
Putty, Catherine: (B) 1848, (CO) Stone, (A) 22, (BP) ?, (CMTS) 1870 Census
Putty, Catherine: (B) 1853, (CO) Stone, (A) 17, (BP) MO, (CMTS) 1870 Census
Putty, Obiel: (B) 1838, (CO) Stone, (A) 32, (BP) TN, (CMTS) 1870 Census
Querry, John: (B) 1838, (CO) Pulaski, (A) 22, (BP) TN, (CMTS) 1860 Census
Querry, Sarah: (B) 1843, (CO) Pulaski, (A) 17, (BP) TN, (CMTS) 1860 Census
Quick, Joseph P: (B) 1851, (CO) Stone, (A) 19, (BP) MO, (CMTS) 1870 Census
Quick, Sophia: (B) 1830, (CO) Stone, (A) 40, (BP) TN, (CMTS) 1870 Census
Quinn, George: (B) 1830, (CO) Pulaski, (A) 30, (BP) MO, (CMTS) 1860 Census
Quinn, John: (B) 1815, (CO) Pulaski, (A) 45, (BP) TN, (CMTS) 1860 Census
Quinn, Mary: (B) Nov. 2, 1853, (D) Jan. 1, 1936, (CO) St. Louis, (C) Calvary Cemetery
Quinn, Nancy: (B) 1821, (CO) Pulaski, (A) 39, (BP) TN, (CMTS) 1860 Census
Quinn, Nancy: (B) 1844, (CO) Pulaski, (A) 16, (BP) MO, (CMTS) 1860 Census
Quirk, James A.: (D) Jul. 1, 1909, (CO) St. Louis, (C) Calvary Cemetery
Quirk, Mary F.: (D) Jul. 1, 1909, (CO) St. Louis, (C) Calvary Cemetery
Raggio, Arrigo: (B) 1894, (D) 1957, (CO) St. Louis, (C) Calvary

Cemetery
Rainoldi, Jennie: (B) 1881, (D) 1960, (CO) St. Louis, (C) Calvary Cemetery
Rainwater, Emeline: (B) 1835, (CO) Stone, (A) 35, (BP) TN, (CMTS) 1870 Census
Rainwater, Sarah: (B) 1837, (CO) Stone, (A) 33, (BP) AL, (CMTS) 1870 Census
Randolph, M.: (B) 1835, (CO) Pulaski, (A) 25, (BP) VA, (CMTS) 1860 Census
Rapp, George W.: (B) 1856, (CO) Stone, (A) 14, (BP) MO, (CMTS) 1870 Census
Rapp, Israel B.: (B) 1850, (CO) Stone, (A) 20, (BP) MO, (CMTS) 1870 Census
Rapp, James M.: (B) 1829, (CO) Stone, (A) 41, (BP) TN, (CMTS) 1870 Census
Rapp, Lucretia J.: (B) 1854, (CO) Stone, (A) 16, (BP) MO, (CMTS) 1870 Census
Rapp, Mary: (B) 1853, (CO) Stone, (A) 17, (BP) MO, (CMTS) 1870 Census
Rapp, Nancy J.: (B) 1848, (CO) Stone, (A) 22, (BP) MO, (CMTS) 1870 Census
Rapp, Sarah: (B) 1831, (CO) Stone, (A) 39, (BP) KY, (CMTS) 1870 Census
Rasure, James: (B) 1855, (CO) Stone, (A) 15, (BP) MO, (CMTS) 1870 Census
Rasure, John C.: (B) 1820, (CO) Stone, (A) 50, (BP) KY, (CMTS) 1870 Census
Rasure, John C.: (B) 1852, (CO) Stone, (A) 18, (BP) MO, (CMTS) 1870 Census
Ray, Benjamin: (B) 1837, (CO) Pulaski, (A) 23, (BP) MO, (CMTS) 1860 Census
Ray, Eliza.: (B) Nov. 22, 1824, (D) Oct. 26, 1895, (CO) Barry, (C) Cassville Cemetery
Ray, Elizabeth: (B) 1834, (CO) Pulaski, (A) 26, (BP) IND, (CMTS) 1860 Census
Ray, Eunice: (B) 1830, (CO) Pulaski, (A) 30, (BP) KY, (CMTS) 1860 Census
Ray, Fanny: (B) 1851, (CO) Pulaski, (A) 9, (BP) KY, (CMTS) 1860 Census
Ray, Harriet: (B) 1846, (CO) Pulaski, (A) 14, (BP) KY, (CMTS) 1860 Census
Ray, Jessee: (B) 1830, (CO) Pulaski, (A) 30, (BP) IL, (CMTS) 1860 Census

Ray, John: (B) 1847, (CO) Pulaski, (A) 13, (BP) KY, (CMTS) 1860 Census
Ray, Joshua: (B) 1828, (CO) Pulaski, (A) 32, (BP) IL, (CMTS) 1860 Census
Ray, Joshua: (B) 1837, (CO) Stone, (A) 13, (BP) MO, (CMTS) 1870 Census
Ray, Louisa: (B) 1852, (CO) Pulaski, (A) 8, (BP) MO, (CMTS) 1860 Census
Ray, Lucinda: (B) 1853, (CO) Pulaski, (A) 7, (BP) KY, (CMTS) 1860 Census
Ray, Lucy E.: (B) 1849, (CO) Stone, (A) 1, (BP) MO, (CMTS) 1870 Census
Ray, Mary: (B) 1842, (CO) Pulaski, (A) 18, (BP) KY, (CMTS) 1860 Census
Ray, Mary J.: (B) 1839, (CO) Stone, (A) 11, (BP) MO, (CMTS) 1870 Census
Ray, Patience: (B) 1837, (CO) Pulaski, (A) 23, (BP) NC, (CMTS) 1860 Census
Ray, Polly: (B) 1841, (CO) Pulaski, (A) 19, (BP) MO, (CMTS) 1860 Census
Ray, Price: (B) 1828, (CO) Pulaski, (A) 32, (BP) NC, (CMTS) 1860 Census
Ray, Sarah: (B) 1835, (CO) Pulaski, (A) 25, (BP) MO, (CMTS) 1860 Census
Ray, Sarah: (B) 1837, (CO) Pulaski, (A) 23, (BP) KY, (CMTS) 1860 Census
Ray, Sarah A.: (B) 1815, (CO) Stone, (A) 35, (BP) MO, (CMTS) 1870 Census
Ray, Susan: (B) 1855, (CO) Pulaski, (A) 5, (BP) KY, (CMTS) 1860 Census
Ray, William: (B) 1853, (CO) Pulaski, (A) 7, (BP) MO, (CMTS) 1860 Census
Ray, William H.: (B) 1853, (CO) Pulaski, (A) 7, (BP) MO, (CMTS) 1860 Census
Rayl, Elizabeth: (B) 1840, (CO) Pulaski, (A) 20, (BP) TN, (CMTS) 1860 Census
Rayl, Elizabeth: (B) 1841, (CO) Pulaski, (A) 19, (BP) MO, (CMTS) 1860 Census
Rayl, Harriet: (B) 1850, (CO) Pulaski, (A) 10, (BP) ARK, (CMTS) 1860 Census
Rayl, James E.: (B) 1837, (CO) Pulaski, (A) 23, (BP) MO, (CMTS) 1860 Census
Rayl, Jesse A.: (B) 1848, (CO) Pulaski, (A) 12, (BP) TN, (CMTS)

1860 Census
Rayl, Mary: (B) 1845, (CO) Pulaski, (A) 15, (BP) TN, (CMTS) 1860 Census
Rayl, Nancy: (B) 1819, (CO) Pulaski, (A) 41, (BP) TN, (CMTS) 1860 Census
Rayl, Tennessee: (B) 1857, (CO) Pulaski, (A) 3, (BP) ARK, (CMTS) 1860 Census
Rayl, William: (B) 1820, (CO) Pulaski, (A) 40, (BP) TN, (CMTS) 1860 Census
Raynolds, Anna Kelly: (B) 1882, (D) 1938, (CO) St. Louis, (C) Calvary Cemetery
Raynolds, Mary Roberta: (B) 1912, (D) 1969, (CO) St. Louis, (C) Calvary Cemetery
Rays, Crocia A.: (B) 1849, (CO) Pulaski, (A) 11, (BP) MO, (CMTS) 1860 Census
Rays, Harriett: (B) 1851, (CO) Pulaski, (A) 9, (BP) MO, (CMTS) 1860 Census
Rays, Jesse A.: (B) 1847, (CO) Pulaski, (A) 13, (BP) MO, (CMTS) 1860 Census
Rays, Octarvis: (B) 1838, (CO) Pulaski, (A) 22, (BP) TEN, (CMTS) 1860 Census
Rays, Sarah: (B) 1818, (CO) Pulaski, (A) 42, (BP) TN, (CMTS) 1860 Census
Rays, William: (B) 1841, (CO) Pulaski, (A) 19, (BP) MO, (CMTS) 1860 Census
Ready, Daniel: (D) Jan. 6, 1883, (CO) St. Louis, (C) Calvary Cemetery, (A) 70
Reagan, William B.: (B) Jan. 5, 1836, (D) Dec. 8, 1872, (CO) Bollinger,
Reagan, Jr., Tim: (D) Aug. 21, 1883, (CO) Bollinger,
Reams, Amanda: (B) 1846, (CO) Stone, (A) 24, (BP) TN, (CMTS) 1870 Census
Reams, Henry: (B) 1840, (CO) Stone, (A) 30, (BP) TN, (CMTS) 1870 Census
Reardon, Della Ward: (B) May 30, 1866, (D) Dec. 13, 1954, (CO) St. Louis, (C) Calvary Cemetery
Reardon, Franic A.: (B) Oct. 28, 1898, (D) Dec. 1, 1986, (CO) St. Louis, (C) Calvary Cemetery
Reardon, John J.: (B) Sep. 17, 1869, (D) May 30, 1934, (CO) St. Louis, (C) Calvary Cemetery
Reed, Arathusa: (B) 1847, (CO) Pulaski, (A) 13, (BP) MO, (CMTS) 1860 Census
Reed, Benjamin F: (B) 1841, (CO) Stone, (A) 9, (BP) TX, (CMTS) 1870 Census

Reed, Carlotte Ann: (B) Jul. 2, 1942, (D) Jul. 2, 1942, (CO) Oregon, (C) Falling Springs Cemetery
Reed, Elizabeth: (B) 1854, (CO) Pulaski, (A) 6, (BP) MO, (CMTS) 1860 Census
Reed, George: (B) 1861, (D) 1931, (CO) Barry, (C) Clark Cemetery, Butterfield, MO.
Reed, George W.: (B) 1844, (CO) Stone, (A) 6, (BP) TX, (CMTS) 1870 Census
Reed, James: (B) 1844, (CO) Pulaski, (A) 16, (BP) MO, (CMTS) 1860 Census
Reed, John D.: (B) 1850, (CO) Pulaski, (A) 10, (BP) MO, (CMTS) 1860 Census
Reed, John M.: (B) 1839, (CO) Stone, (A) 11, (BP) MO, (CMTS) 1870 Census
Reed, Joseph: (B) 1856, (CO) Pulaski, (A) 4, (BP) MO, (CMTS) 1860 Census
Reed, Joseph A.: (B) 1822, (CO) Pulaski, (A) 38, (BP) KY, (CMTS) 1860 Census
Reed, Julia A.: (B) 1852, (CO) Pulaski, (A) 8, (BP) MO, (CMTS) 1860 Census
Reed, Leetha E.: (B) 1842, (CO) Stone, (A) 8, (BP) TX, (CMTS) 1870 Census
Reed, Marion A.: (B) 1849, (CO) Stone, (A) 1, (BP) MO, (CMTS) 1870 Census
Reed, Mary Ella: (B) Apr. 9, 1868, (D) Jun. 3, 1941, (CO) Barry, (C) Clark Cemetery, Butterfield, MO.
Reed, Miles: (B) 1816, (CO) Stone, (A) 34, (BP) MO, (CMTS) 1870 Census
Reed, Rebecca: (B) 1791, (CO) Stone, (A) 59, (BP) MO, (CMTS) 1870 Census
Reed, Rebecca: (B) 1855, (CO) Pulaski, (A) 5, (BP) MO, (CMTS) 1860 Census
Reed, Sarah: (B) 1830, (CO) Pulaski, (A) 30, (BP) KY, (CMTS) 1860 Census
Reed, Sarah J.: (B) 1822, (CO) Stone, (A) 28, (BP) TN, (CMTS) 1870 Census
Reed, Tom Louis: , (D) 1878, (CO) Oregon, (C) Falling Springs Cemetery
Reed, Virginia: (B) 1857, (CO) Pulaski, (A) 3, (BP) MO, (CMTS) 1860 Census
Reed, William L.: (B) 1847, (CO) Stone, (A) 3, (BP) TX, (CMTS) 1870 Census
Reed, Zach: (B) 1818, (CO) Pulaski, (A) 42, (BP) TN, (CMTS) 1860 Census

Reed, Zach: (B) 1847, (CO) Pulaski, (A) 13, (BP) MO, (CMTS) 1860 Census
Reed, Zach T.: (B) 1850, (CO) Pulaski, (A) 10, (BP) MO, (CMTS) 1860 Census
Reid, Bessie G.: (B) 1885, (D) 1920, (CO) St. Louis, (C) Calvary Cemetery
Reid, Bridget: (B) 1841, (D) 1922, (CO) St. Louis, (C) Calvary Cemetery
Reid, Charles: (B) 1872, (D) 1949, (CO) St. Louis, (C) Calvary Cemetery
Reid, Hellen: (B) 1869, (D) 1950, (CO) St. Louis, (C) Calvary Cemetery
Reid, James A.: (B) 1884, (D) 1965, (CO) St. Louis, (C) Calvary Cemetery
Reid, John: (B) 1832, (D) 1901, (CO) St. Louis, (C) Calvary Cemetery
Reid, Margaret G.: (B) 1884, (D) 1946, (CO) St. Louis, (C) Calvary Cemetery
Reily, Philip: (D) Jun. 16, 1880, (CO) St. Louis, (C) Calvary Cemetery, (A) 73
Reinert, Ida: (B) 1860, (D) 1934, (CO) St. Louis, (C) Calvary Cemetery
Reinert, Otto: (B) 1854, (D) 1942, (CO) St. Louis, (C) Calvary Cemetery
Relleford, David W.: (B) 1826, (CO) Pulaski, (A) 34, (BP) TN, (CMTS) 1860 Census
Relleford, Delilah: (B) 1837, (CO) Pulaski, (A) 23, (BP) IND, (CMTS) 1860 Census
Renner, Clara A.: (B) Sep. 17, 1897, (D) Aug. 24, 1998, (CO) Boone, (NWS) *Columbia Daily News*, Aug. 26, 1998, (A) 100, (SPOUSE) John Renner, (MD) Jan. 16, 1919, Washington, (BP) Kinkaid, KS, (PRTS) William August Wilmesherr and Katherine Wehmeyer, (FUN) Houser-Millard Funeral Directors Chapel, Jefferson City, (BUR) Aug. 29, 1998, (C) Hawthorn Memorial Gardens Cemetery,
Replogle, Mabel Pauline: (B) Aug. 24, 1930, (CO) Webster,
Replogle, Marilyn Pearl: (B) May 5, 1949, (CO) Webster,
Reynolds, George: (B) 1842, (CO) Stone, (A) 28, (BP) MO, (CMTS) 1870 Census
Reynolds, Haydon B.: (B) 1832, (CO) Pulaski, (A) 28, (BP) IL, (CMTS) 1860 Census
Reynolds, James: (B) 1848, (CO) Pulaski, (A) 12, (BP) TN, (CMTS) 1860 Census
Reynolds, James: (B) 1848, (CO) Stone, (A) 22, (BP) MO, (CMTS) 1870 Census
Reynolds, James T.: (B) 1856, (CO) Pulaski, (A) 4, (BP) MO, (CMTS) 1860 Census
Reynolds, John C.: (B) 1828, (CO) Pulaski, (A) 32, (BP) TN, (CMTS) 1860 Census
Reynolds, Joseph C.: (B) 1852, (CO) Pulaski, (A) 8, (BP) MO, (CMTS) 1860 Census

Reynolds, Martha: (B) 1832, (CO) Pulaski, (A) 28, (BP) TN, (CMTS) 1860 Census
Reynolds, Martha: (B) 1833, (CO) Pulaski, (A) 27, (BP) MO, (CMTS) 1860 Census
Reynolds, Martha: (B) 1837, (CO) Pulaski, (A) 23, (BP) VA, (CMTS) 1860 Census
Reynolds, Mary: (B) 1850, (CO) Pulaski, (A) 10, (BP) IL, (CMTS) 1860 Census
Reynolds, Michael: (B) 1850, (CO) Stone, (A) 20, (BP) MO, (CMTS) 1870 Census
Reynolds, Nancy: (B) 1853, (CO) Pulaski, (A) 7, (BP) MO, (CMTS) 1860 Census
Reynolds, Polly: (B) 1845, (CO) Stone, (A) 25, (BP) MO, (CMTS) 1870 Census
Reynolds, Ronald Earl: (B) Aug. 31, 1947, (D) Apr. 12, 1971, (CO) Henry, (C) Knights of Pythias Cemetery, Deepwater, MO
Reynolds, Ruth H.: (B) 1855, (CO) Pulaski, (A) 5, (BP) MO, (CMTS) 1860 Census
Reynolds, Sarah: (B) 1852, (CO) Pulaski, (A) 8, (BP) IL, (CMTS) 1860 Census
Reynolds, William: (B) 1828, (CO) Pulaski, (A) 32, (BP) VA, (CMTS) 1860 Census
Reynolds, William: (B) 1854, (CO) Pulaski, (A) 6, (BP) IL, (CMTS) 1860 Census
Rhodes, Catherine: (B) 1819, (CO) Stone, (A) 51, (BP) MO, (CMTS) 1870 Census
Rhodes, Celia S.: (B) 1847, (CO) Stone, (A) 3, (BP) MO, (CMTS) 1870 Census
Rhodes, Cordelia A.: (B) 1831, (CO) Stone, (A) 19, (BP) AR, (CMTS) 1870 Census
Rhodes, Delina: (B) 1847, (CO) Stone, (A) 3, (BP) MO, (CMTS) 1870 Census
Rhodes, Eliza B.: (B) 1831, (CO) Stone, (A) 19, (BP) TX, (CMTS) 1870 Census
Rhodes, Elizabeth: (B) 1854, (CO) Stone, (A) 16, (BP) MO, (CMTS) 1870 Census
Rhodes, Faithey A.: (B) 1835, (CO) Stone, (A) 15, (BP) MO, (CMTS) 1870 Census
Rhodes, James L.: (B) 1840, (CO) Stone, (A) 10, (BP) MO, (CMTS) 1870 Census
Rhodes, Riley: (B) 1823, (CO) Stone, (A) 27, (BP) MO, (CMTS) 1870 Census
Rhodes, David: (B) 1829, (CO) Stone, (A) 21, (BP) MO, (CMTS) 1870

Census

Rhodes, William J.: (B) 1832, (CO) Stone, (A) 18, (BP) MO, (CMTS) 1870 Census

Rice, David: (B) 1795, (CO) Stone, (A) 55, (BP) MA, (CMTS) 1870 Census

Rice, David: (B) 1839, (D) 1924, (CO) Cedar, (C) Brashear Cemetery

Rice, Hay B.: (B) 1848, (D) 1920, (CO) Cedar, (C) Brashear Cemetery

Rice, Jordan: (B) 1840, (CO) Stone, (A) 10, (BP) TX, (CMTS) 1870 Census

Rice, Missouri A.: (B) 1842, (D) 1928, (CO) Cedar, (C) Brashear Cemetery

Rice, Paulina: (B) 1825, (CO) Stone, (A) 25, (BP) PA, (CMTS) 1870 Census

Rice, Peter: (B) 1839, (CO) Stone, (A) 11, (BP) TX, (CMTS) 1870 Census

Rice, W. A.: (B) 1836, (D) 1901, (CO) Cedar, (C) Brashear Cemetery

Rice, William: (B) 1847, (CO) Stone, (A) 3, (BP) TX, (CMTS) 1870 Census

Rich, John R.: (B) 1864, (D) 1944, (CO) Henry, (C) Knights of Pythias Cemetery, Deepwater, MO

Richards, Martha A.: (B) Aug. 24, 1835, (D) Apr. 4, 1896, (CO) Audrain, (C) Pisgah Cemetery

Richardson, George N.: (B) 1853, (CO) Pulaski, (A) 7, (BP) MO, (CMTS) 1860 Census

Richardson, Isaac N.: (B) 1854, (CO) Pulaski, (A) 6, (BP) MO, (CMTS) 1860 Census

Richardson, John M.: (B) 1822, (CO) Pulaski, (A) 38, (BP) TEN, (CMTS) 1860 Census

Richardson, Margaret A.: (B) 1855, (CO) Pulaski, (A) 5, (BP) MO, (CMTS) 1860 Census

Richardson, Mary E.: (B) 1852, (CO) Pulaski, (A) 8, (BP) MO, (CMTS) 1860 Census

Richardson, Nancy E.: (B) 1856, (CO) Pulaski, (A) 4, (BP) MO, (CMTS) 1860 Census

Richardson, Susan: (B) 1828, (CO) Pulaski, (A) 32, (BP) MO, (CMTS) 1860 Census

Rickett, John W.: (D) Feb.24, 1857, (CO) Audrain, (C) Old Village Cemetery

Ricketts, Mary: (B) 1833, (CO) Pulaski, (A) 27, (BP) IND, (CMTS) 1860 Census

Ricketts, William F.: (B) 1855, (CO) Pulaski, (A) 5, (BP) IND, (CMTS) 1860 Census

Rickman, Adeline M.: (B) 1828, (CO) Stone, (A) 22, (BP) AR, (CMTS)

1870 Census
Rickman, David L.: (B) 1843, (CO) Stone, (A) 27, (BP) AR, (CMTS) 1870 Census
Rickman, Eliza Jane: (B) 1840, (CO) Stone, (A) 10, (BP) AR, (CMTS) 1870 Census
Rickman, Ellen: (B) 1848, (CO) Stone, (A) 22, (BP) MO, (CMTS) 1870 Census
Rickman, John: (B) 1834, (CO) Stone, (A) 16, (BP) AR, (CMTS) 1870 Census
Rickman, Martha J.: (B) 1829, (CO) Stone, (A) 21, (BP) MO, (CMTS) 1870 Census
Rickman, Mary M.: (B) 1826, (CO) Stone, (A) 24, (BP) AR, (CMTS) 1870 Census
Rickman, Sarah M.: (B) 1832, (CO) Stone, (A) 18, (BP) AR, (CMTS) 1870 Census
Riddle, Benjamin: (B) 1850, (CO) Pulaski, (A) 10, (BP) MO, (CMTS) 1860 Census
Riddle, Elias: (B) 1845, (CO) Pulaski, (A) 15, (BP) MO, (CMTS) 1860 Census
Riddle, Harriet: (B) 1853, (CO) Pulaski, (A) 7, (BP) MO, (CMTS) 1860 Census
Riddle, Isaac: (B) 1842, (CO) Pulaski, (A) 18, (BP) MO, (CMTS) 1860 Census
Riddle, James W.: (B) 1845, (CO) Pulaski, (A) 15, (BP) KY, (CMTS) 1860 Census
Riddle, Jepthah: (B) 1846, (CO) Pulaski, (A) 14, (BP) MO, (CMTS) 1860 Census
Riddle, John F.: (B) 1822, (CO) Pulaski, (A) 38, (BP) TN, (CMTS) 1860 Census
Riddle, Lovisa: (B) 1847, (CO) Pulaski, (A) 13, (BP) MO, (CMTS) 1860 Census
Riddle, Margaret: (B) 1815, (CO) Pulaski, (A) 45, (BP) TN, (CMTS) 1860 Census
Riddle, Mary: (B) 1844, (CO) Pulaski, (A) 16, (BP) KY, (CMTS) 1860 Census
Riddle, Mirriam J.: (B) 1842, (CO) Pulaski, (A) 18, (BP) MO, (CMTS) 1860 Census
Riddle, Nancy: (B) 1850, (CO) Pulaski, (A) 10, (BP) MO, (CMTS) 1860 Census
Riddle, Paradigm: (B) 1856, (CO) Pulaski, (A) 4, (BP) MO, (CMTS) 1860 Census
Riddle, Sarah: (B) 1844, (CO) Pulaski, (A) 16, (BP) MO, (CMTS) 1860 Census

Riddle, Sarah E.: (B) 1840, (CO) Pulaski, (A) 20, (BP) MO, (CMTS) 1860 Census
Riddle, Susan: (B) 1823, (CO) Pulaski, (A) 37, (BP) KY, (CMTS) 1860 Census
Riden, Charles M.: (B) 1844, (CO) Pulaski, (A) 16, (BP) MO, (CMTS) 1860 Census
Riden, Delilah: (B) 1839, (CO) Pulaski, (A) 21, (BP) MO, (CMTS) 1860 Census
Riden, Elender: (B) 1823, (CO) Pulaski, (A) 37, (BP) KY, (CMTS) 1860 Census
Riden, Elizabeth: (B) 1849, (CO) Pulaski, (A) 11, (BP) MO, (CMTS) 1860 Census
Riden, Elizabeth: (B) 1849, (CO) Pulaski, (A) 11, (BP) MO, (CMTS) 1860 Census
Riden, Elvira: (B) 1847, (CO) Pulaski, (A) 13, (BP) MO, (CMTS) 1860 Census
Riden, Francis M.: (B) 1839, (CO) Pulaski, (A) 21, (BP) MO, (CMTS) 1860 Census
Riden, James: (B) 1852, (CO) Pulaski, (A) 8, (BP) MO, (CMTS) 1860 Census
Riden, Joseph: (B) 1849, (CO) Pulaski, (A) 11, (BP) MO, (CMTS) 1860 Census
Riden, Mahala: (B) 1848, (CO) Pulaski, (A) 12, (BP) MO, (CMTS) 1860 Census
Riden, Melissa: (B) 1831, (CO) Pulaski, (A) 29, (BP) IL, (CMTS) 1860 Census
Riden, Nancy: (B) 1823, (CO) Pulaski, (A) 37, (BP) MO, (CMTS) 1860 Census
Riden, Wesley: (B) 1818, (CO) Pulaski, (A) 42, (BP) SC, (CMTS) 1860 Census
Riden, William: (B) 1851, (CO) Pulaski, (A) 9, (BP) MO, (CMTS) 1860 Census
Riggs, George W.: (B) 1844, (CO) Stone, (A) 26, (BP) MO, (CMTS) 1870 Census
Riggs, Louisa: (B) 1845, (CO) Stone, (A) 25, (BP) IL, (CMTS) 1870 Census
Right, Amanda: (B) 1832, (D) 1870, (CO) Adair, (A) 38, (CMTS) 1870 Mortality Schedule
Rigney, William: (D) Oct. 24, 1852, (CO) Andrew, (C) Oak Ridge Cemetery, (A) 28Y 2M 5D
Rigsby, Frances: (B) 1841, (CO) Pulaski, (A) 19, (BP) MO, (CMTS) 1860 Census
Rigsby, Jacob: (B) 1841, (CO) Pulaski, (A) 19, (BP) MO, (CMTS)

1860 Census
Rigsby, Kelly: (B) 1835, (CO) Pulaski, (A) 25, (BP) TN, (CMTS) 1860 Census
Rigsby, Mary: (B) 1855, (CO) Pulaski, (A) 5, (BP) MO, (CMTS) 1860 Census
Rilerford, Artemesa: (B) 1856, (CO) Pulaski, (A) 4, (BP) MO, (CMTS) 1860 Census
Rilerford, Catharine: (B) 1858, (CO) Pulaski, (A) 2, (BP) MO, (CMTS) 1860 Census
Rilerford, Francis M.: (B) 1858, (CO) Pulaski, (A) 2, (BP) MO, (CMTS) 1860 Census
Rilerford, James: (B) 1852, (CO) Pulaski, (A) 8, (BP) MO, (CMTS) 1860 Census
Rilerford, Polly: (B) 1827, (CO) Pulaski, (A) 33, (BP) KY, (CMTS) 1860 Census
Rilerford, Polly Ann: (B) 1849, (CO) Pulaski, (A) 11, (BP) MO, (CMTS) 1860 Census
Rilerford, Silas: (B) 1821, (CO) Pulaski, (A) 39, (BP) KY, (CMTS) 1860 Census
Riley, Isabell: (B) 1845, (CO) Pulaski, (A) 15, (BP) MO, (CMTS) 1860 Census
Riley, John: (D) Sep. 27, 1890, (CO) St. Louis, (C) Calvary Cemetery, (A) 57
Riley, Luther: (B) 1823, (CO) Pulaski, (A) 37, (BP) TN, (CMTS) 1860 Census
Riley, William: (B) 1842, (CO) Pulaski, (A) 18, (BP) MO, (CMTS) 1860 Census
Ring, Jennie A.: (B) 1865, (D) 1950, (CO) Henry, (C) Knights of Pythias Cemetery, Deepwater, MO
Ring, Robert L.: (B) 1866, (D) 1948, (CO) Henry, (C) Knights of Pythias Cemetery, Deepwater, MO
Risdon, Lorenzo D.: (B) Sep. 3, 1832, (D) Jul. 18, 1895, (CO) Barry, (C) Cassville Cemetery
Ritchie, Alonzo: (B) 1844, (CO) Pulaski, (A) 16, (BP) MO, (CMTS) 1860 Census
Ritchie, Cynthia H.: (B) 1846, (CO) Pulaski, (A) 14, (BP) AR, (CMTS) 1860 Census
Ritchie, Elizabeth: (B) 1822, (CO) Pulaski, (A) 38, (BP) KY, (CMTS) 1860 Census
Ritchie, Ellen: (B) 1856, (CO) Pulaski, (A) 4, (BP) MO, (CMTS) 1860 Census
Ritchie, Emily J.: (B) 1851, (CO) Pulaski, (A) 9, (BP) MO, (CMTS) 1860 Census

Ritchie, Ewing: (B) 1849, (CO) Pulaski, (A) 11, (BP) KY, (CMTS) 1860 Census
Ritchie, Frank A.: (B) 1854, (D) 1938, (CO) St. Louis, (C) Calvary Cemetery
Ritchie, James: (B) 1818, (CO) Pulaski, (A) 42, (BP) TN, (CMTS) 1860 Census
Ritchie, LeRoy: (B) 1855, (CO) Pulaski, (A) 5, (BP) MO, (CMTS) 1860 Census
Ritchie, Malvina: (B) 1819, (CO) Pulaski, (A) 41, (BP) KY, (CMTS) 1860 Census
Ritchie, Margaret: (B) 1856, (CO) Pulaski, (A) 4, (BP) MO, (CMTS) 1860 Census
Ritchie, Mary: (B) 1852, (CO) Pulaski, (A) 8, (BP) MO, (CMTS) 1860 Census
Ritchie, Mary A.: (B) 1856, (D) 1940, (CO) St. Louis, (C) Calvary Cemetery
Ritchie, Polk D.: (B) 1849, (CO) Pulaski, (A) 11, (BP) MO, (CMTS) 1860 Census
Ritchie, Rev. Paul J.: (B) May 14, 1887, (D) Aug. 26, 1941, (CO) St. Louis, (C) Calvary Cemetery
Ritter, Helen M.: (D) Dec. 21, 1999, (CO) Bates, (DP) Butler, MO, (NWS) *Allentown, Pennslyvania Morning Call*, Dec. 23, 1999.
Ritter, TomWilliam: (B) Aug. 26, 1905, (D) Jun. 22, 1994, (CO) Henry, (C) Knights of Pythias Cemetery, Deepwater, MO
Roach, Myrtle Ivy: (B) Aug. 25, 1906, (D) Jan. 4, 1992, (CO) Henry, (C) Knights of Pythias Cemetery, Deepwater, MO
Roberson, Catherine: (B) 1844, (CO) Stone, (A) 6, (BP) OH, (CMTS) 1870 Census
Roberson, Charles F: (B) 1842, (CO) Stone, (A) 8, (BP) OH, (CMTS) 1870 Census
Roberson, Cornelius: (B) 1838, (CO) Stone, (A) 12, (BP) IL, (CMTS) 1870 Census
Roberson, Ellen: (B) 1841, (CO) Stone, (A) 9, (BP) IL, (CMTS) 1870 Census
Roberson, Fledwood: (B) 1836, (CO) Stone, (A) 14, (BP) IL, (CMTS) 1870 Census
Roberson, John N: (B) 1838, (CO) Stone, (A) 32, (BP) OH, (CMTS) 1870 Census
Roberson, Joseph O: (B) 1841, (CO) Stone, (A) 9, (BP) OH, (CMTS) 1870 Census
Roberson, Lerenrean: (B) 1847, (CO) Stone, (A) 23, (BP) ENG, (CMTS) 1870 Census
Roberson, Mary: (B) 1816, (CO) Stone, (A) 34, (BP) OH, (CMTS) 1870

Census

Roberson, Maud: (B) 1846, (CO) Stone, (A) 4, (BP) OH, (CMTS) 1870 Census

Roberts, Aron: (B) 1829, (CO) Stone, (A) 21, (BP) KY, (CMTS) 1870 Census

Roberts, Asa F: (B) 1855, (CO) Stone, (A) 15, (BP) AR, (CMTS) 1870 Census

Roberts, David: (B) 1834, (CO) Pulaski, (A) 26, (BP) TN, (CMTS) 1860 Census

Roberts, Elizabeth J.: (B) 1837, (CO) Pulaski, (A) 23, (BP) TN, (CMTS) 1860 Census

Roberts, George: (B) 1853, (CO) Stone, (A) 17, (BP) AR, (CMTS) 1870 Census

Roberts, Joel: (B) 1835, (CO) Stone, (A) 15, (BP) KY, (CMTS) 1870 Census

Roberts, John R.: (B) 1831, (CO) Stone, (A) 19, (BP) KY, (CMTS) 1870 Census

Roberts, Lord M.: (B) 1832, (CO) Stone, (A) 18, (BP) KY, (CMTS) 1870 Census

Roberts, Mary: (B) 1795, (CO) Pulaski, (A) 65, (BP) VA, (CMTS) 1860 Census

Roberts, Mary Jane: (B) 1836, (CO) Stone, (A) 14, (BP) KY, (CMTS) 1870 Census

Roberts, Mary T.: (B) 1855, (CO) Pulaski, (A) 5, (BP) TN, (CMTS) 1860 Census

Roberts, Milly: (B) 1840, (CO) Stone, (A) 10, (BP) KY, (CMTS) 1870 Census

Roberts, Sarah F.: (B) 1857, (CO) Pulaski, (A) 3, (BP) TN, (CMTS) 1860 Census

Roberts, Susan P: (B) 1839, (CO) Stone, (A) 11, (BP) KY, (CMTS) 1870 Census

Roberts, Thomas F: (B) 1843, (CO) Stone, (A) 7, (BP) KY, (CMTS) 1870 Census

Roberts, Thomas M.: (B) 1793, (CO) Pulaski, (A) 67, (BP) NC, (CMTS) 1860 Census

Robertson, Caroline: (B) 1848, (CO) Pulaski, (A) 12, (BP) MO, (CMTS) 1860 Census

Robertson, Elizabeth: (B) 1827, (CO) Pulaski, (A) 33, (BP) IND, (CMTS) 1860 Census

Robertson, Isaac: (B) 1819, (CO) Pulaski, (A) 41, (BP) TN, (CMTS) 1860 Census

Robertson, Jane: (B) 1838, (CO) Pulaski, (A) 22, (BP) MO, (CMTS) 1860 Census

Robertson, Nancy: (B) 1850, (CO) Pulaski, (A) 10, (BP) MO, (CMTS) 1860 Census
Robertson, Rachael: (B) 1851, (CO) Pulaski, (A) 9, (BP) MO, (CMTS) 1860 Census
Robertson, Starling C.: (B) 1852, (CO) Pulaski, (A) 8, (BP) MO, (CMTS) 1860 Census
Robeson, Eleanor H.: (D) 1974, (CO) St. Louis, (C) Calvary Cemetery
Robinson, Ann M.: (B) 1854, (CO) Pulaski, (A) 6, (BP) IL, (CMTS) 1860 Census
Robinson, Berthana: (B) 1829, (CO) Pulaski, (A) 31, (BP) NC, (CMTS) 1860 Census
Robinson, Catharine W.: (B) 1837, (CO) Pulaski, (A) 23, (BP) VA, (CMTS) 1860 Census
Robinson, Eliza: (B) 1847, (CO) Pulaski, (A) 13, (BP) MO, (CMTS) 1860 Census
Robinson, Elizabeth F.: (B) 1842, (CO) Pulaski, (A) 18, (BP) VA, (CMTS) 1860 Census
Robinson, Ezekiel: (B) 1836, (CO) Pulaski, (A) 24, (BP) MO, (CMTS) 1860 Census
Robinson, Frances J.: (B) 1834, (CO) Pulaski, (A) 26, (BP) KY, (CMTS) 1860 Census
Robinson, Francis J.: (B) 1835, (D) 1885, (CO) Cedar, (C) Brashear Cemetery
Robinson, George: (B) 1845, (CO) Pulaski, (A) 15, (BP) KY, (CMTS) 1860 Census
Robinson, Isaac: (B) 1853, (CO) Pulaski, (A) 7, (BP) MO, (CMTS) 1860 Census
Robinson, James: (B) 1838, (CO) Pulaski, (A) 22, (BP) KY, (CMTS) 1860 Census
Robinson, James: (B) 1851, (CO) Pulaski, (A) 9, (BP) MO, (CMTS) 1860 Census
Robinson, James M.: (B) 1850, (CO) Pulaski, (A) 10, (BP) IL, (CMTS) 1860 Census
Robinson, James: (B) 1833, (D) 1916, (CO) Cedar, (C) Brashear Cemetery
Robinson, John: (B) 1841, (CO) Pulaski, (A) 19, (BP) KY, (CMTS) 1860 Census
Robinson, John: (B) 1856, (CO) Pulaski, (A) 4, (BP) TN, (CMTS) 1860 Census
Robinson, John T.: (B) 1847, (CO) Pulaski, (A) 13, (BP) IL, (CMTS) 1860 Census
Robinson, Josiah: (B) 1834, (CO) Pulaski, (A) 26, (BP) VA, (CMTS) 1860 Census
Robinson, Mahala: (B) 1844, (CO) Pulaski, (A) 16, (BP) MO, (CMTS)

1860 Census
Robinson, Margaret V.: (B) 1844, (CO) Pulaski, (A) 16, (BP) VA, (CMTS) 1860 Census
Robinson, Marmaduke: (B) 1827, (CO) Pulaski, (A) 33, (BP) NC, (CMTS) 1860 Census
Robinson, Martha W.: (B) 1845, (CO) Pulaski, (A) 15, (BP) VA, (CMTS) 1860 Census
Robinson, Mary: (B) 1795, (CO) Pulaski, (A) 65, (BP) NC, (CMTS) 1860 Census
Robinson, Mary: (B) 1844, (CO) Pulaski, (A) 16, (BP) IL, (CMTS) 1860 Census
Robinson, Mary: (B) 1856, (CO) Pulaski, (A) 4, (BP) MO, (CMTS) 1860 Census
Robinson, Mary E.: (B) 1840, (CO) Pulaski, (A) 20, (BP) VA, (CMTS) 1860 Census
Robinson, P.: (B) 1826, (CO) Pulaski, (A) 34, (BP) KY, (CMTS) 1860 Census
Robinson, Rhoda: (B) 1822, (CO) Pulaski, (A) 38, (BP) NC, (CMTS) 1860 Census
Robinson, Samuel H.: (B) 1836, (CO) Pulaski, (A) 24, (BP) KY, (CMTS) 1860 Census
Robinson, Sarah: (B) 1822, (CO) Pulaski, (A) 38, (BP) IL, (CMTS) 1860 Census
Robinson, Sarah A. O.: (B) 1853, (CO) Pulaski, (A) 7, (BP) VA, (CMTS) 1860 Census
Robinson, Susan: (B) 1842, (CO) Pulaski, (A) 18, (BP) IL, (CMTS) 1860 Census
Robinson, Virgil A. I.: (B) 1849, (CO) Pulaski, (A) 11, (BP) VA, (CMTS) 1860 Census
Robinson, William: (B) 1843, (CO) Pulaski, (A) 17, (BP) KY, (CMTS) 1860 Census
Rockwell, Henry: (B) 1854, (CO) Stone, (A) 16, (BP) OH, (CMTS) 1870 Census
Rockwell, Kenneth C.: (B) 1839, (CO) Stone, (A) 31, (BP) OH, (CMTS) 1870 Census
Rockwell, Lewis: (B) 1815, (CO) Stone, (A) 55, (BP) OH, (CMTS) 1870 Census
Rodgers, Thomas J.: (B) Jul. 19, 1808, (D) Feb. 20, 1870, (CO) Barry, (C) Old Corsicana Cemetery
Rogers, Isabella: (B) 1856, (D) 1930, (CO) Henry, (C) Knights of Pythias Cemetery, Deepwater, MO
Rollins, Courtenay: (B) 1848, (CO) Pulaski, (A) 12, (BP) MO, (CMTS) 1860 Census

Rollins, David: (B) 1822, (CO) Pulaski, (A) 38, (BP) TN, (CMTS) 1860 Census
Rollins, Emily E.: (B) 1852, (CO) Pulaski, (A) 8, (BP) VA, (CMTS) 1860 Census
Rollins, George W.: (B) 1845, (CO) Pulaski, (A) 15, (BP) MO, (CMTS) 1860 Census
Rollins, Harrison: (B) 1856, (CO) Pulaski, (A) 4, (BP) TN, (CMTS) 1860 Census
Rollins, James: (B) 1831, (CO) Pulaski, (A) 29, (BP) VA, (CMTS) 1860 Census
Rollins, Jamesper: (B) 1852, (CO) Pulaski, (A) 8, (BP) MO, (CMTS) 1860 Census
Rollins, Jeremiah: (B) 1853, (CO) Pulaski, (A) 7, (BP) MO, (CMTS) 1860 Census
Rollins, Martha J.: (B) 1843, (CO) Pulaski, (A) 17, (BP) TN, (CMTS) 1860 Census
Rollins, Rachael: (B) 1825, (CO) Pulaski, (A) 35, (BP) TN, (CMTS) 1860 Census
Rollins, Sarah J.: (B) 1837, (CO) Pulaski, (A) 23, (BP) VA, (CMTS) 1860 Census
Rollins, Susan: (B) 1856, (CO) Pulaski, (A) 4, (BP) MO, (CMTS) 1860 Census
Roseman, Alford L.: (B) 1845, (D) 1925, (CO) Cedar, (C) Brashear Cemetery
Roseman, Elizabeth: (B) 1845, (CO) Cedar, (C) Brashear Cemetery
Rosenauer, Veronika: (B) Jan. 16, 1820, (D) Sep. 14, 1917, (CO) Jefferson, (C) Old St. John's Catholic Cemetery
Rosenthal, George O.: (B) 1869, (D) 1913, (CO) St. Louis, (C) Calvary Cemetery
Rosenthal, Josephine: (B) 1874, (D) 1953, (CO) St. Louis, (C) Calvary Cemetery
Roser, Amanda: (B) 1829, (CO) Stone, (A) 21, (BP) MO, (CMTS) 1870 Census
Roser, James: (B) 1832, (CO) Stone, (A) 18, (BP) MO, (CMTS) 1870 Census
Roser, Mary: (B) 1838, (CO) Stone, (A) 12, (BP) MO, (CMTS) 1870 Census
Roser, William: (B) 1835, (CO) Stone, (A) 15, (BP) MO, (CMTS) 1870 Census
Rosnick, Mary E.: (B) 1842, (CO) Stone, (A) 28, (BP) TN, (CMTS) 1870 Census
Ross, Lucinda: (B) 1844, (CO) Pulaski, (A) 16, (BP) MO, (CMTS) 1860 Census

Ross, Nancy Priscilla: (B) Sep. 25, 1819, (D) Mar. 3, 1871, (CO) Missouri, (DP) Mt. Pleasant, IA
Ross, W.: (B) 1841, (CO) Pulaski, (A) 19, (BP) MO, (CMTS) 1860 Census
Ross, William C.: (D) Jan. 12, 1935, (CO) St. Louis, (C) Calvary Cemetery
Routh, Loves A.: (B) Feb. 1, 1829, (D) Apr. 6, 1857, (CO) Barry, (C) Cassville Cemetery
Rovane, Annie: (D) Sep. 25, 1924, (CO) St. Louis, (C) Calvary Cemetery
Roy, John: (B) 1829, (CO) Stone, (A) 21, (BP) MO, (CMTS) 1870 Census
Roy, Luciln Sr.: (B) 1907, (D) 1984, (CO) St. Louis, (C) Calvary Cemetery
Roy, Martha *: (B) 1912, (D) 1983, (CO) St. Louis, (C) Calvary Cemetery
Roy, Rebecca: (B) 1849, (CO) Stone, (A) 1, (BP) MO, (CMTS) 1870 Census
Roy, Sarah: (B) 1830, (CO) Stone, (A) 20, (BP) AR, (CMTS) 1870 Census
Rufner, Mary E.: (B) Apr. 5, 1894, (D) Jun. 9, 1979, (CO) Jackson,
Ruhr, Conrad: (B) Mar. 30, 1884, (D) Mar. 28, 1939, (CO) St. Louis, (C) Calvary Cemetery
Ruhr, Henry: (B) May 9, 1883, (D) Feb. 21, 1903, (CO) St. Louis, (C) Calvary Cemetery
Rum, George: (B) 1855, (CO) Pulaski, (A) 5, (BP) MO, (CMTS) 1860 Census
Rum, Henry: (B) 1830, (CO) Pulaski, (A) 30, (BP) TN, (CMTS) 1860 Census
Rum, Jane: (B) 1852, (CO) Pulaski, (A) 8, (BP) MO, (CMTS) 1860 Census
Rum, Mary: (B) 1832, (CO) Pulaski, (A) 28, (BP) TN, (CMTS) 1860 Census
Rum, Nancy: (B) 1851, (CO) Pulaski, (A) 9, (BP) MO, (CMTS) 1860 Census
Runells, Emeline: (B) 1829, (CO) Stone, (A) 41, (BP) TN, (CMTS) 1870 Census
Runells, John: (B) 1832, (CO) Stone, (A) 38, (BP) MO, (CMTS) 1870 Census
Runold, Daniel D.: (B) 1842, (CO) Pulaski, (A) 18, (BP) IL, (CMTS) 1860 Census
Runold, Jesse L.: (B) 1844, (CO) Pulaski, (A) 16, (BP) IL, (CMTS) 1860 Census
Runold, Judith: (B) 1853, (CO) Pulaski, (A) 7, (BP) IL, (CMTS) 1860 Census

Runold, Mary C.: (B) 1846, (CO) Pulaski, (A) 14, (BP) IL, (CMTS) 1860 Census
Runold, Matilda J.: (B) 1847, (CO) Pulaski, (A) 13, (BP) IL, (CMTS) 1860 Census
Runold, Nancy: (B) 1855, (CO) Pulaski, (A) 5, (BP) IL, (CMTS) 1860 Census
Runold, Nathanial: (B) 1819, (CO) Pulaski, (A) 41, (BP) NC, (CMTS) 1860 Census
Runold, William C.: (B) 1841, (CO) Pulaski, (A) 19, (BP) IL, (CMTS) 1860 Census
Russell, Charles E.: (D) Feb. 3, 1967, (CO) St. Louis, (C) Calvary Cemetery
Russell, Elizabeth: (B) 1841, (CO) Pulaski, (A) 19, (BP) MO, (CMTS) 1860 Census
Russell, James S.: (B) 1842, (CO) Stone, (A) 8, (BP) MO, (CMTS) 1870 Census
Russell, John: (B) 1815, (CO) Stone, (A) 35, (BP) TN, (CMTS) 1870 Census
Russell, John B.: (B) 1834, (CO) Stone, (A) 36, (BP) TN, (CMTS) 1870 Census
Russell, Malissa: (B) 1834, (CO) Stone, (A) 36, (BP) TN, (CMTS) 1870 Census
Russell, Mary M.: (B) 1838, (CO) Stone, (A) 12, (BP) MO, (CMTS) 1870 Census
Russell, Mary M.: (B) 1856, (CO) Stone, (A) 14, (BP) MO, (CMTS) 1870 Census
Russell, Melissa: (B) 1815, (CO) Stone, (A) 35, (BP) TN, (CMTS) 1870 Census
Russell, Nancy P S.: (B) 1841, (CO) Stone, (A) 9, (BP) AR, (CMTS) 1870 Census
Russell, Rollins: (D) Aug. 15, 1921, (CO) St. Louis, (C) Calvary Cemetery
Russell, Sarah E.: (B) 1839, (CO) Stone, (A) 11, (BP) AR, (CMTS) 1870 Census
Russell, Thomas S.: (B) 1848, (CO) Stone, (A) 2, (BP) MO, (CMTS) 1870 Census
Russell, William: (B) 1839, (CO) Pulaski, (A) 21, (BP) TN, (CMTS) 1860 Census
Russell, William N S.: (B) 1844, (CO) Stone, (A) 6, (BP) MO, (CMTS) 1870 Census
Russman, Fritz: (B) 1842, (CO) Stone, (A) 28, (BP) HAMBUR, (CMTS) 1870 Census
Russman, Hulda: (B) 1845, (CO) Stone, (A) 25, (BP) IN, (CMTS) 1870

Census
Ruthsatz, Herman: (D) Dec. 2, 1868, (CO) St. Louis, (C) Calvary Cemetery
Ryan, Alice: (B) 1846, (CO) Pulaski, (A) 14, (BP) OH, (CMTS) 1860 Census
Ryan, Ann G.: (D) Jun. 4, 1905, (CO) St. Louis, (C) Calvary Cemetery
Ryan, Edward A.: (D) Apr. 23, 1949, (CO) St. Louis, (C) Calvary Cemetery
Ryan, James A.: (B) 1844, (CO) Pulaski, (A) 16, (BP) OH, (CMTS) 1860 Census
Ryan, Jeremiah J.: (D) May 7, 1924, (CO) St. Louis, (C) Calvary Cemetery
Ryan, John W.: (B) 1878, (D) 1930, (CO) St. Louis, (C) Calvary Cemetery
Ryan, William L.: (D) Sep. 27, 1880, (CO) St. Louis, (C) Calvary Cemetery, (A) 79
Ryan, Jr.,Edward J.: (D) Aug. 17, 1995, (CO) St. Louis, (C) Calvary Cemetery
Ryner, William: (B) 1831, (CO) Pulaski, (A) 29, (BP) Ireland, (CMTS) 1860 Census
Saake, Anton J.: (B) May 19, 1819, (D) Dec. 4, 1881, (CO) Jefferson, (C) Old St. John's Catholic Cemetery
Sack, Marie F.: (B) 1898, (D) 1979, (CO) St. Louis, (C) Calvary Cemetery
Saettele, Frenricke E.: (B) 1873, (D) 1927, (CO) St. Louis, (C) Calvary Cemetery
Sain, Constance K.: (D) Apr. 18, 1972, (CO) St. Louis, (C) Calvary Cemetery
Sally, Irving: (B) 1837, (CO) Pulaski, (A) 23, (BP) KY, (CMTS) 1860 Census
Sally, Orlena: (B) 1842, (CO) Pulaski, (A) 18, (BP) TN, (CMTS) 1860 Census
Saltsman, Daniel G.: (B) 1849, (CO) Pulaski, (A) 11, (BP) KY, (CMTS) 1860 Census
Saltsman, Eva: (B) 1844, (CO) Pulaski, (A) 16, (BP) KY, (CMTS) 1860 Census
Saltsman, Harriet J.: (B) 1855, (CO) Pulaski, (A) 5, (BP) MO, (CMTS) 1860 Census
Saltsman, Margaret: (B) 1853, (CO) Pulaski, (A) 7, (BP) MO, (CMTS) 1860 Census
Saltsman, Mary: (B) 1846, (CO) Pulaski, (A) 14, (BP) KY, (CMTS) 1860 Census
Saltsman, Mary: (B) 1836, (CO) Pulaski, (A) 24, (BP) TN, (CMTS) 1860 Census
Saltsman, William: (B) 1833, (CO) Pulaski, (A) 27, (BP) IL, (CMTS)

1860 Census
Sanders, Callaway: (B) 1856, (CO) Stone, (A) 14, (BP) TX, (CMTS) 1870 Census
Sanders, Henry N: (B) 1852, (CO) Stone, (A) 18, (BP) TN, (CMTS) 1870 Census
Sanders, James L.: (B) 1826, (CO) Stone, (A) 24, (BP) MO, (CMTS) 1870 Census
Sanders, John H.: (B) 1849, (CO) Stone, (A) 21, (BP) TN, (CMTS) 1870 Census
Sanders, John M.: (B) 1823, (CO) Stone, (A) 27, (BP) TN, (CMTS) 1870 Census
Sanders, Lola Edith: (B) Feb. 18, 1907, (D) Mar. 7, 1987, (CO) Henry, (C) Knights of Pythias Cemetery, Deepwater, MO
Sanders, Mack P: (B) 1835, (CO) Stone, (A) 15, (BP) MO, (CMTS) 1870 Census
Sanders, Mary E.: (B) 1850, (CO) Stone, (A) 20, (BP) AL, (CMTS) 1870 Census
Sanders, Prior: (B) 1847, (CO) Stone, (A) 23, (BP) TN, (CMTS) 1870 Census
Sanders, Rachel: (B) 1825, (CO) Stone, (A) 25, (BP) AR, (CMTS) 1870 Census
Sanders, Rena: (B) 1820, (CO) Stone, (A) 50, (BP) TN, (CMTS) 1870 Census
Sanders, Susan: (B) 1830, (CO) Stone, (A) 20, (BP) MO, (CMTS) 1870 Census
Sanders, William: (B) 1847, (CO) Stone, (A) 23, (BP) MO, (CMTS) 1870 Census
Sanduskey, Levi: (B) Dec. 13, 1868, (D) Jul. 9, 1905, (CO) Henry, (C) Knights of Pythias Cemetery, Deepwater, MO
Sanifer, James T.: (B) 1837, (CO) Pulaski, (A) 23, (BP) KY, (CMTS) 1860 Census
Sanifer, Mary E.: (B) 1838, (CO) Pulaski, (A) 22, (BP) KY, (CMTS) 1860 Census
Santino, Elice: (B) 1871, (D) 1926, (CO) St. Louis, (C) Calvary Cemetery
Sappinton, John: (B) Nov. 21, 1866,, (CO) Missouri, (SPOUSE) Anna Bledsoe
Sappinton, Mary: (B) Nov. 27, 1805, (D) Sep. 5, 1876, (CO) Missouri, (C) New Salem Church Cemetery, (BP) Ashland, (SPOUSE) Squire Burnam
Sappinton, Milton: (B) Apr. 4, 1859, (CO) Missouri, (SPOUSE) Emma Bledsoe
Sappinton, Sarah A.: (B) Aug. 13, 1861, (D) Nov. 3, 1908, (CO) Polk, (C) Turkey Creek Cemetery

Sartini, Anthony: (B) 1854, (D) 1931, (CO) St. Louis, (C) Calvary Cemetery

Sartini, James: (B) Sep. 4, 1886, (D) Mar. 11, 1908, (CO) St. Louis, (C) Calvary Cemetery

Sartini, Mary: (B) 1850, (D) 1917, (CO) St. Louis, (C) Calvary Cemetery

Savage, Annie: (D) Feb. 5, 1920, (CO) St. Louis, (C) Calvary Cemetery

Savage, Thomas L.: (D) Dec. 9, 1901, (CO) St. Louis, (C) Calvary Cemetery

Sawyer, Julia O.: (B) 1849, (D) 1916, (CO) Henry, (C) Knights of Pythias Cemetery, Deepwater, MO

Scaggs, Jacob: (B) 1852, (CO) Pulaski, (A) 8, (BP) MO, (CMTS) 1860 Census

Scaggs, James: (B) 1850, (CO) Pulaski, (A) 10, (BP) MO, (CMTS) 1860 Census

Scaggs, James M.: (B) 1847, (CO) Pulaski, (A) 13, (BP) MO, (CMTS) 1860 Census

Scaggs, Jane: (B) 1830, (CO) Pulaski, (A) 30, (BP) TN, (CMTS) 1860 Census

Scaggs, Maston: (B) 1796, (CO) Pulaski, (A) 64, (BP) TN, (CMTS) 1860 Census

Scaggs, Polly: (B) 1855, (CO) Pulaski, (A) 5, (BP) MO, (CMTS) 1860 Census

Scaggs, Susan: (B) 1822, (CO) Pulaski, (A) 38, (BP) MO, (CMTS) 1860 Census

Scaggs, William A.: (B) 1821, (CO) Pulaski, (A) 39, (BP) TN, (CMTS) 1860 Census

Schafluetzel, Jacob: (B) Sep. 12, 1854, (D) Feb. 9, 1939, (CO) St. Louis, (C) Calvary Cemetery

Scheele, John H.: (B) Sep. 7, 1887, (D) May 18, 1987, (CO) St. Louis, (C) Calvary Cemetery

Schell, Willard: (B) Apr. 19, 1922, (D) Oct. 4, 1998, (CO) Joplin, (NWS) *Joplin Globe, Oct. 5, 1998*, (BP) Rocky Comfort, (MD) Oct. 13, 1969, Miami, OK, (SPOUSE) Aline Charlestain, (C) Ozark Memorial Cemetery, (CMTS) Sharon Johnson, daughter; JoAnn Howe, sister

Schiller, Charles: (B) 1854, (CO) Pulaski, (A) 6, (BP) MO, (CMTS) 1860 Census

Schiller, Henry: (B) 1841, (CO) Pulaski, (A) 19, (BP) MO, (CMTS) 1860 Census

Schiller, Henry: (B) 1847, (CO) Pulaski, (A) 13, (BP) Prussia, (CMTS) 1860 Census

Schiller, Lewis: (B) 1843, (CO) Pulaski, (A) 17, (BP) MO, (CMTS) 1860 Census

Schiller, Mary: (B) 1825, (CO) Pulaski, (A) 35, (BP) Prussia, (CMTS) 1860 Census
Schiller, William: (B) 1819, (CO) Pulaski, (A) 41, (BP) Prussia, (CMTS) 1860 Census
Schlacht, Anton: (B) Apr. 15, 1815, (D) Jun. 5, 1861, (CO) Jefferson, (C) Old St. John's Catholic Cemetery
Schmidt, Lois: (B) Sep. 7, 1927, (D) Jul. 24, 1976, (CO) St. Louis, (C) Calvary Cemetery
Schmidt, Louise: (B) Sep. 7, 1887, (D) Oct. 29, 1976, (CO) St. Louis, (C) Calvary Cemetery
Schneider, Anna: (B) Oct. 4, 1820, (D) Oct. 2, 1887, (CO) Andrew, (C) Oak Ridge Cemetery
Schneider, Anna: (B) Oct. 4, 1820, (D) Oct. 2, 1887, (CO) Andrew, (C) Oak Ridge Cemetery
Schneider, Chaterine: (B) Aug. 9, 1823, (D) Oct. 23, 1876, (CO) Andrew, (C) Oak Ridge Cemetery
Schneider, Elizabeth: (B) Nov. 15, 1800, (D) Jul. 7, 1876, (CO) Andrew, (C) Oak Ridge Cemetery
Schneider, Henry: (B) 1820, (CO) Pulaski, (A) 40, (BP) Ruttenburg, (CMTS) 1860 Census
Schneider, Johann: (B) Oct. 15, 1809, (D) Nov. 4,1883, (CO) Andrew, (C) Oak Ridge Cemetery
Schneider, Katherina: (B) Jan. 27, 1823, (D) Dec. 8, 1890, (CO) Andrew, (C) Oak Ridge Cemetery
Schneider, Nicklaus: (B) 1833, (D) 1896, (CO) Andrew, (C) Oak Ridge Cemetery
Schneller, Mary Alice: (B) Dec. 30, 1866, (D) Dec. 30, 1960, (CO) Callaway, (DP) Portland, MO
Scholten, Eva J.: (B) 1845, (CO) Stone, (A) 5, (BP) MO, (CMTS) 1870 Census
Scholten, Frederic: (B) 1848, (CO) Stone, (A) 2, (BP) MO, (CMTS) 1870 Census
Scholten, John: (B) 1842, (CO) Stone, (A) 8, (BP) MO, (CMTS) 1870 Census
Scholten, Mary E.: (B) 1821, (CO) Stone, (A) 29, (BP) MO, (CMTS) 1870 Census
Scholten, Mattie: (B) 1840, (CO) Stone, (A) 10, (BP) MO, (CMTS) 1870 Census
Schramm, William C.: (B) Nov. 4, 1885, (D) Feb. 17, 1953, (CO) St. Louis, (C) Calvary Cemetery
Schrenk, Anna: (B) 1834, (D) 1903, (CO) St. Louis, (C) Calvary Cemetery
Schrenk, John: (B) 1844, (D) 1904, (CO) St. Louis, (C) Calvary Cemetery
Schulte, Alvin H.: (B) 1921, (CO) St. Louis, (C) Calvary Cemetery

Schulte, Lorraine A.: (B) 1920, (CO) St. Louis, (C) Calvary Cemetery
Schulze, Charles F.: (B) Oct. 26, 1886, (D) Mar. 23, 1905, (CO) St. Louis, (C) Calvary Cemetery
Schulze, Henry A.: (B) May 2, 1858, (D) Jun. 6, 1935, (CO) St. Louis, (C) Calvary Cemetery
Schwab, Mrs. Theresia: (D) Jan. 13, 1883, (CO) St. Louis, (C) Calvary Cemetery, (A) 63
Schwartz, Joseph: (D) Aug.20, 2000, (CO) Cole, (NWS) *Jefferson City, Missouri News-Tribune*, Aug. 22, 2000, (RES) Freeburg
Schwarztrauber, Jacob: (B) 1894, (D) 1968, (CO) St. Louis, (C) Calvary Cemetery
Schwarztrauber, Mary A.: (B) 1897, (D) 1946, (CO) St. Louis, (C) Calvary Cemetery
Schweiss, Sr.,Benard P.: (B) Sep. 20, 1930, (CO) St. Louis, (C) Calvary Cemetery
Sciortino, Jean A.: (B) 1916, (CO) St. Louis, (C) Calvary Cemetery
Score, Ellen: (D) 1922, (CO) St. Louis, (C) Calvary Cemetery
Score, William John: (D) 1906, (CO) St. Louis, (C) Calvary Cemetery
Scott, Ardillera: (B) 1855, (CO) Pulaski, (A) 5, (BP) TN, (CMTS) 1860 Census
Scott, Auphema: (B) 1856, (CO) Pulaski, (A) 4, (BP) TN, (CMTS) 1860 Census
Scott, Cooper B.: (B) 1858, (CO) Pulaski, (A) 2, (BP) TN, (CMTS) 1860 Census
Scott, Daniel: (B) 1858, (CO) Pulaski, (A) 2, (BP) MO, (CMTS) 1860 Census
Scott, Daniel B.: (B) 1827, (CO) Pulaski, (A) 33, (BP) IL, (CMTS) 1860 Census
Scott, Elizabeth: (B) 1850, (CO) Pulaski, (A) 10, (BP) MO, (CMTS) 1860 Census
Scott, Fanny: (B) 1835, (CO) Pulaski, (A) 25, (BP) KY, (CMTS) 1860 Census
Scott, Jackson: (B) 1832, (CO) Pulaski, (A) 28, (BP) KY, (CMTS) 1860 Census
Scott, John: (B) 1856, (CO) Pulaski, (A) 4, (BP) KY, (CMTS) 1860 Census
Scott, John B.: (B) 1852, (CO) Pulaski, (A) 8, (BP) MO, (CMTS) 1860 Census
Scott, Levi: (B) 1831, (CO) Pulaski, (A) 29, (BP) TN, (CMTS) 1860 Census
Scott, Lucinda: (B) 1837, (CO) Pulaski, (A) 23, (BP) TN, (CMTS) 1860 Census

Scott, Malinda: (B) 1830, (CO) Pulaski, (A) 30, (BP) IL, (CMTS) 1860 Census
Scott, Nancy: (B) 1854, (CO) Pulaski, (A) 6, (BP) KY, (CMTS) 1860 Census
Scott, Reubin: (B) 1853, (CO) Pulaski, (A) 7, (BP) KY, (CMTS) 1860 Census
Scott, Robert: (B) 1851, (CO) Pulaski, (A) 9, (BP) KY, (CMTS) 1860 Census
Scott, William J.: (B) 1856, (CO) Pulaski, (A) 4, (BP) MO, (CMTS) 1860 Census
Scribner, Martha: (B) 1846, (CO) Pulaski, (A) 14, (BP) MO, (CMTS) 1860 Census
Seling,: (B) 1885, (D) 1939, (CO) St. Louis, (C) Calvary Cemetery
Selzer, Angie: (D) Apr. 27, 1933, (CO) St. Louis, (C) Calvary Cemetery
Setser, Elizabeth: (B) 1841, (CO) Pulaski, (A) 19, (BP) NC, (CMTS) 1860 Census
Setser, Emanuel: (B) 1854, (CO) Pulaski, (A) 6, (BP) NC, (CMTS) 1860 Census
Setser, John: (B) 1846, (CO) Pulaski, (A) 14, (BP) NC, (CMTS) 1860 Census
Setser, Mary: (B) 1847, (CO) Pulaski, (A) 13, (BP) NC, (CMTS) 1860 Census
Setser, Rua H.: (B) 1849, (CO) Pulaski, (A) 11, (BP) NC, (CMTS) 1860 Census
Setser, Sarah: (B) 1856, (CO) Pulaski, (A) 4, (BP) NC, (CMTS) 1860 Census
Sexton, Rolla K: (B) 1845, (CO) Stone, (A) 25, (BP) TN, (CMTS) 1870 Census
Sexton, Sopha J.: (B) 1850, (CO) Stone, (A) 20, (BP) TN, (CMTS) 1870 Census
Shaha, Benjamin: (B) 1858, (CO) Pulaski, (A) 2, (BP) MO, (CMTS) 1860 Census
Shaha, Cynthia J.: (B) 1852, (CO) Pulaski, (A) 8, (BP) OH, (CMTS) 1860 Census
Shaha, Elizabeth: (B) 1835, (CO) Pulaski, (A) 25, (BP) VA, (CMTS) 1860 Census
Shaha, Jackson: (B) 1832, (CO) Pulaski, (A) 28, (BP) OH, (CMTS) 1860 Census
Shaha, Sarah E.: (B) 1855, (CO) Pulaski, (A) 5, (BP) OH, (CMTS) 1860 Census
Shaijh, James: (B) 1833, (CO) Pulaski, (A) 27, (BP) Ireland, (CMTS) 1860 Census
Sharp, Charles: (B) 1828, (CO) Pulaski, (A) 32, (BP) TN, (CMTS)

1860 Census
Sharp, Eli: (B) 1852, (CO) Pulaski, (A) 8, (BP) MO, (CMTS) 1860 Census
Sharp, Eliza: (B) 1832, (CO) Pulaski, (A) 28, (BP) TN, (CMTS) 1860 Census
Sharp, George W.: (B) 1850, (CO) Pulaski, (A) 10, (BP) MO, (CMTS) 1860 Census
Sharp, Lucinda: (B) 1818, (CO) Pulaski, (A) 42, (BP) KY, (CMTS) 1860 Census
Sharp, Oliver: (B) 1855, (CO) Pulaski, (A) 5, (BP) MO, (CMTS) 1860 Census
Sharp, Polly Ann: (B) 1847, (CO) Pulaski, (A) 13, (BP) MO, (CMTS) 1860 Census
Shaw, Columbus: (B) 1854, (CO) Pulaski, (A) 6, (BP) MO, (CMTS) 1860 Census
Shaw, Eliza: (B) 1858, (CO) Pulaski, (A) 2, (BP) MO, (CMTS) 1860 Census
Shaw, George: (B) 1831, (CO) Pulaski, (A) 29, (BP) Prussia, (CMTS) 1860 Census
Shaw, Grenville: (B) 1851, (CO) Pulaski, (A) 9, (BP) MO, (CMTS) 1860 Census
Shaw, James R.: (B) 1853, (CO) Pulaski, (A) 7, (BP) MO, (CMTS) 1860 Census
Shaw, John A.: (B) Apr. 7, 1828, (D) Jan. 18, 1892, (CO) Barry, (C) Old Corsicana Cemetery
Shaw, Levi: (B) 1818, (CO) Pulaski, (A) 42, (BP) OH, (CMTS) 1860 Census
Shaw, Martha J.: (B) 1849, (CO) Pulaski, (A) 11, (BP) MO, (CMTS) 1860 Census
Shaw, Mary: (B) 1819, (D) Jan. 17. 1884, (CO) Barry, (C) Old Corsicana Cemetery
Shaw, Rebecca: (B) 1816, (CO) Pulaski, (A) 44, (BP) TN, (CMTS) 1860 Census
Shaw, Rebecca: (B) 1832, (CO) Pulaski, (A) 28, (BP) KY, (CMTS) 1860 Census
Shaw, Samantha: (B) 1852, (CO) Pulaski, (A) 8, (BP) MO, (CMTS) 1860 Census
Shaw, Sarah: (B) 1855, (CO) Pulaski, (A) 5, (BP) MO, (CMTS) 1860 Census
Shaw, William: (B) 1849, (CO) Pulaski, (A) 11, (BP) MO, (CMTS) 1860 Census
Shaw, William: (B) Aug. 31, 1819, (D) Mar. 28, 1885, (CO) Barry, (C) Old Corsicana Cemetery

Sheehan, Celeste M.: (B) 1898, (D) 1974, (CO) St. Louis, (C) Calvary Cemetery
Sheehan, Donald J.: (B) 1926, (D) 1972, (CO) St. Louis, (C) Calvary Cemetery
Sheehan, John J.: (B) 1896, (D) 1971, (CO) St. Louis, (C) Calvary Cemetery
Shellhorn, Jacobine: (B) 1850, (D) 1929, (CO) Cedar, (C) Brashear Cemetery
Shelton, Ann W.: (B) 1798, (CO) Pulaski, (A) 62, (BP) SC, (CMTS) 1860 Census
Shelton, Charlotte: (B) 1823, (CO) Pulaski, (A) 37, (BP) TN, (CMTS) 1860 Census
Shelton, Clarissa: (B) 1843, (CO) Pulaski, (A) 17, (BP) TN, (CMTS) 1860 Census
Shelton, Donisda: (B) 1849, (CO) Pulaski, (A) 11, (BP) MO, (CMTS) 1860 Census
Shelton, Eliza: (B) 1848, (CO) Pulaski, (A) 12, (BP) TN, (CMTS) 1860 Census
Shelton, Elmira: (B) 1852, (CO) Pulaski, (A) 8, (BP) MO, (CMTS) 1860 Census
Shelton, Isaac: (B) 1841, (CO) Pulaski, (A) 19, (BP) MO, (CMTS) 1860 Census
Shelton, Isaac: (B) 1841, (CO) Pulaski, (A) 19, (BP) MO, (CMTS) 1860 Census
Shelton, J.: (B) 1839, (CO) Pulaski, (A) 21, (BP) KY, (CMTS) 1860 Census
Shelton, Jacob: (B) 1854, (CO) Pulaski, (A) 6, (BP) MO, (CMTS) 1860 Census
Shelton, James: (B) 1849, (CO) Pulaski, (A) 11, (BP) TN, (CMTS) 1860 Census
Shelton, James C.: (B) 1819, (CO) Pulaski, (A) 41, (BP) TN, (CMTS) 1860 Census
Shelton, John: (B) 1843, (CO) Pulaski, (A) 17, (BP) MO, (CMTS) 1860 Census
Shelton, Julia: (B) 1856, (CO) Pulaski, (A) 4, (BP) MO, (CMTS) 1860 Census
Shelton, Louisa: (B) 1851, (CO) Pulaski, (A) 9, (BP) TN, (CMTS) 1860 Census
Shelton, Mary: (B) 1847, (CO) Pulaski, (A) 13, (BP) KY, (CMTS) 1860 Census
Shelton, Mary: (B) 1854, (CO) Pulaski, (A) 6, (BP) MO, (CMTS) 1860 Census
Shelton, Nancy: (B) 1821, (CO) Pulaski, (A) 39, (BP) TN, (CMTS)

1860 Census
Shelton, Samantha: (B) 1854, (CO) Pulaski, (A) 6, (BP) TN, (CMTS) 1860 Census
Shelton, Sarah: (B) 1832, (CO) Pulaski, (A) 28, (BP) AL, (CMTS) 1860 Census
Shelton, Sarah: (B) 1846, (CO) Pulaski, (A) 14, (BP) TN, (CMTS) 1860 Census
Shelton, Sarah: (B) 1853, (CO) Pulaski, (A) 7, (BP) IL, (CMTS) 1860 Census
Shelton, Shepard: (B) 1825, (CO) Pulaski, (A) 35, (BP) AL, (CMTS) 1860 Census
Shelton, William: (B) 1844, (CO) Pulaski, (A) 16, (BP) IL, (CMTS) 1860 Census
Shepherd, Daniel?: (B) 1858, (CO) Stone, (A) 12, (BP) AR, (CMTS) 1870 Census
Shepherd, John: (B) 1856, (CO) Stone, (A) 14, (BP) IN, (CMTS) 1870 Census
Shepherd, Tilman: (B) 1850, (CO) Stone, (A) 20, (BP) IN, (CMTS) 1870 Census
Shibley, Elizabeth: (B) 1798, (D) 1870, (CO) Adair, (A) 72, (CMTS) 1870 Mortality Schedule
Shoaf, Bessie Mae: (B) Apr.11, 1895, (D) Mar. 23, 1964, (CO) Callaway, (C) Old Salem Cemetery, Reform, MO
Shoat, Alsie J.: (B) 1848, (CO) Stone, (A) 22, (BP) AL, (CMTS) 1870 Census
Shoat, Emmanuel: (B) 1846, (CO) Stone, (A) 24, (BP) TN, (CMTS) 1870 Census
Shoat, John: (B) 1845, (CO) Stone, (A) 25, (BP) TN, (CMTS) 1870 Census
Shoat, Margaret M.: (B) 1851, (CO) Stone, (A) 19, (BP) AL, (CMTS) 1870 Census
Shoehn, Charles: (B) 1832, (CO) Pulaski, (A) 28, (BP) Saxony, (CMTS) 1860 Census
Short, Deborah: (B) 1821, (CO) Stone, (A) 49, (BP) TN, (CMTS) 1870 Census
Short, Elizabeth: (B) 1833, (CO) Stone, (A) 37, (BP) TN, (CMTS) 1870 Census
Short, Franklin S.: (B) 1819, (CO) Stone, (A) 51, (BP) TN, (CMTS) 1870 Census
Short, George: (B) 1853, (CO) Stone, (A) 17, (BP) MO, (CMTS) 1870 Census
Short, John: (B) 1826, (CO) Stone, (A) 44, (BP) TN, (CMTS) 1870 Census

Short, John: (B) 1855, (CO) Pulaski, (A) 5, (BP) IL, (CMTS) 1860 Census
Short, John W.: (B) 1850, (CO) Stone, (A) 20, (BP) MO, (CMTS) 1870 Census
Short, Margarette: (B) 1845, (CO) Stone, (A) 25, (BP) TN, (CMTS) 1870 Census
Short, Martha: (B) 1835, (CO) Pulaski, (A) 25, (BP) OH, (CMTS) 1860 Census
Short, Nancy: (B) 1848, (CO) Stone, (A) 22, (BP) TN, (CMTS) 1870 Census
Short, Nancy: (B) 1855, (CO) Stone, (A) 15, (BP) MO, (CMTS) 1870 Census
Short, Sarah: (B) 1857, (CO) Stone, (A) 13, (BP) MO, (CMTS) 1870 Census
Short, William A.: (B) 1817, (CO) Pulaski, (A) 43, (BP) TN, (CMTS) 1860 Census
Shryrock, Martha Ann: (D) Apr. 24, 1863, (CO) Audrain, (C) Old Village Cemetery, (A) 51Y 27D
Shryrock, W.: (D) Oct. 30, 1863, (CO) Audrain, (C) Old Village Cemetery, (A) 37Y 9M 26D
Shusterson, Vandover L. T.: (B) 1849, (CO) Pulaski, (A) 11, (BP) MO, (CMTS) 1860 Census
Signaigo, Zetta May: (D) Jul. 2, 1909, (CO) St. Louis, (C) Calvary Cemetery, (A) 51
Sill, William: (B) 1828, (CO) Stone, (A) 22, (BP) PA, (CMTS) 1870 Census
Simmons, Emily: (B) 1849, (D) 1943, (CO) Henry, (C) Knights of Pythias Cemetery, Deepwater, MO
Simms, Francis: (B) 1856, (CO) Stone, (A) 14, (BP) MO, (CMTS) 1870 Census
Simms, James M.: (B) 1850, (CO) Stone, (A) 20, (BP) TN, (CMTS) 1870 Census
Simms, LukeC: (B) 1854, (CO) Stone, (A) 16, (BP) TN, (CMTS) 1870 Census
Simms, Mary A..: (B) 1825, (CO) Stone, (A) 45, (BP) TN, (CMTS) 1870 Census
Simpson, Herbert H.: (B) 1930, (CO) St. Louis, (C) Calvary Cemetery
Simpson, Rosita: (B) 1927, (D) 1992, (CO) St. Louis, (C) Calvary Cemetery
Simpson, Sarah E.: (B) Mar. 20, 1858, (D) Jun. 11, 1893, (CO) Camden,
Sims, Franklin: (B) 1852, (CO) Stone, (A) 18, (BP) MO, (CMTS) 1870 Census
Sims, James: (B) 1849, (CO) Stone, (A) 21, (BP) TN, (CMTS) 1870

Census
Sims, James W.: (B) 1822, (CO) Stone, (A) 48, (BP) TN, (CMTS) 1870 Census
Sims, Lucinda: (B) 1835, (CO) Stone, (A) 35, (BP) TN, (CMTS) 1870 Census
Sims, Mary E.: (B) 1855, (CO) Stone, (A) 15, (BP) MO, (CMTS) 1870 Census
Sims, Nancy J.: (B) 1855, (CO) Stone, (A) 15, (BP) MO, (CMTS) 1870 Census
Sims, Thomas: (B) 1857, (CO) Stone, (A) 13, (BP) MO, (CMTS) 1870 Census
Singleton, Burris P.: (B) 1855, (CO) Pulaski, (A) 5, (BP) NC, (CMTS) 1860 Census
Singleton, Cynthia: (B) 1836, (CO) Pulaski, (A) 24, (BP) NC, (CMTS) 1860 Census
Singleton, Ossina: (B) 1823, (CO) Pulaski, (A) 37, (BP) NC, (CMTS) 1860 Census
Singleton, Phillip: (B) 1851, (CO) Pulaski, (A) 9, (BP) NC, (CMTS) 1860 Census
Singleton, Robert H.: (B) 1845, (CO) Pulaski, (A) 15, (BP) NC, (CMTS) 1860 Census
Singleton, Vincent A.: (B) 1853, (CO) Pulaski, (A) 7, (BP) NC, (CMTS) 1860 Census
Singleton, William C.: (B) 1847, (CO) Pulaski, (A) 13, (BP) NC, (CMTS) 1860 Census
Sizemore, Jobi Isaac: (B) Feb. 12, 1916, (D) Feb. 18, 1965, (CO) Henry, (C) Knights of Pythias Cemetery, Deepwater, MO
Skaggs, Caroline: (B) 1856, (CO) Pulaski, (A) 4, (BP) MO, (CMTS) 1860 Census
Skaggs, Elizabeth: (B) 1850, (CO) Pulaski, (A) 10, (BP) MO, (CMTS) 1860 Census
Skaggs, Emily: (B) 1836, (CO) Pulaski, (A) 24, (BP) OH, (CMTS) 1860 Census
Skaggs, Jacob: (B) 1835, (CO) Pulaski, (A) 25, (BP) MO, (CMTS) 1860 Census
Skaggs, John: (B) 1848, (CO) Pulaski, (A) 12, (BP) MO, (CMTS) 1860 Census
Skaggs, Patsy: (B) 1853, (CO) Pulaski, (A) 7, (BP) MO, (CMTS) 1860 Census
Skidmore, Rubin: (B) 1843, (CO) Pulaski, (A) 17, (BP) MO, (CMTS) 1860 Census
Skinner, Exile: (B) 1820, (CO) Pulaski, (A) 40, (BP) OH, (CMTS) 1860 Census

Skinner, Isabel: (B) 1856, (CO) Pulaski, (A) 4, (BP) IL, (CMTS) 1860 Census

Skulley,: (B) 1826, (CO) Pulaski, (A) 34, (BP) Ireland, (CMTS) 1860 Census

Slankard, Russell: (B) Apr. 22, 1914, (D) Oct. 3, 1998, (NWS) *Joplin Globe, Oct. 5, 1998*, (BP) Ft. Smith, AR, (MD) Mar. 4, 1937, (SPOUSE) Lola Crandall, (C) Forrest Park Cemetery, (CMTS) Gerald Slankard, son; Wayne Slankard, son; Virginia Clark, daughter; Sharon Booth, daughter; Marvin Slankard, brother;

Slattery, Alyce May: (B) 1898, (D) 1950, (CO) St. Louis, (C) Calvary Cemetery

Slattery, Lester A.: (B) 1898, (D) 1973, (CO) St. Louis, (C) Calvary Cemetery

Sloan, Charles: (B) 1838, (CO) Stone, (A) 32, (BP) SC, (CMTS) 1870 Census

Sloan, Martha: (B) 1842, (CO) Stone, (A) 28, (BP) TN, (CMTS) 1870 Census

Slone, Burton: (B) 1836, (CO) Stone, (A) 14, (BP) OH, (CMTS) 1870 Census

Slone, Daniel: (B) 1820, (CO) Stone, (A) 30, (BP) TN, (CMTS) 1870 Census

Slone, Daniel: (B) 1820, (CO) Stone, (A) 30, (BP) IL, (CMTS) 1870 Census

Slone, George M.: (B) 1829, (CO) Stone, (A) 21, (BP) OH, (CMTS) 1870 Census

Slone, Hampton H.: (B) 1843, (CO) Stone, (A) 7, (BP) IO, (CMTS) 1870 Census

Slone, Louisa: (B) 1840, (CO) Stone, (A) 10, (BP) IO, (CMTS) 1870 Census

Slone, Margaret M.: (B) 1849, (CO) Stone, (A) 1, (BP) MO, (CMTS) 1870 Census

Slone, Margarette: (B) 1848, (CO) Stone, (A) 2, (BP) MO, (CMTS) 1870 Census

Slone, Mary: (B) 1846, (CO) Stone, (A) 4, (BP) MO, (CMTS) 1870 Census

Slone, Mary: (B) 1847, (CO) Stone, (A) 3, (BP) MO, (CMTS) 1870 Census

Slone, William Holt: (B) 1835, (CO) Stone, (A) 15, (BP) IO, (CMTS) 1870 Census

Sloss, Brooke: (D) Aug. 20, 2000, (CO) Cole, (NWS) *Jefferson City, Missouri News-Tribune*, Aug. 22, 2000, (RES) Fulton

Smallwood, Emm C.: (B) 1851, (CO) Pulaski, (A) 9, (BP) IND, (CMTS) 1860 Census

Smallwood, Enseba: (B) 1831, (CO) Pulaski, (A) 29, (BP) IND, (CMTS) 1860 Census
Smallwood, George A.: (B) 1856, (CO) Pulaski, (A) 4, (BP) IND, (CMTS) 1860 Census
Smallwood, James W.: (B) 1854, (CO) Pulaski, (A) 6, (BP) IND, (CMTS) 1860 Census
Smallwood, John M.: (B) 1849, (CO) Pulaski, (A) 11, (BP) IND, (CMTS) 1860 Census
Smallwood, Martha C.: (B) 1862, (D) 1948, (CO) Henry, (C) Knights of Pythias Cemetery, Deepwater, MO
Smallwood, William M.: (B) 1826, (CO) Pulaski, (A) 34, (BP) IND, (CMTS) 1860 Census
Smiser, Arabella Perrin: (B) Feb. 26, 1835, (D) Sep. 1, 1863, (CO) Monroe
Smiser, Darius Layton: (B) Jul. 4, 1814, (D) 1909, (CO) Bates
Smiser, George Perrin: (B) Sep. 23, 1833, (D) Jul. 18, 1857, (CO) Monroe
Smiser, Henry Thomas Allen: (B) Aug. 2, 1845, (CO) Monroe
Smiser, John Edward: (B) Jul. 6, 1839, (D) Jan. 19, 1925, (CO) Monroe
Smiser, John Milton: (B) Feb. 10, 1807, (D) Apri. 10, 1894, (CO) Monroe, (DP) Paris, MO, (BP) Harrison Co., KY, (SPOUSE) Julia Ann Edwards, (MD) Nov. 22, 1832
Smiser, Llewellyn Davis: (B) Dec. 9, 1860, (D) May 16, 1939, (CO) Monroe
Smiser, Mary Elizabeth: (B) Jun. 28, 1850, (D) Jan. 5, 1888, (CO) Monroe
Smiser, Milton Berry: (B) Oct. 9, 1857, (D) Jan. 1, 1902, (CO) Monroe
Smiser, Wesley Taylor: (B) Jan. 10, 1848, (D) May 2, 1920, (CO) Monroe
Smiser, William Garret: (B) Jul. 14, 1842, (D) 1913, (CO) Monroe
Smith, Albert: (B) 1838, (CO) Pulaski, (A) 22, (BP) KY, (CMTS) 1860 Census
Smith, Alvin: (B) 1845, (CO) Pulaski, (A) 15, (BP) MO, (CMTS) 1860 Census
Smith, Amanda: (B) 1852, (CO) Pulaski, (A) 8, (BP) MO, (CMTS) 1860 Census
Smith, Andrew: (B) 1848, (CO) Pulaski, (A) 12, (BP) MO, (CMTS) 1860 Census
Smith, Andrew: (B) 1855, (CO) Pulaski, (A) 5, (BP) MO, (CMTS) 1860 Census
Smith, Catherine E.: (B) 1855, (CO) Stone, (A) 15, (BP) TN, (CMTS) 1870 Census
Smith, Cory Domn.: (B) 1834, (D) 1926, (CO) Henry, (C) Knights of Pythias Cemetery, Deepwater, MO

Smith, Curtis E.: (D) Oct. 11, 1887, (CO) Audrain
Smith, Daniel: (B) 1846, (CO) Pulaski, (A) 14, (BP) MO, (CMTS) 1860 Census
Smith, Daniel R.: (B) 1855, (CO) Pulaski, (A) 5, (BP) MO, (CMTS) 1860 Census
Smith, David H.: (D) 10, 1960, (CO) St. Louis, (C) Calvary Cemetery
Smith, David T.: (B) 1848, (CO) Stone, (A) 22, (BP) AR, (CMTS) 1870 Census
Smith, Eli: (B) 1858, (CO) Pulaski, (A) 2, (BP) MO, (CMTS) 1860 Census
Smith, Eliza Ann: (B) 1827, (CO) Stone, (A) 43, (BP) NC, (CMTS) 1870 Census
Smith, Eliza G: (B) 1843, (CO) Stone, (A) 7, (BP) MO, (CMTS) 1870 Census
Smith, Elizabeth: (B) 1820, (CO) Stone, (A) 30, (BP) TN, (CMTS) 1870 Census
Smith, Elizabeth: (B) 1826, (CO) Stone, (A) 24, (BP) TN, (CMTS) 1870 Census
Smith, Elizabeth: (B) 1830, (CO) Pulaski, (A) 30, (BP) TN, (CMTS) 1860 Census
Smith, Elizabeth: (B) 1839, (CO) Stone, (A) 31, (BP) TN, (CMTS) 1870 Census
Smith, Elizabeth: (B) Oct. 6, 1820, (D) May 26, 1886, (CO) Barry, (C) Old Corsicana Cemetery
Smith, Emeline: (B) 1841, (CO) Stone, (A) 29, (BP) TN, (CMTS) 1870 Census
Smith, Emily: (B) 1828, (CO) Pulaski, (A) 32, (BP) MO, (CMTS) 1860 Census
Smith, Everett: (B) 1830, (CO) Stone, (A) 40, (BP) TN, (CMTS) 1870 Census
Smith, Frank: (B) 1841, (CO) Pulaski, (A) 19, (BP) KY, (CMTS) 1860 Census
Smith, Fred L.: (D) Mar. 17, 1885, (CO) Audrain
Smith, George Paul: (D) Aug. 8, 1959, (CO) St. Louis, (C) Calvary Cemetery
Smith, George W.: (B) 1847, (CO) Pulaski, (A) 13, (BP) MO, (CMTS) 1860 Census
Smith, Gilbert: (B) 1833, (CO) Pulaski, (A) 27, (BP) KY, (CMTS) 1860 Census
Smith, Harriet: (B) 1831, (CO) Pulaski, (A) 29, (BP) MO, (CMTS) 1860 Census
Smith, Harriet: (B) 1836, (CO) Pulaski, (A) 24, (BP) IND, (CMTS) 1860 Census

Smith, Henson: (D) Aug. 5, 1887, (CO) Audrain
Smith, Hugh M.: (B) 1823, (CO) Stone, (A) 47, (BP) VA, (CMTS) 1870 Census
Smith, Isam M.: (B) 1826, (CO) Stone, (A) 24, (BP) TN, (CMTS) 1870 Census
Smith, James: (B) 1827, (CO) Stone, (A) 43, (BP) IN, (CMTS) 1870 Census
Smith, James: (B) 1844, (CO) Pulaski, (A) 16, (BP) MO, (CMTS) 1860 Census
Smith, James: (B) 1846, (CO) Stone, (A) 24, (BP) MO, (CMTS) 1870 Census
Smith, James A.: (B) Nov. 5, 1846, (CO) Carroll (PRTS) William Henry Smith and Susannah Walker
Smith, James Michael: (B) Aug. 12, 1845, (CO) Perry, (PRTS) James Smith and Mary Elizabeth Tucker
Smith, Jane C: (B) 1835, (CO) Stone, (A) 35, (BP) VA, (CMTS) 1870 Census
Smith, Jarvis: (D) Feb. 20, 1876, (CO) Andrew, (C) Oak Ridge Cemetery, (A) 78Y 8M 9D
Smith, Jessie A.: (B) 1846, (CO) Stone, (A) 4, (BP) MO, (CMTS) 1870 Census
Smith, John: (B) 1851, (CO) Pulaski, (A) 9, (BP) MO, (CMTS) 1860 Census
Smith, John B.: (D) Mar. 25, 1888, (CO) Audrain
Smith, John W.: (B) 1830, (CO) Pulaski, (A) 30, (BP) IL, (CMTS) 1860 Census
Smith, John W.: (B) 1847, (CO) Pulaski, (A) 13, (BP) MO, (CMTS) 1860 Census
Smith, Joseph: (B) 1834, (CO) Pulaski, (A) 26, (BP) KY, (CMTS) 1860 Census
Smith, Mahala E.: (B) 1846, (CO) Stone, (A) 4, (BP) MO, (CMTS) 1870 Census
Smith, Malinda: (B) 1841, (CO) Pulaski, (A) 19, (BP) MO, (CMTS) 1860 Census
Smith, Malinda: (B) 1842, (CO) Pulaski, (A) 18, (BP) MO, (CMTS) 1860 Census
Smith, Mallissa E.: (B) 1850, (CO) Pulaski, (A) 10, (BP) MO, (CMTS) 1860 Census
Smith, Margaret: (B) 1833, (CO) Pulaski, (A) 27, (BP) MO, (CMTS) 1860 Census
Smith, Marshall G.: (B) 1841, (CO) Pulaski, (A) 19, (BP) MO, (CMTS) 1860 Census
Smith, Martha: (B) 1845, (CO) Stone, (A) 5, (BP) MO, (CMTS) 1870

Census
Smith, Martha E.: (B) 1849, (CO) Stone, (A) 1, (BP) MO, (CMTS) 1870 Census
Smith, Mary C.: (B) 1827, (CO) Stone, (A) 43, (BP) TN, (CMTS) 1870 Census
Smith, Mary C.: (B) 1850, (CO) Stone, (A) 20, (BP) MO, (CMTS) 1870 Census
Smith, Mary E.: (B) 1856, (CO) Stone, (A) 14, (BP) MO, (CMTS) 1870 Census
Smith, Mary E.: (B) 1850, (CO) Pulaski, (A) 10, (BP) MO, (CMTS) 1860 Census
Smith, Mary Estelle: (D) Oct. 10, 1953, (CO) St. Louis, (C) Calvary Cemetery
Smith, Mary J.: (B) 1848, (CO) Stone, (A) 2, (BP) MO, (CMTS) 1870 Census
Smith, Mary J.: (B) 1856, (CO) Pulaski, (A) 4, (BP) MO, (CMTS) 1860 Census
Smith, Mary C: (B) 1851, (CO) Stone, (A) 19, (BP) MO, (CMTS) 1870 Census
Smith, Matilda: (B) 1851, (CO) Pulaski, (A) 9, (BP) MO, (CMTS) 1860 Census
Smith, Moses: (B) 1836, (CO) Pulaski, (A) 24, (BP) KY, (CMTS) 1860 Census
Smith, Mrs. Martha A.: (D) Sep. 18, 1885, (CO) Audrain,
Smith, Mrs. Orlando: (D) Feb. 18, 1888, (CO) Audrain,
Smith, Nancy: (B) 1830, (CO) Pulaski, (A) 30, (BP) TN, (CMTS) 1860 Census
Smith, Nancy: (B) 1850, (CO) Pulaski, (A) 10, (BP) MO, (CMTS) 1860 Census
Smith, Narcisie: (B) 1826, (CO) Stone, (A) 44, (BP) AR, (CMTS) 1870 Census
Smith, Niles: (B) 1839, (CO) Stone, (A) 31, (BP) NY, (CMTS) 1870 Census
Smith, Patsy A.: (D) Sep. 17, 1864, (CO) Andrew, (C) Oak Ridge Cemetery, (A) 60Y 6M 18D
Smith, Phillip: (B) 1854, (CO) Pulaski, (A) 6, (BP) MO, (CMTS) 1860 Census
Smith, Polly: (B) Nov. 2, 1802, (D) Sep. 31, 1866, (CO) Andrew, (C) Oak Ridge Cemetery
Smith, Rachel: (B) 1838, (CO) Stone, (A) 32, (BP) TN, (CMTS) 1870 Census
Smith, Robert F: (B) 1853, (CO) Stone, (A) 17, (BP) TN, (CMTS) 1870 Census

Smith, Sarah: (B) 1838, (CO) Stone, (A) 32, (BP) TN, (CMTS) 1870 Census
Smith, Sarah E.: (B) 1855, (CO) Stone, (A) 15, (BP) MO, (CMTS) 1870 Census
Smith, Sarah F: (B) 1844, (CO) Stone, (A) 6, (BP) MO, (CMTS) 1870 Census
Smith, Sarah F.: (B) 1852, (CO) Pulaski, (A) 8, (BP) MO, (CMTS) 1860 Census
Smith, Sarah L.: (B) 1841, (CO) Stone, (A) 9, (BP) MO, (CMTS) 1870 Census
Smith, Sarah C: (B) 1856, (CO) Stone, (A) 14, (BP) MO, (CMTS) 1870 Census
Smith, Thomas: (B) 1854, (CO) Pulaski, (A) 6, (BP) MO, (CMTS) 1860 Census
Smith, Thomas: (D) Jan. 21, 1888, (CO) Audrain
Smith, Thomas D: (B) 1852, (CO) Stone, (A) 18, (BP) TN, (CMTS) 1870 Census
Smith, Victory J.: (B) 1857, (CO) Stone, (A) 13, (BP) MO, (CMTS) 1870 Census
Smith, Wayne Lee: (B) Jul. 16, 1924, (D) May 28, 1980, (CO) Henry, (C) Knights of Pythias Cemetery, Deepwater, MO
Smith, William: (B) 1825, (CO) Pulaski, (A) 35, (BP) IL, (CMTS) 1860 Census
Smith, William: (B) 1832, (CO) Pulaski, (A) 28, (BP) KY, (CMTS) 1860 Census
Smith, William: (B) 1842, (CO) Stone, (A) 28, (BP) TN, (CMTS) 1870 Census
Smith, William: (B) 1842, (CO) Pulaski, (A) 18, (BP) MO, (CMTS) 1860 Census
Smith, William S.: (B) 1851, (CO) Pulaski, (A) 9, (BP) MO, (CMTS) 1860 Census
Smith,: (D) Dec. 15, 1889, (CO) Audrain,
Smith,Jesse: (D) Jun. 29, 1885, (CO) Audrain,RCH
Smith,Melvina: (B) 1832, (D) 1887, (CO) Johnson, (C) Pemberton Cemetery
Smith,Oliver: (B) 1824, (D) 1903, (CO) Johnson, (C) Pemberton Cemetery
Smith,Viola: (B) Jan. 23, 1891, (D) Feb. 14, 1969, (CO) Johnson, (C) Pemberton Cemetery
Smith,Walter Edward: (B) Jun. 29, 1914, (D) Oct. 10, 1923, (CO) Johnson, (C) Pemberton Cemetery
Smyth, Martha: (B) 1832, (CO) Stone, (A) 38, (BP) MO, (CMTS) 1870 Census
Smyth, Mary J. C.: (B) 1825, (CO) Stone, (A) 45, (BP) IN, (CMTS) 1870

Census
Snider, James: (B) 1823, (CO) Pulaski, (A) 37, (BP) England, (CMTS) 1860 Census
Snider, Sarah: (B) 1829, (CO) Pulaski, (A) 31, (BP) MO, (CMTS) 1860 Census
Snider, Sarah: (B) 1852, (CO) Pulaski, (A) 8, (BP) MO, (CMTS) 1860 Census
Snowden, Charles: (B) 1827, (CO) Stone, (A) 23, (BP) KY, (CMTS) 1870 Census
Snowden, George L.: (B) 1848, (CO) Stone, (A) 2, (BP) IL, (CMTS) 1870 Census
Snowden, Henry: (B) 1835, (CO) Stone, (A) 15, (BP) IL, (CMTS) 1870 Census
Snowden, Joseph L.: (B) 1791, (CO) Stone, (A) 59, (BP) MD, (CMTS) 1870 Census
Snowden, Mary E.: (B) 1833, (CO) Stone, (A) 17, (BP) TN, (CMTS) 1870 Census
Snowden, Mary Jane: (B) 1828, (CO) Stone, (A) 22, (BP) KY, (CMTS) 1870 Census
Snowden, Samuel: (B) 1822, (CO) Stone, (A) 28, (BP) IL, (CMTS) 1870 Census
Snyder, John T.: (B) 1835, (D) 1924, (CO) Henry, (C) Knights of Pythias Cemetery, Deepwater, MO
Snyder, Louvisa A.: (B) 1842, (D) 1937, (CO) Henry, (C) Knights of Pythias Cemetery, Deepwater, MO
Sommer, Frederic: (B) Aug. 22, 1818, (D) Jun. 27, 1886, (CO) Andrew, (C) Oak Ridge Cemetery
Sorrell, Mary M.: (B) 1843, (D) 1935, (CO) Henry, (C) Knights of Pythias Cemetery, Deepwater, MO
Southerland, James: (B) 1849, (CO) Pulaski, (A) 11, (BP) MO, (CMTS) 1860 Census
Southerland, William: (B) 1845, (CO) Pulaski, (A) 15, (BP) MO, (CMTS) 1860 Census
Sparks, James A.: (B) 1840, (D) 1919, (CO) Oregon, (C) Falling Springs Cemetery
Sparks, Martha A.: (B) 1840, (CO) Pulaski, (A) 20, (BP) MO, (CMTS) 1860 Census
Spelsey, Dennis: (B) 1828, (CO) Pulaski, (A) 32, (BP) Ireland, (CMTS) 1860 Census
Spence, Smith: (D) Mar. 6, 1887, (CO) Audrain
Spencer, Charles L.: (B) 1886, (D) 1947, (CO) St. Louis, (C) Calvary Cemetery
Spencer, Eliza C.: (B) 1855, (CO) Pulaski, (A) 5, (BP) MO, (CMTS)

1860 Census
Spencer, Ellen M.: (B) 1852, (D) 1925, (CO) St. Louis, (C) Calvary Cemetery
Spencer, Margaret A.: (B) 1842, (CO) Pulaski, (A) 18, (BP) MO, (CMTS) 1860 Census
Spencer, Milla: (B) 1842, (CO) Pulaski, (A) 18, (BP) IA, (CMTS) 1860 Census
Spencer, Nelson A.: (B) 1847, (CO) Pulaski, (A) 13, (BP) MO, (CMTS) 1860 Census
Spencer, Patrick: (B) 1849, (D) 1922, (CO) St. Louis, (C) Calvary Cemetery
Spencer, Sarah H.: (B) 1853, (CO) Pulaski, (A) 7, (BP) MO, (CMTS) 1860 Census
Spencer, Thomas: (B) 1845, (CO) Pulaski, (A) 15, (BP) MO, (CMTS) 1860 Census
Spencer, William J.: (B) 1882, (D) 1930, (CO) St. Louis, (C) Calvary Cemetery
Spencer, William W.: (B) 1838, (CO) Pulaski, (A) 22, (BP) MO, (CMTS) 1860 Census
Sper, Elisabeth: (B) 1847, (CO) Stone, (A) 23, (BP) TN, (CMTS) 1870 Census
Sper, William: (B) 1847, (CO) Stone, (A) 23, (BP) AR, (CMTS) 1870 Census
Spradlin, Samuel H.: (B) Nov. 9, 1874, (D) Aug. 31, 1952, (CO) Crawford, (DP) Wyandotte Co., KS.
Sprock, Johan: (B) 1790, (D) Dec. 11, 1872, (CO) Jefferson, (C) Old St. John's Catholic Cemetery
Sprock, Theresia: (B) 1791, (D) Sep. 17, 1862, (CO) Jefferson, (C) Old St. John's Catholic Cemetery
Spurgeon, George W.: (B) 1848, (CO) Stone, (A) 2, (BP) MO, (CMTS) 1870 Census
Spurgeon, Martha Jane: (B) 1832, (CO) Stone, (A) 18, (BP) MO, (CMTS) 1870 Census
Spurgeon, Phebe E.: (B) 1839, (CO) Stone, (A) 11, (BP) MO, (CMTS) 1870 Census
Spurgeon, Richard: (B) 1843, (CO) Stone, (A) 7, (BP) MO, (CMTS) 1870 Census
Spurgeon, Seigle: (B) 1841, (CO) Stone, (A) 9, (BP) MO, (CMTS) 1870 Census
Spurgeon, Stephen: (B) 1834, (CO) Stone, (A) 16, (BP) MO, (CMTS) 1870 Census
Spurgeon, William: (B) 1845, (CO) Stone, (A) 5, (BP) MO, (CMTS) 1870 Census

Staats, Agnes B.: (B) 1821, (D) 1912, (CO) Henry, (C) Knights of Pythias Cemetery, Deepwater, MO

Stabblefield, Catherine: (B) 1896, (D) 1918, (CO) St. Louis, (C) Calvary Cemetery

Stacy, Elvira: (B) 1844, (CO) Stone, (A) 26, (BP) MO, (CMTS) 1870 Census

Stall, Alice M.: (B) 1850, (D) 1926, (CO) Johnson, (C) Pemberton Cemetery

Stall, David L.: (B) 1846, (D) 1941, (CO) Johnson, (C) Pemberton Cemetery

Stall, Henry H.: (B) 1868, (CO) Johnson, (C) Pemberton Cemetery

Stall, Isabel E.: (B) 1882, (D) 1952, (CO) Johnson, (C) Pemberton Cemetery

Stall, Jessie W.: (B) 1878, (D) 1880, (CO) Johnson, (C) Pemberton Cemetery

Stall, Weathly: (B) 1883, (D) 1884, (CO) Johnson, (C) Pemberton Cemetery

Stallins, Ephraim A.: (B) 1797, (CO) Stone, (A) 53, (BP) KY, (CMTS) 1870 Census

Stallins, F E Alexander: (B) 1849, (CO) Stone, (A) 1, (BP) MO, (CMTS) 1870 Census

Stallins, John W.: (B) 1833, (CO) Stone, (A) 17, (BP) MO, (CMTS) 1870 Census

Stallins, Lucinda: (B) 1838, (CO) Stone, (A) 12, (BP) MO, (CMTS) 1870 Census

Stallins, Rebecca: (B) 1828, (CO) Stone, (A) 22, (BP) KY, (CMTS) 1870 Census

Stallins, Reubin: (B) 1830, (CO) Stone, (A) 20, (BP) KY, (CMTS) 1870 Census

Stamsburg, Samuel: (B) Mar. 6, 1839, (D) Dec. 7, 1895, (CO) Barry, (C) Old Corsicana Cemetery

Standefer, Isaac Bradford: (D) Jan. 28, 1924, (CO) Callaway, (NWS) *Fulton Telegraph and Callaway Weekly Gazette*

Standefer, Willie: (D) Nov. 2, 1884, (CO) Callaway, (NWS) *Callaway Weekly Gazette*

Standifer, Mrs. Parnina: (D) Jun. 16, 1890, (CO) Callaway, (NWS) *Callaway Weekly Gazette*, (A) 80Y

Stanley, Hannah M.: (B) 1836, (CO) Stone, (A) 14, (BP) AR, (CMTS) 1870 Census

Stanley, Joseph: (B) 1794, (CO) Stone, (A) 56, (BP) IL, (CMTS) 1870 Census

Stanley, Joseph: (B) 1825, (CO) Stone, (A) 25, (BP) AR, (CMTS) 1870 Census

Stanley, Mary R.: (B) 1832, (CO) Stone, (A) 18, (BP) AR, (CMTS) 1870 Census
Stanley, Milley: (B) 1797, (CO) Stone, (A) 53, (BP) NC, (CMTS) 1870 Census
Stanly, Jane: (B) 1829, (CO) Stone, (A) 21, (BP) MO, (CMTS) 1870 Census
Stanly, John: (B) 1818, (CO) Stone, (A) 32, (BP) AR, (CMTS) 1870 Census
Stanly, Joseph T.: (B) 1846, (CO) Stone, (A) 4, (BP) AR, (CMTS) 1870 Census
Stanly, Leuretta: (B) 1849, (CO) Stone, (A) 1, (BP) MO, (CMTS) 1870 Census
Stanton, John W.: (B) Dec. 21, 1827, (D) Jul. 5, 1905, (CO) Andrews,
Stark, William: (B) 1840, (CO) Pulaski, (A) 20, (BP) MO, (CMTS) 1860 Census
Stearns, Frank E.: (B) Sep. 12, 1929, (CO) Oregon, (C) Falling Springs Cemetery
Steel, Henry H.: (B) 1853, (CO) Stone, (A) 17, (BP) MO, (CMTS) 1870 Census
Steel, John T.: (B) 1821, (CO) Stone, (A) 49, (BP) TN, (CMTS) 1870 Census
Steel, Lucinda J.: (B) 1836, (CO) Stone, (A) 34, (BP) MO, (CMTS) 1870 Census
Steel, Manlius: (B) 1850, (CO) Stone, (A) 20, (BP) MO, (CMTS) 1870 Census
Steel, Martha M.: (B) 1835, (CO) Stone, (A) 35, (BP) TN, (CMTS) 1870 Census
Steel, Mary J.: (B) 1853, (CO) Stone, (A) 17, (BP) MO, (CMTS) 1870 Census
Steel, Richard R.: (B) 1854, (CO) Stone, (A) 16, (BP) MO, (CMTS) 1870 Census
Steely, Elijah G: (B) 1839, (CO) Stone, (A) 11, (BP) IL, (CMTS) 1870 Census
Steely, Elijah J.: (B) 1849, (CO) Stone, (A) 21, (BP) MO, (CMTS) 1870 Census
Steely, James P: (B) 1844, (CO) Stone, (A) 6, (BP) IL, (CMTS) 1870 Census
Steely, Jeramiah: (B) 1828, (CO) Stone, (A) 42, (BP) IN, (CMTS) 1870 Census
Steely, John: (B) 1853, (CO) Stone, (A) 17, (BP) MO, (CMTS) 1870 Census
Steely, Julia A.: (B) 1841, (CO) Stone, (A) 9, (BP) IL, (CMTS) 1870 Census

Steely, Martha L C.: (B) 1819, (CO) Stone, (A) 31, (BP) IL, (CMTS) 1870 Census
Steely, May Elizabeth: (B) 1847, (CO) Stone, (A) 3, (BP) IN, (CMTS) 1870 Census
Steely, Missouri: (B) 1851, (CO) Stone, (A) 19, (BP) MO, (CMTS) 1870 Census
Steely, Tennessee: (B) 1856, (CO) Stone, (A) 14, (BP) MO, (CMTS) 1870 Census
Steely, Virginia: (B) 1855, (CO) Stone, (A) 15, (BP) MO, (CMTS) 1870 Census
Steely, Wiley B.: (B) 1849, (CO) Stone, (A) 1, (BP) MO, (CMTS) 1870 Census
Steinbeck, Christian Frederick: (B) May 21 1832, (CO) Cape Girardeau
Steinbeck, Dorothea Louisa: (B) Dec. 19, 1812, (D) Apr. 19, 1852, (CO) Cape Girardeau
Steinbeck, Frederick William: (B) Mar. 19, 1814, (D) Dec. 1, 1815, (CO) Cape Girardeau,
Steinbeck, George Lewis: (B) Dec. 15, 1810, (D) Oct. 11, 1850, (CO) Cape Girardeau
Stephens, Allen: (B) 1849, (CO) Pulaski, (A) 11, (BP) IL, (CMTS) 1860 Census
Stephens, Amanda: (B) 1855, (CO) Pulaski, (A) 5, (BP) IL, (CMTS) 1860 Census
Stephens, Benjamin: (B) 1856, (CO) Pulaski, (A) 4, (BP) IL, (CMTS) 1860 Census
Stephens, James: (B) 1827, (CO) Pulaski, (A) 33, (BP) IL, (CMTS) 1860 Census
Stephens, Mary: (B) 1838, (CO) Pulaski, (A) 22, (BP) IL, (CMTS) 1860 Census
Stevens, Bennett: (B) 1850, (CO) Stone, (A) 20, (BP) AR, (CMTS) 1870 Census
Stevens, Catherine: (B) 1835, (CO) Stone, (A) 35, (BP) TN, (CMTS) 1870 Census
Stevens, Hugh: (B) 1854, (CO) Pulaski, (A) 6, (BP) AL, (CMTS) 1860 Census
Stevens, James: (B) 1850, (CO) Pulaski, (A) 10, (BP) AL, (CMTS) 1860 Census
Stevens, John: (B) 1828, (CO) Pulaski, (A) 32, (BP) TN, (CMTS) 1860 Census
Stevens, John: (B) 1853, (CO) Pulaski, (A) 7, (BP) AL, (CMTS) 1860 Census
Stevens, Josiah: (B) 1820, (CO) Stone, (A) 50, (BP) MO, (CMTS) 1870 Census

Stevens, Polly: (B) 1828, (CO) Pulaski, (A) 32, (BP) AL, (CMTS) 1860 Census
Stevens, Ruth: (B) 1855, (CO) Stone, (A) 15, (BP) AR, (CMTS) 1870 Census
Stevens, Sarah J.: (B) 1856, (CO) Pulaski, (A) 4, (BP) AL, (CMTS) 1860 Census
Stevens, William: (B) 1851, (CO) Stone, (A) 19, (BP) AR, (CMTS) 1870 Census
Stevenson, Mary: (B) 1847, (CO) Stone, (A) 23, (BP) IN, (CMTS) 1870 Census
Stevenson, Nathan: (B) 1840, (CO) Stone, (A) 30, (BP) TN, (CMTS) 1870 Census
Stevenson, Sarah: (B) 1842, (CO) Stone, (A) 28, (BP) TN, (CMTS) 1870 Census
Stewart, Beryl Jack: (B) Aug. 4, 1908, (D) Apr. 6, 1978, (CO) Henry, (C) Knights of Pythias Cemetery, Deepwater, MO
Stewart, Charles: (B) 1858, (CO) Pulaski, (A) 2, (BP) MO, (CMTS) 1860 Census
Stewart, Deborah: (B) 1826, (CO) Stone, (A) 24, (BP) OH, (CMTS) 1870 Census
Stewart, Elija J.: (B) 1850, (CO) Pulaski, (A) 10, (BP) MO, (CMTS) 1860 Census
Stewart, Elizabeth: (B) 1847, (CO) Pulaski, (A) 13, (BP) MO, (CMTS) 1860 Census
Stewart, H.: (B) 1838, (CO) Pulaski, (A) 22, (BP) MO, (CMTS) 1860 Census
Stewart, Henry: (B) 1822, (CO) Stone, (A) 28, (BP) IL, (CMTS) 1870 Census
Stewart, J.: (B) 1844, (CO) Pulaski, (A) 16, (BP) MO, (CMTS) 1860 Census
Stewart, James: (B) 1854, (CO) Pulaski, (A) 6, (BP) MO, (CMTS) 1860 Census
Stewart, Jane: (B) 1834, (CO) Pulaski, (A) 26, (BP) MO, (CMTS) 1860 Census
Stewart, John W.: (B) 1835, (CO) Pulaski, (A) 25, (BP) IL, (CMTS) 1860 Census
Stewart, Lucinda: (B) 1835, (CO) Pulaski, (A) 25, (BP) KY, (CMTS) 1860 Census
Stewart, Margaret M.: (B) 1853, (CO) Pulaski, (A) 7, (BP) MO, (CMTS) 1860 Census
Stewart, Martha: (B) 1855, (CO) Pulaski, (A) 5, (BP) MO, (CMTS) 1860 Census
Stewart, Mary M.: (B) 1820, (CO) Pulaski, (A) 40, (BP) MO, (CMTS)

1860 Census
Stewart, Matilda: (B) 1831, (CO) Pulaski, (A) 29, (BP) KY, (CMTS) 1860 Census
Stewart, Michael: (B) 1839, (CO) Pulaski, (A) 21, (BP) MO, (CMTS) 1860 Census
Stewart, Minerva: (B) 1853, (CO) Pulaski, (A) 7, (BP) MO, (CMTS) 1860 Census
Stewart, Miranda: (B) 1827, (CO) Pulaski, (A) 33, (BP) KY, (CMTS) 1860 Census
Stewart, Rebecca: (B) 1844, (CO) Pulaski, (A) 16, (BP) MO, (CMTS) 1860 Census
Stewart, Rebecca: (B) 1857, (CO) Pulaski, (A) 3, (BP) MO, (CMTS) 1860 Census
Stewart, Sarah: (B) 1850, (CO) Pulaski, (A) 10, (BP) MO, (CMTS) 1860 Census
Stewart, Sarah: (B) 1853, (CO) Pulaski, (A) 7, (BP) MO, (CMTS) 1860 Census
Stewart, Sarah: (B) 1853, (CO) Pulaski, (A) 7, (BP) MO, (CMTS) 1860 Census
Stewart, Silas: (B) 1851, (CO) Pulaski, (A) 9, (BP) MO, (CMTS) 1860 Census
Stewart, Thomas: (B) 1854, (CO) Pulaski, (A) 6, (BP) MO, (CMTS) 1860 Census
Stewart, Vinet V: (B) 1847, (CO) Stone, (A) 3, (BP) WI, (CMTS) 1870 Census
Stewart, W.: (B) 1825, (CO) Pulaski, (A) 35, (BP) MO, (CMTS) 1860 Census
Stewart, Wallace: (B) 1830, (CO) Pulaski, (A) 30, (BP) MO, (CMTS) 1860 Census
Stewart, William R.: (B) 1831, (CO) Pulaski, (A) 29, (BP) MO, (CMTS) 1860 Census
Stinard, Charles A..: (B) 1843, (CO) Stone, (A) 27, (BP) GER, (CMTS) 1870 Census
Stinard, Martha E.: (B) 1837, (CO) Stone, (A) 33, (BP) TN, (CMTS) 1870 Census
Stitt, James H.: (D) Sep. 17, 1999, (CO), (DP) Columbia, MO, (PRTS) James Wilson Stitt and Dorothy Gladys Jewett, (NWS) *Allentown, Pennsylvania Morning Call*, Oct. 8, 1999.
Stockstill, Harvey Samuel: (B) Nov. 15, 1836, (D) Sep. 7, 1910, (CO) Christian, (DP) Highlandville, MO.
Stockwell, Calvin: (B) 1834, (CO) Stone, (A) 16, (BP) IN, (CMTS) 1870 Census
Stockwell, Emma: (B) 1842, (CO) Stone, (A) 8, (BP) MO, (CMTS) 1870

Census
Stockwell, Harrison: (B) 1839, (CO) Stone, (A) 11, (BP) MO, (CMTS) 1870 Census
Stockwell, Martha E.: (B) 1831, (CO) Stone, (A) 19, (BP) IN, (CMTS) 1870 Census
Stockwell, Melvina: (B) 1833, (CO) Stone, (A) 17, (BP) IN, (CMTS) 1870 Census
Stokes, Joel R.: (B) 1830, (D) 1886, (CO) Cedar, (C) Brashear Cemetery
Stokes, Mary E.: (B) 1841, (D) 1903, (CO) Cedar, (C) Brashear Cemetery
Stone, Almeda: (B) 1837, (CO) Stone, (A) 13, (BP) MO, (CMTS) 1870 Census
Stone, Christina M.: (B) 1848, (CO) Stone, (A) 2, (BP) MO, (CMTS) 1870 Census
Stone, Clinton: (B) 1838, (CO) Stone, (A) 12, (BP) MO, (CMTS) 1870 Census
Stone, Cordelia: (B) 1834, (CO) Stone, (A) 16, (BP) MO, (CMTS) 1870 Census
Stone, Cynthia A.: (B) 1828, (CO) Stone, (A) 22, (BP) MO, (CMTS) 1870 Census
Stone, Elijah B.: (B) 1835, (CO) Stone, (A) 15, (BP) MO, (CMTS) 1870 Census
Stone, Eliza: (B) 1818, (CO) Pulaski, (A) 42, (BP) KY, (CMTS) 1860 Census
Stone, Elizabeth: (B) Mar. 2, 1799, (D) Nov. 18, 1815, (CO) Barry, (C) Old Corsicana Cemetery
Stone, Ermine: (B) 1830, (CO) Stone, (A) 20, (BP) MO, (CMTS) 1870 Census
Stone, Eusitias: (B) 1848, (CO) Stone, (A) 2, (BP) MO, (CMTS) 1870 Census
Stone, Francis A.: (B) 1835, (CO) Pulaski, (A) 25, (BP) TN, (CMTS) 1860 Census
Stone, George G.: (B) 1841, (CO) Pulaski, (A) 19, (BP) TN, (CMTS) 1860 Census
Stone, George L.: (B) 1845, (CO) Stone, (A) 5, (BP) MO, (CMTS) 1870 Census
Stone, Henry L.: (B) 1849, (CO) Stone, (A) 1, (BP) MO, (CMTS) 1870 Census
Stone, Jane: (B) 1846, (CO) Stone, (A) 4, (BP) MO, (CMTS) 1870 Census
Stone, John: (B) 1839, (CO) Stone, (A) 11, (BP) MO, (CMTS) 1870 Census
Stone, John C.: (B) 1838, (CO) Pulaski, (A) 22, (BP) TN, (CMTS) 1860 Census

Stone, Joseph L.: (B) 1847, (CO) Stone, (A) 3, (BP) MO, (CMTS) 1870 Census
Stone, Julia A.: (B) 1848, (CO) Stone, (A) 2, (BP) MO, (CMTS) 1870 Census
Stone, Martha E.: (B) 1837, (CO) Stone, (A) 13, (BP) MO, (CMTS) 1870 Census
Stone, Mary C.: (B) 1849, (CO) Stone, (A) 1, (BP) MO, (CMTS) 1870 Census
Stone, Mary E.: (B) 1854, (CO) Pulaski, (A) 6, (BP) KY, (CMTS) 1860 Census
Stone, Nancy J.: (B) 1837, (CO) Pulaski, (A) 23, (BP) KY, (CMTS) 1860 Census
Stone, Rebecca: (B) 1822, (CO) Stone, (A) 28, (BP) MO, (CMTS) 1870 Census
Stone, Rosetta: (B) 1849, (CO) Stone, (A) 1, (BP) MO, (CMTS) 1870 Census
Stone, Sarah E.: (B) 1846, (CO) Stone, (A) 4, (BP) MO, (CMTS) 1870 Census
Stone, Sarah P: (B) 1839, (CO) Stone, (A) 11, (BP) MO, (CMTS) 1870 Census
Stone, Talitha C.: (B) 1832, (CO) Stone, (A) 18, (BP) MO, (CMTS) 1870 Census
Stone, Thomas: (B) 1844, (CO) Stone, (A) 6, (BP) MO, (CMTS) 1870 Census
Stone, Usabias: (B) 1827, (CO) Stone, (A) 23, (BP) MO, (CMTS) 1870 Census
Stone, William E.: (B) 1836, (CO) Stone, (A) 14, (BP) MO, (CMTS) 1870 Census
Stone, William T.: (B) 1827, (CO) Stone, (A) 23, (BP) MO, (CMTS) 1870 Census
Stone, Willis C.: (B) 1846, (CO) Pulaski, (A) 14, (BP) KY, (CMTS) 1860 Census
Stone, Woodson J.: (B) 1792, (CO) Stone, (A) 58, (BP) TN, (CMTS) 1870 Census
Story, James: (B) 1849, (CO) Pulaski, (A) 11, (BP) MO, (CMTS) 1860 Census
Story, James: (B) 1837, (CO) Pulaski, (A) 23, (BP) NC, (CMTS) 1860 Census
Story, John M.: (B) 1855, (CO) Pulaski, (A) 5, (BP) NC, (CMTS) 1860 Census
Story, Joseph: (B) 1845, (CO) Pulaski, (A) 15, (BP) MO, (CMTS) 1860 Census
Story, Malinda: (B) 1844, (CO) Pulaski, (A) 16, (BP) MO, (CMTS)

1860 Census
Story, Nancy: (B) 1833, (CO) Pulaski, (A) 27, (BP) TN, (CMTS) 1860 Census
Story, Phebe: (B) 1820, (CO) Pulaski, (A) 40, (BP) NC, (CMTS) 1860 Census
Story, Sarah: (B) 1830, (CO) Pulaski, (A) 30, (BP) NC, (CMTS) 1860 Census
Story, Smith: (B) 1835, (CO) Pulaski, (A) 25, (BP) NC, (CMTS) 1860 Census
Story, Tabitha: (B) 1821, (CO) Pulaski, (A) 39, (BP) NC, (CMTS) 1860 Census
Story, Thomas: (B) 1851, (CO) Pulaski, (A) 9, (BP) NC, (CMTS) 1860 Census
Story, Vincent: (B) 1856, (CO) Pulaski, (A) 4, (BP) MO, (CMTS) 1860 Census
Strain, Ellen: (B) 1841, (CO) Pulaski, (A) 19, (BP) TN, (CMTS) 1860 Census
Strain, Lydia: (B) 1815, (CO) Pulaski, (A) 45, (BP) TN, (CMTS) 1860 Census
Strain, Samuel: (B) 1845, (CO) Pulaski, (A) 15, (BP) TN, (CMTS) 1860 Census
Strain, Thomas: (B) 1846, (CO) Pulaski, (A) 14, (BP) TN, (CMTS) 1860 Census
Strain, William: (B) 1840, (CO) Pulaski, (A) 20, (BP) TN, (CMTS) 1860 Census
Strange, George: (B) Mar. 24, 1848, (CO) Johnson, (C) Pemberton Cemetery
Strange, Mary E.: (B) Jul. 30, 1852, (D) Jan. 8, 1909, (CO) Johnson, (C) Pemberton Cemetery
Strange, Mona: (B) Jan. 27, 1896, (D) Mar. 23, 1910, (CO) Johnson, (C) Pemberton Cemetery
Stuber, Elizabeth: (B) Jan. 16, 1817, (D) Oct. 19, 1895, (CO) Andrew, (C) Oak Ridge Cemetery
Stumpff, Lon: (B) Sep. 13, 1861, (D) May 2, 1928, (CO) Johnson, (C) Pemberton Cemetery
Sublet, Nancy: (B) 1839, (CO) Pulaski, (A) 21, (BP) MO, (CMTS) 1860 Census
Sublet, William: (B) 1838, (CO) Pulaski, (A) 22, (BP) IL, (CMTS) 1860 Census
Sucka, Kasper: (B) Feb. 14, 1836, (D) May 4, 1897, (CO) Jefferson, (C) Old St. John's Catholic Cemetery
Sullivan, Allen: (B) 1835, (CO) Pulaski, (A) 25, (BP) TN, (CMTS) 1860 Census

Sullivan, Elizabeth: (B) 1832, (CO) Pulaski, (A) 28, (BP) TN, (CMTS) 1860 Census
Sullivan, George W.: (B) 1858, (CO) Pulaski, (A) 2, (BP) MO, (CMTS) 1860 Census
Sullivan, James: (B) 1847, (CO) Pulaski, (A) 13, (BP) MO, (CMTS) 1860 Census
Sullivan, Jesse: (B) 1830, (CO) Pulaski, (A) 30, (BP) TN, (CMTS) 1860 Census
Sullivan, Mary: (B) 1851, (CO) Pulaski, (A) 9, (BP) MO, (CMTS) 1860 Census
Sullivan, Matilda: (B) 1836, (CO) Pulaski, (A) 24, (BP) TN, (CMTS) 1860 Census
Sullivan, Nicholas: (B) 1849, (CO) Pulaski, (A) 11, (BP) MO, (CMTS) 1860 Census
Sullivan, Patrick: (B) 1836, (CO) Pulaski, (A) 24, (BP) TN, (CMTS) 1860 Census
Sullivan, Robert C.: (B) 1857, (CO) Pulaski, (A) 3, (BP) MO, (CMTS) 1860 Census
Sullivan, Sarah: (B) 1820, (CO) Pulaski, (A) 40, (BP) AL, (CMTS) 1860 Census
Sullivan, Sarah E.: (B) 1857, (CO) Pulaski, (A) 3, (BP) MO, (CMTS) 1860 Census
Summerland, George: (B) 1833, (CO) Pulaski, (A) 27, (BP) IL, (CMTS) 1860 Census
Summerland, Martha A.: (B) 1836, (CO) Pulaski, (A) 24, (BP) KY, (CMTS) 1860 Census
Summerland, William B.: (B) 1854, (CO) Pulaski, (A) 6, (BP) TX, (CMTS) 1860 Census
Summers, Ailsie J.: (B) 1839, (CO) Stone, (A) 11, (BP) MO, (CMTS) 1870 Census
Summers, Annie E.: (B) 1858, (D) 1942, (CO) Henry, (C) Knights of Pythias Cemetery, Deepwater, MO
Summers, Cordelia E.: (B) 1835, (CO) Stone, (A) 15, (BP) MO, (CMTS) 1870 Census
Summers, John W.: (B) 1855, (D) 1925, (CO) Henry, (C) Knights of Pythias Cemetery, Deepwater, MO
Summers, Martha: (B) 1820, (CO) Stone, (A) 30, (BP) MO, (CMTS) 1870 Census
Summers, Martha E.: (B) 1846, (CO) Stone, (A) 4, (BP) MO, (CMTS) 1870 Census
Summers, Price: (B) 1820, (CO) Stone, (A) 30, (BP) TN, (CMTS) 1870 Census
Surber, David W.: (B) 1850, (CO) Stone, (A) 20, (BP) KY, (CMTS) 1870

Census

Surber, Elizabeth: (B) 1830, (CO) Stone, (A) 40, (BP) VA, (CMTS) 1870 Census

Surber, Henry B.: (B) 1828, (CO) Stone, (A) 42, (BP) KY, (CMTS) 1870 Census

Sutton, Caroline: (B) 1828, (CO) Stone, (A) 22, (BP) AR, (CMTS) 1870 Census

Sutton, Cyrenia P: (B) 1849, (CO) Stone, (A) 1, (BP) MO, (CMTS) 1870 Census

Sutton, Nancy C.: (B) 1867, (D) 1951, (CO) Henry, (C) Knights of Pythias Cemetery, Deepwater, MO

Svehlas, Barbara: (D) Aug. 29, 1809, (CO) Jefferson, (C) Old St. John's Catholic Cemetery, (A) 73

Svehlas, Jakuba: (D) Oct. 18, 1896, (CO) Jefferson, (C) Old St. John's Catholic Cemetery, (A) 75

Swarthout, Charles: (B) 1855, (D) 1927, (CO) Henry, (C) Knights of Pythias Cemetery, Deepwater, MO

Swarthout, Harriet: (B) 1855, (D) 1912, (CO) Henry, (C) Knights of Pythias Cemetery, Deepwater, MO

Swartz, Henry: (B) 1832, (CO) Pulaski, (A) 28, (BP) Baden, (CMTS) 1860 Census

Swehla, Jane: (B) 1822, (D) Dec. 15, 1881, (CO) Jefferson, (C) Old St. John's Catholic Cemetery, (A) 59

Swink, Llewellen: (B) 1831, (CO) Pulaski, (A) 29, (BP) AL, (CMTS) 1860 Census

Switser, Hester N.: (B) 1844, (CO) Pulaski, (A) 16, (BP) MO, (CMTS) 1860 Census

Switser, Pleasant: (B) 1836, (CO) Pulaski, (A) 24, (BP) TN, (CMTS) 1860 Census

Synder, Margaret: (B) 1815, (D) 1870, (CO) Adair, (A) 55, (CMTS) 1870 Mortality Schedule

Tabor, Dora E.: (B) Jan.1, 1884, (D) Sep. 6, 1971, (CO) Greene

Tabor, Elizabeth: (B) Jun. 30, 1856, (D) Apr. 15, 1898, (CO) Johnson, (C) Pemberton Cemetery

Tabor, Sarah J.: (B) Mar. 9, 1842, (D) Apr. 29, 1919, (CO) Johnson, (C) Pemberton Cemetery

Tabor, Thomas J.: (B) Apr. 24, 1839, (D) Oct. 23, 1908, (CO) Johnson, (C) Pemberton Cemetery

Tait, Huson Dora: (B) Jul. 13, 1893, (D) May 26, 1927, (CO) Henry, (C) Knights of Pythias Cemetery, Deepwater, MO

Tatam, Ann Eliza: (B) 1818, (CO) Stone, (A) 52, (BP) TN, (CMTS) 1870 Census

Tatam, Elizabeth: (B) 1849, (CO) Stone, (A) 21, (BP) TN, (CMTS) 1870

Census

Tatam, James M.: (B) 1852, (CO) Stone, (A) 18, (BP) TN, (CMTS) 1870 Census

Tatam, John: (B) 1851, (CO) Stone, (A) 19, (BP) TN, (CMTS) 1870 Census

Tatam, John B.: (B) 1820, (CO) Stone, (A) 50, (BP) TN, (CMTS) 1870 Census

Taylor, Alice: (B) Seo. 11, 1906, (D) Jan. 27, 1998, (CO) Stone, (DP) Crane, MO.

Taylor, Anna I: (B) 1845, (CO) Stone, (A) 25, (BP) MO, (CMTS) 1870 Census

Taylor, Bethana: (B) 1855, (CO) Stone, (A) 15, (BP) AL, (CMTS) 1870 Census

Taylor, Carrie: (B) Mar. 15, 1893, (D) Jun., 1976, (CO) Stone, (DP) Reeds Spring, MO.

Taylor, Cleo: (B) Oct. 29, 1895, (D) Jul. 11, 1974, (CO) Stone, (DP) Blue-Eye, MO.

Taylor, David: (B) 1838, (CO) Stone, (A) 32, (BP) TN, (CMTS) 1870 Census

Taylor, Edmond: (B) 1840, (CO) Stone, (A) 30, (BP) OH, (CMTS) 1870 Census

Taylor, Edna: (B) Jun. 23, 1927, (D) Sep. 15, 1996, (CO) Stone, (DP) Reeds Spring, MO.

Taylor, Elizabeth: (B) 1839, (CO) Stone, (A) 31, (BP) TN, (CMTS) 1870 Census

Taylor, Elizabeth: (B) 1847, (CO) Stone, (A) 23, (BP) MO, (CMTS) 1870 Census

Taylor, Elizabeth: (B) 1858, (CO) Stone, (A) 12, (BP) MO, (CMTS) 1870 Census

Taylor, Francis M.: (B) 1847, (CO) Stone, (A) 3, (BP) MO, (CMTS) 1870 Census

Taylor, George A.: (B) 1855, (CO) Pulaski, (A) 5, (BP) KY, (CMTS) 1860 Census

Taylor, George W.: (B) 1837, (CO) Stone, (A) 13, (BP) MO, (CMTS) 1870 Census

Taylor, Haydon: (B) 1822, (CO) Pulaski, (A) 38, (BP) KY, (CMTS) 1860 Census

Taylor, Isaac: (B) 1849, (CO) Stone, (A) 21, (BP) MO, (CMTS) 1870 Census

Taylor, James: (B) 1844, (CO) Stone, (A) 26, (BP) TN, (CMTS) 1870 Census

Taylor, James: (B) 1844, (CO) Stone, (A) 26, (BP) AL, (CMTS) 1870 Census

Taylor, James W.: (B) 1853, (CO) Pulaski, (A) 7, (BP) KY, (CMTS) 1860 Census
Taylor, Jeffery: (B) Oct. 13, 1956, (D) Sep. 13, 1993, (CO) Stone, (DP) Kimberling City, MO
Taylor, John: (B) Oct. 26, 1886, (CO) Morgan
Taylor, John F.: (B) Jun. 7, 1865, (CO) Perry
Taylor, John H.: (D) Dec. 1, 1909, (CO) Buchannan
Taylor, John James: (B) Dec. 28, 1853, (D) Dec. 23, 1916, (CO) Lincoln, (C) New Salem Cemetery
Taylor, John M.: (B) 1839, (CO) Stone, (A) 11, (BP) MO, (CMTS) 1870 Census
Taylor, John T.: (B) 1856, (CO) Stone, (A) 14, (BP) TN, (CMTS) 1870 Census
Taylor, John W.: (B) Jun. 23, 1855, (CO) Saline,
Taylor, Josephine: (B) 1840, (CO) Stone, (A) 30, (BP) KY, (CMTS) 1870 Census
Taylor, Landers L.: (B) 1848, (CO) Stone, (A) 22, (BP) AL, (CMTS) 1870 Census
Taylor, Lottie: (B) Dec. 9, 1894, (D) May 15, 1974, (CO) Stone, (DP) Galena, MO.
Taylor, Louisa: (B) 1851, (CO) Stone, (A) 19, (BP) MO, (CMTS) 1870 Census
Taylor, Mack: (B) 1826, (CO) Stone, (A) 44, (BP) TN, (CMTS) 1870 Census
Taylor, Margaret: (B) 1842, (CO) Stone, (A) 28, (BP) MO, (CMTS) 1870 Census
Taylor, Martha: (B) 1819, (CO) Stone, (A) 51, (BP) TN, (CMTS) 1870 Census
Taylor, Martha: (B) 1852, (CO) Stone, (A) 18, (BP) MO, (CMTS) 1870 Census
Taylor, Martha: (B) 1856, (CO) Stone, (A) 14, (BP) IL, (CMTS) 1870 Census
Taylor, Martha J.: (B) 1856, (CO) Stone, (A) 14, (BP) MO, (CMTS) 1870 Census
Taylor, Mary E.: (B) 1854, (CO) Stone, (A) 16, (BP) MO, (CMTS) 1870 Census
Taylor, Mary J.: (B) 1829, (CO) Pulaski, (A) 31, (BP) KY, (CMTS) 1860 Census
Taylor, Pamelia: (B) 1843, (CO) Stone, (A) 27, (BP) MO, (CMTS) 1870 Census
Taylor, Patrick C.: (B) 1845, (CO) Stone, (A) 25, (BP) MO, (CMTS) 1870 Census
Taylor, Polly Ann: (B) 1853, (CO) Stone, (A) 17, (BP) AL, (CMTS) 1870

Census
Taylor, Raymond: (B) 1854, (CO) Pulaski, (A) 6, (BP) KY, (CMTS) 1860 Census
Taylor, Samuel: (B) 1846, (CO) Stone, (A) 24, (BP) AL, (CMTS) 1870 Census
Taylor, Sarah: (B) 1832, (CO) Stone, (A) 38, (BP) AL, (CMTS) 1870 Census
Taylor, Sarah: (B) 1842, (CO) Stone, (A) 28, (BP) TN, (CMTS) 1870 Census
Taylor, Sarah: (B) 1851, (CO) Stone, (A) 19, (BP) AL, (CMTS) 1870 Census
Taylor, Sarah Jane: (B) 1855, (CO) Stone, (A) 15, (BP) MO, (CMTS) 1870 Census
Taylor, T.: (B) 1834, (CO) Pulaski, (A) 26, (BP) PA, (CMTS) 1860 Census
Taylor, Thomas: (B) 1845, (CO) Stone, (A) 25, (BP) AL, (CMTS) 1870 Census
Taylor, Valentine: (B) 1794, (CO) Stone, (A) 56, (BP) TN, (CMTS) 1870 Census
Taylor, William A.: (B) 1855, (CO) Pulaski, (A) 5, (BP) KY, (CMTS) 1860 Census
Taylor, William D: (B) 1842, (CO) Stone, (A) 8, (BP) MO, (CMTS) 1870 Census
Taylor, Zebedee: (B) 1840, (CO) Stone, (A) 30, (BP) AL, (CMTS) 1870 Census
Taylor, Zebedee: (B) 1856, (CO) Stone, (A) 14, (BP) MO, (CMTS) 1870 Census
Teasley, Cynthia A.: (B) 1834, (CO) Pulaski, (A) 26, (BP) IL, (CMTS) 1860 Census
Teasley, Rebecca: (B) 1844, (CO) Pulaski, (A) 16, (BP) TN, (CMTS) 1860 Census
Teeples, Diana: (B) 1847, (CO) Pulaski, (A) 13, (BP) MO, (CMTS) 1860 Census
Teeples, Hannah: (B) 1851, (CO) Pulaski, (A) 9, (BP) MO, (CMTS) 1860 Census
Teeples, Isaac: (B) 1838, (CO) Pulaski, (A) 22, (BP) MO, (CMTS) 1860 Census
Teeples, Jacob: (B) 1840, (CO) Pulaski, (A) 20, (BP) MO, (CMTS) 1860 Census
Teeples, Margaret: (B) 1842, (CO) Pulaski, (A) 18, (BP) MO, (CMTS) 1860 Census
Teeples, Nancy: (B) 1840, (CO) Pulaski, (A) 20, (BP) MO, (CMTS) 1860 Census

Teeples, Nancy: (B) 1849, (CO) Pulaski, (A) 11, (BP) MO, (CMTS) 1860 Census
Tellams, Ferman: (B) 1833, (CO) Stone, (A) 37, (BP) NJ, (CMTS) 1870 Census
Tellams, Margaret: (B) 1844, (CO) Stone, (A) 26, (BP) England, (CMTS) 1870 Census
Templeton, George: (B) 1839, (CO) Pulaski, (A) 21, (BP) MO, (CMTS) 1860 Census
Templeton, Mary E.: (B) 1844, (CO) Pulaski, (A) 16, (BP) MO, (CMTS) 1860 Census
Templeton, Prior M.: (B) 1837, (CO) Pulaski, (A) 23, (BP) TN, (CMTS) 1860 Census
Tennis, Christina: (B) 1831, (CO) Stone, (A) 19, (BP) AR, (CMTS) 1870 Census
Teppet, Emily: (B) 1846, (CO) Pulaski, (A) 14, (BP) MO, (CMTS) 1860 Census
Teppet, George: (B) 1845, (CO) Pulaski, (A) 15, (BP) TN, (CMTS) 1860 Census
Teppet, James: (B) 1845, (CO) Pulaski, (A) 15, (BP) TN, (CMTS) 1860 Census
Teppet, Jesse: (B) 1849, (CO) Pulaski, (A) 11, (BP) TN, (CMTS) 1860 Census
Teppet, Mary: (B) 1849, (CO) Pulaski, (A) 11, (BP) TN, (CMTS) 1860 Census
Teppet, Rebecca: (B) 1820, (CO) Pulaski, (A) 40, (BP) TN, (CMTS) 1860 Census
Teppet, Sarah J.: (B) 1851, (CO) Pulaski, (A) 9, (BP) TN, (CMTS) 1860 Census
Teppet, Thomas: (B) 1842, (CO) Pulaski, (A) 18, (BP) TN, (CMTS) 1860 Census
Terrell, Albert N.: (B) 1851, (CO) Pulaski, (A) 9, (BP) TN, (CMTS) 1860 Census
Terrell, Arnold B.: (B) 1849, (CO) Pulaski, (A) 11, (BP) TN, (CMTS) 1860 Census
Terrell, Celestia J.: (B) 1845, (CO) Pulaski, (A) 15, (BP) NC, (CMTS) 1860 Census
Terrell, James A.: (B) 1839, (CO) Pulaski, (A) 21, (BP) NC, (CMTS) 1860 Census
Terrell, Laura J.: (B) 1851, (CO) Pulaski, (A) 9, (BP) TN, (CMTS) 1860 Census
Terrell, Susan: (B) 1857, (CO) Pulaski, (A) 3, (BP) MO, (CMTS) 1860 Census
Terrell, Susan B.: (B) 1815, (CO) Pulaski, (A) 45, (BP) NC, (CMTS)

1860 Census

Terrill, Henr G.: (B) 1833, (CO) Pulaski, (A) 27, (BP) NC, (CMTS) 1860 Census

Terrill, Jemima: (B) 1842, (CO) Pulaski, (A) 18, (BP) MO, (CMTS) 1860 Census

Terry, Rebecca C.: (B) 1876, (CO) Missouri, (RES) Graves Co., TX, (CMTS) 1920 Census, p. 111

Thogmartin, Pelina: (B) 1841, (CO) Stone, (A) 29, (BP) MO, (CMTS) 1870 Census

Thogmartin, William: (B) 1832, (CO) Stone, (A) 38, (BP) TN, (CMTS) 1870 Census

Thomas, Charlie L.: (B) Mar. 28, 1891, (D) Mar. 28, 1955, (CO) Pettis, Black Baptist Cemetery, Prairie Township

Thomas, Elizabeth: (B) Feb. 25, 1846, (D) Aug. 25, 1902, (CO) Henry, (C) Knights of Pythias Cemetery, Deepwater, MO

Thomas, Orval: (B) Dec. 8, 1910, (D) Feb. 5, 1924, (CO) Henry, (C) Knights of Pythias Cemetery, Deepwater, MO

Thomason, George W.: (B) 1844, (CO) Stone, (A) 6, (BP) MO, (CMTS) 1870 Census

Thomason, William J.: (B) 1841, (CO) Stone, (A) 9, (BP) MO, (CMTS) 1870 Census

Thompson, Alexander C.: (B) 1856, (CO) Pulaski, (A) 4, (BP) TN, (CMTS) 1860 Census

Thompson, Carrol: (B) 1839, (CO) Pulaski, (A) 21, (BP) VA, (CMTS) 1860 Census

Thompson, Elizabeth: (B) 1851, (CO) Pulaski, (A) 9, (BP) VA, (CMTS) 1860 Census

Thompson, Emeline: (B) 1849, (CO) Pulaski, (A) 11, (BP) VA, (CMTS) 1860 Census

Thompson, Isaac A.: (B) 1853, (CO) Pulaski, (A) 7, (BP) TN, (CMTS) 1860 Census

Thompson, James: (B) 1841, (CO) Pulaski, (A) 19, (BP) VA, (CMTS) 1860 Census

Thompson, James: (B) 1846, (CO) Pulaski, (A) 14, (BP) MO, (CMTS) 1860 Census

Thompson, James: (B) 1840, (CO) Pulaski, (A) 20, (BP) TN, (CMTS) 1860 Census

Thompson, James A.: (B) 1855, (CO) Pulaski, (A) 5, (BP) MO, (CMTS) 1860 Census

Thompson, Joanna: (B) 1831, (CO) Pulaski, (A) 29, (BP) TN, (CMTS) 1860 Census

Thompson, John: (B) 1791, (CO) Pulaski, (A) 69, (BP) PA, (CMTS) 1860 Census

Thompson, John: (B) 1834, (CO) Pulaski, (A) 26, (BP) TN, (CMTS) 1860 Census
Thompson, John C.: (B) 1831, (CO) Pulaski, (A) 29, (BP) TN, (CMTS) 1860 Census
Thompson, John F.: (B) 1855, (CO) Pulaski, (A) 5, (BP) TN, (CMTS) 1860 Census
Thompson, L.: (B) Apr. 6, 1805, (D) Jan. 31, 1875, (CO) Audrain, (C) Old Village Cemetery
Thompson, Margaret: (B) 1856, (CO) Pulaski, (A) 4, (BP) IL, (CMTS) 1860 Census
Thompson, Margaret J.: (B) 1850, (CO) Pulaski, (A) 10, (BP) MO, (CMTS) 1860 Census
Thompson, Martha: (B) 1841, (CO) Pulaski, (A) 19, (BP) MO, (CMTS) 1860 Census
Thompson, Martha S.: (B) 1855, (CO) Pulaski, (A) 5, (BP) TN, (CMTS) 1860 Census
Thompson, Mary: (B) 1830, (CO) Pulaski, (A) 30, (BP) TN, (CMTS) 1860 Census
Thompson, Mirand: (B) 1827, (CO) Pulaski, (A) 33, (BP) VA, (CMTS) 1860 Census
Thompson, Nancy: (B) 1842, (CO) Pulaski, (A) 18, (BP) MO, (CMTS) 1860 Census
Thompson, Nancy E.: (B) 1854, (CO) Pulaski, (A) 6, (BP) MO, (CMTS) 1860 Census
Thompson, Orlena: (B) 1831, (CO) Pulaski, (A) 29, (BP) TN, (CMTS) 1860 Census
Thompson, Phebe A.: (B) 1834, (CO) Pulaski, (A) 26, (BP) VA, (CMTS) 1860 Census
Thompson, Rebecca: (B) 1848, (CO) Pulaski, (A) 12, (BP) MO, (CMTS) 1860 Census
Thompson, Sarah: (B) 1842, (CO) Pulaski, (A) 18, (BP) IL, (CMTS) 1860 Census
Thompson, Sarah: (B) 1844, (CO) Pulaski, (A) 16, (BP) VA, (CMTS) 1860 Census
Thompson, Sarah: (B) 1853, (CO) Pulaski, (A) 7, (BP) MO, (CMTS) 1860 Census
Thompson, Tally A.: (B) 1836, (CO) Pulaski, (A) 24, (BP) TN, (CMTS) 1860 Census
Thompson, William: (B) 1836, (CO) Pulaski, (A) 24, (BP) TN, (CMTS) 1860 Census
Thompson, William: (B) 1847, (CO) Pulaski, (A) 13, (BP) MO, (CMTS) 1860 Census
Thompson, William: (B) 1854, (CO) Pulaski, (A) 6, (BP) VA, (CMTS)

1860 Census
Thompson, William K.: (B) 1853, (CO) Pulaski, (A) 7, (BP) TN, (CMTS) 1860 Census
Thornton, Elizabeth: (B) 1841, (CO) Pulaski, (A) 19, (BP) AL, (CMTS) 1860 Census
Thornton, Milton: (B) 1828, (CO) Pulaski, (A) 32, (BP) IL, (CMTS) 1860 Census
Thornton, Permelia K.: (B) Dec. 18m 1859, (D) ????, (CO) DeKalb,
Thorton, James: (B) Mar. 13, 1827, (D) Aug. 16, 1903, (CO) Howard,
Tilley, Charlotte: (B) 1839, (CO) Pulaski, (A) 21, (BP) MO, (CMTS) 1860 Census
Tilley, LeRoy: (B) 1841, (CO) Pulaski, (A) 19, (BP) MO, (CMTS) 1860 Census
Tilley, Mahala: (B) 1843, (CO) Pulaski, (A) 17, (BP) MO, (CMTS) 1860 Census
Tilley, Mipanaiah: (B) 1849, (CO) Pulaski, (A) 11, (BP) MO, (CMTS) 1860 Census
Tilley, Newton: (B) 1835, (CO) Pulaski, (A) 25, (BP) MO, (CMTS) 1860 Census
Tilmon, Lola E.: (B) Aug. 25, 1901, (D) Jan. 27, 1980, (CO) Henry, (C) Knights of Pythias Cemetery, Deepwater, MO
Timmons, Clark: (B) 1855, (D) 1936, (CO) Cedar, (C) Brashear Cemetery
Tinker, George W.: (B) Mar. 25, 1824, (D) Jan. 11, 1904, (CO) St. Louis,
Tinker, Hannah J.: (B) Feb. 19, 1857, (CO) St. Louis,
Tippet, Permelia: (B) 1853, (CO) Pulaski, (A) 7, (BP) MO, (CMTS) 1860 Census
Tippett, Josiah: (B) 1849, (CO) Pulaski, (A) 11, (BP) MO, (CMTS) 1860 Census
Tippett, Mary A.: (B) 1842, (CO) Pulaski, (A) 18, (BP) TN, (CMTS) 1860 Census
Tippett, Nancy: (B) 1845, (CO) Pulaski, (A) 15, (BP) MO, (CMTS) 1860 Census
Tipton, Calvin: (B) 1833, (CO) Stone, (A) 37, (BP) TN, (CMTS) 1870 Census
Tipton, Poly: (B) 1838, (CO) Stone, (A) 32, (BP) KY, (CMTS) 1870 Census
Tipton, Thomas A.: (B) 1857, (CO) Stone, (A) 13, (BP) AR, (CMTS) 1870 Census
Tolby, T.: (B) May 3, 1833, (D) Sep. 13, 1890, (CO) Barry, (C) Cassville Cemetery
Tony, Peter: (B) 1832, (CO) Pulaski, (A) 28, (BP) Saxony, (CMTS) 1860 Census
Torbet, James A.: (B) 1849, (CO) Stone, (A) 21, (BP) TN, (CMTS) 1870

Census
Torbet, John C.: (B) 1856, (CO) Stone, (A) 14, (BP) MO, (CMTS) 1870 Census
Torbet, Margaret: (B) 1818, (CO) Stone, (A) 52, (BP) TN, (CMTS) 1870 Census
Torbet, Nancy E.: (B) 1847, (CO) Stone, (A) 23, (BP) TN, (CMTS) 1870 Census
Townsend, C.: (B) Aug.24, 1815, (D) Oct. 15, 1890, (CO) Barry, (C) Cassville Cemetery
Townsend, Susan: (B) Dec. 3 1812, (D) Mar. 1, 1894, (CO) Barry, (C) Cassville Cemetery
Townsend, Will: (B) Mar. 3, 1794, (D) Jul. 13, 1875, (CO) Barry, (C) Cassville Cemetery
Towson, James A.: (B) Sep. 30, 1819, (D) Jan. 13, 1871, (CO) Audrain, (C) Old Village Cemetery
Trautenmiller, Charles: (D) Sep., 1913, (CO) St. Louis, (C) Calvary Cemetery
Trautmann, Edna G.: (D) Apr. 28, 1903, (CO) St. Louis, (C) Calvary Cemetery, (A) 17
Trautmann, John F.: (B) 1843, (D) 1909, (CO) St. Louis, (C) Calvary Cemetery
Trautmann, Susan M.: (B) 1845, (D) 1911, (CO) St. Louis, (C) Calvary Cemetery
Trautmann, Theo J. M.*: (B) 1876, (D) 1916, (CO) St. Louis, (C) Calvary Cemetery
Travis, Nathaniel: (B) 1838, (CO) Pulaski, (A) 22, (BP) TN, (CMTS) 1860 Census
Travis, Sarah: (B) 1845, (CO) Pulaski, (A) 15, (BP) TN, (CMTS) 1860 Census
Trenner, Phillip: (B) 1822, (CO) Pulaski, (A) 38, (BP) Ireland, (CMTS) 1860 Census
Tribble, Effa: (B) 1833, (CO) Pulaski, (A) 27, (BP) IND, (CMTS) 1860 Census
Tribble, L.: (B) 1830, (CO) Pulaski, (A) 30, (BP) IND, (CMTS) 1860 Census
Tribble, Mary: (B) 1853, (CO) Pulaski, (A) 7, (BP) IND, (CMTS) 1860 Census
Trobo, Samuel: (B) 1849, (CO) Pulaski, (A) 11, (BP) TN, (CMTS) 1860 Census
Trower, Almeda: (B) 1851, (CO) Pulaski, (A) 9, (BP) MO, (CMTS) 1860 Census
Trower, John: (B) 1848, (CO) Pulaski, (A) 12, (BP) Mo, (CMTS) 1860 Census

Trower, Mary A.: (B) 1854, (CO) Pulaski, (A) 6, (BP) MO, (CMTS) 1860 Census
Trower, Samantha J.: (B) 1845, (CO) Pulaski, (A) 15, (BP) MO, (CMTS) 1860 Census
Trower, William: (B) 1849, (CO) Pulaski, (A) 11, (BP) MO, (CMTS) 1860 Census
Truemper, Florence: (B) Mar. 9, 1893, (D) Feb. 28, 1988, (CO) St. Louis, (C) Calvary Cemetery
Truemper, Louis: (B) May 28, 1859, (D) Jun. 15, 1919, (CO) St. Louis, (C) Calvary Cemetery
Tucker, Sarah: (B) Aug. 19, 1835, (CO) Perry, (SPOUSE) James Smith, (MD) Feb. 2, 1855, (PRTS) Nicholas P. Tucker and Sarah Ann Moore
Tudor, William E.: (B) Sep. 22, 1892, (D) 1972, (CO) St. Louis, (C) Calvary Cemetery
Turnbull, Ann J.: (B) 1852, (CO) Pulaski, (A) 8, (BP) MO, (CMTS) 1860 Census
Turnbull, Hezekiah: (B) 1830, (CO) Pulaski, (A) 30, (BP) MO, (CMTS) 1860 Census
Turnbull, Margaret: (B) 1820, (CO) Pulaski, (A) 40, (BP) AL, (CMTS) 1860 Census
Turnbull, Margaret: (B) 1839, (CO) Pulaski, (A) 21, (BP) MO, (CMTS) 1860 Census
Turnbull, Squire: (B) 1848, (CO) Pulaski, (A) 12, (BP) MO, (CMTS) 1860 Census
Turner, Elijah: (B) 1847, (CO) Pulaski, (A) 13, (BP) MO, (CMTS) 1860 Census
Turner, Elizabeth: (B) 1829, (D) 1896, (CO) Barry, (C) Old Corsicana Cemetery
Turner, G.: (B) 1821, (CO) Pulaski, (A) 39, (BP) KY, (CMTS) 1860 Census
Turner, Margaret: (B) 1834, (CO) Pulaski, (A) 26, (BP) TN, (CMTS) 1860 Census
Turner, Mary: (B) 1850, (CO) Pulaski, (A) 10, (BP) MO, (CMTS) 1860 Census
Turner, Nancy: (B) 1843, (CO) Pulaski, (A) 17, (BP) MO, (CMTS) 1860 Census
Turner, Ollie: (B) Oct. 6, 1875, (D) Oct. 19, 1939, (CO) Barry, (C) Clark Cemetery, Butterfield, MO.
Turner, Rebecca: (B) Jan. 25, 1802, (D) Jan. 25, 1877, (CO) Barry, (C) Old Corsicana Cemetery
Turner, Robert: (B) 1854, (CO) Pulaski, (A) 6, (BP) MO, (CMTS) 1860 Census

Turner, Slias: (B) Ferb. 13, 1872, (D) Mar. 11, 1943, (CO) Barry, (C) Clark Cemetery, Butterfield, MO.
Turner, William: (B) 1844, (CO) Pulaski, (A) 16, (BP) MO, (CMTS) 1860 Census
Turpin, Eliza A.: (B) 1851, (CO) Pulaski, (A) 9, (BP) MO, (CMTS) 1860 Census
Turpin, John M.: (B) 1842, (CO) Pulaski, (A) 18, (BP) KY, (CMTS) 1860 Census
Turpin, Joseph H.: (B) 1846, (CO) Pulaski, (A) 14, (BP) KY, (CMTS) 1860 Census
Turpin, Mary J.: (B) 1843, (CO) Pulaski, (A) 17, (BP) KY, (CMTS) 1860 Census
Turpin, Thomas M.: (B) 1848, (CO) Pulaski, (A) 12, (BP) MO, (CMTS) 1860 Census
Underwood, Eliza Margaret: (D) Mar. 22, 1847, (CO) Andrew, (C) Oak Ridge Cemetery, (A) 30Y 12D
Underwood, Rebecca: (B) 1838, (CO) Pulaski, (A) 22, (BP) TN, (CMTS) 1860 Census
Uterback, Donald: (B) Nov. 2, 1928, (D) Oct. 17, 1993, (CO) Texas, (DP) Success, MO.
Utterback, Adolphus: (B) Mar. 7, 1904, (CO) Pike, (DP) Louisana, MO.
Utterback, Agnes: (B) Dec. 24, 1879, (DP) Joplin, MO.
Utterback, Almeda: (B) Jun. 22, 1934, (D) Jan. 15, 1988, (CO) Greene, (DP) Springfield, MO.
Utterback, Altye: (B) Sep. 22, 1909, (CO) Monroe, (DP) Paris, MO.
Utterback, Bertha: (B) Sep. 19, 1902, (CO) Clay
Utterback, Bessie: (B) Mar. 2, 1900, (CO) St. Louis, (DP) St. Louis, MO
Utterback, Beula: (B) Aug. 21, 1909, (CO) Audrain, (DP) Mexico, MO
Utterback, Bob: (B) Apr. 1, 1930, (D) Jul. 17, 1995, (CO) Montgomery, (DP) Middletown, MO
Utterback, Calvin: (B) Feb. 28, 1920, (D) Sep. 19, 1998, (CO) Ralls, (DP) Perry, MO
Utterback, Catherine: (B) Jul. 11, 1910, (D) Dec. 1, 1996, (CO) St. Louis, (DP) St. Louis, MO.
Utterback, Cora: (B) Feb. 3, 1918, (D) Apr., 1996, (CO) Audrain, (DP) Mexico, MO.
Utterback, David: (B) Dec. 3, 1915, (D) 1985, (CO) Audrain, (DP) Mexico, MO.
Utterback, Delbert: (B) Dec. 2, 1908, (CO) Marion, (DP) Hannibal, MO.
Utterback, Sarah C.: (B) Jan. 3, 1834, (CO) Ralls
Utterback, William: (B) Nov. 5, 1822, (D) Nov. 25, 1902, (DP) Carls Junction, MO

Utterback, William S.: (B) Mar. 12, 1848, (CO) Vernon
Van Winkle, Ezekiel: (B) 1886, (D) 7 Oct 1907, (CO) Oregon, (C) Falling Springs Cemetery
Vanbuskirk, Bessie: (B) 1837, (D) 1917, (CO) Cedar, (C) Brashear Cemetery
Vance, Elizabeth: (B) 1842, (CO) Pulaski, (A) 18, (BP) MO, (CMTS) 1860 Census
Vance, Harrison: (B) 1837, (CO) Pulaski, (A) 23, (BP) TN, (CMTS) 1860 Census
Vance, Jackson: (B) 1849, (CO) Pulaski, (A) 11, (BP) MO, (CMTS) 1860 Census
Vance, Jane: (B) 1847, (CO) Pulaski, (A) 13, (BP) MO, (CMTS) 1860 Census
Vance, William: (B) 1835, (CO) Pulaski, (A) 25, (BP) TN, (CMTS) 1860 Census
Vance,Jesse: (B) Aug. 12, 1800, (D) May 29, 1874, (CO) Audrain, (C) Pisgah Cemetery
Vaughan, Bramlett W.: (B) 1828, (CO) Pulaski, (A) 32, (BP) KY, (CMTS) 1860 Census
Vaughan, Franklin: (B) 1840, (CO) Pulaski, (A) 20, (BP) MO, (CMTS) 1860 Census
Vaughan, James: (B) 1853, (CO) Pulaski, (A) 7, (BP) MO, (CMTS) 1860 Census
Vaughan, James: (B) 1844, (CO) Pulaski, (A) 16, (BP) MO, (CMTS) 1860 Census
Vaughan, Jeremiah: (B) 1855, (CO) Pulaski, (A) 5, (BP) MO, (CMTS) 1860 Census
Vaughan, Joseph: (B) 1839, (CO) Pulaski, (A) 21, (BP) MO, (CMTS) 1860 Census
Vaughan, Laton: (B) 1854, (CO) Pulaski, (A) 6, (BP) MO, (CMTS) 1860 Census
Vaughan, Lucinda: (B) 1838, (CO) Pulaski, (A) 22, (BP) KY, (CMTS) 1860 Census
Vaughan, Nancy: (B) 1844, (CO) Pulaski, (A) 16, (BP) MO, (CMTS) 1860 Census
Vaughan, Permelia: (B) 1831, (CO) Pulaski, (A) 29, (BP) TN, (CMTS) 1860 Census
Vaughan, Plly: (B) 1841, (CO) Pulaski, (A) 19, (BP) MO, (CMTS) 1860 Census
Vaughan, William: (B) 1851, (CO) Pulaski, (A) 9, (BP) MO, (CMTS) 1860 Census
Vaughan, William R.: (B) 1851, (CO) Pulaski, (A) 9, (BP) MO, (CMTS) 1860 Census

Vaught, Elizabeth: (B) 1840, (CO) Pulaski, (A) 20, (BP) TN, (CMTS) 1860 Census
Vaught, Joseph: (B) 1827, (CO) Pulaski, (A) 33, (BP) AL, (CMTS) 1860 Census
Vento, Steve: (B) Sep. 8, 1882, (D) Dec. 16, 1955, (CO) St. Louis, (C) Calvary Cemetery
Vermilion, Francis J.: (B) 1840, (CO) Stone, (A) 10, (BP) MO, (CMTS) 1870 Census
Vermilion, John B.: (B) 1834, (CO) Stone, (A) 16, (BP) MO, (CMTS) 1870 Census
Vermilion, Malissa J.: (B) 1838, (CO) Stone, (A) 12, (BP) MO, (CMTS) 1870 Census
Vermilion, Martha E.: (B) 1845, (CO) Stone, (A) 5, (BP) MO, (CMTS) 1870 Census
Vermilion, Reubin D: (B) 1847, (CO) Stone, (A) 3, (BP) MO, (CMTS) 1870 Census
Vermillion, Jessie C.: (B) 1843, (CO) Stone, (A) 7, (BP) MO, (CMTS) 1870 Census
Vermillion, John: (B) 1848, (CO) Stone, (A) 2, (BP) MO, (CMTS) 1870 Census
Vermillion, Mary: (B) 1830, (CO) Stone, (A) 20, (BP) MO, (CMTS) 1870 Census
Vickers, Emaline: (B) 1844, (CO) Pulaski, (A) 16, (BP) MO, (CMTS) 1860 Census
Vickers, Nancy: (B) 1828, (CO) Pulaski, (A) 32, (BP) MO, (CMTS) 1860 Census
Vickers, Nancy: (B) 1847, (CO) Pulaski, (A) 13, (BP) MO, (CMTS) 1860 Census
Vickers, Reubin: (B) 1856, (CO) Pulaski, (A) 4, (BP) MO, (CMTS) 1860 Census
Vickers, William V.: (B) 1832, (CO) Pulaski, (A) 28, (BP) IND, (CMTS) 1860 Census
Vincent, Bennett: (B) 1854, (CO) Pulaski, (A) 6, (BP) MO, (CMTS) 1860 Census
Vincent, Eliza: (B) 1834, (CO) Pulaski, (A) 26, (BP) IL, (CMTS) 1860 Census
Vincent, Hiram: (B) 1852, (CO) Pulaski, (A) 8, (BP) MO, (CMTS) 1860 Census
Vincent, James: (B) 1837, (CO) Pulaski, (A) 23, (BP) MO, (CMTS) 1860 Census
Vincent, James A.: (B) 1847, (CO) Pulaski, (A) 13, (BP) MO, (CMTS) 1860 Census
Vincent, John: (B) 1827, (CO) Pulaski, (A) 33, (BP) TN, (CMTS)

1860 Census
Vincent, Nancy E.: (B) 1856, (CO) Pulaski, (A) 4, (BP) MO, (CMTS) 1860 Census
Vincent, Nancy N.: (B) 1828, (CO) Pulaski, (A) 32, (BP) IL, (CMTS) 1860 Census
Vincent, Robert F.: (B) 1853, (CO) Pulaski, (A) 7, (BP) MO, (CMTS) 1860 Census
Vincent, Sarah: (B) 1849, (CO) Pulaski, (A) 11, (BP) MO, (CMTS) 1860 Census
Vineyard, Charles M.: (B) 1852, (CO) Pulaski, (A) 8, (BP) TN, (CMTS) 1860 Census
Vineyard, Elizabeth: (B) 1833, (CO) Pulaski, (A) 27, (BP) MO, (CMTS) 1860 Census
Vineyard, John: (B) 1832, (CO) Pulaski, (A) 28, (BP) TN, (CMTS) 1860 Census
Viviano, Phillip: (B) 1893, (D) 1985, (CO) St. Louis, (C) Calvary Cemetery
Vogeli, Julius L.: (B) Jul. 24, 1908, (D) Sep. 15, 1908, (CO) Henry, (C) Knights of Pythias Cemetery, Deepwater, MO
Vohs, Helen: (B) Apr. 24, 1859, (D) Apr. 27, 1934, (CO) Missouri,
Vohs, William A.: (B) Jul. ??, 1862, (CO),
Votan, Artemesa: (B) 1830, (CO) Pulaski, (A) 30, (BP) IL, (CMTS) 1860 Census
Votan, Henry: (B) 1821, (CO) Pulaski, (A) 39, (BP) MO, (CMTS) 1860 Census
Wagenblast, John: (B) Feb. 14, 1826, (D) Nov. 27, 1847, (CO) Andrew, (C) Oak Ridge Cemetery
Waggoer, Louisa: (B) Apr. 19, 1849, (CO) Oregon, (PRTS) Henry Waggoner
Wagner, Dorcas E.: (B) 1851, (CO) Pulaski, (A) 9, (BP) MO, (CMTS) 1860 Census
Wagner, Frederic: (B) 1833, (CO) Pulaski, (A) 27, (BP) Prussia, (CMTS) 1860 Census
Wagner, George W.: (B) 1850, (CO) Pulaski, (A) 10, (BP) MO, (CMTS) 1860 Census
Wagner, Julius: (B) 1829, (CO) Pulaski, (A) 31, (BP) Prussia, (CMTS) 1860 Census
Wagner, Lucinda: (B) 1826, (CO) Pulaski, (A) 34, (BP) VA, (CMTS) 1860 Census
Wagner, Martha J.: (B) 1851, (CO) Pulaski, (A) 9, (BP) MO, (CMTS) 1860 Census
Wagner, Sarah E.: (B) 1848, (CO) Pulaski, (A) 12, (BP) KY, (CMTS) 1860 Census

Waldon, Barbara: (B) 1830, (CO) Stone, (A) 20, (BP) MO, (CMTS) 1870 Census
Waldon, James: (B) 1828, (CO) Stone, (A) 22, (BP) TN, (CMTS) 1870 Census
Waldroof, Jane: (B) 1830, (CO) Stone, (A) 40, (BP) NC, (CMTS) 1870 Census
Waldroof, John: (B) 1852, (CO) Stone, (A) 18, (BP) AR, (CMTS) 1870 Census
Waldroof, Margarette: (B) 1853, (CO) Stone, (A) 17, (BP) AR, (CMTS) 1870 Census
Waldroof, Meak: (B) 1827, (CO) Stone, (A) 43, (BP) AR, (CMTS) 1870 Census
Walker, Caroline: (B) 1845, (CO) Pulaski, (A) 15, (BP) MO, (CMTS) 1860 Census
Walker, Dow: (B) 1855, (CO) Pulaski, (A) 5, (BP) IL, (CMTS) 1860 Census
Walker, George: (B) 1847, (CO) Stone, (A) 23, (BP) MO, (CMTS) 1870 Census
Walker, Henry: (B) 1830, (CO) Pulaski, (A) 30, (BP) TN, (CMTS) 1860 Census
Walker, James: (B) 1835, (CO) Pulaski, (A) 25, (BP) IL, (CMTS) 1860 Census
Walker, James M.: (B) 1842, (CO) Stone, (A) 8, (BP) MO, (CMTS) 1870 Census
Walker, Louisa: (B) 1850, (CO) Stone, (A) 20, (BP) MO, (CMTS) 1870 Census
Walker, Margaret C.: (B) 1841, (CO) Stone, (A) 9, (BP) MO, (CMTS) 1870 Census
Walker, Martilla J.: (B) 1841, (CO) Pulaski, (A) 19, (BP) MO, (CMTS) 1860 Census
Walker, Mary J.: (B) 1848, (CO) Stone, (A) 2, (BP) MO, (CMTS) 1870 Census
Walker, Merrill C.: (B) 1853, (CO) Pulaski, (A) 7, (BP) MO, (CMTS) 1860 Census
Walker, Nancy: (B) 1837, (CO) Pulaski, (A) 23, (BP) IL, (CMTS) 1860 Census
Walker, Pamela Mermis: (B) 6 January 1956, (D) May 1, 1998, (CO) Oregon, (C) Falling Springs Cemetery
Walker, Priscilla: (B) 1825, (CO) Pulaski, (A) 35, (BP) MO, (CMTS) 1860 Census
Walker, Sally: (B) 1839, (CO) Pulaski, (A) 21, (BP) MO, (CMTS) 1860 Census
Walker, Samuel: (B) 1844, (CO) Stone, (A) 6, (BP) MO, (CMTS) 1870

Census
Walker, Sarah A.: (B) 1846, (CO) Stone, (A) 4, (BP) MO, (CMTS) 1870 Census
Walker, William E.: (B) 1836, (CO) Pulaski, (A) 24, (BP) TN, (CMTS) 1860 Census
Walkup, Samuel J.: (B) 1857, (D) 1945, (CO) Henry, (C) Knights of Pythias Cemetery, Deepwater, MO
Walkup, Sarah Ann: (B) 1859, (D) 1955, (CO) Henry, (C) Knights of Pythias Cemetery, Deepwater, MO
Waller, John: (B) Sep. 25, 1818, (D) Dec. 2, 1885, (CO) Barry, (C) Old Corsicana Cemetery
Walls, Cynthia: (B) 1854, (CO) Pulaski, (A) 6, (BP) MO, (CMTS) 1860 Census
Walls, Frances: (B) 1828, (CO) Stone, (A) 22, (BP) AR, (CMTS) 1870 Census
Walls, Isaac: (B) 1828, (CO) Stone, (A) 22, (BP) AR, (CMTS) 1870 Census
Walls, Lorenzo D.: (B) 1833, (CO) Pulaski, (A) 27, (BP) MO, (CMTS) 1860 Census
Walls, Nancy: (B) 1835, (CO) Pulaski, (A) 25, (BP) TN, (CMTS) 1860 Census
Ward, Ala: (B) 1820, (CO) Pulaski, (A) 40, (BP) TN, (CMTS) 1860 Census
Ward, Andrew: (B) 1852, (CO) Pulaski, (A) 8, (BP) IL, (CMTS) 1860 Census
Ward, Clarissa: (B) 1854, (CO) Pulaski, (A) 6, (BP) IL, (CMTS) 1860 Census
Ward, Ernest: (B) Jul. 23, 1888, (D) Apr. 21, 1961, (CO) Henry, (C) Knights of Pythias Cemetery, Deepwater, MO
Ward, Judith: (B) 1849, (CO) Pulaski, (A) 11, (BP) IL, (CMTS) 1860 Census
Ward, Mahala F: (B) 1850, (CO) Stone, (A) 20, (BP) MO, (CMTS) 1870 Census
Ward, Moses S.: (B) 1843, (CO) Stone, (A) 27, (BP) MO, (CMTS) 1870 Census
Warnell, Elizabeth: (B) 1837, (CO) Pulaski, (A) 23, (BP) IL, (CMTS) 1860 Census
Warnell, Richard: (B) 1823, (CO) Pulaski, (A) 37, (BP) KY, (CMTS) 1860 Census
Warner, Anna Mae: (B) Jan. 9, 1869, (D) Aug. 14, 1941, (CO) Cass, (C) Strasburg Cemetery, Strasburg, MO.
Warner, William R.: (B) May 16, 1867, (D) Sep. 11, 1941, (CO) Cass, (C) Strasburg Cemetery, Strasburg, MO.

Warren, Charles C.: (B) 1834, (CO) Stone, (A) 16, (BP) AR, (CMTS) 1870 Census
Warren, Frances: (B) 1826, (CO) Pulaski, (A) 34, (BP) TN, (CMTS) 1860 Census
Warren, Isaac: (B) 1839, (CO) Pulaski, (A) 21, (BP) TN, (CMTS) 1860 Census
Warren, Isaac: (B) 1839, (CO) Pulaski, (A) 21, (BP) TN, (CMTS) 1860 Census
Warren, James: (B) 1852, (CO) Pulaski, (A) 8, (BP) TN, (CMTS) 1860 Census
Warren, Jane: (B) 1850, (CO) Pulaski, (A) 10, (BP) TN, (CMTS) 1860 Census
Warren, John: (B) 1855, (CO) Pulaski, (A) 5, (BP) TN, (CMTS) 1860 Census
Warren, Robert: (B) 1847, (CO) Pulaski, (A) 13, (BP) TN, (CMTS) 1860 Census
Warren, Seyrine: (B) 1843, (CO) Pulaski, (A) 17, (BP) TN, (CMTS) 1860 Census
Warren, Tina: (B) 1855, (CO) Pulaski, (A) 5, (BP) TN, (CMTS) 1860 Census
Warthen, Alva: (B) 1851, (CO) Pulaski, (A) 9, (BP) MO, (CMTS) 1860 Census
Warthen, Benjamin: (B) 1826, (CO) Pulaski, (A) 34, (BP) TN, (CMTS) 1860 Census
Warthen, Dan: (B) 1856, (CO) Pulaski, (A) 4, (BP) MO, (CMTS) 1860 Census
Warthen, Jane: (B) 1821, (CO) Pulaski, (A) 39, (BP) TN, (CMTS) 1860 Census
Waterfall, Emiline: (B) 1830, (CO) Stone, (A) 20, (BP) TN, (CMTS) 1870 Census
Waterfall, Samuel: (B) 1825, (CO) Stone, (A) 25, (BP) Swizterland, (CMTS) 1870 Census
Waters, Eliza: (D) Oct. 8, 1867, (CO) Audrain, (C) Old Village Cemetery, (A) 53
Waters, S.: (B) 1805, (D) Oct. 7, 1867, (CO) Audrain, (C) Old Village Cemetery, (A) 62
Watkins, Eliza E.: (B) 1854, (CO) Stone, (A) 16, (BP) AR, (CMTS) 1870 Census
Watkins, Eliza J.: (B) 1851, (CO) Pulaski, (A) 9, (BP) MO, (CMTS) 1860 Census
Watkins, Julia: (B) 1845, (CO) Pulaski, (A) 15, (BP) MO, (CMTS) 1860 Census
Watkins, Martin: (B) 1839, (CO) Pulaski, (A) 21, (BP) MO, (CMTS)

1860 Census
Watkins, Mary E.: (B) 1856, (CO) Stone, (A) 14, (BP) AR, (CMTS) 1870 Census
Watkins, Mary L.: (B) 1830, (CO) Stone, (A) 40, (BP) AL, (CMTS) 1870 Census
Watkins, Nancy: (B) 1827, (CO) Stone, (A) 23, (BP) MO, (CMTS) 1870 Census
Watkins, Sarah E.: (B) 1852, (CO) Stone, (A) 18, (BP) TN, (CMTS) 1870 Census
Watkins, Silvey: (B) 1848, (CO) Pulaski, (A) 12, (BP) MO, (CMTS) 1860 Census
Watson, Elizabeth: (B) 1843, (CO) Pulaski, (A) 17, (BP) MO, (CMTS) 1860 Census
Watson, Melissa: (B) 1828, (CO) Stone, (A) 22, (BP) AR, (CMTS) 1870 Census
Watson, Richard: (B) 1823, (CO) Stone, (A) 27, (BP) KY, (CMTS) 1870 Census
Watson, Richard: (B) 1835, (CO) Pulaski, (A) 25, (BP) IL, (CMTS) 1860 Census
Watson, Thomas: (B) 1856, (CO) Pulaski, (A) 4, (BP) MO, (CMTS) 1860 Census
Watson, William T.: (B) 1849, (CO) Stone, (A) 1, (BP) MO, (CMTS) 1870 Census
Wayne, Turner: (B) Sep. 29, 1920, (D) Oct. 3, 1998, (NWS) *Joplin Globe*, Oct. 5, 1998, (BP) Hammon, OK, (SPOUSE) Mildred Jessie Blundell, (MD) Aug. 9, 1953, Ft. Smith, AR
Weatherspoon, Delia: (B) 1832, (CO) Stone, (A) 18, (BP) MO, (CMTS) 1870 Census
Weatherspoon, Wesley: (B) 1828, (CO) Stone, (A) 22, (BP) AR, (CMTS) 1870 Census
Weaver, Samuel: (B) 1829, (CO) Stone, (A) 41, (BP) AL, (CMTS) 1870 Census
Weaver, Sarah J.: (B) 1835, (CO) Stone, (A) 35, (BP) TN, (CMTS) 1870 Census
Webb, Thomas: (B) 1840, (CO) Pulaski, (A) 20, (BP) Ireland, (CMTS) 1860 Census
Weber, Albert: (D) May 5, 1888, (CO) Jefferson, (C) Old St. John's Catholic Cemetery, (A) 77Y 6M
Weber, Theresa: (D) Aug 24, 1893, (CO) Jefferson, (C) Old St. John's Catholic Cemetery, (A) 80Y
Webster, Elizure M.: (B) 1839, (CO) Stone, (A) 11, (BP) MO, (CMTS) 1870 Census
Webster, Sarah E.: (B) 1849, (CO) Stone, (A) 1, (BP) MO, (CMTS) 1870

Census

Webster, William D: (B) 1841, (CO) Stone, (A) 9, (BP) MO, (CMTS) 1870 Census

Webster, Willie P: (B) 1837, (CO) Stone, (A) 13, (BP) MO, (CMTS) 1870 Census

Weeks, John W.: (B) 1850, (CO) Pulaski, (A) 10, (BP) MO, (CMTS) 1860 Census

Weeks, Keziah: (B) 1830, (CO) Pulaski, (A) 30, (BP) MO, (CMTS) 1860 Census

Weeks, Shelby: (B) 1820, (CO) Pulaski, (A) 40, (BP) TN, (CMTS) 1860 Census

Weeks, Thomas H.: (B) 1852, (CO) Pulaski, (A) 8, (BP) MO, (CMTS) 1860 Census

Weil, James R.: (B) 1854, (CO) Stone, (A) 16, (BP) AR, (CMTS) 1870 Census

Weil, Mary Ann: (B) 1820, (CO) Stone, (A) 50, (BP) TN, (CMTS) 1870 Census

Weil, Samuel: (B) 1816, (CO) Stone, (A) 54, (BP) NC, (CMTS) 1870 Census

Weil, Samuel: (B) 1857, (CO) Stone, (A) 13, (BP) AR, (CMTS) 1870 Census

Weindel, Caroline Ann: (D) Dec. 3, 1929, (CO) St. Louis, (C) Calvary Cemetery

Weindel, Emelie: (D) Jan. 22, 1951, (CO) St. Louis, (C) Calvary Cemetery

Weindel, John A.: (B) 1852, (D) 1925, (CO) St. Louis, (C) Calvary Cemetery

Weindel, Valeria: (B) 1881, (D) 1919, (CO) St. Louis, (C) Calvary Cemetery

Weis, Joseph F.: (B) 1891, (D) 1918, (CO) St. Louis, (C) Calvary Cemetery

Weissmann, Mary: (B) 1908, (D) 1936, (CO) St. Louis, (C) Calvary Cemetery

Weissmann, Walter: (B) 1910, (D) 1988, (CO) St. Louis, (C) Calvary Cemetery

Welch, M.: (B) 1837, (CO) Pulaski, (A) 23, (BP) MO, (CMTS) 1860 Census

Wells, Betsy J.: (B) 1837, (CO) Stone, (A) 13, (BP) AL, (CMTS) 1870 Census

Wells, George W.: (B) 1834, (CO) Stone, (A) 16, (BP) AL, (CMTS) 1870 Census

Wells, Mary A.: (B) 1839, (CO) Stone, (A) 11, (BP) AL, (CMTS) 1870 Census

Wells, Miranda E.: (B) 1842, (CO) Stone, (A) 8, (BP) MO, (CMTS) 1870 Census

Welsh, Earl W.: (B) Aug. 23, 1911, (D) Sep. 25, 1986, (CO) Henry, (C) Knights of Pythias Cemetery, Deepwater, MO

Welsh, Emily L.: (B) 1856, (CO) Pulaski, (A) 4, (BP) MO, (CMTS) 1860 Census

Welsh, James: (B) 1840, (CO) Stone, (A) 30, (BP) MO, (CMTS) 1870 Census

Welsh, John: (B) 1823, (CO) Pulaski, (A) 37, (BP) TN, (CMTS) 1860 Census

Welsh, John: (B) 1833, (CO) Pulaski, (A) 27, (BP) Ireland, (CMTS) 1860 Census

Welsh, Lefa E.: (B) 1849, (CO) Pulaski, (A) 11, (BP) MO, (CMTS) 1860 Census

Welsh, Margaret: (B) 1829, (CO) Pulaski, (A) 31, (BP) KY, (CMTS) 1860 Census

Welsh, Mary: (B) 1848, (CO) Stone, (A) 22, (BP) MO, (CMTS) 1870 Census

Welsh, Mary H.: (B) 1851, (CO) Pulaski, (A) 9, (BP) Mo, (CMTS) 1860 Census

Weltin,: (D) Feb. 2, 1908, (CO) St. Louis, (C) Calvary Cemetery

Wenger, John: (B) 1820, (D) 1870, (CO) Adair, (A) 50, (CMTS) 1870 Mortality Schedule

West, Ayola: (B) 1930, (CO) Oregon, (C) Falling Springs Cemetery

West, Benjamin: (B) 1827, (CO) Pulaski, (A) 33, (BP) TN, (CMTS) 1860 Census

West, Lucinda: (B) 1840, (CO) Pulaski, (A) 20, (BP) MO, (CMTS) 1860 Census

West, Nancy Williams: (D) Nov. 23, 1848, (CO) Audrain, (C) Old Village Cemetery, (A) 78

Wethers, Charles: (B) 1836, (CO) Pulaski, (A) 24, (BP) KY, (CMTS) 1860 Census

Wethers, Delilah: (B) 1836, (CO) Pulaski, (A) 24, (BP) KY, (CMTS) 1860 Census

Wetmore, Francis: (B) 1838, (CO) Pulaski, (A) 22, (BP) NY, (CMTS) 1860 Census

Wheeler, Cage: (B) 1844, (CO) Stone, (A) 6, (BP) MO, (CMTS) 1870 Census

Wheeler, Harvey: (B) 1839, (CO) Stone, (A) 11, (BP) IL, (CMTS) 1870 Census

Wheeler, John: (B) 1833, (CO) Stone, (A) 17, (BP) IL, (CMTS) 1870 Census

Wheeler, Lucinda: (B) 1848, (CO) Stone, (A) 2, (BP) IL, (CMTS) 1870

Census
Wheeler, Margaretta: (B) 1825, (CO) Stone, (A) 25, (BP) MO, (CMTS) 1870 Census
Wheeler, Mary F: (B) 1847, (CO) Stone, (A) 3, (BP) MO, (CMTS) 1870 Census
Wheeler, Nancy: (B) 1845, (CO) Stone, (A) 5, (BP) MO, (CMTS) 1870 Census
Wheeler, Rubin: (B) 1828, (CO) Stone, (A) 22, (BP) IL, (CMTS) 1870 Census
Wheeler, Sarah: (B) 1795, (CO) Pulaski, (A) 65, (BP) TN, (CMTS) 1860 Census
Wheeler, Sarah: (B) 1841, (CO) Stone, (A) 9, (BP) IL, (CMTS) 1870 Census
Wheeler, Willard: (B) 1836, (CO) Stone, (A) 14, (BP) IL, (CMTS) 1870 Census
Whelan, Elizabeth M.: (D) Mar. 12, 1971, (CO) St. Louis, (C) Calvary Cemetery
Whelan, Mary E.: (D) Aug. 30, 1932, (CO) St. Louis, (C) Calvary Cemetery
Whelan, Thomas: (D) Feb. 9, 1924, (CO) St. Louis, (C) Calvary Cemetery
Wherry, Charlotte: (B) 1843, (CO) Pulaski, (A) 17, (BP) MO, (CMTS) 1860 Census
Wherry, David: (B) 1832, (CO) Pulaski, (A) 28, (BP) TN, (CMTS) 1860 Census
White, Amanda: (B) 1840, (CO) Stone, (A) 10, (BP) MO, (CMTS) 1870 Census
White, Annie W.: (B) 1838, (CO) Pulaski, (A) 22, (BP) TN, (CMTS) 1860 Census
White, Eliza: (B) 1842, (CO) Stone, (A) 8, (BP) MO, (CMTS) 1870 Census
White, Elizabeth: (B) 1822, (CO) Stone, (A) 48, (BP) TN, (CMTS) 1870 Census
White, Florence E.: (D) Aug. 26, 1945, (CO) St. Louis, (C) Calvary Cemetery
White, Frances: (B) 1832, (CO) Stone, (A) 18, (BP) MO, (CMTS) 1870 Census
White, Hannah: (B) 1838, (CO) Stone, (A) 12, (BP) MO, (CMTS) 1870 Census
White, Henry: (B) 1826, (D) 1870, (CO) Adair, (A) 44, (CMTS) 1870 Mortality Schedule
White, John: (B) 1830, (CO) Pulaski, (A) 30, (BP) Ireland, (CMTS) 1860 Census
White, John B.: (B) 1850, (D) 1934, (CO) Henry, (C) Knights of Pythias

Cemetery, Deepwater, MO
White, John James: (B) May 26, 1862, (D) Jun. 24, 1863, (CO) St. Louis, (C) Calvary Cemetery
White, John C.: (B) 1851, (CO) Stone, (A) 19, (BP) TN, (CMTS) 1870 Census
White, Jonathan: (B) 1815, (CO) Stone, (A) 55, (BP) TN, (CMTS) 1870 Census
White, Louisa: (B) 1850, (CO) Stone, (A) 20, (BP) TN, (CMTS) 1870 Census
White, Lucinda: (B) 1847, (CO) Stone, (A) 23, (BP) TN, (CMTS) 1870 Census
White, Margaret: (B) 1853, (CO) Stone, (A) 17, (BP) MO, (CMTS) 1870 Census
White, Mary: (B) 1840, (CO) Pulaski, (A) 20, (BP) NC, (CMTS) 1860 Census
White, Mary Jane: (B) 1855, (CO) Stone, (A) 15, (BP) MO, (CMTS) 1870 Census
White, Minerva: (B) 1846, (CO) Pulaski, (A) 14, (BP) MO, (CMTS) 1860 Census
White, Orlena: (B) 1850, (D) 1932, (CO) Henry, (C) Knights of Pythias Cemetery, Deepwater, MO
White, Robert: (B) 1847, (CO) Stone, (A) 23, (BP) TN, (CMTS) 1870 Census
White, Samuel: (B) 1837, (CO) Pulaski, (A) 23, (BP) TN, (CMTS) 1860 Census
White, Sarah P: (B) 1857, (CO) Stone, (A) 13, (BP) MO, (CMTS) 1870 Census
White, William W.: (B) 1845, (CO) Stone, (A) 25, (BP) TN, (CMTS) 1870 Census
Whitelaw, Hannah: (D) 1954, (CO) St. Louis, (C) Calvary Cemetery
Whitelaw, Mary Jane: (D) 1956, (CO) St. Louis, (C) Calvary Cemetery
Whitelaw, Thomas David: (D) 1933, (CO) St. Louis, (C) Calvary Cemetery
Whitelaw, Thomas Reese: (D) Aug. 15, 1947, (CO) St. Louis, (C) Calvary Cemetery
Whitmier, Catharine: (B) 1827, (CO) Pulaski, (A) 33, (BP) MO, (CMTS) 1860 Census
Whitmier, Isaac: (B) 1849, (CO) Pulaski, (A) 11, (BP) MO, (CMTS) 1860 Census
Whitmier, Jackson: (B) 1845, (CO) Pulaski, (A) 15, (BP) MO, (CMTS) 1860 Census
Whitmier, Mary: (B) 1855, (CO) Pulaski, (A) 5, (BP) MO, (CMTS) 1860 Census

Whitmier, Sarah A.: (B) 1853, (CO) Pulaski, (A) 7, (BP) MO, (CMTS) 1860 Census
Whitmier, Theodenc: (B) 1857, (CO) Pulaski, (A) 3, (BP) MO, (CMTS) 1860 Census
Whitney, Anna L.: (B) 10-May-11, (D) Jul. 9, 1984, (CO) Pettis, (C) Black Baptist Cemetery, Prairie Township
Whitney, Charles W.: (B) Nov. 7, 1910, (D) Nov. 3, 1973, (CO) Pettis, (C) Black Baptist Cemetery, Prairie Township
Whittington, Edward: (B) Apr. 8, 1837, (D) Jun. 24, 1897, (CO) Barry, (C) Old Corsicana Cemetery
Wight, John E.: (B) Nov. 18, 1909, (CO) Clay,
Wilcox, Polly: (B) 1834, (CO) Stone, (A) 16, (BP) MO, (CMTS) 1870 Census
Wilcox, William: (B) 1835, (CO) Pulaski, (A) 25, (BP) MO, (CMTS) 1860 Census
Wilhelm, Carl L.: (B) 1898, (D) 1958, (CO) St. Louis, (C) Calvary Cemetery
Wilhelm, Lorraine: (B) 1904, (D) 1966, (CO) St. Louis, (C) Calvary Cemetery
Wilhelms, Elizabeth: (B) 1850, (CO) Stone, (A) 20, (BP) AL, (CMTS) 1870 Census
Wilhelms, Mary: (B) 1830, (CO) Stone, (A) 40, (BP) AL, (CMTS) 1870 Census
Wilhight, Holloway: (B) 1852, (CO) Stone, (A) 18, (BP) TN, (CMTS) 1870 Census
Wilke, Adolph: (B) 1865, (D) 1942, (CO) St. Louis, (C) Calvary Cemetery
Wilke, Josephine: (B) 1873, (D) 1949, (CO) St. Louis, (C) Calvary Cemetery
Wilkinson, Catharine: (B) 1822, (CO) Pulaski, (A) 38, (BP) KY, (CMTS) 1860 Census
Wilkinson, Catharine A.: (B) 1838, (CO) Pulaski, (A) 22, (BP) KY, (CMTS) 1860 Census
Wilkinson, Hue: (B) 1844, (CO) Pulaski, (A) 16, (BP) KY, (CMTS) 1860 Census
Wilkinson, Marvelle: (B) 1855, (CO) Pulaski, (A) 5, (BP) IL, (CMTS) 1860 Census
Wilkinson, Nancy M.: (B) 1842, (CO) Pulaski, (A) 18, (BP) KY, (CMTS) 1860 Census
Wilkinson, William: (B) 1847, (CO) Pulaski, (A) 13, (BP) IL, (CMTS) 1860 Census
Williams, Albert G.: (B) 1845, (CO) Pulaski, (A) 15, (BP) MO, (CMTS) 1860 Census
Williams, Caleb: (B) 1848, (CO) Pulaski, (A) 12, (BP) KY, (CMTS)

1860 Census
Williams, Caroline: (B) 1836, (CO) Pulaski, (A) 24, (BP) TN, (CMTS) 1860 Census
Williams, Clara H.: (D) Dec., 1931, (CO) St. Louis, (C) Calvary Cemetery
Williams, Comfort: (B) 1826, (CO) Pulaski, (A) 34, (BP) MO, (CMTS) 1860 Census
Williams, Cynthia: (B) 1849, (CO) Stone, (A) 21, (BP) AR, (CMTS) 1870 Census
Williams, David: (B) 1842, (CO) Pulaski, (A) 18, (BP) TN, (CMTS) 1860 Census
Williams, David B.: (B) Aug. 25, 1797, (D) Feb. 28, 1875, (CO) Audrain, (C) Old Village Cemetery
Williams, Elizabeth: (B) 1841, (CO) Pulaski, (A) 19, (BP) KY, (CMTS) 1860 Census
Williams, George: (B) 1844, (CO) Pulaski, (A) 16, (BP) TN, (CMTS) 1860 Census
Williams, Henry: (B) 1834, (CO) Stone, (A) 16, (BP) MO, (CMTS) 1870 Census
Williams, Irvena: (B) 1848, (CO) Stone, (A) 2, (BP) MO, (CMTS) 1870 Census
Williams, Isaac: (B) 1853, (CO) Pulaski, (A) 7, (BP) KY, (CMTS) 1860 Census
Williams, James: (B) 1828, (CO) Stone, (A) 42, (BP) TN, (CMTS) 1870 Census
Williams, Jane Amanda: (B) 1841, (CO) Stone, (A) 9, (BP) MO, (CMTS) 1870 Census
Williams, John: (B) 1832, (CO) Pulaski, (A) 28, (BP) MO, (CMTS) 1860 Census
Williams, John: (B) 1843, (CO) Stone, (A) 27, (BP) KY, (CMTS) 1870 Census
Williams, John: (B) 1853, (CO) Pulaski, (A) 7, (BP) KY, (CMTS) 1860 Census
Williams, John M.: (B) 1815, (CO) Stone, (A) 35, (BP) TN, (CMTS) 1870 Census
Williams, Joseph C: (B) 1855, (CO) Stone, (A) 15, (BP) MO, (CMTS) 1870 Census
Williams, Joshua: (B) 1846, (CO) Pulaski, (A) 14, (BP) KY, (CMTS) 1860 Census
Williams, Lewis: (B) 1844, (CO) Pulaski, (A) 16, (BP) KY, (CMTS) 1860 Census
Williams, Lizzie: (B) 1853, (CO) Stone, (A) 17, (BP) MO, (CMTS) 1870 Census

Williams, Lotta: (B) 1834, (CO) Stone, (A) 36, (BP) MO, (CMTS) 1870 Census
Williams, Mack L.: (B) 1826, (CO) Stone, (A) 24, (BP) MO, (CMTS) 1870 Census
Williams, Malinda: (B) 1820, (CO) Pulaski, (A) 40, (BP) KY, (CMTS) 1860 Census
Williams, Margarette: (B) 1846, (CO) Stone, (A) 24, (BP) TN, (CMTS) 1870 Census
Williams, Mary: (B) 1835, (CO) Stone, (A) 15, (BP) MO, (CMTS) 1870 Census
Williams, Mary: (B) 1851, (CO) Pulaski, (A) 9, (BP) KY, (CMTS) 1860 Census
Williams, Mary: (B) Feb. 8, 1798, (D) Jan. 26, 1881, (CO) Audrain, (C) Old Village Cemetery
Williams, Mary J.: (B) 1831, (CO) Stone, (A) 39, (BP) TN, (CMTS) 1870 Census
Williams, Meredith: (B) 1822, (CO) Pulaski, (A) 38, (BP) SC, (CMTS) 1860 Census
Williams, Mrs. Mary: (D) Feb., 19, 1877, (CO) St. Louis, (C) Calvary Cemetery, (A) 25
Williams, Nancy: (B) 1848, (CO) Pulaski, (A) 12, (BP) TN, (CMTS) 1860 Census
Williams, Nancy: (B) 1854, (CO) Pulaski, (A) 6, (BP) MO, (CMTS) 1860 Census
Williams, Nathan: (B) 1838, (CO) Stone, (A) 32, (BP) IL, (CMTS) 1870 Census
Williams, Olive M.: (B) 1839, (CO) Pulaski, (A) 21, (BP) KY, (CMTS) 1860 Census
Williams, Oliver: (B) 1815, (CO) Pulaski, (A) 45, (BP) TN, (CMTS) 1860 Census
Williams, Owen: (B) 1829, (CO) Stone, (A) 41, (BP) TN, (CMTS) 1870 Census
Williams, Sarah E.: (B) 1849, (CO) Pulaski, (A) 11, (BP) MO, (CMTS) 1860 Census
Williams, Sina: (B) 1845, (CO) Stone, (A) 25, (BP) MO, (CMTS) 1870 Census
Williams, Smith: (B) 1843, (CO) Pulaski, (A) 17, (BP) MO, (CMTS) 1860 Census
Williams, Sophia E.: (B) 1829, (CO) Stone, (A) 21, (BP) AR, (CMTS) 1870 Census
Williams, Thomas M.: (B) 1850, (CO) Pulaski, (A) 10, (BP) MO, (CMTS) 1860 Census
Williams, Thomas B.: (B) 1834, (CO) Stone, (A) 36, (BP) IL, (CMTS)

1870 Census

Williams, William: (B) 1831, (CO) Pulaski, (A) 29, (BP) KY, (CMTS) 1860 Census

Willis, Clifton Morgan: (B) Aug. 31, 1897, (D) Jul. 28, 1964, (CO) Carroll (NWS) *Carrollton Daily Democrat*, Jul. 28, 1964, (PRTS) Cullun Willis and Minnie Magee, (SPOUSE) Elsie Hoffman, (MD) Sep. 27, 1919, (CMTS) Ray Willis, son; Sidney Willis, son; Maj. Clyde Willis (Airforce), son; Mrs. Lucile Butler sister; ; Mrs. Glen Dell Cary of Independence, two sisters, Mrs. Lucille Butler and Mrs. Ruby Dunlap of Kansas City, one brother, Emmett Willis of Kansas City, (C) Carroll Memory Gardens, (FUN) Gibson Funeral Home

Wills, James: (B) 1837, (CO) Stone, (A) 33, (BP) TN, (CMTS) 1870 Census

Wills, Permelia: (B) 1850, (CO) Stone, (A) 20, (BP) MO, (CMTS) 1870 Census

Wiloby, Elizabeth: (B) 1855, (CO) Stone, (A) 15, (BP) MO, (CMTS) 1870 Census

Wilson, Dan: (B) 1856, (CO) Pulaski, (A) 4, (BP) MO, (CMTS) 1860 Census

Wilson, David: (B) 1847, (CO) Stone, (A) 23, (BP) TN, (CMTS) 1870 Census

Wilson, Eliza J.: (B) 1854, (CO) Stone, (A) 16, (BP) TN, (CMTS) 1870 Census

Wilson, Elizabeth: (B) 1831, (CO) Stone, (A) 39, (BP) TN, (CMTS) 1870 Census

Wilson, Elizabeth: (B) 1833, (CO) Stone, (A) 17, (BP) AL, (CMTS) 1870 Census

Wilson, Elizabeth: (B) 1837, (CO) Stone, (A) 13, (BP) MO, (CMTS) 1870 Census

Wilson, Emily: (B) 1854, (CO) Stone, (A) 16, (BP) MO, (CMTS) 1870 Census

Wilson, George W.: (B) 1842, (CO) Stone, (A) 8, (BP) MO, (CMTS) 1870 Census

Wilson, Hedgeman: (B) Jul. 28, 1802, (D) May 10, 1869, (CO) Ralls, (C) Salt River Cemetery

Wilson, James: (B) 1837, (CO) Pulaski, (A) 23, (BP) MO, (CMTS) 1860 Census

Wilson, James L.: (B) 1849, (CO) Stone, (A) 21, (BP) MO, (CMTS) 1870 Census

Wilson, John: (B) 1834, (CO) Pulaski, (A) 26, (BP) TN, (CMTS) 1860 Census

Wilson, John Edward: (B) Sep. 5, 1874, (D) Jun. 16, 1940, (CO) Livingston

Wilson, John Madison: (B) Aug. 4, 1842, (CO) Clay, (PRTS) Richard Wilson and Pacey Noland
Wilson, John W.: (B) 1845, (CO) Stone, (A) 25, (BP) TN, (CMTS) 1870 Census
Wilson, Joseph L.: (B) 1825, (CO) Stone, (A) 45, (BP) TN, (CMTS) 1870 Census
Wilson, Leroy: (B) 1845, (CO) Stone, (A) 5, (BP) MO, (CMTS) 1870 Census
Wilson, Leroy: (B) 1850, (CO) Stone, (A) 20, (BP) IN, (CMTS) 1870 Census
Wilson, Margaret: (B) 1855, (CO) Pulaski, (A) 5, (BP) MO, (CMTS) 1860 Census
Wilson, Margaret J.: (B) 1838, (CO) Pulaski, (A) 22, (BP) TN, (CMTS) 1860 Census
Wilson, Margarett: (B) 1850, (CO) Stone, (A) 20, (BP) TN, (CMTS) 1870 Census
Wilson, Marion: (B) 1847, (CO) Pulaski, (A) 13, (BP) MO, (CMTS) 1860 Census
Wilson, Martha J.: (B) 1816, (CO) Stone, (A) 34, (BP) IN, (CMTS) 1870 Census
Wilson, Mary: (B) 1834, (CO) Pulaski, (A) 26, (BP) TN, (CMTS) 1860 Census
Wilson, Mary E.: (B) 1847, (CO) Stone, (A) 3, (BP) MO, (CMTS) 1870 Census
Wilson, Mary J.: (B) 1842, (CO) Pulaski, (A) 18, (BP) IL, (CMTS) 1860 Census
Wilson, Melissa: (B) 1851, (CO) Stone, (A) 19, (BP) MO, (CMTS) 1870 Census
Wilson, Nancy: (B) 1834, (CO) Pulaski, (A) 26, (BP) MO, (CMTS) 1860 Census
Wilson, Nancy: (B) 1852, (CO) Stone, (A) 18, (BP) MO, (CMTS) 1870 Census
Wilson, Otis K.: (B) Dec. 25, 1898, (D) Oct. 16, 1961, (CO) Henry, (C) Knights of Pythias Cemetery, Deepwater, MO
Wilson, Paul Eugene: (B) Feb. 20, 1918, (D) Feb. 20, 1918, (CO) Gentry, (C) High Ridge Cemetery, Stanberry, MO.
Wilson, Rousora: (B) 1851, (CO) Stone, (A) 19, (BP) TN, (CMTS) 1870 Census
Wilson, Ruthy: (B) 1846, (CO) Stone, (A) 24, (BP) TN, (CMTS) 1870 Census
Wilson, Sarah: (B) 1840, (CO) Pulaski, (A) 20, (BP) MO, (CMTS) 1860 Census
Wilson, Silvester: (B) 1836, (CO) Stone, (A) 14, (BP) MO, (CMTS) 1870

Census

Wilson, Stephen A.: (B) 1832, (CO) Stone, (A) 18, (BP) IN, (CMTS) 1870 Census

Wilson, Thomas: (B) 1839, (CO) Pulaski, (A) 21, (BP) ., (CMTS) 1860 Census

Wilson, Thomas: (B) 1848, (CO) Stone, (A) 22, (BP) TN, (CMTS) 1870 Census

Wilson, William: (B) 1822, (CO) Pulaski, (A) 38, (BP) TN, (CMTS) 1860 Census

Wilson, Harve Earl: (B) 1886, (D) 1851, (CO) Gentry, (C) High Ridge Cemetery, Stanberry, MO.

Winchester, Mary: (B) 1842, (CO) Pulaski, (A) 18, (BP) TN, (CMTS) 1860 Census

Wingate, Virgil Cyrus: (B) Feb. 2, 1888, (D) Mar. 17, 1984, (CO) Henry, (C) Knights of Pythias Cemetery, Deepwater, MO

Winn, Charles Lee: (B) Jul. 20, 1921, (D) Oct. 22, 1949, (CO) Henry, (C) Knights of Pythias Cemetery, Deepwater, MO

Wise, Effie: (B) 1839, (CO) Stone, (A) 31, (BP) OH, (CMTS) 1870 Census

Wise, Joshua M.: (B) 1837, (CO) Stone, (A) 33, (BP) OH, (CMTS) 1870 Census

Witt, Daniel: (B) 1849, (CO) Pulaski, (A) 11, (BP) KY, (CMTS) 1860 Census

Witt, Edmund: (B) 1851, (CO) Pulaski, (A) 9, (BP) KY, (CMTS) 1860 Census

Witt, Janes: (B) 1846, (CO) Pulaski, (A) 14, (BP) KY, (CMTS) 1860 Census

Witt, John V.: (B) 1847, (CO) Pulaski, (A) 13, (BP) KY, (CMTS) 1860 Census

Witt, Nancy: (B) 1820, (CO) Pulaski, (A) 40, (BP) KY, (CMTS) 1860 Census

Wittig, William C.: (B) Dec. 10, 1889, (D) Jul. 2, 1970, (CO) Henry, (C) Knights of Pythias Cemetery, Deepwater, MO

Wolf, Edda: (B) 1830, (CO) Stone, (A) 40, (BP) MO, (CMTS) 1870 Census

Wolf, Fred C.: (B) 1894, (D) 1968, (CO) St. Louis, (C) Calvary Cemetery

Wolf, Mary: (B) 1830, (CO) Stone, (A) 40, (BP) MO, (CMTS) 1870 Census

Wood, Andrew J.: (B) Mar. 31, 1833, (D) Jun. 13, 1857, (CO) Audrain, (C) Old Village Cemetery

Wood, Charles A.: (B) 1848, (CO) Stone, (A) 2, (BP) MO, (CMTS) 1870 Census

Wood, Eliza E.: (B) 1858, (CO) Pulaski, (A) 2, (BP) MO, (CMTS) 1860 Census
Wood, Georgergia Amelia: (B) Sep. 18, 1861, (D) Dec. 28, 1927, (CO) Johnson, (C) Pemberton Cemetery
Wood, James C.: (B) 1856, (CO) Pulaski, (A) 4, (BP) MO, (CMTS) 1860 Census
Wood, John: (B) 1835, (CO) Stone, (A) 15, (BP) MO, (CMTS) 1870 Census
Wood, Lucinda: (B) 1822, (CO) Stone, (A) 28, (BP) MO, (CMTS) 1870 Census
Wood, Martha A.: (B) 1832, (CO) Pulaski, (A) 28, (BP) MO, (CMTS) 1860 Census
Wood, Martha J.: (B) 1848, (CO) Stone, (A) 2, (BP) MO, (CMTS) 1870 Census
Wood, Mary E.: (B) 1846, (CO) Stone, (A) 4, (BP) MO, (CMTS) 1870 Census
Wood, Mary H.: (B) 1829, (CO) Stone, (A) 21, (BP) MO, (CMTS) 1870 Census
Wood, Nelson: (B) 1823, (CO) Pulaski, (A) 37, (BP) NC, (CMTS) 1860 Census
Wood, William: (B) 1831, (CO) Stone, (A) 19, (BP) MO, (CMTS) 1870 Census
Wood, William P: (B) 1825, (CO) Stone, (A) 25, (BP) MO, (CMTS) 1870 Census
Woodard, Catherine: (B) 1856, (D) 1945, (CO) Henry, (C) Knights of Pythias Cemetery, Deepwater, MO
Woodard, David D.: (B) 1851, (D) 1945, (CO) Henry, (C) Knights of Pythias Cemetery, Deepwater, MO
Woodard, Sr., Leon C.: (B) Aug. 9, 1897, (D) Dec. 2, 1982, (CO) Henry, (C) Knights of Pythias Cemetery, Deepwater, MO
Woodcock, Cecil Arnold: (D) Aug. 19, 2000, (CO) Cole, (NWS) *Jefferson City, Missouri News-Tribune*, Aug. 22, 2000, (RES) Edwards
Woods, Anna: (B) 1848, (D) 1924, (CO) Henry, (C) Knights of Pythias Cemetery, Deepwater, MO
Woods, Caroll: (B) 1837, (CO) Pulaski, (A) 23, (BP) TN, (CMTS) 1860 Census
Woods, Harriet J.: (B) 1837, (CO) Pulaski, (A) 23, (BP) MO, (CMTS) 1860 Census
Woods, Jeremiah: (B) 1858, (D) 1914, (CO) Henry, (C) Knights of Pythias Cemetery, Deepwater, MO
Woods, Jesse M.: (B) 1844, (CO) Pulaski, (A) 16, (BP) MO, (CMTS) 1860 Census
Woods, John: (B) 1834, (CO) Stone, (A) 16, (BP) AR, (CMTS) 1870

Census
Woods, Louisa: (B) 1854, (CO) Pulaski, (A) 6, (BP) MO, (CMTS) 1860 Census
Woods, Margaret: (B) 1818, (CO) Pulaski, (A) 42, (BP) TN, (CMTS) 1860 Census
Woods, Martha: (B) 1836, (CO) Pulaski, (A) 24, (BP) IL, (CMTS) 1860 Census
Woods, Riley: (B) 1831, (CO) Pulaski, (A) 29, (BP) MO, (CMTS) 1860 Census
Woods, Samuel: (B) 1852, (CO) Pulaski, (A) 8, (BP) MO, (CMTS) 1860 Census
Woods, Sarah: (B) 1842, (CO) Pulaski, (A) 18, (BP) TN, (CMTS) 1860 Census
Woods, Thomas A.: (B) 1841, (CO) Pulaski, (A) 19, (BP) MO, (CMTS) 1860 Census
Woods, William T.: (B) 1837, (CO) Pulaski, (A) 23, (BP) MO, (CMTS) 1860 Census
Woodworth, John C.: (B) 1873, (D) 1929, (CO) St. Louis, (C) Calvary Cemetery
Woody, Angie: (B) 1839, (CO) Stone, (A) 11, (BP) MO, (CMTS) 1870 Census
Woody, Charity A.: (B) 1834, (CO) Pulaski, (A) 26, (BP) MO, (CMTS) 1860 Census
Woody, Jameson: (B) 1840, (CO) Pulaski, (A) 20, (BP) MO, (CMTS) 1860 Census
Woody, Louisa: (B) 1846, (CO) Stone, (A) 24, (BP) MO, (CMTS) 1870 Census
Woody, Louisa: (B) 1852, (CO) Pulaski, (A) 8, (BP) MO, (CMTS) 1860 Census
Woody, Lydia J.: (B) 1851, (CO) Stone, (A) 19, (BP) MO, (CMTS) 1870 Census
Woody, Margaret: (B) 1845, (CO) Pulaski, (A) 15, (BP) MO, (CMTS) 1860 Census
Woody, Marion: (B) 1833, (CO) Pulaski, (A) 27, (BP) KY, (CMTS) 1860 Census
Woody, Mary: (B) 1833, (CO) Stone, (A) 17, (BP) MO, (CMTS) 1870 Census
Woody, Rebecca A.: (B) 1854, (CO) Pulaski, (A) 6, (BP) MO, (CMTS) 1860 Census
Woody, Robert: (B) 1838, (CO) Pulaski, (A) 22, (BP) MO, (CMTS) 1860 Census
Woody, Samuel M.: (B) 1856, (CO) Stone, (A) 14, (BP) MO, (CMTS) 1870

Census

Woody, Sarah: (B) 1837, (CO) Stone, (A) 13, (BP) MO, (CMTS) 1870 Census

Woody, Sarah E.: (B) 1857, (CO) Pulaski, (A) 3, (BP) MO, (CMTS) 1860 Census

Woolf, Robert: (D) Jan. 18, 1999, (CO), (DP) Lebanon, MO, (RES) Hartville, MO, (SPOUSE) Kathryn Davitt, (PRTS) S. Dale Woolf and Harriet Housel, (NWS) *Allentown, Pennsylvania Morning Call*, Jan. 21, 1999

Woolly, Margaret: (B) 1832, (CO) Stone, (A) 18, (BP) MO, (CMTS) 1870 Census

Worthen, Alvin: (B) 1850, (CO) Pulaski, (A) 10, (BP) MO, (CMTS) 1860 Census

Worthen, Catharine: (B) 1849, (CO) Pulaski, (A) 11, (BP) MO, (CMTS) 1860 Census

Worthen, Elizabeth: (B) 1847, (CO) Pulaski, (A) 13, (BP) MO, (CMTS) 1860 Census

Worthen, James: (B) 1840, (CO) Pulaski, (A) 20, (BP) MO, (CMTS) 1860 Census

Worthen, Peasant: (B) 1839, (CO) Pulaski, (A) 21, (BP) TN, (CMTS) 1860 Census

Worthen, Phebe: (B) 1843, (CO) Pulaski, (A) 17, (BP) MO, (CMTS) 1860 Census

Worthen, Sarah: (B) 1845, (CO) Pulaski, (A) 15, (BP) MO, (CMTS) 1860 Census

Worthig, George: (B) Sep. 9, 1915, (D) 1987, (CO) St. Louis, Mo, (DP) Eureka, MO.

Worthing, Alma: (B) Aug, 3, 1896, (D) Dec., 1984, (CO) Jackson, (DP) Kansas City, MO.

Worthing, Elizabeth: (B) 1826, (CO) Pulaski, (A) 34, (BP) TN, (CMTS) 1860 Census

Worthing, Garrott: (B) 1851, (CO) Pulaski, (A) 9, (BP) MO, (CMTS) 1860 Census

Worthing, Hampton: (B) 1827, (CO) Pulaski, (A) 33, (BP) TN, (CMTS) 1860 Census

Worthing, Mary: (B) 1856, (CO) Pulaski, (A) 4, (BP) MO, (CMTS) 1860 Census

Worthing, Matilda: (B) 1847, (CO) Pulaski, (A) 13, (BP) TN, (CMTS) 1860 Census

Worthing, Nancy: (B) 1849, (CO) Pulaski, (A) 11, (BP) MO, (CMTS) 1860 Census

Worthing, Sarah E.: (B) 1855, (CO) Pulaski, (A) 5, (BP) MO, (CMTS) 1860 Census

Worthing, Smith B.: (B) 1843, (CO) Pulaski, (A) 17, (BP) TN, (CMTS) 1860 Census
Wrape, Emma: (B) 1858, (D) 1905, (CO) St. Louis, (C) Calvary Cemetery
Wrape, Henry: (B) 1851, (D) 1923, (CO) St. Louis, (C) Calvary Cemetery
Wren, Cordelia A.: (B) 1855, (CO) Stone, (A) 15, (BP) MS, (CMTS) 1870 Census
Wright, Andrew M.: (B) 1855, (CO) Pulaski, (A) 5, (BP) MO, (CMTS) 1860 Census
Wright, Catherine: (B) 1842, (CO) Stone, (A) 28, (BP) TN, (CMTS) 1870 Census
Wright, Frances: (B) 1832, (CO) Pulaski, (A) 28, (BP) VA, (CMTS) 1860 Census
Wright, George: (B) 1840, (CO) Stone, (A) 30, (BP) PA, (CMTS) 1870 Census
Wright, Green Lee: (B) Jan. 31, 1853, (D) Mar. 15, 1941, (CO) Cole,
Wright, Henry W.: (B) 1851, (CO) Pulaski, (A) 9, (BP) MO, (CMTS) 1860 Census
Wright, Isabella: (B) 1831, (CO) Pulaski, (A) 29, (BP) MO, (CMTS) 1860 Census
Wright, James E.: (B) 1847, (CO) Pulaski, (A) 13, (BP) MO, (CMTS) 1860 Census
Wright, James L.: (B) Jan. 6, 1818, (CO) Miller, (DP) Tuscumbia, MO.
Wright, James P.: (B) Nov. 14, 1850, (D) Jun. 19, 1953, (CO) Cole,
Wright, John F.: (B) 1843, (CO) Pulaski, (A) 17, (BP) MO, (CMTS) 1860 Census
Wright, John Monroe: (B) Oct. 7, 1847, (CO) Johnson, (PRTS) John A. Wright
Wright, John W.: (B) Mar. 23, 1863, (D) Feb. 9, 1939, (CO) Miller,
Wright, Joseph: (B) 1831, (CO) Stone, (A) 39, (BP) TN, (CMTS) 1870 Census
Wright, Louisa V.: (B) 1851, (CO) Pulaski, (A) 9, (BP) VA, (CMTS) 1860 Census
Wright, Mary: (B) 1825, (CO) Pulaski, (A) 35, (BP) IL, (CMTS) 1860 Census
Wright, Mary J.: (B) 1840, (CO) Stone, (A) 30, (BP) PA, (CMTS) 1870 Census
Wright, Nancy Elizabeth: (B) Feb. 2, 1875, (CO) Warren,
Wright, Rachel M.: (B) 1852, (CO) Stone, (A) 18, (BP) MO, (CMTS) 1870 Census
Wright, Richard N.: (B) 1853, (CO) Pulaski, (A) 7, (BP) MO, (CMTS) 1860 Census

Wright, Robert: (B) 1821, (CO) Stone, (A) 49, (BP) TN, (CMTS) 1870 Census
Wright, Robert B.: (B) 1849, (CO) Pulaski, (A) 11, (BP) MO, (CMTS) 1860 Census
Wright, Warren: (B) 1820, (CO) Pulaski, (A) 40, (BP) KY, (CMTS) 1860 Census
Wright, William J.: (B) 1845, (CO) Pulaski, (A) 15, (BP) MO, (CMTS) 1860 Census
Wright, William R.: (B) 1827, (CO) Pulaski, (A) 33, (BP) VA, (CMTS) 1860 Census
Wrinkles, Catharine: (B) 1828, (CO) Pulaski, (A) 32, (BP) TN, (CMTS) 1860 Census
Wrinkles, Charles: (B) 1838, (CO) Pulaski, (A) 22, (BP) IL, (CMTS) 1860 Census
Wrinkles, Clifford: (B) Jul. 28, 1923, (CO) Wright, (DP) Norwood, MO.
Wrinkles, Elbert: (B) 1856, (CO) Pulaski, (A) 4, (BP) TX, (CMTS) 1860 Census
Wrinkles, Elias: (B) 1829, (CO) Pulaski, (A) 31, (BP) TN, (CMTS) 1860 Census
Wrinkles, Elias J.: (B) 1840, (CO) Pulaski, (A) 20, (BP) TN, (CMTS) 1860 Census
Wrinkles, Ernie: (B) Jan. 20, 1912, (D) Sep. 7, 1996, (CO) Greene, (DP) Springfield, MO.
Wrinkles, George: (B) 1851, (CO) Pulaski, (A) 9, (BP) MO, (CMTS) 1860 Census
Wrinkles, James: (B) 1835, (CO) Pulaski, (A) 25, (BP) IL, (CMTS) 1860 Census
Wrinkles, John: (B) 1844, (CO) Pulaski, (A) 16, (BP) AR, (CMTS) 1860 Census
Wrinkles, John F.: (B) 1855, (CO) Pulaski, (A) 5, (BP) MO, (CMTS) 1860 Census
Wrinkles, Kathleen: (B) Jun. 8, 1923, (D) Apr. 24, 1987, (CO) Greene, (DP) Springfield, MO.
Wrinkles, Lura E.: (B) 1850, (CO) Pulaski, (A) 10, (BP) MO, (CMTS) 1860 Census
Wrinkles, Margaret J.: (B) 1855, (CO) Pulaski, (A) 5, (BP) MO, (CMTS) 1860 Census
Wrinkles, Martha: (B) 1842, (CO) Pulaski, (A) 18, (BP) NC, (CMTS) 1860 Census
Wrinkles, Mary: (B) 1847, (CO) Pulaski, (A) 13, (BP) AR, (CMTS) 1860 Census
Wrinkles, Mary M.: (B) 1856, (CO) Pulaski, (A) 4, (BP) MO, (CMTS)

1860 Census

Wrinkles, Nancy: (B) 1833, (CO) Pulaski, (A) 27, (BP) TN, (CMTS) 1860 Census

Wrinkles, Orlena: (B) 1851, (CO) Pulaski, (A) 9, (BP) MO, (CMTS) 1860 Census

Wrinkles, Rebecca: (B) 1837, (CO) Pulaski, (A) 23, (BP) TN, (CMTS) 1860 Census

Wrinkles, Shadrak: (B) 1842, (CO) Pulaski, (A) 18, (BP) TN, (CMTS) 1860 Census

Wrinkles, Silas: (B) 1820, (CO) Pulaski, (A) 40, (BP) TN, (CMTS) 1860 Census

Wrinkles, William: (B) 1846, (CO) Pulaski, (A) 14, (BP) MO, (CMTS) 1860 Census

Wyman, James L.: (B) 1841, (CO) Pulaski, (A) 19, (BP) MO, (CMTS) 1860 Census

Wyman, John: (B) 1833, (CO) Pulaski, (A) 27, (BP) MO, (CMTS) 1860 Census

Wyman, John: (B) 1844, (CO) Pulaski, (A) 16, (BP) MO, (CMTS) 1860 Census

Yates, Ellender: (B) 1855, (CO) Stone, (A) 15, (BP) MO, (CMTS) 1870 Census

Yates, John P: (B) 1828, (CO) Stone, (A) 42, (BP) TN, (CMTS) 1870 Census

Yates, Mary Jane: (B) 1835, (CO) Stone, (A) 35, (BP) TN, (CMTS) 1870 Census

Yeackel, Charles Peter: (B) May 12, 1845, (D) Feb. 13, 1907, (CO) St. Louis, (C) Calvary Cemetery

Yeackel, Louis G.: (B) 1869, (D) 1950, (CO) St. Louis, (C) Calvary Cemetery

Yoachum, Bernice: (B) Dec. 16, 1910, (D) Jan., 1980, (CO) Greene, (RES) Springfield, MO.

Yoachum, Christena: (B) 1827, (CO) Stone, (A) 23, (BP) MO, (CMTS) 1870 Census

Yoachum, Claude: (B) Jun. 12, 1891, (D) Apr., 1982, (CO) Christian, (DP) Billings, MO.

Yoachum, Elizabeth: (B) 1839, (CO) Stone, (A) 31, (BP) TN, (CMTS) 1870 Census

Yoachum, Jacob: (B) 1818, (CO) Stone, (A) 32, (BP) MO, (CMTS) 1870 Census

Yoachum, Jacob: (B) 1842, (CO) Stone, (A) 28, (BP) MO, (CMTS) 1870 Census

Yoachum, Louise: (B) Nov. 28, 1905, (CO) Greene, (RES) Springfield, MO.

Yoachum, Madge: (B) Feb. 12, 1911, (D) Jul., 1986, (CO) Jackson, (RES) Kansas City, MO.
Yoachum, Margaret: (B) Sep. 12, 1921, (D) May 16, 1997, (CO),
Yoachum, William E.: (B) 1847, (CO) Stone, (A) 3, (BP) MO, (CMTS) 1870 Census
Yochum, Della Pearl: (B) Jun. 10, 1898, (CO) Stone,
Yochum, Elizabeth: (B) 1829, (CO) Stone, (A) 21, (BP) MO, (CMTS) 1870 Census
Yochum, Jacob: (B) 1837, (CO) Stone, (A) 13, (BP) MO, (CMTS) 1870 Census
Yochum, Loren M..: (B) Feb. 3, 1901, (CO) Stone,
Yochum, Malinda: (B) 1838, (CO) Stone, (A) 12, (BP) MO, (CMTS) 1870 Census
Yochum, Martin: (B) 1849, (CO) Stone, (A) 1, (BP) MO, (CMTS) 1870 Census
Yochum, Thomas: (B) 1835, (CO) Stone, (A) 15, (BP) MO, (CMTS) 1870 Census
Yochum, William: (B) 1834, (CO) Stone, (A) 16, (BP) MO, (CMTS) 1870 Census
Yoder, John D: (B) 1828, (CO) Stone, (A) 22, (BP) IN, (CMTS) 1870 Census
Young, Alexander: (B) 1843, (D) 1924, (CO) St. Louis, (C) Calvary Cemetery
Young, ColeWilliam: (B) 1849, (D) 1939, (CO) Henry, (C) Knights of Pythias Cemetery, Deepwater, MO
Young, Florence: (B) 1871, (D) 1894, (CO) St. Louis, (C) Calvary Cemetery
Young, Mary E.: (B) 1848, (D) 1926, (CO) St. Louis, (C) Calvary Cemetery
Young, Upton: (B) 1837, (D) 1905, (CO) St. Louis, (C) Calvary Cemetery
Young, William H.: (D) Mar. 10, 1924, (CO) St. Louis, (C) Calvary Cemetery
Zeibig, Capen: (D) Jan. 22, 1888, (CO) St. Louis, (C) Calvary Cemetery
Zeibig, Charles: (D) Nov. 22, 1891, (CO) St. Louis, (C) Calvary Cemetery
Zeibig, Hunt: (D) Dec. 29, 1987, (CO) St. Louis, (C) Calvary Cemetery
Ziegler, Barbara: (B) Jan. 28, 1820, (D) Nov. 13, 1872, (CO) Andrew, (C) Oak Ridge Cemetery
Zumwalt, Benjamin F.: (B) 1838, (D) 1920, (CO) Pike,
Zumwalt, Josiah: (B) Jul. 5, 1822, (D) May 14, 1911, (CO) Callaway, (DP) Cedar City, MO, (MD) Mar. 20, 1845, (SPOUSE) Susan McNeil.
Zumwalt, Levi: (B) Apr. 15, 1818, (D) Sep. 1, 1900, (CO) Calloway,

Buried Name Index